Three Purgatory Poems

The Gast of Gy
Sir Owain
The Vision of Tundale

Middle English Texts

General Editor

Russell A. Peck
University of Rochester

Associate Editor

Alan Lupack
University of Rochester

Assistant Editor

Dana M. Symons
University of Rochester

Advisory Board

Rita Copeland
University of Pennsylvania

Thomas G. Hahn
University of Rochester

Lisa Kiser
Ohio State University

R. A. Shoaf
University of Florida

Bonnie Wheeler
Southern Methodist University

The Middle English Texts Series is designed for classroom use. Its goal is to make available to teachers and students texts that occupy an important place in the literary and cultural canon but have not been readily available in student editions. The series does not include those authors, such as Chaucer, Langland, or Malory, whose English works are normally in print in good student editions. The focus is, instead, upon Middle English literature adjacent to those authors that teachers need in compiling the syllabuses they wish to teach. The editions maintain the linguistic integrity of the original work but within the parameters of modern reading conventions. The texts are printed in the modern alphabet and follow the practices of modern capitalization, word formation, and punctuation. Manuscript abbreviations are silently expanded, and *u/v* and *j/i* spellings are regularized according to modern orthography. Yogh is transcribed as *g*, *gh*, *y*, or *s*, according to the letter in modern English spelling to which it corresponds. Distinction between the second person pronoun and the definite article is made by spelling the one *thee* and the other *the*, and final *-e* that receives full syllabic value is accented (e.g., *charité*). Hard words, difficult phrases, and unusual idioms are glossed on the page, either in the right margin or at the foot of the page. Explanatory and textual notes appear at the end of the text, along with a glossary. The editions include short introductions on the history of the work, its merits and points of topical interest, and also contain briefly annotated bibliographies.

Three Purgatory Poems

The Gast of Gy
Sir Owain
The Vision of Tundale

Edited by
Edward E. Foster

Published for TEAMS
(The Consortium for the Teaching of the Middle Ages)
in Association with the University of Rochester

by

MEDIEVAL INSTITUTE PUBLICATIONS
College of Arts and Sciences
Western Michigan University
Kalamazoo, Michigan
2004

Library of Congress Cataloging-in-Publication Data

Three purgatory poems / edited by Edward E. Foster.
    p. cm. -- (Middle English texts series)
 Includes bibliographical references.
 ISBN 1-58044-082-7 (paperbound : alk. paper)
 1. English poetry--Middle English, 1100-1500. 2. English poetry--Middle English, 1100-1500--History and criticism. 3. Christian poetry, English (Middle)--History and criticism. 4. Christian poetry, English (Middle) 5. Purgatory in literature. 6. Purgatory--Poetry. 7. Visio Tnugdali. 8. Owayne Miles. 9. Gast of Gy. I. Foster, Edward E. II. Consortium for the Teaching of the Middle Ages. III. Gast of Gy. IV. Owayne Miles. English (Middle English) V. Visio Tnugdali. English (Middle English) VI. Middle English texts (Kalamazoo, Mich.)
 PR1203.T48 2004
 821'.108--dc22

                                 2004002164

ISBN 1–58044–082–7

Contents

Acknowledgments   vii

General Introduction   1
    General Bibliography   11
    Standard Abbreviations   13

Three Purgatory Poems

The Gast of Gy
    Introduction   15
    Select Bibliography   24
    Text   27
    Explanatory Notes   81
    Textual Notes   101

Sir Owain
    Introduction   109
    Select Bibliography   119
    Text   121
    Explanatory Notes   163
    Textual Notes   175

The Vision of Tundale
    Introduction   179
    Select Bibliography   189
    Text   191
    Explanatory Notes   255
    Textual Notes   273

Glossary   281

Acknowledgments

I would like to thank the National Library of Scotland for access to Advocates' MS 19.3.1, my base text for *The Vision of Tundale* and for access to Advocates' MS 19.2.1 (the Auchinleck Manuscript), my base text for *Sir Owain*; to Scolar Press, whose 1977 facsimile gave me continuing access to the Auchinleck Manuscript; to the Bodleian Library for access to MS Rawlinson Poet. 175, my base text for *The Gast of Gy*; and to the British Library for access to MS Cotton Tiberius E.vii to check readings in *The Gast of Gy* and access to MS Cotton Caligula A.ii to check readings in *The Vision of Tundale*.

I am grateful to Whitman College for a sabbatical leave in 2001–2002, during which most of my work was completed. I am also grateful to the administration and staff of the Queen Mother Library at the University of Aberdeen for access and assistance during my sabbatical, and to the administration and staff, especially Lee Keene and Denise Shorey, of Penrose Library at Whitman College for their usual splendid help.

At the University of Rochester, Russell A. Peck gave the manuscript its initial reading, made suggestions on glosses and explanatory notes, and supervised revisions. Michael Livingston formatted the volume, entered corrections, and prepared camera-ready copy; he also checked the text of *Sir Owain* against photocopies of the manuscripts used as base texts and added various textual notes. Emily Rebekah Huber read the text of *The Vision of Tundale* against a facsimile of the manuscript, proposed some glossing changes and explanatory notes, and entered corrections. Andrew Wadoski read the manuscript at a late stage in its preparation and offered useful suggestions toward revision. The final reading at Rochester was done by Dana M. Symons.

Patricia Hollahan and her crew at Medieval Institute Publications gave the volume one last assessment and registered the volume with the Library of Congress. Julie Scrivener marked the volume for the printer. We are grateful to the National Endowment for the Humanities for their continued support of the Middle English Texts Series.

Three Purgatory Poems

General Introduction

The genesis of the idea of Purgatory lies ultimately in the inevitability, finality, and mystery of death. To be human is to be aware of death and to be aware of death is to wonder what becomes of us when this quotidian life comes to an end. In the history of Christianity the consideration of the nature of life after death took varied and complex forms. From the time of the four evangelists and St. Paul, the idea of an afterlife of reward or punishment is clearly present. The acceptance of Purgatory as a middle place or state between Heaven and Hell was slower to develop. In the Middle Ages, Purgatory became a central, perhaps crucial, issue in the contemplation of the hereafter. Although speculation, theological and literary, existed from as early as the second century, it was not until the Second Council of Lyons (1274) that the doctrine was dogmatically asserted, and it was not until the Council of Trent (1545–63), during the Counter-Reformation, that it was extensively defined.

In one sense, the doctrine of Purgatory is essential to medieval Christianity in that it accommodates God's justice and mercy and connects the living and the dead. However, the nature of the "middle state" never enjoyed a clear and monolithic clarification. Hazy ideas become clearer, but are often only put into sharp relief to be debated yet again. The doctrine emerged, in fits and starts, without any clear sequence, and was an often confusing and contentious mixture of Scripture, folklore, popular belief, ecclesiastical pronouncements, and theological speculation.

The history of Purgatory is a concatenation of questions, variously and non-sequentially addressed — and then once again debated or left in abeyance. The core of the doctrine is that after death souls not directly received into Heaven or consigned to Hell experience a period of purgation or purification that eventually allows for beatitude. Beyond this, there were numerous questions, foremost of which was whether Purgatory was a place or a state. Related and subsidiary questions abounded from the inception of the Church through the Middle Ages. What, precisely, is the condition of the souls therein? How can souls, spiritual entities, suffer corporeal punishments? Is their punishment a matter of degree? How long does it last? Is the punishment, punitive or purificatory, by fire or by ice, or is it by an assault on all the senses? (In this matter, fire of some sort remained the most popular and enduring torment.) Are the souls aware that they will eventually be saved and, if so, do they know when? What do they know of the affairs of this world, and are they ever able to revisit it for any reason? Can the prayers and offerings, called suffrages, of the living do any good for the souls in Purgatory? If Purgatory is a place, what is its geography?

Such questions as these were not taken up in a systematic way. Indeed, Jacques Le Goff in *The Birth of Purgatory*, the most comprehensive history of the doctrine, argues that such a basic question as whether Purgatory was a place or state was not even provisionally resolved until the late twelfth century — and then not definitively or permanently, as the ambiguities of the Council of Trent suggest.[1] This question, like all the others, appeared in a kind of peek-a-boo development over the centuries, often complicated by the incorporation of suspect sources, doubtful datings of authorities by other authorities, and a substantial admixture of folk beliefs and alternative pagan traditions such as the Irish otherworld. If any direction is discernable, it is an evolution in which the idea of Purgatory shifts from a "temporary Hell" to a process of purification that emphasizes cleansing at least as much as torment.

Some idea of Purgatory existed from the earliest days of Christianity. The scriptural basis, however, is slender and ambiguous and is, perhaps, one of the reasons for the somewhat chaotic development of the idea. References to baptism by fire occur in Matthew 3:11 and Luke 3:16; punishment for sin with a possible end of the punishment, in Matthew 5:25–26 and 12:32; Christ's "descent into Hell" between His Crucifixion and Resurrection in Matthew 12:40, Acts 2:31, and Romans 10:6–7; the existence of souls "under the earth" in Apocalypse (Revelation)[2] 5:3, 13; approval of prayers for the dead in 1 Corinthians 15:29–30 and 2 Machabees 12:41–46; and, perhaps most influentially in the Middle Ages, the "test by fire" in 1 Corinthians 3:11–15.

Scriptural accounts were supplemented with a variety of non-Christian authorities whose ideas circulated from antiquity: Zoroastrian beliefs about darkness, fire, and tests after death; elaborate Egyptian accounts of the torments of the dead; Plato's idea of justice, which required variations in the nature of the afterlife; Virgil's underworld, in which there are not only gradations of torment, but also a relationship between the punishment and the crime. Even more significant is the large body of apocryphal literature that circulated during the early centuries of the Church, much of which has survived: the Book of Enoch, the Apocalypses of St. Peter, Ezra, St. Paul, and St. John (only the last of which eventually achieved canonicity), and the Gospel of Nicodemus. Though these works are generally fanciful accounts of Heaven or Hell, they were easily assimilated into discussions of Purgatory.

Perhaps the most influential text in later centuries is the *Apocalypse of St. Paul*, which tells of a visit to the "Heavens" and Hell by St. Paul. The earliest version is thought to have been written in Greek and was advertised as an additional writing by St. Paul recovered from his house in Tarsus, along with a pair of Paul's shoes, in 388. The story was translated into Armenian, Coptic,

---

[1] See Jacques Le Goff, *The Birth of Purgatory*, pp. 84, 357.

[2] Since the Vulgate was the primary source for biblical information during the Middle Ages, I have utilized the Douay-Rheims translation of the Vulgate for all references to Scripture. Some attributions, particularly those among the Psalms, may differ in both chapter and verse from those found in Protestant Bibles.

Introduction

Old Slavonic, Syriac, Greek, and into eight Latin redactions from the fourth to the twelfth centuries, as well as many European vernacular languages, of which the most important for our purposes is the thirteenth-century English "Visio Sancti Pauli," based on the fourth redaction of the Latin version.[3] In the English text Paul is taken by St. Michael to meet the guardian angels and to the "Place of the Righteous"; he sees what happens to the good when they die and go to a kind of "New Jerusalem" of salvation; he meets the Hebrew prophets and speaks with Enoch, who was subsumed, body and soul, into Heaven.[4] But he also sees the world of torment; though it is Hell, what he sees became embodied in numerous later accounts of Purgatory. He sees sinners immersed to varying degrees in a river of fire, cast into pits by demons, and invaded by hideous vermin. Across Hell stretches a bridge from which it is possible to fall into torment. In addition to these details which became part of the literary iconography of Purgatory, it is made clear that souls are judged at the time of death in a "Particular Judgment" and thus do not have to wait until Doomsday, the "General Judgment," for assignment to their eternal destiny. Many later writers seem to have converted the sufferings seen by Paul into the sufferings of Purgatory, thus contributing to occasional overlappings of views of Purgatory and Hell and sometimes to a conception of Purgatory as a kind of temporary Hell.

But serious theological considerations of Purgatory were well underway before the *Apocalypse of St. Paul*. The earliest theological commentaries on Purgatory were by Tertullian (late second century), St. Clement of Alexandria (early third century), and Origen (mid third century).[5] Tertullian, who later was declared a heretic because of other beliefs, proposed a place of "refreshment" for the dead awaiting the Second Coming of Christ. Tertullian also held, on the basis of 2 Machabees 12:41–46 and 1 Corinthians 15:29–30, that the prayers of the living could benefit the dead. These views, expressed so early by a renowned theologian, provide a notable example of how doctrine can weave simultaneously through authoritative theological argument and dubious apocrypha.

The apocryphal *Book of Nicodemus*, mentioned above, although not written until the fourth century and truly influential only much later, told that the fate of souls could be altered after death and presented a vague idea of a limbo that was rather a place of waiting than punishment, but not strictly reserved for the pre-Christian patriarchs. To further exemplify this interpenetration of theology, apocrypha, and legend, there is the early-third-century story of "The Passion of Perpetua and Felicitas," a vision in which Perpetua prays for a "place of refreshment" for her deceased little brother as she sees him trying unsuccessfully to drink from a fountain. Thus, the story is illustrative of early concerns about what the living can do for the dead. So we are left with a second-century

---

[3] For an edition of "Visio Sancti Pauli" based on the version in the Vernon Manuscript, see Carl Horstmann, "Die Vision der heiligen Paulus," *Englische Studien* 1 (1877), 295–99.

[4] For the translation of Enoch, see Genesis 5:23–24.

[5] See Le Goff, pp. 46–47, 52–57.

3

theologian, a fourth-century apocryphon, and a third-century legend all commenting, with various nuances, on incipient notions of Purgatory.

Although the idea of Purgatory is more a product and concern of the Western Latin Church (indeed the Greek Eastern Church had to be brought into line with Western thought at the Second Council of Lyons in 1274), it was Clement of Alexandria and Origen, writing in Greek, who argued that punishment by God must be to educate and, thereby, contribute to salvation. Neither went so far as Tertullian, who seemed to believe that eventually all would be saved. Basing his ideas especially on Old Testament notions of fire as a divine means of punishment and St. Paul's notion, in Corinthians, of a purifying fire after death, Clement concluded that the fire mentioned in Scripture must be purifying or "cleansing," because God cannot be vindictive. Origen went further in speculating on the fate of souls after death. Indeed, he seems to have seen Hell as a kind of Purgatory in which redemptive suffering is unfortunately eternal. Although vague on the circumstances of souls until the Last Judgment, he held that on Doomsday there occurs a fire that purifies; for some the fire lasts only an instant; the truly sinful must endure longer periods. Origen, unlike Tertullian and Clement, does not suggest that praying for the dead can have any effect on their fate, but he does introduce the idea of gradations of punishment, or necessary purification, and it is clear in Origen that the experience of souls is individual in the sense that each person's experience is related to the life he or she has lived.[6]

Late in the third century, St. Ambrose took these ideas further by distinguishing three categories: the righteous (the saved), the truly wicked (the damned), and those who would endure a Pauline trial by fire. For the third group, St. Ambrose believed that the prayers of the living could be efficacious even though some degree of fire was inevitable for all of them. Thus, Ambrose perpetuated the idea of gradations of punishment (or purification) and trial, but, more explicitly than anyone before, emphasized the hopeful note that the living could help the dead. He thereby advanced the doctrine of suffrages: prayers, masses, or other devotions offered on behalf of the dead to reduce or eliminate their remaining time in Purgatory.

It is St. Augustine (354–430), however, who, learning so much from St. Ambrose about how to read Scripture, made the earliest comments that would inform later debates about the organization of the afterlife. The idea that suffrages are efficacious is clear in his prayers for his mother, Monica, in *The Confessions*, though there is no hint of the idea of purchased masses and memorials. Although it seems that Augustine is more interested in Hell in *The Enchiridion*, he does refer to a fire that is different from the fire of damnation (*Enchiridion* 18.69 / *PL* 40.265).[7] Most importantly in these works, he divides the afterlife into four segments, a division that would be influential well into the twelfth century and beyond. The first Augustinian part of the afterlife was

---

[6] For a full exposition of the views of Clement and Origen, see Le Goff, pp. 52–57.

[7] The citations are from Louis A. Arand's translation of the *Enchiridion*, cited in the Bibliography, followed by the Latin citations from the *Patrologia Latina*, ed. J.-P. Migne.

for the *boni*, the truly virtuous such as saints and martyrs, and this place is Paradise. At the other end of the spectrum are the *mali*, the unmistakably evil, who are damned to eternal punishment in the retributive fires of Hell. The two middle groups are the *mali non valde*, the not completely wicked, and the *non valde boni*, the not completely good. Both of these groups could be assisted by suffrages (*Enchiridion* 29.110 / *PL* 40.283), though it seems that for the former repentance and the prayers of the living created a "more tolerable" Hell, while the latter would pass through a penitential fire at the time of the Last Judgment and be admitted to Heaven, though the purgative fire could be lessened by the benefactions of the living.

Augustine is not entirely clear on the fate of the two middle groups; indeed, he saw their existence in a "state" rather than a "place" and was more concerned about repentance by human beings while living. Nevertheless, he established for succeeding centuries a clear connection between repentance and purgation, a major theme of later purgatorial literature, and suggested a kind of non-spatial geography of the afterlife that was crucial in later developments. St. Gregory the Great, who became pope in 590, held in his *Dialogues* an essentially Augustinian view that provided succeeding centuries with *exempla* for sermons that were of great significance in defining the more familiar Purgatory of Dante and his successors. It would be hard to overemphasize the importance of Gregory's *Dialogues* in establishing the torments of Purgatory as a powerful motive for repentance in this life.

Jacques Le Goff suggests that even though learned debate on the doctrine of Purgatory was muted from the fifth to the eleventh centuries, Purgatory did not disappear from folk-consciousness and penitential practices.[8] The doctrine thrived in this period in a plethora of works dealing with visions and journeys. Although these are usually of Heaven or Hell, the infernal parts kept vividly alive the images of purgatorial torment which were to re-emerge in the twelfth century, for it should be remembered that in the ambiguous and non-sequential development of doctrine, ideas of Hell and Purgatory often overlapped to the point that Purgatory was seen as a mild or temporary version of the Hell of these spiritual visions. Thus, these visions and voyages, which are so well chronicled by Eileen Gardiner,[9] provide the bridge between Augustine and the revival of theological speculation on Purgatory in the twelfth century.

St. Gregory the Great provided the appropriate link between Augustine and what was to occur from the fifth to the eleventh centuries, when the theologians and didacts once again took up their quills with purgatorial fervor. St. Gregory's *Dialogues*, as has been noted, incorporated *exempla* that kept the consideration of Purgatory alive in the sermons of the succeeding centuries, but many other works contributed as well. Most prominent was Bede's "Vision of Drythelm" in his *Ecclesiastical History* (c. 731), recorded under the year 696. Drythelm is a good man, who

---

[8] See Le Goff, pp. 100–07.

[9] See Eileen Gardiner, *Visions of Heaven and Hell before Dante*. Professor Gardiner includes excellent commentary with her translations of twelve "visions."

appears to die; his soul is led to the otherworld by a shining figure, apparently an angel, a characteristic guide for visionaries. Drythelm sees the punishment by fire and ice of diverse sins, a motif that becomes common in subsequent visions. Most importantly, Drythelm sees, between Heaven and Hell, souls whose fate has not yet been decided, who are in an intermediate Purgatory-like state, because they are not so obviously worthy as those who have been certainly saved. Besides raising issues that frequently recur in visions and tracts, the "Vision of Drythelm" reminds us of an especially significant question about the state of souls after death: will they receive their assignment immediately, or will they have to wait until the Last Judgment for permanent disposition? This remarkably clear question remains a matter of controversy in the fourteenth century and beyond.

"The Vision of Drythelm" is not alone in Bede's *Ecclesiastical History* as an example of a purgatorial visit. Bede also reports, under the year 633, the "Vision of Furseus," the first example of a visionary who apparently visited the afterworld physically, since he returns with burn marks on his shoulder, a sign that he himself has suffered, if only slightly, during his visionary journey. And Bede's work is only a part of a continuing vision tradition during the "silence" of the early Middle Ages. There are numerous others, including "Wetti's Vision" (ninth century) and "Charles the Fat's Vision" (late ninth century). These visions seem infernal rather than purgatorial, but they do provide later centuries with glimpses of various punishments and much of the furniture that will decorate later, more clearly purgatorial visions and visits. One might even include in this catalogue "The Voyages of St. Brendan" (c. 486–578), a ninth-century legend preserved in an early-tenth-century work, which includes Brendan's journeys to magical, mystical islands. Although still less obviously purgatorial than the previous examples, the journeys of St. Brendan remind us of the Celtic contribution to developing ideas of otherworlds, especially significant because Ireland will become so important in later visions, especially those of "St. Patrick's Purgatory," but many others as well.

That these visions and journeys provide a continuity between the fifth century and the eleventh becomes apparent when one notices that they are not simply folktales that live (and perhaps die) in popular imagination, but are told and retold by chroniclers like Bede, William of Malmesbury (c. 1095–1143) in *Gesta regum Anglorum*, Roger of Wendover (d. 1236) in his *Chronicles*, Vincent of Beauvais (c. 1190–1264) in his *Speculum*, and Jacobus de Voragine (1231–98) in his extraordinarily popular *Legenda aurea*. Two facts make these works especially important. First, multiple versions of the same stories seem to have survived and been passed on. For example, Bede's version of "Drythelm" dates the event in 696, Roger of Wendover places it in 699, and Vincent of Beauvais in 941. Second, the chroniclers wrote well past the time by which theological speculation on Purgatory had resumed in earnest.

Although little new was added to the formation of the doctrine of Purgatory until its resurgence in theological speculation in the twelfth century, the visions and voyages helped to keep the considerations of Purgatory alive. In addition, practical problems, such as the question of the efficacy of suffrages, continue to crop up. Indeed, the Cluniac Benedictines established All Souls'

Introduction

Day in the early eleventh century, indicating that prayers for the dead remained a matter of concern. Le Goff, on whom I have relied for much of the chronology of early speculations on Purgatory, argues that, although vague elements and indistinct notions of some kind of purgatorial experience, engendered by early theologians, survived through the second half of the first millennium, it was not until the late twelfth century that Purgatory really achieved the status of a "place," a true geographical location. Although there is no doubt that interest in Purgatory as a physical reality intensified in the late twelfth century, Le Goff may have tried to be more definitive in establishing a precise dating for "the birth of Purgatory" as a place than the facts allow. He cites two concrete pieces of evidence for his strict historical line of demarcation: the use of Purgatory as a noun (*purgatorium*) rather than as an adjective (*purgatorius, -a, -um*) by Peter the Chanter in 1170, and the composition of the Latin account of Sir Owain's entry, body and soul, into "St. Patrick's Purgatory" (Lough Derg, County Donegal, Ireland) in the late 1180s. The origin of the idea of Purgatory as a place cannot, I think, be dated so specifically. Certainly there was much attention given to Purgatory as a place at this time, but, as early as the seventh century, Furseus' burns suggest that he visited a real place, and, at the other extreme, the Council of Trent (1545–63) was still not dogmatic about "place" in the sixteenth century.

There is no doubt, however, that ideas of Purgatory were being clarified and challenged. Significant contributions were made throughout the twelfth century before Peter the Chanter. Hugh of St. Victor (d. 1141) was interested both in the problem of place and in the other very old question of how physical punishments could be applied to incorporeal souls. Bernard of Clairvaux (d. 1153) suggested a three-part division composed of Hell, of some kind of "place" of purification, and of a location on the face of the earth where the just waited in peace for eventual entry into Heaven. Thus, the question of when entry to Heaven was possible had not been resolved, but one can see hints of a drift towards a simplified three-part afterlife consisting of Hell, Purgatory, and Heaven, despite the retention of some kind of "place of waiting."[10] Gratian of Bologna, in his *Decretum* (1140) reinforced the long-developing idea of an antechamber, or "place of waiting" between death and the resurrection of the body, during which suffrages (once again) were efficacious. And Peter Lombard, in his *Sentences* (1155–57), began more clearly to merge the two middle parts of Augustine's four-part division into a single "middle" place.

---

[10] The "place of waiting" was sometimes, especially in literary works, transformed into the "terrestrial paradise," a spiritual Garden of Eden at the end of Purgatory, where souls waited in a state of pre-lapsarian bliss for their assured eventual entry into Heaven. See the explanatory note to lines 775 ff. of *Sir Owain*. The idea is most highly elaborated and given the greatest theological significance in Dante's *Purgatorio*, xxix–xxxiii.

7

In any case, the twelfth and thirteenth centuries are replete with commentaries essentially consistent with a three-part afterlife.[11] The idea of a single Purgatory was widely promulgated, at first especially by the mendicant orders of Franciscans and Dominicans. One might cynically argue that the doctrine was well suited to the situation of the mendicant friars, who could use gruesome *exempla* based on the pains (now made more graphic by the visions discussed earlier) of a single, unified Purgatory to encourage repentance and to provide income, because of the now quite firmly established doctrine of suffrages, which usually took the form of almsgiving, memorial masses for a price, and even donation of endowments for perpetual prayers for the deceased. The possibilities for corruption were great and resulted, by the fourteenth century, in many satiric caricatures of fat, greedy friars. The situation was further complicated by the development of the doctrine of Indulgences — remissions in whole (plenary) or part (partial) of the purgatorial punishment required for venial (less serious) sins and for mortal (damnable) sins that had been forgiven in the Sacrament of Penance but not completely satisfied by repentance at the time of death. Moreover, the living could help the dead by securing indulgences on their behalf — a somewhat elaborate way of providing suffrages. In 1300, Pope Boniface VIII offered a plenary indulgence, at considerable cost, for pilgrimages to the Holy Land and later put the indulgences on offer more flexibly simply for the donation to the Church of the cost of a pilgrimage to the Holy Land. Indulgences have their own history, too lengthy to probe here, but they were clearly related to the enduring question of suffrages found in almsgiving and memorial masses.

The reality, however, cannot be reduced to cynical generalizations. One motive does not necessarily destroy the validity of others. Thus, Franciscans and Dominicans might benefit from doctrines of indulgences and suffrages even while believing devoutly in the doctrine of Purgatory to which especially the Dominicans contributed so much intellectually over the centuries. In fact, it was rather the Cistercians, the austere reformers of Benedictine monasticism, led by the venerable St. Bernard of Clairvaux, who were the first and foremost promulgators of the doctrine as it came to be understood by the beginning of the thirteenth century. Regardless of motives, the eleventh through thirteenth centuries are replete with serious considerations of the doctrine of Purgatory. Theological treatises flourished in the works of commentators such as Peter Damian, Alberic, Anselm, Gratian, Peter Lombard, and St. Bonaventure, and didactic tracts, such as "St. Patrick's Purgatory" (the story of Sir Owain) and "The Vision of Tundale."

Foremost among thirteenth-century theologians who addressed the doctrine of Purgatory was the great Dominican "angelic doctor," St. Thomas Aquinas. It was Aquinas who most clearly and powerfully asserted the sense of the doctrine for the later Middle Ages, and provided the clarity

---

[11] Two additional places or states were sporadically mentioned in the discussion, although they were not directly relevant to the central problem of organizing Hell, Purgatory, and Heaven. They are the *Limbus Patrum*, where Old Testament patriarchs awaited the coming of Christ, and the *Limbus Infantium*, where unbaptized children were placed. See Le Goff, pp. 220–21.

and coherence so influential on Dante's ultimate imaginative embodiment of the doctrine at the beginning of the fourteenth century.

While admitting that Scripture says nothing of the location of Purgatory, Aquinas, especially in the *Summa contra Gentiles* (3.140–46) and the *Summa theologiae* (repeatedly), including the "Supplementum" added by his students and doubtlessly Thomistic in its opinions, gave shape and clarity even when simply articulating the significant questions we have seen emerge over and over. Aquinas did not try to resolve all disputes, but he did lay a firm foundation for the doctrine in the idea that Divine Justice requires a place for the purification of souls who have not completed their penance for sins forgiven. In accordance with the canons of the Fourth Lateran Council (1215), Aquinas believed that the priest could absolve the "culpa" of mortal sin but the "poena" (pain or punishment) still had to be satisfied by repentance (*ST* 3.qu.84–90). Aquinas held that such repentance could be achieved in this life, but Divine Justice required a second chance, in Purgatory, if the repentance had begun and the purpose of amendment was firm. He distinguished between contrition, sorrow for sin because it is an offense against God, and attrition, sorrow engendered by the fear of punishment. Attrition was efficacious, but more clearly required purgatorial purification (*ST* Suppl.qu.1–5, 12–15). Likewise, less serious venial sins could be expiated after death. The foundation of Aquinas' views was in the doctrine of "the Communion of Saints." Following his Dominican colleague, Albertus Magnus, Aquinas saw the Church as composed of three interrelated groups: the "Church Triumphant," those souls who had achieved salvation; the "Church Militant," human beings in the process of working out their salvation; and the "Church Suffering," the dead who need purification before beatitude (*ST* Suppl.71).

The doctrine does not seem astonishingly innovative, and indeed Aquinas was not the first or only theologian to articulate it, but Aquinas emphasized the essential unity of the three groups, under a just God, and thereby was able to show an interdependence, a community of all Christians at whatever stage in their existence. As a result, the doctrine of the "Communion of Saints" implies a kind of reciprocity among all Christians. The saved souls, all of them saints because they have achieved beatitude, may be invoked through prayer by both living Christians and suffering souls to assist them in their journey to beatitude. Even more striking for the doctrine of Purgatory is the reciprocity between human souls on earth and the suffering souls after death. The living may pray for the dead, one of the few ideas about Purgatory with some scriptural justification, and thereby assist them towards Paradise. Aquinas avoided mathematical calculations about how long various souls would suffer and how much quantitative good human prayer could do, but he was clear that the actions of the living can benefit the undamned dead. Then, of course, when the suffering souls achieve salvation, they can be invoked by members of the "Church Militant." The relationship is not simple *quid pro quo*, but an enduring connection of charity.

Aquinas' formulation has important consequences. First, it implies that souls are judged at the time of their death and therefore begin their purification immediately, not having to await the General Judgment. Second, suffrages are firmly defined as efficacious. The best suffrages, according to Aquinas, are prayer, masses, and almsgiving — and their efficacy is based on the fundamental Christian doctrine of charity, the greatest of the theological virtues. Third, the union between the living and the souls in Purgatory implies a connection that, without denying the necessity of personal penance and satisfaction for sin, creates a world in which the living and the dead are not entirely cut off from each other. Although not a wholly new idea, indeed Aquinas often formulates or consolidates earlier ideas, it is a vibrant connection, founded as it is in the doctrine of the "Communion of Saints." The damned are damned and, therefore, beyond consideration. The saved may be invoked, but it is the continuing "conversation" between souls on earth and souls in Purgatory that gives an especially human and humane cast to Aquinas' explication of the doctrine. The dead are not completely lost to us. Suffrages, long an important part of the doctrine especially for Dominicans, are given a human face in that they become not only a financial opportunity for friars and a theological duty for the living, but also a solace to the grief-stricken.

Aquinas had spoken, but, unsurprisingly, controversy did not disappear, not even after the ultimate total rejection of the doctrine by Luther and Calvin. Aquinas did not answer all of the questions, and, as had long been the case, resolved matters became unresolved, earlier opinions were periodically revived, and later versions of literary works often renewed issues from sources centuries earlier. The three poems in this volume provide a good example. Two, *Sir Owain* and *The Vision of Tundale*, are fourteenth-century works in Middle English that preserve and also put their own imprint on doctrines from twelfth-century Latin sources; one, *The Gast of Gy*, also written in the fourteenth century, seems at least in part a Dominican attempt to dissuade Pope John XXII from his tendency to relegate judgment on all souls until Doomsday, by this time an almost heretical view. Thus, revival and reconsideration and dispute endured. What remains clear is that the doctrine, no matter what the nuances of interpretation, had an enormous appeal and poignancy into the fourteenth century and well beyond. After all, it had everything: adventure and adversity, suffering and excitement, and, most importantly, a profound theological warning wrapped in the joyful solace of communion with the departed and hope for our own sinful selves.

General Bibliography

Anderson, Heather Jerrim. "The Terrestrial Paradise: A Study in the 'Intermediacy' and Multi-Levelled Nature of the Medieval Garden of Eden." Ph.D. Dissertation: SUNY Buffalo, 1973. *DAI* 34.9A (1974), p. 5830A.

Andersson, Otto, et al. *The Bowed-Harp: A Study in the History of Early Musical Instruments*. Ed. Kathleen Schlesinger. London: W. Reeves, 1930; rpt. New York: AMS Press, 1973.

Introduction

Aquinas, St. Thomas. *Summa contra Gentiles*. Trans. Anton C. Pegis, James F. Anderson, Vernon J. Bourke, and Charles J. O'Neil. 4 vols. published as 5. Notre Dame, IN: University of Notre Dame Press, 1975.

—————. *The Summa Theologica*. Trans. Fathers of the English Dominican Province. 5 vols. Westminster, MD: Christian Classics, 1981.

Augustine, St. *Faith, Hope, and Charity*. Trans. and annotated Louis A. Arand. *Ancient Christian Writers* 3. New York: Newman Press, 1947; rpt. Westminster, MD: Newman Press, 1963. [*Enchiridion de fide, spe et caritate*.]

Becker, Ernest. *A Contribution to the Comparative Study of the Medieval Visions of Heaven and Hell*. Baltimore: John Murphy Co., 1899; rpt. 1976.

Bliss, A. J. "Notes on the Auchinleck Manuscript." *Speculum* 26 (1951), 652–58.

Burrows, Jean Harpham. "The Auchinleck Manuscript: Contexts, Texts and Audience." Ph.D. Dissertation: Washington University, 1984. *DAI* 45.12A (1985), p. 3633A.

Carter, Henry Holland. *A Dictionary of Middle English Musical Terms*. Ed. George B. Gerhard. Bloomington, IN: Indiana University Press, 1961.

Chaucer, Geoffrey. *The Riverside Chaucer*. Gen. ed. Larry D. Benson. Third ed. Boston: Houghton Mifflin, 1987.

Cursor Mundi: A Northumbrian Poem of the XIVth Century in Four Versions. Ed. Richard Morris, et al. EETS o.s. 57, 59, 62, 66, 68, 99, 101. London: K. Paul, Trench, Trübner, & Co., 1876; rpt. London: Oxford University Press, 1961.

Delumeau, Jean. *Sin and Fear: The Emergence of a Western Guilt Culture, 13th–18th Centuries*. Trans. Eric Nicholson. New York: St. Martin's Press, 1990.

Easting, Robert. "Peter of Bramham's Account of a Chaplain's View of Purgatory (c. 1343?)." *Medium Ævum* 65 (1996), 211–29.

—————. *Visions of the Other World in Middle English*. Cambridge, UK: D.S. Brewer, 1997.

Fenn, Richard K. *The Persistence of Purgatory*. Cambridge, UK: Cambridge University Press, 1995.

Three Purgatory Poems

Gardiner, Eileen, ed. *Visions of Heaven and Hell before Dante*. New York: Italica Press, 1989.

Harley, Marta Powell. "The Origin of a Revelation of Purgatory." *Reading Medieval Studies* 12 (1986), 87–91.

Jeffrey, David L., ed. *A Dictionary of Biblical Tradition in English Literature*. Grand Rapids, MI: William B. Eerdmans, 1992.

Keiser, George R. "The Progress of Purgatory: Visions of the Afterlife in Later Middle English Literature." In *Zeit, Tod und Ewigkeit in der Renaissance Literatur*. Vol. 3. Ed. James Hogg. Salzburg: Institut für Anglistik und Amerikanistik, 1987. Pp. 72–100.

Le Goff, Jacques. *The Birth of Purgatory*. Trans. Arthur Goldhammer. Chicago: University of Chicago Press, 1984.

Matsuda, Takami. *Death and Purgatory in Middle English Didactic Poetry*. Cambridge, UK: D. S. Brewer, 1997.

Mumford, J., and Richard Ashby. *Two Ancient Treatises on Purgatory*. London: Burns and Oates, 1893.

Murphy, John Lancaster. "The Idea of Purgatory in Middle English Literature." Ph.D. Dissertation: UCLA, 1994. *DAI* 56.3A (1995), p. 944A.

Oakden, J. P. *Alliterative Poetry in Middle English*. Manchester: Manchester University Press, 1930; rpt. Hamden, CT: Archon Books, 1968.

Ombres, Robert. *Theology of Purgatory*. Dublin: Mercier Press, 1978.

Os, Arnold Barel van. *Religious Visions: The Development of the Eschatological Elements in Mediaeval English Religious Literature*. Amsterdam: H. J. Paris, 1932.

Pantin, W. A. *The English Church in the Fourteenth Century*. Cambridge, UK: Cambridge University Press, 1955; rpt. Toronto: University of Toronto Press, 1980.

Patch, Howard Rollin. *The Other World, According to Descriptions in Medieval Literature*. Cambridge, MA: Harvard University Press, 1950.

Introduction

Spearing, A. C. *Medieval Dream-Poetry*. Cambridge, UK: Cambridge University Press, 1976.

Taylor, Michael J. *Purgatory*. Huntington, IN: Our Sunday Visitor Publications, 1998.

Standard Abbreviations

CT   *Canterbury Tales*
MED Middle English Dictionary
OCD Oxford Classical Dictionary
OED Oxford English Dictionary
PL   *Patrologia Latina* (Ed. J.-P. Migne)
TC   *Troilus and Criseyde*

The Gast of Gy

Introduction

The Gast of Gy puts a human face on the doctrine of Purgatory, not only in the amiable, logical, and patient person of the Gast of Gy himself, who is a purgatorial spirit whom we hear but do not see, but also in the careful and cautious dialogue between the Gast and the Pryor who questions him. That informative, didactic exchange, leavened with several sections that emphasize the human and humane ambience of the poem, is not invigorated with gruesome, pictorial visions of the afterlife designed to terrify the wicked into virtue or frighten us with the fearful details of the punishment that may await sinners even after sins have been confessed and forgiven. Rather, the dialogue, in its concern for the Gast's wife and for the suffering of all souls, presents a rational and compassionate context in which Purgatory emerges as a doctrine of hope rather than of horror. Much of the matter would have been familiar to an audience already fascinated by the torments of Purgatory and consoled by the comfort the doctrine implied in its maintenance of a connection between the living and the dead. They would have heard many other stories of the torments of the dead and would have heard vivid *exempla* in the preaching of learned if sometimes disingenuous friars, and in the sermons of their parish priests who relied on the teachings of their more learned colleagues. Besides its terrifying fire-and-brimstone side, Purgatory offers a comforting note, a theory of hope revisited both for the living and for their departed loved ones. *The Gast of Gy* shows an awareness of *post-mortem* tortures, but concentrates its logic and feeling on a more reassuring doctrine, namely the comfort that spiritual reciprocity between the living and the dead can provide.

The Gast of Gy was enormously popular, partly because of its morbidity, partly because of its consolation, and partly because of its historicity. Based roughly on *De Spiritu Guidonis*, a first-person account by the Dominican Jean Gobi of his experiences with the spirit of Gy in the Southern French town of Alés, or Alais, from late December 1323 to 12 January 1324, the poem reports strange events. There is controversy about who wrote the original account in Latin; although there does seem to have been a Dominican named Jean Gobi in Alés in the 1320s, and he does identify himself in the original account, there is no evidence that he was a prior. Johannes de Fordun (d. c. 1384), in his *Scotichronicon*, claims to have a letter from Gobi to Pope John XXII explaining the events, but the circumstances are by no means clear. There does exist a letter, sent in 1327 from John de Rosse, later bishop of Carlisle, to Walter Reynolds, bishop of Worcester and later archbishop of Canterbury, attesting to the events. Certainly by the early 1330s, there was a longer, more detailed account in Latin in the third person, which does not mention Gobi by name, but likely was presented to John XXII as a correction to the pope's semi-heretical flirtation with the idea that souls began neither purgation nor salvation until the Last Judgment. It is probably from this extended version that the narrative exploded into the popularity it enjoyed during the fourteenth and fifteenth centuries. If one includes several fragments, there are extant at least sixty versions of the narrative: thirty-six Latin, nine English, six French, four German, and one each in Italian, Swedish, Irish, Welsh, and Spanish. The popularity was undoubtedly widespread. The English versions include two in four-stress couplets, three in quatrains, three in prose, and a five-stress couplet printed fragment. The present edition is based on the better preserved of the four-stress couplet versions, written in the mid-fourteenth century in a Northern, probably Yorkshire, dialect and preserved in Bodleian Library MS Rawlinson Poet. 175. All of the versions long enough to provide evidence agree on the basic elements of the story, although one English prose version mistakenly states the year as 1333, and both of the four-stress English couplet versions identify Alés (Alexty in the Middle English) as thirty miles from Bayonne. This is clearly erroneous, probably influenced by an early Italian version that located the events near Bologna, thus the error. All other versions print some form of Avignon, a much more likely location since it is indeed about thirty miles from Alés and was the seat of John XXII's papacy during the so-called "Babylonian Captivity" (1309–1417).

The story is a simple narrative even if its theological issues and implications are complex. On 20 November 1323, Gy, a citizen of Alés, dies. Eight days later, strange noises in his home begin to terrify his wife, who, fearing either a demonic spirit or perhaps a malevolent Gy, seeks help from the Dominican convent on 27 December, the Feast of St. John the Evangelist. After proper preparations and precautions, the Dominican Pryor goes to Gy's house and engages in an extensive conversation with the disembodied spirit of Gy. The conversation elucidates fourteenth-century, especially Dominican, views on Purgatory. The Pryor, much enlightened by the Gast and assured that the Gast will enter Heaven at Easter, leaves and then returns with a larger clerical entourage on the Feast of the Epiphany for another shorter but significant conversation. The poem then concludes with a report that representatives of the pope visited Gy's house at Easter, found no sign of him, and concluded that the Gast had indeed gone to Heaven. The fascination and joy in the poem itself are in the enlightened nature of the dialogue between the Gast and the Pryor, in the elucidation of many features of purgatorial doctrine whose terrors are more than overcome by its consolations, in its gentle but clear moral advice to the living, and perhaps most importantly, in the humane ambience and human context in which the conversation occurs.

The narrative belongs to the genre of the "ghost story," a popular form of moral instruction, in which a spirit returns to guide the living or to seek help for himself. It is to be distinguished from the even more popular "vision literature," which appeared in early Christian times and flourished from the late twelfth through the fifteenth centuries, and in which the "visionary" sees, often quite vividly, or visits the terrifying sights of purgatorial punishment. *The Gast of Gy* offers no visit to the horrific worlds of Purgatory or Hell and no graphic representations of the sufferings of the damned or of souls undergoing purgation. *Gy* rather belongs to the tradition of narratives in which spirits return temporarily to this world for their own benefit or to give salutary advice.

Introduction

The early Church had resisted and discouraged such stories and ideas as superstitious or perhaps even demonic in origin. There is a long tradition dating from classical antiquity of damned souls returning for their own purposes; but early Christian commentators discouraged belief in visitors from the next world. St. Augustine (354–430) rejected the possibility of purgatorial spirits returning to earth for any reason, arguing in *De Cura pro Mortuis*, that a "spiritual image" could appear, but not a truly ghostly visitor. There persisted, however, a clerical tradition that there was a distinction between good and bad ghosts, and there was continuing speculation about whether the saved could reappear to help or whether the damned could reappear to beguile or torment. Thus, despite official discouragement by many theologians, ideas of the malevolent damned and the beneficent saved would not entirely disappear. As early as Sulpicius Severus' *Life of St. Martin* (c. 420), Martin is reported to have dispelled the spirit of a robber around whom a cult had developed.

Although a history of such accounts is quite beyond the scope of an introduction to *The Gast of Gy*, some landmarks may be noted. St. Gregory the Great, in his influential *Dialogi* (593–94), which provided a source of purgatorial *exempla* for centuries of preachers to come, recounts the story of Geronimus, bishop of Capua, who came upon the spirit of the deceased deacon Paschanius doing penance in the Roman baths at Angulus where Paschanius had committed an unnamed sin. In a few days the prayers of Geronimus deliver Paschanius from his purgatorial duties in the baths. The story establishes, with the eminent authority of St. Gregory, that souls from Purgatory may not only return to earth but also, at least in some cases, be sent to the scene of their sin as a part of their punishment. A few centuries after Gregory, from about the ninth century, there appeared, mostly in monastic circles, stories in which the doctrine of suffrages, the idea that prayers, masses, and almsgiving done or provided by the living could help the dead, is emphasized in narrative examples. It is not, however, until the eleventh and twelfth centuries, that period of renewed interest in Purgatory, that narratives of visits from the dead became more common in the works of chroniclers and clerics such as William of Malmesbury (1096–1142), Geoffrey of Monmouth (c. 1100–1155), Walter Map (c. 1140–1208), Giraldus Cambrensis (c. 1146–1220), and Gervase of Tilbury (d. c. 1235).

In the *Trental of St. Gregory*, Pope Gregory's disfigured mother appears to him during Mass and admits that she killed an illegitimate child and was embarrassed to confess such a heinous sin. That she should even be in Purgatory is generous, but, after saying a cycle of thirty masses, Gregory sees her beautified and beatified. The value of suffrages is clear and prominent in the especially influential story of "The Ghost of Beaucaire" recounted by Gervase of Tilbury. A dissolute young man is exiled and dies in a brawl. After first appearing to an eleven-year-old virgin, he is questioned by others, including the prior of Terascon, between July and September 1211. The ghost explains that after death good and bad angels fight over the soul; after a period of wandering, souls go to Purgatory and gradually progress to the Beatific Vision. The geography is fuzzy, but it is significant that suffrages help the souls along the way. The form is that of a rigid interrogation and, although much is said of Purgatory, the story lacks the theological complexity, human ambience, and charitable disposition of *The Gast of Gy*, though it contains an abundance of controversial details.

Such narratives were disseminated by mendicant preachers and often used as *exempla* in admonitory sermons, especially by Dominicans, but also in the Sunday sermons of less well-educated parsons. The idea even appears in secular literature in the appearance of Guenevere's mother from a purgatorial place in *The Awntyrs of Arthur*.[1] Debates abounded and accounts proliferated from the late eleventh century on.

Enter *The Gast of Gy*, now a mid-fourteenth-century version in English. Although most earlier ghost stories had appeared in the form of the "tractatus" or "chronicle," *The Gast of Gy* is a work of imaginative literature as well as a presentation of purportedly authoritative doctrine. In Wells' *Manual of the Writings in Middle English*, the poem had been listed under "Tales"; Francis Lee Utley in Severs and Hartung's revision of the *Manual* includes the poem under "Dialogues, Debates, and Catechisms" and asserts that it is of "no great merit in style or structure," though perhaps deserving of attention for theological and historical reasons.[2] I would suggest, however, that it is precisely its merit as imaginative literature that sets *Gy* apart and accounts for its extraordinary popularity in the vernacular in its own time. In the Middle English couplet version, *Gy* emerges as more than a report or *exemplum* or even an interrogation in the manner of "The Ghost of Beaucaire." It offers fascinating insights into the workings of the world.

Certainly *The Gast of Gy* conveys much of the information of a "tract," providing opinions on many topics of debate. It is, thus, on one level, an exposition of the whole discourse on Purgatory: Purgatory is a place, not just a state; purgatorial pain is by purifying fire; there is a Particular Judgment shortly after death when the soul is assigned its fate and proceeds to experience it; souls are privy to what happens on earth, at least in part, but have no special knowledge of Heaven or Hell; there is a dual Purgatory — a "common" Purgatory beneath the earth and a "departable" Purgatory, one set apart for a particular person, where the soul suffers at the place of the sin; souls not only know that they will eventually complete their sufferings and go to Heaven, they even know when; the sentence can be commuted by God after death; suffrages, and this is the dominant theological point of the poem, benefit the dead; nevertheless, repentance in this world is much to be preferred to purgation in the next. This catalogue may seem benign, but most points were subjects of acrimonious debate from the time of the efflorescence of the doctrine of Purgatory in the late twelfth century to the time of *Gy* and well beyond to the Sessions of the Council of Trent (1545–63), despite repeated attempts to settle some of the issues even at the Second Council of Lyons (1274) and the Council of Florence (1438–45).

---

[1] See *Awntyrs of Arthur* in *Sir Gawain: Eleven Romances and Tales*, ed. Thomas Hahn (Kalamazoo: Medieval Institute Publications, 1995), pp. 169–226.

[2] John Edwin Wells, ed., *A Manual of the Writings in Middle English, 1050–1400*, pp. 170–72, and Albert E. Hartung, ed., *A Manual of the Writings in Middle English, 1050–1500*, 3.698–700.

Introduction

The Gast of Gy, however, deserves our attention as more than a catalogue of disputes about Purgatory. As imaginative fiction, it is structured around the dialogue between the Gast and the Pryor, a searching interlocutor who engages the Gast in discussion for his own benefit and for the benefit of the reader. The Pryor is neither the grim inquisitor that some would have him, nor an ignorant buffoon in serious need of basic instruction. Thus, it is hard to agree with those who would see his role as a satire on the ignorance of the clergy. Rather, the Pryor is a patient questioner, always careful, as he should be, about whether the Gast is demonic or benign, as he indicates in his first question: "Whether ertow ane ill gast or a gud?" (line 235). He is an honest searcher for precise truth with regard to hard questions. The literary interlocutor, as with the narrator in *Pearl* or Chaucer's *Book of the Duchess*, must, as part of his role, seem to be ignorant or unsure concerning important matters, but genuinely interested in the discovery of the truth from a reliable source. Indeed, his persistent curiosity redounds within the fiction of the poem to the credit of the Dominicans, the main interpreters of Purgatory to the later Middle Ages. Therefore, as a tract, as well as a work of literature, *The Gast of Gy* gives the Pryor the opportunity to evoke a doctrine of Purgatory that appears authoritative without being coercive. The popularity of the poem in an age when Chaucer could make his Tale of Melibee a kind of centerpiece of *The Canterbury Tales* should not be surprising. Edification, generously and humanely presented, was a source of literary as well as moral pleasure. The appeal of the poem, however, goes beyond edification by truths of theology to the attraction of a story made richer, fuller, and more humane by a ghost who is logical, articulate, patient, and sympathetic.

Despite the fact that most of the poem is in the form of questions and answers, it is hard to characterize *The Gast of Gy* as a debate (the Gast is by definitive experience the best authority, always right), or a dialogue (the development is too catechetic), or a catechism (too much else is going on in the poem). The poem has a narrative energy and a human sympathy that place the conversation in a literary context that not only elucidates doctrine but is a generous representation of the human condition. It is not poetically spectacular: the couplets are efficient, often graceful, but they serve more to expedite the narrative rather than as literary ornaments. Nor does it rely on vividly gruesome images of the suffering souls. It appeals, in its competent verse form, as a clear and rational exposition of matters of profound importance. To this end, the poem is careful to establish its authenticity, by precise dating, locating, and description of ambient circumstances. It is, however, in its tone and context that *Gy* rises above simple exposition.

The questioning is relentless and systematic, but it is inquisitive rather than inquisitory. It is appropriate that the Pryor be quite careful to determine that he is speaking to a genuine and reliable soul rather than to a demonic deceiver. The conversation itself is civil, intelligent, and rational. That the Pryor should repeatedly begin his queries with an assertion to the effect that the Gast has given himself away as ignorant or untruthful is not contentious. For example, the Pryor says: "Thou says noght right, and here now whi" (line 252) and "Me think thou ert noght stabill, / Bot thou ert fals and desayvabill, / And in this matere makes thou lyes. / That may I prove thee on this wyse" (lines 443–46). (There are many comparable examples.) The Pryor's objections are not

19

offensive, but cautious and presented with some rational justification, not confrontation. The Gast of Gy is calm, patient, and civil in his responses. There is a dignity in their dialogue. The bulk of the poem is composed of over fifty such exchanges (more if you count minor forays within the main inquiries), and, if they are not arranged in a systematically climactic way, they proceed with the sequential logic of serious conversation.

Thus, it is in context, character, and tone that *The Gast of Gy* achieves its success. The Pryor initially takes on the encounter with the Gast not out of ecclesiastical self-importance but out of concern for the condition of Gy's distressed wife, who seeks his assistance. The Pryor is prudent in the way he accepts his mission. He first consults the chapter of friars, because:

> . . . sykerer may it so be tane   *more certainly; accepted*
> Than of a man bi him allane. (lines 101–02)   *by himself alone*

He is accompanied by two learned masters, one of theology and the other of philosophy. He alerts the mayor to his enterprise and secures the accompaniment of two hundred men as witnesses or as protectors in case of trouble (though it is difficult to see what good the men might do if the spirit is infernal). All are shriven and receive the Eucharist before proceeding. The Pryor enters Gy's home with rituals appropriate to the undertaking: he uses both liturgical forms for the sprinkling of holy water and a full recitation of the Office of the Dead. It is in response to these prayers that we first hear the Gast as he utters a feeble "Amen" (line 208). The questions that the Pryor then raises, neither stupid nor confrontational, as we have seen, are parallel to the questions raised and discussed by the students of the greatest of the Dominicans, Thomas Aquinas, in the *Supplementum* to the *Summa theologiae*, such as whether suffrages for individuals benefit all souls in Purgatory and, conversely, what good suffrages for All Souls do for the individual. The Gast's answers to the questions reflect sound Thomism: a Requiem for Gy benefits all, and prayers on behalf of all benefit Gy. The Pryor and the Gast range over many issues, some of them without sure grounding, e.g., the idea of a dual Purgatory, the knowledge of the soul of the time of his release, and the "grace period" for two hours after death during which prayers, like those of Gy's friar friend, are especially helpful. However, it is the question of suffrages that is central and most prominent in the Pryor's examination and the Gast's expositions: what prayers and observances are most efficacious for the dead. This primary issue is extensively explained by the Gast in his witnessing that a Requiem Mass, a Mass of the Holy Spirit, or a Marian Mass, is of great benefit, but that the Office of the Dead, based as it is on the scriptural Psalms, and almsgiving, because it is a fundamental manifestation of Christian charity, are also of inestimable value.

Despite the fact that the underlying form of the poem is largely a series of exchanges between the Pryor and the Gast, the poem does not degenerate into a list. Even after the long introduction (lines 1–205), which establishes the historicity of the events, the Pryor's concerned responses to the suffering of Gy's wife, and his care in making proper preparations in the event that he will be dealing with a demon, the poem is modulated by variation in the length of the Gast's responses.

For example, he gives a comprehensive answer (lines 599–766) to the Pryor's question about what helps souls most. The Gast's answer is long, but entirely appropriate to the poem's primary concern with the doctrine of suffrages. He attributes the greatest, indeed essential, assistance to the Incarnation of Christ, which allows for the Redemption without which no soul could achieve salvation. Second, the Gast asserts the importance of the intercession of the Blessed Virgin, entirely appropriate to her special place as the mother of Christ and a sympathetic view because of the special devotion of the Dominicans to Mary. Indeed, the Gast quotes Mary at some length in a speech that validates her power by her assertion that she is "empress of Hell," a clever play on the more familiar epithet of "Regina Coeli" (Queen of Heaven). Third, the Gast explains that the intercession of the saints and the suffrages of the living are also beneficial.

Shortly thereafter, the Gast says that, of all suffrages, the Mass of the Holy Spirit is most helpful. In response the Pryor makes a somewhat contentious defense of the efficacy of the Requiem Mass he had said that morning:

> . . . I se, thou ert noght trew.
> Of Requiem I sang, certaine,
> For Cristen saules, that er in payne.
> Tharfor thou says noght sothfastly. (lines 812–15)

The Gast's lengthy response (lines 817–997) allows the spirit to expatiate not only on the special importance of the Mass of the Holy Spirit, but also the Marian Mass, and other suffrages provided by both clergy and laity. The concentration on suffrages is directly pertinent and the length of the answer loosens the rhythm of the developing exchanges. Likewise, the Gast's exposition (lines 1098–1208) on the importance of the Office of the Dead, mollifies the Pryor, endorses the power of scriptural prayer (the Office is primarily based on Psalms), and reinforces yet again the help that the living can provide for the suffering souls. This section may seem tedious to a modern audience, and it certainly is repetitious, but it is both pertinent as doctrine and clever in the way that the Gast plays with the symbolic significance of the numbers of Psalms in various parts of the Office of the Dead.

It is not only in these variations in the rhythm of the exchanges, however, that the poem transcends the dangers of formal rigidity. There are, for example, small instances like the insertion, immediately after the Gast first says he will enter Heaven at Easter, of the comment that the Pryor later checked and found the statement to be true (lines 998–1001). Even more consonant with the generosity of spirit in the poem is the concerned hiatus at lines 1212–38, when the Gast says that the Pryor should hurry because his pain is increasing. The response is more than fear that the Pryor will lose his knowledgeable witness. The surrounding company, at the Gast's direction, quickly recite the prayers, probably the joyful mysteries of the rosary, a devotion much promoted by the Dominicans, and the prayers immediately provide temporary relief for Gy. The tone is more sympathetic than expedient and is a small but direct suggestion of how the living can improve the condition of purgatorial souls.

However, the most important demonstration of the magnanimous tone of the poem comes in lines 1355–1511, where attention is turned to the distress of Gy's wife and the importance of marital love and mutuality. After a long description of the suffering of Gy's wife, the Pryor asks the Gast why she mourns so. The Gast's response is a chivalrous suggestion that the Pryor ask her directly. But she will not, or cannot, respond. The Pryor then asks the Gast again, and he once more directs him to his wife:

> Ask hirself, scho kan thee say. (line 1404)

The Gast is not evading the issue; rather, he is refusing to invade his wife's spiritual privacy, as later events make clear. So the Pryor tries the Gast again, and the Gast responds only with a broad statement that there are many sins that can be committed between husband and wife. Some commentators have suggested that Gy and his wife are guilty of infanticide, but this seems extreme in view of the tone of the narrative. More likely, it was one of the sexual behaviors proscribed by the Church even between husband and wife, perhaps simply the enjoyment of sex without the primary purpose of procreation. This is highly speculative, but fits the love and mutuality the poem implies. The Gast makes quite clear that it is not the business of the Pryor to inquire into the precise nature of a sin that has already been forgiven in the Sacrament of Penance (lines 1438–46). Repentance and satisfaction must be made, but the confidential "seal of Confession" need not be broken even by the penitent, and the dignity and privacy of the repentant deserve to be respected, another doctrinally orthodox and humanly compassionate insistence that is congruent with the tone of the poem. At this point, however, the Gast's wife, no longer able to restrain herself, asks the Gast the main question:

> Gud Gy, for luf of me,
> Say if I sall saved be
> Or I sall dwell in dole ever mare   *sorrow*
> For that syn that thou nevend are,   *mentioned before*
> Wharof, I wate, God was noght payd. (lines 1467–71)   *know; requited*

The Gast assures her, though the orthodoxy of his certainty is debatable, that she will be saved if she will give alms in satisfaction for her sin. The best way to avoid Purgatory is, of course, to repent and make amends in this life, but the Gast reinforces the doctrine of suffrages by asking her to remember him in her penitential actions. The doctrine is sound and the mutual love is attractive.

Introduction

The Pryor cannot help but ask why the Gast did not come directly to the clergy to make his revelation to his wife, because the clergy are closer to God than any woman. The Gast's answer is movingly appropriate to the tone of the scene:

> . . . I lufed mare my wyfe   *loved more*
> Than any other man on lyfe,   *alive*
> And tharfor first to hir I went. (lines 1497–99)

The questioning resumes at this point, but the scene has formidably given doctrine a powerful human form, and the egalitarian character of the poem is again reinforced by the Gast's statement (lines 1676–82) that no estate or "degree" is preferred over another in this world. And shortly afterwards (lines 1865 ff.) the sympathetic, if stern, Pryor adjures the Gast to cease haunting. The Gast, returning to the doctrine of suffrages fundamental to the poem, appropriately replies that he will comply if his wife lives in chaste widowhood and has three hundred masses said "for us twa" (line 1873). She quickly agrees to do so and the Pryor adds that he will say Mass for her and Gy every day until Easter. The Gast goes away and the Pryor is satisfied.

That his wife is still not easy in her mind is evidenced in her fear to return to her house and her eventual return to the convent for help and assurance at the Epiphany, which results in the much shorter second visit to Gy's house and the culmination of the poem. The Pryor brings with them twenty friars plus a number of parish priests. That the friars include Augustinians and Franciscans suggests that the Pryor intends not only to provide solace for the wife, but also authentication of the events by including clergy beyond the Dominicans. When the Pryor conjures up the Gast again, one of the friars is even allowed to ask some questions. This scene is, however, not so interrogatory as the rest of the poem. After a few questions about Gy's suffering and what they can do to help him at this stage, the Pryor intrudes one of his few "trick" questions, if that is what it is. He asks the Gast for a "mervaile" (line 2007), something that defies the ordinary laws of Nature, so as to persuade the pope of the veracity of the Pryor's account of his experience. The Gast, properly, says he knows no marvels and proceeds to present a strong admonition to the clergy to do better in preaching the doctrine of Purgatory and repentance. This, after all, is why the Gast was allowed to return. True, the primary warning is to his wife and by extension to all of the faithful, but here he focuses on the deficiencies of the clergy and urges them to do better. Consonant with the spirit of the poem, the Gast's indictment is not a diatribe. It is vigorous and pointed and predicts vengeance if there is not reform, but it is tempered with the magnanimity that pervades the poem.

The Pryor tries again to elicit some authenticating information from the Gast by asking how many popes there will be before Doomsday. Earlier, during the first visit, the Pryor had attempted something similar in asking the Gast when the Antichrist would come. But the Gast again refuses to do magic tricks; he does not know the future. Instead he returns to his admonition to the clergy to revive the vigor of the past in preaching and prayer concerning the dead, lest they suffer divine punishment. And then the Gast is gone to continue the suffering that will result in his salvation at

Easter, that appropriate season of the celebration of the Resurrection of Christ. All report the events to the pope, who, perhaps somewhat improbably, sends a delegation to confirm the Gast's disappearance and assumed salvation. They are satisfied and the instructive, magnanimous, compassionate story of the Gast of Gy concludes.

Select Bibliography

Manuscripts

Bodleian Library MS Rawlinson Poet. 175 (*SC* 14667), fols. 96r–108v. [c. 1350]

British Library MS Cotton Tiberius E. vii, fols. 90r–101r. [c. 1325–50]

Editions

Horstmann, Carl, ed. *Yorkshire Writers: Richard Rolle of Hampole, an English Father of the Church, and his Followers*. Library of Early English Writers 2. London: S. Sonnenschein and Co., 1895–96. Vol. 2, pp. 292–333.

Schleich, Gustav, ed. *The Gast of Gy: Eine englische Dichtung des 14. Jahrhunderts nebst ihrer lateinischen Quelle De spiritu Guidonis*. Palaestra 1. Berlin: Mayer and Müller, 1898.

Commentary

Bowers, R. H. *The Gast of Gy: A Middle-English Religious Prose Tract Preserved in Queen's College, Oxford, MS. 383*. Beiträge zur englischen Philologie 32. Leipzig: B. Tauchnitz, 1938.

Eleazer, Ed. "*The Gast of Gy*: An Edition of the Quatrain Version with Critical Commentary." Ph.D. Dissertation: Florida State University, 1984. *DAI* 45.9A (1985), p. 2868A.

Gobi, Jean. *Dialogue avec un Fantôme*. Trans. Marie-Anne Polo de Beaulieu. Paris: Les Belles Lettres, 1994.

Greenblatt, Stephen. *Hamlet in Purgatory*. Princeton: Princeton University Press, 2001. [Paperback rpt. 2002.]

Introduction

Hartung, Albert E., ed. *A Manual of the Writings in Middle English, 1050–1500*. Vol. 3. New Haven, CT: Connecticut Academy of Arts and Sciences, 1972. Pp. 698–700.

Kaluza, Max. Rev. of *The Gast of Gy*, ed. Gustav Schleich. *Literaturblatt für germanische und romanische Philologie* 10 (1900), 330–34.

Schmitt, Jean-Claude. *Ghosts in the Middle Ages: The Living and the Dead in Medieval Society.* Trans. Teresa L. Fagan. Chicago: University of Chicago Press, 1998.

Wells, John Edwin, ed. *A Manual of the Writings in Middle English, 1050–1400*. New Haven, CT: Connecticut Academy of Arts and Sciences, 1916. Pp. 170–72.

The Gast of Gy

	Saint Michael, the aungell clere,	*angel bright*
	And Saint Austyn, the doctour dere,	*Augustine*
	And other maisters mare and myn	*masters greater and lesser*
	Sais that men gret mede may wyn	*Say; reward*
5	(And namely clerkes, that kan of lare),	*know of learning*
	If thai thair connyng will declare	*understanding*
	Unto lewed men, that kan les,	*uneducated; know less*
	And namely thing, that nedefull es,	*needful is*
	That whylk may ger tham sese of syn	*which; prepare them [to] cease*
10	And help tham unto Heven at wyn;	*to win*
	And Saint Paule, Godes apostell dere,	
	Says till us on this manere:	*to*
	"All, that clerkes in bokes rede,	*books read*
	Es wryten all anely for our spede,"	*only; benefit*
15	That we may thareof ensaumple take	*example*
	To save our saules and syn forsake,	*souls*
	And lede our lives, both mare and les,	*more and less*
	Als haly bokes beres witnes.	*books; bear witness*
	And for that God of His gret grace	*because; great*
20	Will His pople in ilk a place	*people; every*
	Trow in thinges that er to come,	*Believe; are*
	Of ded and of the Day of Dome,	*death; Judgment*
	And how ilk man sall have his mede,	*each; shall; reward*
	Be saved or dampned after thair dede,	*damned according to; deeds*
25	Tharfor He schewes ensaumpels sere	*shows various examples*
	On this mold omang us here,	*earth among*
	To ger us in oure trowth be stabill	*To prepare; fidelity [to] be steadfast*
	And lif in faith withowten fabill.	*live; deception*
	And so in world He will us wys	*guide (advise)*
30	To kepe us clene and com to blys.	*bliss*
	So it bifell in a sesoune	*season*
	Efter Cristes Incarnacioune	*Incarnation*
	A thowsand wynter, be yhe bald,	*be you assured*

	And thre hundreth, als clerkes tald,	*hundred; counted*
35	And thareto thre and twenty yhere.	*years*
	Than bifell on this manere	*happened*
	In Alexty, a noble toune,	
	That thretty mylle es fro Bayoune,	*thirty miles; Bayonne*
	The XII kalendes, als clerkes call,	*20 November*
40	Of Decembre, als it gan fall,	*occurred*
	A gret burges, that named was Gy,	*citizen*
	In that same ceté gan dy.	*city died*
	And, when the cors in erth was layd,	*corpse*
	Than was his gast full smertly grayd.	*spirit; sharply troubled*
45	Unto his wyfe he went ogayne	*[back] again*
	And suede hir with mykell payne,	*afflicted; great pain*
	And did hir dole both day and nyght	*caused her suffering*
	Bot of him myght scho have no sight;	*Though; she*
	And in his chaumber myght scho here	*chamber might she hear*
50	Mikell noys and hydous bere,	*Great noise; dreadful commotion*
	And oft scho was so rugged and rent,	*distraught and torn*
	That for sorow scho was nere schent.	*almost overcome*
	Thus was scho turment in that stede	*she tormented; place*
	Eghtene days after he was dede;	*On the eighth day (i.e., after a week)*
55	And scho ne wist noght witerly	*she did not know truly*
	Whether it war the gast of Gy	*was; spirit*
	Or it war fandyng of the fende,	*was torment; fiend*
	That so had soght hir for to schende.	*sought; destroy*
	Tharfore sone efter on a day	*soon after*
60	Till the freres scho toke the way,	*To the friars she*
	That prechours war of that ceté,	*preachers; city*
	Wele lyfand men of gud degré;	*Good living; status*
	And till the Pryor gan scho tell	*And to the Prior she proceeded [to] tell*
	This ferly all how it bifell	*wonder; occurred*
65	On Saint John Day the Evangelyste,	*St. John's Day; Evangelist*
	The thred day after the brithe of Criste.	*third; birth*
	Scho tald unto him lest and maste,	*She told; least and most (i.e., every detail)*
	How scho was greved with the gaste,	*troubled*
	And how scho was sted in that stede,	*beset; place*
70	Sen tyme that hir husband was dede,	*Since [the] time*
	And how scho hoped ryght wyterly,	*truly*
	It was the gast of hir lord Gy;	*spirit*

	For in that chaumbre oft herd was he,	*chamber*
	Whare hir lord was wont to be,	*accustomed*
75	To spyll that bed wald he noght blyn,	*make desolate; would; cease*
	That Gy, hir lord, and scho lay in.	*she*
	"Tharfor," scho said with symple chere,	*open manner*
	"That hows dar I no mare com nere;	*house*
	Bot hyder I come to ask counsaile,	*hither; counsel*
80	What thing myght in this case availe."	
	When the Pryor herd all this case,	
	Gret mournyng in his hert he mase;	*made*
	Bot, for scho suld noght be affrayd,	*so she should not*
	Unto the woman thus he sayd:	
85	"Dame," he said, "ne dred thee noght,	*dread you not at all*
	For out of bale thou sall be broght;	*difficulty; shall*
	And have na mervail in thi mynde	*no marvel*
	Of cases that falles omang mankynde.	*circumstances; among*
	Forwhy," he said, "als kennes thir clerkes,	*Therefore; as these clerks know*
90	God is wonderfull in His werkes;	*works*
	And wele I wate, that He will now	*well I know*
	Ordayn som poynt for our prow	*Set some point; testing*
	To schew omang His servandes dere	*show among; servants dear*
	Till thair helpying, als men sall here.	*For; shall hear*
95	Tharfor, dame, gyf thee noght ill,	*do not distress yourself (be troubled)*
	Bot be blythe and byde here styll,	*But; glad; stay*
	For to my brether I will a space	*brothers; a while*
	To ask thair counsail in this case;	*counsel*
	For omang many wytty men	*among; intelligent*
100	Som gud counsail may thai ken,	*good advice; know*
	And sykerer may it so be tane	*more certainly; accepted*
	Than of a man bi him allane.	*by himself alone*
	Bot dame," he said, "I sall noght dwell."	*shall not delay*
	Than gert he ryng the chapter bell	*began; chapter*
105	And gedyrd his brether all togyder,	*gathered; brothers; together*
	And hastily when thai come thider,	*there*
	He declared tham all this case,	*told them; situation*
	Als the woman said it wase,	*As; was*
	And prayd tham for to tell him to	*asked*
110	Tharof what best es to do?	
	Unto this tale thai tuke gud tent	*listened carefully*

	And ordaind be thair comon assent,	*decided by*
	That the Pryor sone suld ga	*soon should go*
	And with him other maisters twa,	*masters two*
115	That wysest war in thair degré	
	Unto the mayre of that ceté	*mayor; city*
	To tell this ilk aventure him tyll	*same occurrence; to*
	And pray him, if it war his will,	*were*
	That he wald vouchesave to send	*would promise*
120	Som sertaine men with tham to wend	*A number of; them to go*
	To Gy hows, that was newly dede,	*Gy's house, who*
	To se tha wonders in that stede	*place*
	And to bere witnes of thaire dede	*bear witness; actions*
	And mayntene tham, if it war nede.	*protect; if it were necessary*
125	And thus thai did with al thaire maine:	*strength*
	The woman was thareof ful fayne.	*glad*
	When the mayre had herd this thing,	*mayor*
	Twa hundreth men sone gert he bring	*Two hundred; prepared*
	And armed tham fra top to ta	*from top to toe*
130	And bad tham with the Pryor ga	*ordered; go*
	And baynly do, what he will byd.	*obediently*
	And, als he bad, ryght swa thai dyd.	*as he ordered; so*
	The Pryor bad tha men bidene,	*those; forthwith*
	That thai suld all be schryven clene	*should; shriven clean*
135	And here Messe with devocyoune,	*hear Mass; devotion*
	And sithen baldly mak tham boune.	*then boldly; ready*
	Of Requiem he sang a Messe	*Mass*
	For Cristen saules both more and lesse,	*Christian souls; more and less (all)*
	And in his mynde than toke he Gy	*took*
140	And prayd for him full specially.	
	And all that than wald Howsell take	*who then wished to receive the Eucharist*
	War howsyld sone for Godes sake,	*Were soon given the Eucharist*
	For that the fende suld noght tham fere	*So that; fiend should not; frighten*
	Ne in thair dedes do tham no dere.	*Nor; actions; harm*
145	And than the Pryor full prevely	*secretly*
	In a bost tok Godes body	*pendant; God's body (i.e., the Host)*
	Under his gere with gud entent,	*clothing; purpose*
	Bot na man wist, that with him went.	*But no; knew*
	He and his forsayd brether twa	*aforementioned brothers two*
150	Unto Gy hows gon thai ga.	*house they went*

	The armed men than ordand he	*then arranged*
	All obout the hows to be,	*about; house*
	All umsett on ilk a syde	*All set around on every side*
	To se what aventure wald betyde:	*event would occur*
155	Som in the windows, som in the dore,	*by; by the door*
	With wapen that war styf and store;	*weapons; sturdy and strong*
	And som in the gardyns gert he lyg,	*he caused to lie*
	And som upon the howses ryg,	*house's roof*
	And ever in ilk a place bot thre	*And always in each place just three*
160	In takenyng of the Trinité;	*token; Trinity*
	And, thus, when thai war sett obout,	*set about*
	He bad that thai suld have no dout.	*ordered; should*
	Than entred he into that place,	
	And his twa brether with him gase,	*two brothers; went*
165	And thir wordes he said in hy:	*these; immediately*
	"Pax huic domui!"	*Peace to this house*
	That es on Ynglysch thus to say:	*is in English*
	"Pese be to this hows allway!"	*Peace; house always*
	To chaumber he went withouten rest,	*chamber*
170	And haly water obout he kest	*holy; about; cast*
	With "Vidi aquam" and than said thus:	*I have seen water*
	"Veni, Creator Spiritus"	*Come, Creator Spirit*
	With the Colett, that sall efter come,	*Collect; should after*
	"Deus, qui corda fidelium";	*O God, who the hearts of the faithful . . .*
175	And haly water obout kest he	*holy; about cast*
	Eftsones and said: "Asperges me."	*Soon after; Sprinkle me*
	He cald the wyfe withouten mare;	*called; without more [delay]*
	Scho come wepand wonder sare.	*She came weeping very bitterly*
	He said: "Dame, teche me unto the stede	*show; place*
180	And to the bed, whare Gy was dede."	*where; died*
	The woman was full mased and mad:	*distraught; beside herself*
	Scho trembyld than, scho was so rad.	*She trembled; frightened*
	Unto the bed sone scho him tald;	*soon she; took*
	The care was at hir hert full cald,	*worry; cold*
185	Bot in hir wa, yhit als scho was,	*But; woe, as yet she was*
	Scho said: "Sir Pryor, or yhe pas,	*before you leave*
	I pray yhow for the luf of me,	*you; love*
	And als in dede of charyté,	*also as an act of charity*
	That yhe wald byd som haly bede	*you would make some holy petition*

31

190	And mak prayers in this stede	*place*
	For Gy saule, that noble man."	*Gy's soul*
	And than the Pryor thus bigan	
	And said: "Dominus vobiscum";	*The Lord be with you*
	His brether answerd all and som.	*every one of them*
195	And efterward he said onone	*afterwards; at once*
	The fyrst gosspell of Saint Jone	*John*
	("In principio" clerkes it call).	*In the beginning*
	When it was said, than satt thai all	*sat*
	Doune on a burde the bed besyde	*Down; bench*
200	And said the servyce in that tyde,	*service of that season*
	That for the ded aw for to be:	*ought to be*
	"Placebo" with the "Dirige,"	*I will please (i.e., appease); Guide [me]*
	And after the Laudes thai said in hy	*immediately*
	The seven Psalmes with the Letany.	*Litany [of the Saints]*
205	"Agnus Dei" than said thai thryse,	*thrice*
	And ane than answerd on this wyse:	*someone; manner*
	A febyll voyce than might thai ken	*feeble; apprehend*
	Als a child sayand: "Amen."	*As; saying*
	Tharfor war thai all affraid,	
210	And the Pryor thusgate sayd:	*said as follows*
	"I conjure thee, thou creature,	*command you*
	In the vertu of our Saveoure,	*By the power; Savior*
	That es a God of myghtes maste,	*of greatest power*
	Fader and Son and Haly Gaste,	*Father; Holy Ghost*
215	That was and es and sall be ay,	*shall; always*
	That thou me answer, if thou may,	
	And tell me, what som I will crave,	*whatever; ask for*
	Als fer als thou may power have."	*As far as*
	And than the voyce with lodder bere	*louder tone*
220	Said to him on this manere:	*in*
	"A, Pryor, ask sone, what thou will,	*quickly*
	And I sall tell it thee untyll,	*shall; unto you*
	Als fer als I have myght or mynde	*As far as; power or understanding*
	Or als I may have leve be kynde."	*as; allowance by nature*
225	This ilk voyce than herd thai all	*same*
	(The armed men obout the hall),	
	And in thai come full fast rynand,	*running*
	Ilk ane with wapen in thair hand;	*Each one; weapon*

	For wele it was in thair trowyng	*opinion*
230	That thai suld se som gastly thing.	*should see; ghostly*
	Bot nevertheless yhit saw thai nane,	*yet; none*
	Ne noght herd bot a voyce all ane.	*Nor heard; alone*
	The Pryor bad tham all stand styll,	
	And thus he spak the voyce untyll:	*unto*
235	"Whether ertow ane ill gast or a gud?"	*are you an evil spirit or a good*
	He answerd than with myld mode,	*mild manner*
	"I am a gud gast and nane ill,	*good spirit; none evil*
	I may thee prove be proper skyll.	*to you; reason*
	For Haly Wrytt thus beres witnes:	*Holy Writ (i.e., Scripture); bears witness*
240	When God had made both more and les,	*more and less (i.e., everything)*
	He loked His werkes in ilk a wane,	*works; every one*
	And thai war wonder gud ilk ane.	*wonderfully good each one*
	All war gud, that He gan ma,	*made*
	And, sen that I am ane of tha,	*since; one of those*
245	A gud gast I am forthi.	*good spirit; therefore*
	And, als I am the gast of Gy,	*as; spirit*
	Tharfor may thou have in mynde,	*understand*
	That I am a gud gast be kynde,	*by nature*
	Bot I am evell after my dede,	*evil according to my deeds*
250	And tharfor have I pyne to mede."	*pain for reward*
	The Pryor answerd him in hy:	*quickly*
	"Thou says noght right, and here now whi:	*say not; hear now why*
	That sall I schew thee here in haste.	*shall I show you here quickly*
	Thou sais, thou ert a wicked gaste	*say; are*
255	For the payn that thou has here.	
	I answere thee on this manere:	
	All payns er gud (that prove I thee),	*pains are; you*
	That ordaind er in gud degré,	*ordained are; degree*
	That es to say, that punysch syn	*punish sin*
260	Of tham that in erth wald noght blyn,	*would not stop*
	For it es gyfen thurgh Godes will.	*given by*
	Tharfor I say, it es noght ill,	
	Ne thou es noght wicked thereby."	*Nor are you*
	And than answerd the gast of Gy:	
265	"Ilk payne es gud, I graunt wele,	*Each*
	For fra God es gyfen ilk a dele	*from; given every bit*
	Bi jugement and bi reson clere	*By; by clear reason*

	For evell dedes men has done here.	*evil*
	Bot nevertheless yhit es it ill	*yet*
270	For tham, that it es gyfen untyll.	*given unto*
	Mi payne es yvell to me all ane,	*My; evil; alone*
	For me it ponysch and other nane;	*punish; none other*
	And, sen I have swilk evell payne	*since; such evil*
	For my syns, als es sertayne,	*as is certain*
275	Ane evell spirytt thou may call me	*An evil*
	Unto tyme that I clensed be	*Until; cleansed*
	Of evell dedes, that I have done."	*evil*
	And all thus said the Pryor sone:	
	"Tell me apertely, or thou passe,	*plainly, before; go away*
280	Whase man spirytt that thou wasse."	*Which man's; were*
	Than answerd the voyce in hy	*immediately*
	And said: "I am the gast of Gy,	
	That here was husband in this stede	*place*
	And, als yhe wait, newly dede."	*as you know*
285	The Pryor sayd: "Than wele I fynd	
	Be reson, that thou ert noght kynd,	*By reason; not natural*
	That thou makes slyke sklaunder and stryf	*such scandal; strife*
	Both to thiself and to thi wyf;	
	For, whils that Gy was lyfand man,	*while; living*
290	Ryghtwis was he halden than	*Righteous; considered then*
	And trew in fayth, of noble fame	*true in faith*
	And his wif allso the same;	
	And for thir mervails that thou mase,	*these marvels; make*
	Now will men say in ilk a place,	*everywhere*
295	That Gy was evell in all his lyfe,	
	And tharfor turmentes he his wife,	*torments*
	For lawed folk in ilk a land	*uneducated; every*
	Says evell men er oft walkand,	*are often walking [after death]*
	And Gy was halden gud allway.	*considered; always*
300	Tharfor thou ert unkynd, I say."	*are unnatural (unkind)*
	The voyce answerd, als him thoght,	*as it seemed to him*
	And said: "Unkynd ne am I noght	*Unkind (i.e., unnatural)*
	Nouther to my wyf ne to Gy;	*Neither*
	And, sir, that sall thou here in hye	*shall; hear immediately*
305	Be sawes that thou sall noght forsake;	*By words; shall not ignore*
	For swilk a skyll here I thee make.	*such a proof*

	If thou have gyfen a man to were	*given; wear*
	Cote or hode or other gere	*Coat; hood; clothing*
	And he, that so thi cote has tane,	*taken*
310	Wald suffer for thi luf all ane	*Would; your love alone*
	In gud and evell to lyf and dy,	*to live and die*
	War he noght kynd to thee forthi?"	*Were; thereby*
	The Pryor said: "Yhis, for sertaine."	*Yes, for certain*
	And than answerd the voyce ogayne	*again*
315	And said: "Sir, trewly I thee tell,	
	In Gyes body whils I gan dwell,	*while; did dwell*
	Of him I toke none other thing	
	Bot his cors to my clethyng.	*body; clothing*
	This cors, that I dedely call,	*body; mortal*
320	Gert us bath in folyes fall;	*Made us both fall into sin (follies)*
	And for the wickednes that he wroght,	
	Am I in all thir bales broght;	*these sufferings*
	And his doyng was it ilk a dele.	*every bit*
	Als Haly Wrytt witnes full wele	
325	And says, that lykyng here of fles	*desire; flesh*
	Contrary to the saule es.	*soul is*
	And, if I suffer noght this payne,	
	Both Gy and his saule, for sertayne,	
	Suld suffer payne withouten ende	*Should*
330	In fyre of Hell with many a fende.	*fiend*
	For ilk a man both more and myn	*every man; more and less*
	Sall suffer penaunce for thair syn	*Shall*
	In this erth here, whare thai dwell,	*where*
	Or els in Purgatori or in Hell.	*else*
335	And Gyes body has now na skathe,	*no harm*
	And I am pyned to save us bathe.	*pained; both*
	And efter, when we com to blys,	*later; bliss*
	What joy sa I have sall be his;	*Whatever joy; shall*
	For both togyder sall we be than	*then*
340	In body and saule everilk a man.	*soul every*
	And, sen I suffer thir payns grym,	*since; these; grim*
	I am noght unkynd to him.	*unkind (unnatural)*
	And, sir Pryor, allso thou says,	
	That I of Gy suld sklaunder rays.	*should scandal raise*
345	Tharto I answer on this wyse,	*manner*

That I ger no sklaunder ryse. — *cause no scandal to arise*
Sklaunder es that kyndely kend — *Scandal; sort of knowledge*
That sownes in evell or hase evell end. — *leads to; has; intent*
Wha som it dose, mon dere aby; — *Whoever; does, must dearly pay*
350 For Haly Wryt says openly, — *Holy Writ (i.e., Scripture); clearly*
'Wa unto that man sall be, — *Woe*
Thurgh whame sklaunder comes,' sais He. — *whom scandal*
Tharfor if I answer for Gy,
I do him no velany.
355 Mi spekyng es all for his spede, — *My; well-being*
That I may neven to yhow his nede; — *explain to you*
And als my speche may gretly gayn — *also; greatly benefit*
Till other saules that suffers payn. — *For; souls*
That may thou, syr, thiself se, — *see*
360 For all folk of this ceté
Comes to this hows full hastily,
And specially thai pray for Gy,
That God delyver him out of his care,
Als thou and thi brether dyd are. — *your brothers did already*
365 And in thair prayers that thai ma, — *make*
For other saules thai pray allswa;
And prayers that men prayes for ane, — *one*
May help unto the other ilk ane; — *each one*
And allso tha that er onlyve — *those who are alive*
370 Sall soner of thair syns tham schryve — *sooner; be shriven*
And gyf tham unto penance hard, — *give themselves*
That thai be noght pyned afterward. — *pained*
Tharfor I sklaunder noght, say I, — *scandalize*
Gyes wyf ne his body.
375 Bot all the sauwes, that I say now, — *words*
Es for thair honour and thair prow." — *benefit*
The Pryor said: "This ask I thee,
How any man may evell be,
When he es ded, sen that he was — *after*
380 Schryven clene or he gan pas, — *before; pass*
And was in will gud werkes to wirk — *intended*
And ended in trowth of Haly Kyrk — *truth; Holy Church*
And toke his sacramentes ilk ane."
The voyce answerd sone onane — *at once*

385	And said, that men may evell be	
	On twa maners: "That prove I thee,	*two ways*
	When thai er dede and schryven clene,	*are dead; shriven clean*
	That es on this wise to mene:	*That is to say accordingly*
	Thai er evell, whare so thai wende,	*are; wherever; go*
390	That dampned er withouten ende;	*damned are*
	And thai er evell for certayne space,	
	That suffers payne in any place	
	For thair syns, that es to say,	
	Till tyme that thai be wasted oway.	*washed away*
395	In myself this same es sene,	*is seen*
	For I was schryven in erth full clene,	
	And I am evell, this es certaine,	
	Till I have sufferd sertaine payne.	
	For, als men may in bokes rede,	*as; books read*
400	Clerkes sais that it es nede	*say; necessary*
	That penance alls fer pas,	*as far pass*
	Als lykyng here in the syn was.	*As attachment*
	Tharfor I say it suffyce noght	
	To schryve a man in will and thoght,	
405	Bot if he may in dede fullfyll	*Unless*
	The penaunce that es gyfen him tyll.	*given to him*
	For that at we do noght or we dy,	*Therefore that which we do not before*
	Sall be fullfyld in Purgatory;	*Shall*
	And clerkes proves that a day here	
410	May thare reles us of a yher,	*there release; year*
	And a day thare to suffer payne	*there*
	Es als a yhere here thare ogayne.	*Is as; year*
	Tharfor es gud that men tham schryve	
	And suffer payn here in thair lyve."	
415	The Pryor than of him gan crave,	*desired [to know]*
	If that he wist oght wha war save,	*knew any who*
	Or whilk men war dampned bidene,	*which; damned utterly*
	In the stedes whare he had bene.	*places*
	The voyce answerd than him tyll	*unto*
420	And said: "It es noght Godes will	
	That I suld slyke thing descry.	*should such; reveal*
	I sall thee say encheson why:	*shall; reason*
	All that in Purgatori er dwelland,	*are dwelling*

To blys of Heven er thai ordand.   *are they destined*
425   Tharfor tham aw noght for to say,
   Bot at thai may warand allway;[1]
   And soth hereof may na man tell,   *truth; no*
   Bot thai had bene in Heven and Hell
   And sene what sorow es in the tane,   *the one*
430   And in the tother welth gud wane;   *the other well-being well earned*
   Thus, in tham both wha som had bene,   *whoever*
   Might say the soth, als he had sene.   *truth, as*
   And, sen I am the spirit of Gy   *since*
   And suffyrs payne in Purgatory,
435   The saules in Hell may I noght se.
   I was never thare ne never sall be.
   Ne into Heven may I noght wyn,   *progress*
   Till I be clensed clene of syn.
   Tharfor I may noght sothely say   *truly*
440   Whilk er saved or damned for ay."   *Which are; forever*
   Than the Pryor with gret will
   Spak ogayne the voyce untyll   *again; to*
   And said: "Me think thou ert noght stabill, *stable (i.e., orthodox)*
   Bot thou ert fals and desayvabill,   *deceitful*
445   And in this matere makes thou lyes.   *lies*
   That may I prove thee on this wyse.   *in this way*
   Be Haly Wrytt full wele we knaw
   How prophetes in the Ald Law   *Old Law*
   Spak and tald in feld and toune   *Spoke and told in field and town*
450   Of Cristes Incarnacioune,   *Incarnation*
   And how He suld tak flessch and blode   *should; flesh and blood*
   In Mary, mayden myld of mode;   *mild of manner*
   And als thai tald in many a stede   *told; place*
   How He in erth suld suffer dede,   *should; death*
455   And of His ryseyng tald thai ryght,   *resurrection told*
   And yhit thai saw Him never with sight.   *yet*
   And sen thai war men bodily   *since*
   And tald swilk thinges in prophecy   *told such*

---

[1] Lines 425–26: *Therefore it is not at all fitting for them to say, / Unless they can swear to the truth [of it] in every instance*

	And kend the folk how thai myght knaw	*taught*
460	Thinges that thamself never saw,	
	Bi this reson, thinketh me,	*By; I think*
	A clene spirit, als thou suld be,	*should*
	Suld have mare force swilk thing to tell	*Should; more; such*
	Than any that war in flesch and fell.	*flesh; skin*
465	Tharfor thee aght to witt bi this,	*ought to know by this*
	Whilk er in bale and whilk in blys."	*Which; misery; which*
	The voyce answerd to him in hast:	
	"Sir Pryor, thir wordes er all wast,	*wasted (i.e., useless)*
	I may wele prove thee in this place.	
470	It es na lyknes, that thou mase,	*no similarity; make*
	Betwix prophetes, that standes in story,	
	And sawles, that er in Purgatory.	*souls; are*
	The prophetes had, whils thai war here,	*while; were*
	Of God and of His aungels clere	*bright*
475	And of gyftes of the Haly Gaste,	*gifts; Holy Ghost*
	All thair maters, lest and maste,	*matters; least and most*
	That thai myght tell and preche over all	
	Before what thing suld fall.	*In advance; should occur*
	Swilk power was gyfen tham tyll,	*Such; given; to*
480	And all was for this certayn skyll:	*reason*
	For lawed folk in ilk a land	*uneducated*
	Bi thair stevens myght understand	*By; voices*
	And better trow, how Crist was born,	*believe*
	Be sawes that thai had said biforn.	*By sayings*
485	For, sen thair sawes fra God war sent,	*since*
	Men sall tham trow with gude entent.	*believe*
	And I am sett for sertaine space,	
	Till God will gyf me better grace,	
	Thus for my syns to suffer payne.	
490	And, sir, I say thee for certayne,	
	That I may now nane aungels se	*no; see*
	Bot tham that has kepeyng of me,	*Except those who have keeping*
	And to me will thai tell ryght noght	
	Till I out of this bale be broght.	*misery*
495	Tharfore I may noght say certaine,	
	Whilk er in blys or whilk in payne."	*Which are; which*
	The Pryor than said sone onane:	*at once*

39

"Ryght in thi wordes thou sall be tane.   *caught*
Thou sais, na spirit may tell me,

500   Wha sall saved or dampned be;   *Who*
And bokes beres witnes, be thou bald,   *assuredly*
That fendes somtyme to men has tald   *fiends; have told*
And said the soth, als thai had sene,   *truth, as*
Of tham that saved and dampned had bene."

505   The voyce answerd and said ogayne:
"That spirit that dwelles in payne,
Ne na fendes that dwelles in Hell,   *Nor any*
Has no power for to tell
Ne unto no man here at neven   *to explain (name)*

510   That towches the prevetese of Heven,   *What touches on the hidden matters*
Bot if it be thurgh Godes suffraunce,   *Unless; permission*
Or other aungels tham tell per chaunce.
And unto me thai tell nathing.
Tharfor I may noght have knawyng   *knowledge*

515   Of hevenly blys, how it es thare,
Ne of Hell, how the fendes fare.
The sawles, that thare sall suffyr pyne,   *pain*
Thair penaunce es wele mare than myne;
For I have hope to be in blys,

520   And tharof sall thai ever mys.   *miss*
Tharfor es no lyknes to tell   *similarity*
Betwene me and the fendes in Hell."
Than said the Pryor: "I pray thee now,
Tell me in what stede ertow?"   *place are you*

525   The voyce answerd and said in hy: *immediately*
"I am here in Purgatory."
Than said the Pryor: "Proved thou hase
That Purgatory es in this place.
For ryght als thou es purged here,

530   So may other saules in fere;   *in company*
And, whare saules may be purged all,
Purgatory men may it call.
Tharfor bi thir sawes that thou says,   *these accounts*
Purgatory es here always."

535   The voyce answerd on this manere
And said: "Thare er Purgatoryes sere: *There; several*

	Ane es comon to mare and les,	*One is; to all*
	And departabill aneother es."	*And another is set apart for an individual*
	The Pryor said: "Now wate I wele	*know*
540	That thou ert fals in ilk a dele.	*on every point*
	A saule may noght in a tyme ga	*at one time go*
	To be ponyst in places twa;	*punished; two*
	For, whils he sall be in the tane,	*the one*
	Of the tother he may have nane,	*the other; none*
545	For in a place he suffers payne."	*one place*
	The voice than said: "This es certayne,	
	For I am here, withouten fabyll,	*fable*
	In Purgatory departabyll	*separate*
	Ilk a day, als God vouches save.	*allows*
550	Bot other payn behoves me have:	*must be inflicted upon me*
	For ilk a nyght behoves me	*[it] behooves me*
	In comon Purgatory pyned be	*be pained*
	For to suffyr paynes sare	*agonizing*
	With other saules that er thare."	
555	The Pryor said: "Kan thou me wys,	*Can; explain*
	Whare comon Purgatori is,	
	Whare thou of payns has swilk plenté?"	*such plenty*
	"In mydes of all the erth," says he,	*the middle*
	"Thare es that place ordand for us."	*established*
560	And than the Pryor answerd thus:	
	"Als thou says may it noght be.	
	Be propir skyll that prove I thee.	*reason*
	The mydes of the erth a stede es dyght,	*In the middle; place is set*
	And Purgatory aneother es right;	*another*
565	And twa stedes may noght be in ane.	*one*
	Tharfor I say thou has mysgane.	*erred*
	If Purgatory, whare thou dwelles,	
	War in mydes the erth, whare thou telles,	
	Twa stedes in ane than burd be thare,	*would*
570	And that sall thou se never mare.	
	Tharfor so es it noght arayd."	*arranged*
	The voyce answerd sone and sayd:	
	"Stedes er ordand here full rathe,	*Places are assigned; quickly*
	Bodily and gastly bathe.	*both*
575	The saule es gastly, and forthi	*therefore*

It occupyes na stede bodily.
That es to say, be it all ane
When mans body tharfra es tane.   *is taken from there*
This ilk stede, als thou may se,   *very place*
580   Haldes both the saule and thee,   *the soul and yourself*
And yhit er noght here stedes twa.   *yet are*
And herebi may thou se allswa   *hereby; also*
How rayne and slete, haile and snaw,   *rain; sleet, hail; snow*
Er in the ayre, kyndely to knaw,   *naturally to know*
585   And ilk ane has his cours be kynde.   *each one; according to nature*
So es that place whare we er pynde."   *pained*
The Pryor said: "Tell us in fere,   *all together*
Whi that thou ert ponyst here."   *are punished*
The voyce answerd him in haste:
590   "For in this place I synned maste,   *Because; most*
Of whilk syns I gan me schryve
And did na penaunce in my lyve.
Tharfore here sall I penaunce have
For that syn, till I be save."
595   The Pryor said: "Telle, if thou kan,
What thing noyse mast a man   *troubles (annoys) most*
In tyme of ded when he es tane."   *death; taken*
The voyce answerd sone onane   *at once*
And said: "The syght sall mast him dere   *most; harm*
600   Of foule fendes, that him wald fere;   *would take as a companion*
For than thai sall obout him be
Defygurd all in foule degré,   *Disfigured*
And grysely sall thai gryn and gnayst   *horribly; grimace; gnash [teeth]*
Out of his witt him for to wrayst;   *wrest*
605   And than befor him sall be broght
All wickednes that ever he wroght.
So will thai fande, with any gyn,   *torment; means*
Thurgh wanhope if thai may him wyn."   *By means of despair*
The Pryor said: "Than wald I fayne   *be pleased to*
610   Wytt what remedy war here ogayne,   *Know; against*
And what may help men alther maste   *most of all*
In bandes of ded when thai er braste."   *In bonds of death; overcome*
The voyce said: "Thare es som man
That thar noght hope of na help than.   *there; no*

615	For if a man here lede his lyve	
	In syn and sithen will noght him schryve,	*afterwards*
	Na in hert will have no care	*Nor*
	For the dedes he has done are,	*in the past*
	Than sall his aungell to him tell	
620	How Crist suffyrd payns so fell,	*deadly*
	And how He dyed for his bihove.	*benefit*
	And that sall be to his reprove	*reproof*
	To schew him how he was unkynde	*unnatural*
	Here on this mold, whils he had mynde,	*earth, while*
625	And how that he was mysavysede,	*ill-advised*
	Godes sacramentes when he dispysede,	*despised*
	That wald noght schryve him of his syn,	
	Bot lyked it ever and ended tharein.	*enjoyed*
	And, when thir sawes er thusgate sayd,	*these accusations are thus*
630	Than sall the fendes obout him brayd	*shriek*
	And manase him with all thair myght	*menace*
	And say: 'Com forth, thou wreched wight!'	*creature*
	So sall thai harl him unto Hell	*hurl*
	Withouten end in dole to dwell.	*grief*
635	And, if a man be clensed clene,	
	And schryfen of all his synnes bedene,	*shriven; completely*
	And take his sacramentes ilk ane,	*every one*
	And in that tyme with ded be tane,	*death; taken*
	Yf all his penaunce be noght done,	
640	His gud aungell sais to him sone:	
	'Comforth thee wele, I sall thee were,	*Be well comforted; protect*
	That the devels sall thee noght dere';	*harm*
	And to the fendes than sall he say:	
	'Yhe wicked fendes, wende hethen oway,	*You; go hence away*
645	For yhe have na part in this man.'	
	And the fendes sall answer than	
	And say on this wise: 'Oures he es	
	Be reson and be ryghtwisnes,'	*justice*
	And thare than sall thai schew ful sone	
650	All evell dedes that he has done,	
	Bath in eld and als in yhowth,	*Both; age; also in youth*
	Sen first he kyndely wittes couth,	*Since; human understanding knew*
	And say: 'He synned thus and thus:	

43

Tharfore him aw to wende with us.'   *it is fitting for him to dwell*

655 His gude aungell sall mak debate

And say: 'He synned, wele I wate,   *know*

On this wise als yhe have told;   *way as you; told*

Bot he es borowde, be yhe bald,   *redeemed, be you assured*

For he was schryven and clensed clene,

660 And toke his sacramentes all bidene,   *fully*

And sorow he made for his synnyng.

To clensyng fyre that sall him bring,

And the meryte of Cristes Passyon now   *Passion*

Sall be betwix him and yhow

665 And serve him for scheld and spere,   *shield and spear*

That yhour dartes sall him noght dere;   *your barbs; harm*

And Cristes hend and als His syde,   *Christ's hands; also His side*

That thirled war with woundes wyde,   *pierced*

Sall be bitwix him and yhour hende,   *hands*

670 And fra yhour felnes him defende;   *treachery*

And Cristes face, that buffett was,   *buffeted*

Betwix him and yhour face sall pas,   *Between; shall pass*

So that he sall noght on yhow se

Ne for nathing abaysed be;   *humiliated*

675 All Cristes body spred on the Rode   *Cross*

Sall be unto him armoure gude,

Swa that yhe sall have no powere   *So*

Him for to dere on na manere;   *harm*

All the lymes of Jhesu fre,   *limbs; generous*

680 That for mankynd war pyned on Tre,   *pained; Tree (i.e., the Cross)*

Sall clens him of that foly   *cleanse*

He dyd with lyms of his body.   *limbs*

The saule of Crist, als yhe wele ken,   *know*

That yholden was for erthly men,   *oppressed*

685 Sall purge him now of all the plyght   *guilt*

That saule dyd thurgh his awen myght,   *own power*

So that in him sall leve no gylt   *guilt*

Forwhi he suld with yhow be spylt,   *For which; destroyed*

Ne no payn unto him sall stand

690 Bot Purgatory, that es passand.   *passing (transitory)*

Thare sall he suffer certaine space,

Till he be purged in that place,

44

	And sithen sall he with us wende	*afterwards*
	And won in welth withouten ende.'	*live*
695	And thus es Cristes Passyoune	*Passion*
	Sett bifor us redy boune	*already prepared*
	For to defend us fra the fende,	
	Out of this world when we sall wende;	*go*
	Tharfor us aw, if we be kynde,	*it befits us; natural*
700	To have that Passyoune mast in mynde.	*most*
	And als men may have helpyng gude	*also*
	Of Mary, that es myld of mode.	*mild of disposition*
	If we oght for hir here have done,	*anything*
	Baldli may we ask hir bone,	*Confidently; help*
705	And us to help scho will hir haste,	
	In ded when our myster es maste.	*death; need; greatest*
	For if a man, or he hethen fare,	*before he travels away*
	Be schryven clene, als I said are,	*before*
	That blyssed bryd will be full boune	*woman; ready*
710	To socoure him in that sesoune	*succor*
	And fend fro the fendes in fere	*protect; fiends gathered together*
	And say to tham on this manere:	
	'Mayden and moder both am I	
	Of Jesu, my Son, God allmyghty,	
715	And of Heven am I coround quene	*crowned*
	And lady of all the erth bidene,	*entirely*
	And I am emperys of Hell,	*empress*
	Whare yhe and other devels dwell;	
	And for that I am quene of Heven,	*because*
720	Unto my Son thus sall I neven	*say*
	That He sall deme for luf of me	*judge; love*
	This man in Purgatory to be	
	Till he be clensed clene of syn,	
	And so to Heven I sall him wyn.	
725	In als mykell als I am lady	*Inasmuch as*
	Of all the erth, this ordaine I	
	Thurgh the will of my Son dere,	
	That ilk a bede and ilk a prayere,	*every petition*
	That now in all this warld es sayd,	*world*
730	Untyll his profett be purvayd,	*To; profit*
	And all the messes and almusdede	*masses; almsdeeds*

	May turne this man now unto mede;	*reward*
	And bi tha dedes and be tha messe	*by those deeds; those masses*
	Sall his penaunce be made lesse,	
735	That to him es ordaind for his syn,	*assigned*
	That yhour falshede gert him fall in.	*your; made him fall in*
	For I am emperis of Hell,	
	Tharfor yhour force now sall I fell.	*strength; destroy*
	I comand yhow yhe hethen fare,	*you [that] you go away*
740	And at yhe noy this man no mare,	*that you bother; more*
	That ended in my Son servyse.'	
	And, when scho has said on this wyse,	
	All the halows hegh in Heven	*saints high*
	Hyes all unto hir full even	*Gather; right up to her*
745	And unto Jesu all in fere,	*together*
	And thus than mak thai thair prayere:	
	'Lord Jesu, God allmyghty,	
	Fader of Heven, Man of Mercy,	
	Have mercy of this man that es	
750	Our awen brother and als our flesch.	*own; also; flesh*
	Sen Thou wald com fra Heven on hight	*Since; from; high*
	And suffer payn for mans plyght,	*plight*
	Thou meng Thi mercy with this man.'	*join*
	Thus sall man saule be saved than,	*a man's soul*
755	And his gud aungell sall him take	
	To Purgatory aseth to make,	*reparation*
	And to him he sall tak tent	*pay attention*
	Till he have sufferd his turment.	
	And than the wicked gastes sall ga	*go*
760	Thethen oway with mykell wa.	*Thence; great woe*
	On this wyse may gude prayere	*In these ways*
	And almusdedes, that men dose here,	*almsdeeds; do*
	And meryte of Cristes Passyoune	
	And of halows gud orisoune	*saints' beneficent prayers*
765	May help a man in his dying	
	And unto clensyng fyre him bring."	
	The Pryor said unto him than	
	And asked, if that any man	
	Of Jesu Crist may here have syght	
770	Or of Mary, His moder bryght,	

Or els the halows verraily | *saints truly*
In thair fourme, when thai sall dy. | *shape*
The voyce answerd and said: "Nay,
Bot on this wise, als I sall say, | *Except; as*
775 Bot if it be so haly a man
That has na nede of purging, than
Ne for to dwell in Purgatory,
Thai sall se tham openly,
And synfull men sall noght tham se."
780 The Pryor said: "Than think me,
That thou says now thiself to skorne | *mock yourself*
Ogayns the sawes thou said beforne; | *Against; claims*
For thou said, Cristes Passyoune
And also Mary suld be boune | *prepared*
785 And other halows, that er in Heven, | *saints*
To pray for him with myld steven. | *mild voice*
Than semes it that he se tham may."
The voyce answerd and sayd: "Nay;
Thai sall be thare, I grant thee wele,
790 Bot he sall se tham never a dele | *not a bit*
In thair lyknes verraily. | *truly*
And this es the encheson whi: | *reason*
For the grettest blys of Heven it es
For to se Crist in His lyknes, | *in His own image*
795 That es to say, in His Godhede; | *Divinity*
Than thurt men have nane other mede | *need; reward*
Than in thair dying Him to se,
And in that blys than thai suld be
Sodainly at thair ending, | *Suddenly*
800 And that war noght acordand thing." | *fitting*
Than the Pryor of him asked,
If spirytes, that war hethen passed, | *thither*
May kyndely knaw be morn or none | *by nature; noon*
The dedes that here er for tham done, | *deeds*
805 Or prayer that we for tham ma? | *make*
The voyce answerd and said: "Yha." | *Yes*
The Pryor said: "Than kan thou say,
Wharof I sang Mess this day?" | *Of what; Mass*
The voyce answerd ogayne full tyte | *quickly*

810	And said: "Thou sang of Saint Spiryte."	*Holy Spirit*
	The Pryor answerd, als he knew,	
	And said: "I se, thou ert noght trew.	
	Of Requiem I sang, certaine,	
	For Cristen saules, that er in payne.	
815	Tharfor thou says noght sothfastly."	*truthfully*
	The voyce answerd to him in hy:	*immediately*
	"I graunt graythely, or I gang,	*readily, before I came*
	Of Requiem full ryght thou sang;	
	Bot yhit I say thee, neverthelesse,	*yet; [to] you*
820	Of Saint Spirytt was the Messe.	*the Holy Spirit; Mass*
	That sall thou be ensaumple se:	*example*
	For, custom es, in ilk contré,	*every*
	If any man outher ald or yhing	*either old or young*
	Of aneother suld ask a thing,	*another*
825	What thing so lygges his hert most nere,	*lies; near*
	That in his speche sall fyrst appere	
	And first be in his wordes always.	
	For God thus in His gospell says:	
828a	'Ex habundancia cordis os loquitur';	*(see note)*
	'That of the fulnes of the hert	
830	Spekes the mowth wordes smert.'	*boldly*
	And for the Messe of Saint Spiryte	*Mass; [the] Holy Spirit*
	To my profytt es mast perfyte	*profit; most perfect*
	And allso of the Trinité.	
	Thir messes mykell amendes me;	*These masses greatly*
835	Bot the Mess of the Haly Gast,	*Holy Ghost*
	In my mynde es althir mast.	*the best of all*
	And tharfor I say thou sang	
	Of Saint Spirit, I say noght wrang,	*wrong*
	And here now the encheson whi:	*hear; reason*
840	For, whils I lyfed here bodily,	*while; lived*
	I spended my wyttes and my powere	*spent; wits*
	Full ofte sythes in synnes sere,	*Very many times; various*
	When I suld have tham spended ryght	
	To Godes worschepe with all my myght	*worship*
845	And mensked the Fader with all my mayne;	*honored; strength*
	For of Him comes all power playne	*fully*
	That men has here, whils att thai lyf,	*while that they live*

	After His grace als He will gyf.	*as; give*
	Tharfor, what man so dose unryght	*does*
850	Thurgh his power or his myght	
	Or be his strenkith, if that it be,	*strength*
	Ogayns the Fader, than synnes he;	*Against; then*
	For al power He weldes allways,	*wields*
	Als David in the Psauter says:	*Psalter*
854a	'Omnia, quecunque voluit, Dominus fecit.'	*(see note)*
855	He says: 'The Fader may fullfyll	
	In Heven, in erthe, what som He will.'	*whatever*
	And to Crist, God Son, es gyfen full ryght	
	All wysdom both bi day and nyght.	
	Tharfor God Son thai syn ogayne,	*against*
860	That here dispendes thair wittes in vayne	*uses; vain*
	And settes tham so on werldly gude,	*worldly goods*
	That ryches es mare in thair mode	*mind*
	Than Crist, God Son, that boght tham dere.	*bought (i.e., redeemed) them dearly*
	I have synned on the same manere.	
865	Till the Haly Gast es gyfen all grace	*To*
	And all bountes in ilk a place.	*virtues; every*
	Ogayns Him oft allso synned have I,	*Against*
	When that I used in foule foly	
	The gyftes, that He me gaf of kynde,	*in my nature*
870	And wald noght mensk Him in my mynde.	*honor*
	My gud favor and my fairhede	*excellence*
	Have I oft used in synfull dede,	
	And vertus have I turned to vyce.	*virtues; vice*
	Thus have I wroght als wryche unwyse.	*done; wretch*
875	Tharfore aseth now bus me make	*reparation; must*
	To the Thre Persons for my syn sake.	
	And my gud aungell has me sayd	
	The prayers that er so purvayd,	*provided*
	And messes of the Trinité,	
880	May gretely help now unto me.	
	And, for that I have synned maste	
	Ogayns the gyftes of the Haly Gast,	*Against*
	Covetand here mare ryches	*Coveting; more*
	Than He me gaf of His gudnes,	
885	Or than He vouched safe me to sende;	*promised*

	And tharfor, this myss to amende,	*sin*
	Messes sungen of Saint Spirytt	*[the] Holy Spirit*
	In my payne may do mast respyt.	*relief*
	And tharfor, sir Pryor, I say,	
890	Of Saint Spiritt thou sang this day.	
	All if thine office ordaind ware	*directed*
	For Cristen saules, als thou said are,	*as; earlier*
	Thou said with gud devocioune	
	Of the Haly Gast ane orysoune,	*prayer*
895	And that ilk orysoune, for certayne,	
	Alegged me mare of my payne	*Relieved*
	Than all the other, that thou sayd	
	For tyll all saules thai war purvayd.	*to; provided*
	And, sen that helped me all ane	*since; alone*
900	Wele mare than the other ilk ane,	*more; each one*
	Of the Haly Gast, I say, thou sang.	
	If thou me wyte, thou has the wrang."	*understand; wrong*
	The Pryor askes him than this thing:	
	For how many saules a prest myght syng	
905	On a day and in a stede,	
	Whether thai war quyk or dede,	*alive*
	And ilk ane have in lyke gudenes	*each one; equal value*
	And in lyke meryte of the Mess.	*equal merit*
	The voyce answerd and gan say,	
910	That a prest anely on a day	*priest once*
	For all saules may syng and rede	
	And ilk ane of his mess have mede	*every one; reward*
	Bi vertu of the Sacrament.	*power; Sacrament (i.e., the Eucharist)*
	"And tharfor to this tak tent:	*pay attention*
915	Jesus Crist with Jewes voyce	
	Was anely offyrd on the Croyce,	*once; Cross*
	And thare He dyed and gaf the gast	*gave the ghost (i.e., died)*
	Unto His Fader of myghtes mast	*greatest power*
	For salvacioun of all mankyn	*mankind*
920	And noght anely for a man syn.	*one man's sin*
	Ryght so the prest in ilk a Messe	*each Mass*
	Offers Criste, ryght als He es	
	In hale Godhede, als clerkes ken,	*full Divinity; know*
	In amendement of all Cristen men.	*Christians*

925	Tharfor in a Messe may be tane	*encompassed*
	All Cristen sawles als wele als ane,	*as well as one*
	And better may it part tham tyll.	
	That prove I thee be proper skyll.	*reason*
	For gret difference may men fele	*perceive*
930	Bitwene spirituall thing and temporele.	*temporal*
	Temporall thing, that thou sese here,	*see*
	When it es parted in paracels sere,	*various pieces*
	In the ma parcels it parted es,	*more*
	Itself leves ay wele the les,	*leaves always; less*
935	That es, for porcyoun partyse thar fra.	*for [a] portion parts therefrom*
	Als if thou ane appell ta	*one apple take*
	And part it into many hende,	*divide; hands*
	With thiself sall lytell lende.	*yourself; remain*
	Als wele may thou understand,	
940	That spirituall thing es ay waxand.	*always growing*
	That may thou se be ryght resoune,	
	Als if thou tak this orysoune,	*prayer*
	The Pater Noster, and forth it ken	*(i.e., the Lord's Prayer); make known*
	Kyndely to all Cristen men.	
945	And so when that it teched es,	*taught*
	In itself it es noght les;	
	In understandyng es it mare,	*more*
	When ma it kan than couth it are.	*more; know; knew; before*
	So es the Messe and the prayere	
950	That ordand er for saules sere,	*intended; various*
	For ded and quyk, if that it be,	*living*
	The more it es in it degree."	
	The Pryor answers and says:	
	"Haly Wryt witnes allways	
955	That saules er saved, for certayne,	
	And oft delyverd of thair payne	
	Be speciall prayers and speciall dede,	*deeds*
	That frendes dose here for thair mede;	*friends do; reward*
	And tha frendes dose mare for ane	*those; do more; one*
960	Than for other saules ilk ane.	*each one*
	Than think me that his mede sall fall	*reward*
	Mare than it war done for all,	
	And mare alegge him of his payne."	*relieve*

The voyce answerd thus ogayne:
965 "Ilk a prest, that Messe synges,
Him nedes for to do twa thinges:
First his prayers sall he make
Specially for his frendes sake,
Whilk he es mast halden untyll,   *Whom; most bound to*
970 That God him help of alkyns ill;   *everything bad*
And, when he has so prayed for ane,
Than sall he pray for other ilk ane,
And ilk ane has mede of that Messe.   *reward*
Bot he, for wham it ordaind es,   *whom; directed*
975 Es helped mast fro bale tharby.   *most; suffering*
And on the same manere am I
Delyverd of my penaunce here,
That I suld have sufferd foure yhere,   *years*
For mysdedes als it was dett.   *determined*
980 A lyfand frend thus has it lett.   *living friend; relieved*
I have a cosyn, that thou wele knew,   *kinsman*
A pore frere, that I fynd trew.   *poor friar; find*
I helped him whils he had nede,   *when*
Whils he to the scoles yhede;   *When; schools went*
985 And allso sithen, when he was frere,   *later; friar*
I fand him fully fyve yhere.   *looked after; years*
And for myself full wele I wroght:
That gudenes now forgetes he noght,
For in his mynde he has me maste.   *most*
990 Tharfor I sall be helped in haste.
I sall have penaunce in this place
No ferrer bot fra hethen to Passe.   *farther; from now to Easter*
If thou will witt this for certayne,   *understand*
At Pasch com to this place ogayne,   *Easter; again*
995 And, if thou here noght than of me,   *hear*
Sothly, certayne may thou be,
That I am hent up into Heven."   *taken up*
And, als he bad, he dyd full even: *promised; exactly*
At the Pasch after the hows he soght,   *Easter; house*
1000 And of the voyce he herd ryght noght.
Tharfor he trowed, als he said are.   *believed; before*
Bot in that tyme he asked mare

And said: "Kan thou trewly tell,

If thou in that ilk Heven sall dwell,   *same*

1005   That for Godes halows es purvayd?"   *saints; provided*

The voyce answerd sone and sayd:

"Sire, I tald thee are full even,   *told you before*

That I come never yhit in Heven.   *yet*

Tharfor I may tell thee no mare

1010   Of orders that er ordaind thare.

Bot of blys may I be full bald,   *assured*

For thus myne aungell to me tald:

To Pasch I suld in penance be,   *Easter*

And than, he said, that I suld se

1015   The Kyng of Heven in His Godhede

With His aungels all on brede   *far and wide*

And with His halowes everilk ane.   *saints every one*

And than I answerd sone onane

And sayd: 'A, lord, me think full lang,

1020   That meney till I com omang.'   *company*

Bot He be loved in ilk a place,   *But may He be*

That unto me has gyfen slyke grace!"   *given such*

The Pryor said: "What helpes mast

Unto Heven a saule to hast

1025   Out of the payne of Purgatory?"

The voyce answerd and said in hy: *in haste*

"Messes may mast help tham then,

That er said of haly men

And namely of myld Mary fre."   *generous*

1030   The Pryor said: "Than think me   *I think*

The Office of the Ded, certaine,

Of Requiem, was made in vayne,

Sen other availes tham more than it."   *Since; benefit*

The voyce unto him answerd yhit

1035   And said: "Full mykell avail it may,   *great benefit*

When any men for all will pray;

And, for that lawed men here in land   *uneducated*

Kan noght graythely understand,   *readily*

That saules has nede of other messe,

1040   Tharfor that Offyce ordaind es."

The Pryor said: "Sen thou has kende,   *Since; explained*

	That specyall messes may mast amende,	
	Whilk other prayers withouten tha	*Which; besides those*
	May tyttest saules fra penaunce ta?"	*most quickly; from; take*
1045	The voyce answerd and said in hy:	
	"The seven Psalmes with the Letany."	*Litany [of the Saints]*
	The Pryor said: "That war noght ryght;	
	For God the Pater Noster dyght	*established*
	Als of all prayers pryncipall,	
1050	And aungels made the Ave all	*Ave [Maria] (i.e., Hail Mary)*
	Unto myld Mary for our mede,	*reward*
	And twelve apostels made the Crede.	*the [Apostles'] Creed*
	And the seven Psalmes er erthly werkes	
	Ordand of byshopes and other clerkes,	*Made by*
1055	Men for to say that has mysgane,	*gone astray*
	And David made tham everilk ane;	
	And nouther David, wele we ken,	*neither; know*
	Ne byshopes ne nane other men	
	Unto God er noght at neven,	*not to be compared*
1060	Ne yhit unto aungels of Heven,	
	Ne tyll apostels er thai noght pere.	*to; equal*
	Tharfore me think that thair prayere	
	May noght of slyke bounté be	*benefit*
	Als the Pater Noster and the Ave	
1065	And the Crede, that the apostels purvayde."	
	The voyce answerd than and sayde:	
	"Thir prayers er full mykell of mede	*These; great of help*
	And full haly, if we tak hede,	*take heed*
	In thamself, this es sertayne,	
1070	And for thair makers mykell of mayne.	*great of power*
	We sall tham wirschepe, als worthi es,	*worship*
	Bifor all the other, outtane the Messe.	*except*
	Bot nevertheless, sir, certainly,	
	The seven Psalmes with the Letany	*Litany [of the Saints]*
1075	For to say es mast suffrayne	*beneficial*
	Unto saules, that suffers payne;	
	For thai er ordaind, mare and myn,	
	Ever a Psalme for a syn,	
	And so thai stroy the syns seven.	*destroy*
1080	Tharfor thai er nedefull to neven.	*explain*

The fyrst Psalme gudely grayde		*well performed*
Ogayns pryde es purvayde;		*Against; offered*
And thus to understand it es:		
'Lord, deme us noght in Thi wodenes,		*judge; fury*
1085 Als thou dyd Lucifer, that fell		
For his pryde fro Heven to Hell.'		
And so the other Psalmes on raw		*in order*
Ilk ane a syn oway will draw		*Each one*
Thurgh help of halows in fere,		*saints in company*
1090 That ordaind er in that prayere."		
The Pryor eftsones him assayls		*immediately; attacks*
And said: "Tell me, what it avayls,		*avails*
Or if saules the better be,		
Of 'Placebo' and 'Dirige'		*I will please (i.e., appease); Guide [me]*
1095 With the Offyce that for the ded es dyght."		*prescribed*
The voyce answerd him on hyght		*immediately*
(With gret force out gan he bryst)		*burst*
And said: "A, Pryor, and thou wyst		*if you knew*
How gretly that it may tham gayne,		
1100 Than hope I that thou wald be fayne		*eager*
Oft for to bede that blyssed bede		*offer; prayer*
For thi brether that er dede.		
And, for thou sall it better knaw,		
The privatese I sall thee schaw.		*obscure matters*
1105 In 'Placebo' es purvayd		
Fyve Psalmes, that sall be sayd		
Aneli for the evensang,		*Only; evensong (i.e., vespers)*
With fyve antems als omang.		*anthems (i.e., antiphons)*
Tha ten togeder, when thai er mett,		*performed*
1110 For the saul er thusgat sett,		*appointed*
For to restore, wha to tham tentes,		*who; pays attention*
Unto the saule ten comandementes;		
And makes in mynde, how He tham dyd,		
So that His mede sall noght be hyde.		
1115 Tha fyve Psalmes when thai er mett		*performed*
For fyve wittes of the saule er sett,		*wits (senses); appointed*
Tharfor to schew, be reson ryfe,		*rigorous*
How he tham spended in his lyfe		*used*
And that he spended tham noght in vayne		

1120	That sall lett parcells of his payne.	*remit portions*
	The fyve antems sayd bitwene,	*anthems*
	Fyve myghtes of the saule may mene	*powers; mean*
	That sall bere witness on thair wyse	*in their way*
	How he tham spended in Godes servyse.	*used*
1125	Neghen Psalmes than sayd sall be	*Nine*
	Afterward in the 'Dirige,'	
	And thai sall signify full ryght	
	Neghen orders of aungels bryght,	
	The whilk orders the saule sall be in,	*which*
1130	When he es purged of his syn;	
	That order sa he sall fullfyll,	*so*
	When tha Psalmes er sayd him tyll.	*those*
	The neghen antems next folowand	*nine anthems; following*
	And thre versikles, thou understand,	*three versicles*
1135	The twelve poyntes of trowth thai bring ful chere	
	To him, that thai er sayd fore here,	
	And telles how he trowed tham ryght	*trusted*
	Here on this mold, when he had myght,	*earth; ability*
	Als Haly Kyrk him kyndely kende.	*Holy Church; properly taught*
1140	And so thai may him mykell amende.	*much*
	The neghen lessons bi tham all ane	*nine*
	For the neghen degrese er trewly tane;	*accepted*
	For ilk a saule, bus nedes be,	*must needs be*
	Som of thir neghen in his degré,	*these nine*
1145	That es to say, outher yhong or ald	*either young or old*
	Or pore or of pousté bald,	*poor; power strong*
	Outher in clennes lyfe to lede,	*purity*
	Outher in wedlayke or in wydowhede,	*wedlock; widowhood*
	Outher clerk or lawed man—	*uneducated*
1150	In som of their sall he be than:	*these*
	Thir lessons sall to welth him wyn	*These; well-being*
	In whilk degré sa he was in.	*so*
	And the neghen respons for to rede	*responses*
	Sall mak him tyll have mykell mede.	*to have great reward*
1155	The fyve Psalmes of the 'Laudes' all ane	*all together*
	For fyve wittes may wele be tane	*accepted*
	That ilk a saved saule sall fele.	*avail*
	And thai sall bere witnes full wele	

	And fullfyll it with mayn and myght,	*power and might*
1160	That the saule tham used ryght.	
	The fyve antems than folowand	*anthems; following*
	In witnes for the saul sall stand	
	And faythly help for to fullfyll	
	Fyve strenthes, that God gyfes saules untyll.	*gives to souls*
1165	For God gaf, when this world bigan,	
	Thre strenthes of saules to ilk a man,	
	The whilk strenthes of myght er slyke,	
	That unto God man saule es lyke,	
	And allso other strenthes twa	
1170	Unto mans bodyse gan he ma,	*men's bodies; make*
	That to the saule dose na socoures,	*provide no succor*
	Bot makes tham lyke Godes creatures.	
	First I say, bi strenthe of thoght	*by*
	That saule lyke unto God es wroght;	
1175	The secund es strenthe of understandyng,	
	That es lyke Godes Son in that thing;	
	The thred thingh, strenthe of will,	*third*
	The Haly Gast it es lyke tyll;	*like unto*
	And bi mysgangyng and unwytt	*straying; error*
1180	Lyke ane unskylfull best es it.	*non-rational beast*
	Forwhi the saule dwelles als a stane	*Because; stone*
	And feles als a best all ane	*feels; beast*
	And lyfes als tres, thus clerkes telles,	*lives; trees*
	And understandes als gud aungels.	
1185	Thir strenthes er thus ryght arayd,	*These*
	When this servyse for saules es sayd.	
	Allso the psalme of 'Benedictus'	
	And of 'Magnificat' helpes thus	
	For to save the saules fra skathe	*from harm*
1190	Thurgh Godhede and manhede bathe,	*both*
	Wharof thai sall be certayne	
	To se, when thai er past thare payne,	
	And lat tham witt, how thai sall wende	*know*
	And be in blys withouten ende.	
1195	The twa antemes, that er purvayd	*two anthems; provided*
	With the Psalmes for to be sayd,	
	May be tald the company	*recited [by]*

	Of aungels on the ta party	*one side*
	And of halows on the tother syde,	*saints; the other*
1200	That with the saules in blys sall byde.	*abide*
	The colettes, that men efter mase,	*collects; make (i.e., say)*
	Er demed for dedes of grace,	*directed*
	That saved saules to God sall yeld	*yield*
	With all wirschip that thai may weld.	*wield*
1205	And sa when thai er mended of mys,	*so; sin*
	Than sall thai lende in lastand blys.	*reside; lasting*
	Tharfor, sir Pryor, thir prayers	*these*
	Helpes saules thus, als thou heres."	
	Thus when he had declared this thing,	
1210	All that it herd had gret lykyng,	
	And mery made he, ilk a man.	
	Bot than the gast full sone bigan	
	To morne and mak full simple chere,	*downcast expression*
	And sayd to tham on this manere:	
1215	"Askes of me sone what yhe will;	
	Mi tyme es nere neghand me tyll	*approaching to me*
	That me bus gang, als es my grace,	*must go*
	To suffer payne in other place.	
	To gretter grevance bus me ga."	*must; go*
1220	The Pryor said: "Sen it es swa,	*Since; so*
	This wald I witt, first ar thou wende,	*know; before; go away*
	If we may oght to thee amende."	*anything; help*
	With symple voyce than answerd he,	
	And sayd: "If yhe wald say for me	
1225	Fyve sithes specially	*times*
	The fyve joyes of Our Lady,	
	That myght help mykell me untyll."	*much for me*
	Thai graunted all with full gud will,	
	And on thair knes thai sett tham doune	*knees*
1230	And said with gud devocyoune	
	"Gaude, virgo, mater Christi"	*Rejoice, virgin, mother of Christ*
	With the fyve vers folowand fully,	*verses following*
	Bowsomly, als he tham bad,	*Obediently; bade*
	And tharfor was the gast full glad.	
1235	He thanked tham with wordes fre	*gracious*
	And said: "Wele have yhe comforth me;	

Mi payne es somdele passed now,   *somewhat*
That I may better speke with yhow."
The Prior said: "Kan thou oght tell
1240   What deres mast the fendes of Hell?"   *harms most the fiends*
The gast answerd and said in hy:
"The sacrament of Godes Body;
For, in what stede Goddes Body ware,   *place*
And the fendes of Hell war thare,
1245   Unto it burd tham do honoure,   *must*
And so sall ilk a creatoure."
The Pryor said: "Than think me
That all spirites suld it suthely se,   *truly*
When it es on the auter grayed."   *altar set*
1250   The voyce answerd sone and sayde,
That spirites may it kyndely ken   *by nature know*
Mare verraily than other men.   *More truly*
The Pryor asked him this skyll: *reason (i.e., question)*
"May devels do any dere tharetyll   *harm thereto*
1255   Or disturbe it be any way?"   *by*
The voyce answerd and said: "Nay,
Bot if that a prest be unclene,   *Unless; impure*
In dedly syn, that es to mene,   *say*
Or other syn, what som it be.   *whatsoever*
1260   In swilk prestes has the fende pousté   *power*
For to merre tham in thair Messe,   *mar*
If thai dwell in thair wickednes.   *remain*
And yhit he comes noght comonly   *commonly (i.e., ordinarily)*
To ger tham be abayst thereby.   *cause; humiliated*
1265   Bot, when he wate that thai lyf wrang,   *knows; live wrong*
The ofter wald he that thai sang,   *more often*
And that es to encrese thair payne,   *increase*
For of thair evell fare es he fayne."   *behavior; pleased*
The Pryor asked withouten lett   *delay*
1270   And said: "Es thare nane aungell sett
To yheme the auter fra evell thing,   *protect; altar*
Whils Godes Body es in makyng,
And als the prest wisely to wys?"   *wisely to inform*
He answerd and sayd: "Yhis.   *Yes*
1275   And gude aungels war noght biforne,   *If*

With evyll spirytes myght all be lorne,   *lost*
For thai wald sone disturbe the prest
And putt vayne thoghtes into his brest,
So that he suld noght worthily
1280 Have myght for to mak Godes Body
With honoure, als it aw to be.   *ought*
So suld he think on vanyté."
The Pryor said: "I wald witt fayne   *like to know*
What remedy war here ogayne   *against*
1285 For to defende the fendes fell."   *evil*
Than said the voyce: "I sall thee tell.
If that the prest in Godes presence
Be clene in his awen conscience,   *own*
And mak his prayers with clene thoght,
1290 Than the devels may dere him noght."   *harm*
The Pryor said to him thir sawes: *these words*
"Es thare na prayer that thou knawes,
A prest to say byfore he syng,
That myght fordo swilk evell thing?"   *prevent such*
1295 The voyce said: "What prest so hade
The prayer that Saint Austyn made,   *Augustine*
That 'Summe Sacerdos' es calde,   *'Highest Priest' is called*
And he than with devocyoune walde
Say it ilk day, or he sange,   *before*
1300 To Messe than myght he baldly gang,   *confidently go*
For wathes it wald so wele him were,   *From perils; protect*
Unnethes suld any devels him dere."   *Lest; harm*
The Pryor asked him yhit full ryght,
If he saw oght that solempne syght,   *ever; solemn*
1305 Of Godes Body the sacrament,
Out of this world sen that he went.   *since*
The voyce said: "Yha, I se it yhit,   *Yes; now*
For on thi brest thou beres it
In a box thou has it broght,
1310 Als it was on the auter wroght."   *altar*
Hereof the folk awondred ware,
Forwhi thareof wist thai never are,   *Because; previously*
That the Pryor had Godes Body,
Bot resayved it in his Messe anely.   *received*

1315	The Pryor said: "Than wald I witt,	
	Whi that thou noght honours itt,	
	Sen thou says, ilk a creature	
	Till Godes Body sall do honoure,	
	And thou wate wele, that it es here?"	*know*
1320	The voyce answerd on this manere:	
	"I have it honourd in my kynde	*according to my nature*
	With all my myght and all my mynde,	
	Sen first that thou it hyder broght,	
	All if thou persayved it noght."	*Even if you perceived*
1325	The Pryor than with gud entent	
	Toke the Blyssed Sacrament	
	Out of his clathes, whare it was layd,	*clothes*
	And to the spiryt thus he sayd:	
	"If thou trow it stedfastly,	*believe*
1330	That it is Godes Blyssed Body,	
	And ilk a spirit, wele wate thou,	*know*
	Bihoves unto Godes Body bow;	
	And sen it es of swilk pousté,	*since; such power*
	In vertu thareof I comand thee,	
1335	That thou ga with me playne pase	*go; at a brisk pace*
	To the uttermast ghate of all this place."	*gate*
	The voyce answerd: "I am boune,	*obligated*
	Bot noght to folow thi persoune.	
	Bot with my Lord fayne will I wende,	*eagerly*
1340	That thou haldes betwix thi hende."	
	Than the Pryor toke the gate	*way*
	Fast unto the forsayd ghate,	*aforementioned gate*
	And allso his brether twa	
	With him went and many ma.	*more*
1345	He loked obout and saw ryght noght,	
	Bot in his hereyng wele he thoght,	
	That a noyse after tham come	
	Lyke a besom made of brome,	*swishing; broom*
	That war swepand a pavement.	*sweeping*
1350	Swilk a noyse ay with tham went.	*always*
	And than spak the Prior thus:	
	"Thou spirytt, schew thee unto us	*show yourself*
	Witerly als thou ert wroght!"	*Truly; are*

61

Hereto the spiryt answerd noght.

1355 The Pryor than ogayne gan pass

Unto the wydow, whare scho wass

Lygand sare seke in hir bed,   *Lying sorely sick*

So had scho lang bene evell led.

The voyce folowd, als it did are,   *before*

1360 Untyll thai in the chaumbre ware.

Than sone the woman gan bygyn

Grysely for to gnayst and gryn   *Horribly; gnash (teeth); grimace*

And cryed loud, als scho war wode.   *as [if]; insane*

All war astoned, that thare stode.   *astonished*

1365 Gret sorow thai had that syght to se,

For of hir payne was gret peté.   *pity*

Bot nevertheless all men that myght

Assembled for to se that syght

And persued unto that place,   *followed*

1370 For thai wald witt that wonder case.   *understand; circumstance*

The woman lay lyke unto lede   *lead*

In swounyng doune als scho war dede.   *swooning down*

The Pryor, when he saw this care,

Him thoght full evell that he come thare.

1375 Bot nevertheless yhit stode he styll,

And thus he said the voyce untyll:

"In the vertu of Cristes Passyoune

Say me the soth in this sesoune,   *at this time (season)*

Whi it es and for what thing,

1380 That thi wife mase slyke morning."   *makes such mourning*

Than said the voyce full sarily: *sorrowfully*

"Scho wate hirself, als wele als I."   *knows*

The Pryor than with gud entent

Sone unto the woman went,

1385 And till hir thus gan he say:

"In the name of God, dame, I thee pray,

Tell unto me all thi thought."

And scho lay styll and answerd noght,

And so obout the bed thai stode

1390 To luke, if oght myght mend hir mode.   *look; state of mind*

And many for hir wa gan wepe.   *woe*

And sone than scho bigan to crepe

	Upon hir knes, so als scho may,	
	And cryand loud thus gan scho say:	*crying*
1395	"Lord Jesu, als Thou boght me	
	Of my payne, Thou have peté	*pity*
	And graunt me of Thi help in haste."	
	The Pryor than says unto the gaste:	
	"Whi es thi wife thus travaild here?"	*troubled*
1400	The voyce answerd on this manere:	
	"I tald ryght now here thee untyll,	*unto*
	That hirself wist for what skyll;	*knows; reason*
	And, if thou will witt mare allway,	*know more*
	Ask hirself, scho kan thee say."	
1405	Than the Pryor to hir gase,	*went*
	And mykell mane to hir he mase	*great remonstrance; made*
	And said: "To save thiself of sare	*sorrow*
	Tell me the case of all thi care,	
	And out of bale I sall thee bring."	*misery*
1410	Scho lay and answerd him nothing.	
	And he stode als man amayde,	*amazed*
	And till the spirytt sone he sayde:	
	"Thou creature, I conjure thee	*command*
	Bi Godes myght and His pousté,	*power*
1415	And bi the vertu of His body,	
	And of His moder, myld Mary,	
	And bi the mylk He souke swete,	*sucked*
	And bi the teres scho for Him grete	*wept*
	When scho saw hir Son be slane,	*slain*
1420	And bi the halows everilk ane,	*saints; one*
	The certaine soth that thou me say	*truth*
	Of this mervail, if thou may,	*marvel*
	Whi thi wife has all this payne."	
	And than the voyce answerd ogayne	
1425	And said: "Hir murnyng mare and myn	*mourning; more and less (i.e., entirely)*
	Was all for ane unkyndely syn,	*unnatural*
	That we did bifor my ded	*death*
	Betwix us twa here in this stede,	*place*
	Of whilk we bath war schryven sone.	
1430	Bot the penance was noght done.	
	Tharfor our payne us bus fullfyll	*must*

63

Now als ferre als falles tharetyll."   *as far as falls thereto*
The Prior said: "Now, er thou pass,   *before; go away*
Say to me, what syn it was,
1435   That wedded men may warned be
To do nathing in that degré
Ne lyke to it in dede ne thought."
The voyce said: "God will it noght,
That I that syn suld tyll yhow say,
1440   That thurgh schryft es done oway.   *confession; removed*
Of that syn we bath war schryven.   *forgiven*
Tharfor of God it es forgyven
Als to the blame, that be thou bald.   *assured*
Bot touchand penance I thee tald,   *touching; told*
1445   Aseth bus us make for that syn,   *Reparation must*
Or we any welth may wyn.   *Before; well-being*
And that, that es done fra Godes syght,   *away from*
To tell to men it war noght ryght,
Bot if it war, als God forbede,
1450   Eftsones so done in dede.
Bot unto wedded men sall thou say
And warn tham that thai kepe allway
The rewle of wedyng with thair myght
And duely do both day and nyght.   *duly*
1455   For thare er many comon case   *instances*
In whilk wedded men may trispase.   *trespass*
The cases er kyndeli for to ken   *natural to understand*
On molde omang all witty men.   *earth; intelligent*
This was the suffrayne point," sais he,   *main*
1460   "Whi God lete me speke with thee,
That thou suld trow this stedfastly   *believe*
And other men be mended thareby,
So that thai may thair syns forsake
And in thair lyve amendes make."
1465   The woman, wepand als scho lay,   *weeping*
With sary hert thus gan scho say: *sorry*
"Gud Gy, for luf of me,
Say if I sall saved be
Or I sall dwell in dole ever mare   *sorrow*
1470   For that syn that thou nevend are,   *mentioned before*

64

Wharof, I wate, God was noght payd."   *know; requited*
The spirit answerd sone and sayd:
"For that ded thou dred thee noght;
The penaunce nere tyll end es broght.

1475 Thou sall be saved, for certayne."
And than the woman was full fayne   *glad*
And sayd thare kneland on hir kne   *kneeling*
A Pater Noster and ane Ave.
Scho loved God with word and will.

1480 And than the Pryor said hir tyll:
"Dame, whils thou this lyf may lede,
Ilk day, luke thou do almusdede,   *almsdeeds*
For almusdede may syns waste."   *take away*
Unto that word answerd the gaste:

1485 "Dame," he said, "par charyté,   *for charity*
When thou dose almus, think on me,   *do alms*
For to alegge som of my payne."   *alleviate*
And the Pryor than gan him frayne,   *ask*
Whi he come noght in that sesoune

1490 Unto men of religioune
For to tell to tham his lyfe
Titter than unto his wyfe,   *More readily*
Sen that he wist thai war mare nere   *nearer*
To God than any wemen were,   *women*

1495 And mare wisely thai couth him wys.   *could understand him*
The voyce answerd than unto this
And sayd: "I lufed mare my wyfe   *loved more*
Than any other man on lyfe,   *alive*
And tharfor first to hir I went;

1500 And when me was gyfen the jugement
To suffyr penance in this place,
I asked God of His gret grace
That my wife myght warned be
For to amend hir mys bi me.   *sin*

1505 And of His grace He gaf me leve
On this wise hir for to greve   *grieve*
And for to turment hir biforne,
So that scho suld noght be lorne,   *lost*
Ne that scho suld noght suffyr pyne

1510 For hir syns, als I do for myne,	
Bot do it here in hir lyf days."	*living days*
All sone than the Pryor says:	
"Can thou oght tell me how lang	
That thou sall thole tha payns strang?"	*endure; strong*
1515 The spirit sayd: "I understand,	
To Pasch, that now es next command.	*Easter; coming*
Than sall my payne be broght till ende,	
And unto welth than sall I wende."	*well-being*
The Pryor said: "I mervail me	*I am amazed*
1520 How thou to speke has swilk pousté	*capability*
And has na tong ne other thing	*no tongue*
That instrument es of spekyng."	
The voyce answerd on this manere:	
"Ne sese thou noght, a carpentere,	*Do you not see*
1525 That diverse werkes oft sythes has wroght,	*times*
Withouten ax may he do noght?	
The ax ay will redy be	*always*
With him to hew on ilk a tré,	
And it may nouther styr ne stand	*neither move nor*
1530 Withouten help of mans hand.	
Ryght swa a man here yhow omell	*you among*
Withouten tong may nathing tell.	
And with his tong yhit spekes he noght,	
Bot thurgh the ordenance of the thought:	*guidance*
1535 That es, of the saule allways,	
That ordans all that the tong says.	*guides*
And forthi be this tale tak tent,	*therefore; pay attention*
The body es bot ane instrument	
Of the saule, als thou may se,	
1540 And the saule in himself has fre	*freely*
Alkyns vertuse, myght and mynde.	*All powers of strength and thought*
Swilk gyftes er gyfen to him be kynde.	*by nature*
Tharfor he may speke properly	
Withouten help of the body.	
1545 And whare thou says a man may noght	
Speke the thing that comes of thoght,	
Bot he have mowth and tong als,	*mouth; tongue*
In that, I say, thi sawes er fals.	*sayings are false*

66

	For Haly Wryt witnes full ryght	
1550	That God and all his aungels bryght	
	Spekes wisely to als and yhong,	*old and young*
	And thai ne have nouther mowth ne tong.	
	Ryght so may I and ilk spiryte	
	Fourme voyces full perfyte	
1555	And wirk the wordes, how so we will,	
	And spek withouten tong yhow tyll."	
	The Pryor askes him in what stede	
	The saules dwelles when thai er dede	
	Unto tyme that the dome be done:	*judgment*
1560	"For than thou says thai sall witt sone	*Because*
	Whether thai sall to joy or payne."	
	The gast than answerd sone ogayne	
	And said: "A lytell while beforne	
	Or that the erthly lyf be lorne,	*lost*
1565	The saule sall se and here unhyd	*hear unhidden*
	All the dedes that ever he dyd.	
	The ugly devels and aungels bryght	
	And efter the porcyon of his plyght	*afterwards; affliction*
	In that same tyme sall he se,	
1570	Whider that he sall jugged be	
	To comon Purgatory, that es stabyll,	*stable (i.e., permanent)*
	Or unto Purgatory departabyll	*separated*
	Or els unto the payns of Hell	
	Or unto Heven in blys to dwell."	
1575	The Prior than with wordes hende	*courteous*
	Asked how sone a saule myght wende,	
	When it es past fra the body,	
	To Heven or Hell or Purgatory.	
	The voyce answerd and sayd: "It may	
1580	In a lytell space wend all that way.	
	Sone es it broght whare it sall be,	
	Als thou may be ensaumple se.	
	Thou sese, when the son es rysand,	*sun is rising*
	The lyght gase sone over ilk a land;	*goes quickly*
1585	It passes over all the world full playne,	
	Bot if thare stand oght thareogayne.	*Unless; anything in the way*
	Right swa the saules, when men er ded,	

Al sone er in thair certaine stede.

To Heven or Hell thai wend in hy.   *quickly*

1590 And, if thai pass to Purgatory,

Som tyme wende thai noght so sone,

And that es for thair profett done: *profit*

If thai have any faythfull frende

In this world here, when thai wende,

1595 That for tham will ger syng or rede   *prepare to; read*

Or els do any almusdede,

Thai may so do for tham that tyde,   *at that time*

That in the ayre the saule sall byde,   *bide*

Untyll it have the medes tane   *benefits taken*

1600 Of thair prayers everilk ane.

And so bi help of thair gudenes

May his penaunce be made les.

The dedes that er so done in haste

Unto the saule es helpyng maste,

1605 On the same manere als I say

In this ceté was done this day.   *city*

A frere dyed and demed he was

Till comon Purgatory at pas,   *to pass*

Bot in the tyme of his transyng,   *passing over*

1610 Of his brether he asked this thing,

That thai suld do in dede and saw   *word*

For him als thai war bon bi law.   *bound by*

And the messes that tham aght for to say,   *ought*

Pur charyté he gan tham pray,   *For charity*

1615 That thai suld be said in hy

And everilk ane of Our Lady.

And, als he bad, ryght so thai dyd,

And afterward than thus bityd: *occurred*

When he was dede in flessch and fell,   *flesh; skin*

1620 His aungell demed his saule to dwell   *ordered*

In comon Purgatory playne

Thre monethes to suffer payne,

Als worthy was efter his dede.   *As*

Bot than Our Lady Mary yhede,   *went*

1625 And tyll hir Son scho prayd that tyde,   *at that time*

That the saule in the ayre might byde   *air*

Untyll it had the meryte clere
Of dedes that war done for it here.
And twa oyres than bayde it styll   *hours*
1630 In the ayre, als was Godes wyll,
And swilk mercy of God had he
Thurgh prayer of his moder fre   *gracious*
And thurgh the dedes that here was done,
That he sall be in blys full sone.
1635 In payne he has no lengar tyme
Bot fra now unto to morne at pryme."   *prime (about 6:00 a.m.)*
Than sayd the Prior till him sone:
"Whilk dedes of all, that here er done,
May tyttest help a saule to Heven?"   *most quickly*
1640 The voyce answerd and said full even:
"Parfyte werkes of charyté   *Perfect*
That er done als tham aw to be,   *befits them*
That es to say, to Godes bihove,   *according to God's will*
And our evencristen if we love.   *fellow Christians*
1645 Than of our werkes will God be payd."   *be requited (satsified)*
The Pryor answerd sone and sayd:
"If that thou kan, tell us in haste
What maner of men that now er maste
In Purgatory to suffyr payne."
1650 The gaste answerd sone ogayne:
"Na man comes that place within
Bot anely thai that has done syn;
And all that syns and saved sall be,
Er pyned thare of ilk degré   *pained*
1655 Efter the dedes that thai have done."   *According to*
And than the Pryor asked sone,
What manere of folk that he here fande,   *found*
That in thair lyves war best lyfande.   *living*
The voyce said: "Sir, soth it es
1660 And Haly Wryt wele beres wytnes,
That na man aw other to prays,   *ought; praise*
Whether he do wele or evell always;
For mans lyfe es to prayse nathing,
Bot if he may have gud ending.
1665 For na man in this world here wate,   *knows*

Whether he be worthi to luf or hate,
Ne whether his werkes war evell or wele,
Unto the dome be done ilk dele.   *judgment; every bit*
Than sall he se himself, certayne,
1670   Whether he be worthi joy or payne."
The Pryor said: "This ask I thee:
Whilk es maste parfyte degré
Of all that in this ground es grayde?'   *arranged*
The gast answerd sone and sayde:
1675   "I se in ilk state," he says,   *each*
"Som thinges to lak and som to prays.   *lack; praise*
Tharfor I will prayse na degré,
Ne nane sall be dispraysed for me.
Bot nevertheless this wald I rede,   *advise*
1680   To ilk a man in ilk a stede
To serve God with all thair myght
In what degré so thai be dyght."   *assigned*
The Pryor asked with wordes stabyll,   *resolute*
If that God war oght mercyabyll   *at all merciful*
1685   To saules that war in Purgatory.
The gast said: "Yha, sir, sykerly.
For unto som, this es certayne,
Relese He ferth part of thair payne,   *Releases; one-fourth*
Of som the thred part He releses,   *one-third*
1690   Of som the secund part He seses.   *one-half; remits*
And that es for gude prayers sake,
That frendes here for tham will make.
If any dedes be for tham done,
Than may thai pass fra payns sone.
1695   Lyfand frendes thus may tham lett   *Living; relieve*
Of payn that thai suld dregh be dett,   *suffer by obligation*
And als the prayers of aungels
And of halows, that in Heven dwelles."
The Pryor said: "This wald I crave:
1700   Whatkyn payn thiself sall have,
In Purgatory whils thou sall dwell?"
The voyce said: "I sall thee tell.
In flawme of fyre thus bus me stand,   *flame; must*
That alther hattest es brynand,   *hottest of all; burning*

1705	And have na comforth me to kele."	*cool*
	The Pryor said: "Now se I wele,	
	That thou ert no sothfast gaste.	*true spirit*
	That sall I prove thee here in haste.	
	This wate thou wele, if thou have mynde,	
1710	God dose nathing ogayns kynde.	*contrary to the laws of nature*
	For, if He dyd, this dar I say,	
	His werkes wald sone be wast oway.	*destroyed*
	And bodyly thing the fyre I call,	
	And thou a gast spirytuall;	
1715	And bodily thing may have no myght	
	In gastly thing bath day and nyght.	
	Than be ensaumple may thou se,	
	That fyre may have no myght in thee,	
	All if thou tharein graythely gang."	*properly*
1720	The voyce answerd: "Sir, thou has the wrang,	
	That thou me calles sa dyssayvabyll,	*deceitful*
	Sen thou has fon in me no fabyll.	*caught; fable*
	Bot neverthelesse, sire, whare thou says	
	That bodily thing be nakyn ways	*no kind of*
1725	In gastely thing may have powere,	
	I answer thee on this manere.	
	Thou wate wele that the devels sall lende	*dwell*
	In fyre of Hell withouten ende,	
	And that fyre es als bodily	*as*
1730	Als the fyre of Purgatory,	*As*
	And yhit pynnes it the devels in Hell,	*pains*
	Als God says in His awen Gosspell,	*own*
	And als He to the fendes sall say	
	And to the dampned on Domesday:	*damned; Judgment Day*
1735	'Yhe weryed gastes, I byd yhow wende	*troubled spirits*
	To fyre that lastes withouten ende,	
	That ordand es for nathing els	*ordained*
	Bot to the devell and his aungels.'	
	And, whare thou says, that God does noght	
1740	Ogayns kynde in thinges He wroght,	
	I say, He dose, als folk may fynde,	
	Bi miracle ogayns kynde,	
	Als whilom fell of childre thre,	*once befell*

71

	That ordand war brynt to be.	*ordered; burnt*
1745	In Haly Wrytt er thai named so:	
	Sydrac, Misaac, and Abdenago.	
	Thai war done with full gret ire	*put*
	Intyll a chymné full of fyre;	*furnace*
	And, als it was Our Lordes will,	
1750	The fyre dyd nanekyn harme tham tyll,	*no kind of*
	Bot hale and sounde thai satt and sang,	*healthy*
	Lovand the myght of God omang.	*Loving*
	Thus war thai saved in that stede	*place*
	Fra fyre and fra that kyndely dede.	*natural death*
1755	Ryght so has God ordand in me	
	That the fyre has no pousté	*power*
	To wast me, if I stand tharein,	*destroy*
	Bot for to pyne me for my syn."	*pain*
	Than sayd the Pryor: "Sen thou says,	
1760	That fyre obout the bryns allways,	*burns*
	Than think me that this hows and we	
	Suld bryn all for the fyre of thee,	
	Sen that it es so hate and kene."	*hot; sharp*
	The voyce sayd: "Now es wele sene	
1765	That in thee es full lytell skyll.	*is; rational power*
	For ryght now tald I thee untyll	
	That God may withdraw thurgh His myght	
	The strenthe of fyre both day and nyght	
	So that it no harme may do	
1770	In thing that it es putt unto,	
	Als He dyd of the childre thre,	
	Of whame bifore I tald to thee.	
	Allso thou sese, fyre of levenyng	*see; lightning*
	Wendes obout be alkyn thing	*all kinds of*
1775	Kyndely, als clerkes declare it kan,	
	And nouther bryns it hows ne man.	
	And als thou sese, the son may passe	*sun*
	Thurgh wyndows that er made of glasse,	
	And the glass noght enpayred tharby.	*harmed (impaired)*
1780	So may a spiryt, sikerly,	*surely*
	In ilk a place com in and out	
	And bryn noght that es him obout,	

72

	Howses ne clathes ne other atyre,	*attire*
	All if himself be flaumand in fyre.	*Even if*
1785	And so this hows may resayve me	*receive*
	And itself noght enpayred be.	*harmed*
	Bot, certes, this sall thou understand:	
	If all howses in ilk a land	
	In a sted war brynand schire,	*At once; burning entirely*
1790	It myght noght be so hate a fyre	*hot*
	Als I now suffyr nyght and day."	
	And than the Pryor to him gan say,	
	Askand of him this resoun,	*Asking*
	If he trowed the Incarnacyoune,	*believed*
1795	How Jesu Crist toke flessh and blode.	
	The voyce answerd with eger mode	*sharp manner*
	Till that questyon all with envy,	
	And full loud thus gan he cry:	
	"A, my Pryor, whilk er tha men,	*which*
1800	That the Incarnacyoune will noght ken?	
	Whilk er tha, that will noght knaw,	*those*
	How aungels sayd it in thair saw?	*teaching*
	And devels trowes it wonder wele,	*accept*
	And saules in payne thai may it fele.	
1805	Full mykell wa thai er worthy,	*woe*
	That will noght trow it stedfastly.	
	To ask me yit, it war no need;	
	In Haly Wryt thiself may rede	
	That thus says in the Gospell of Cryste:	
1810	'Wha trewly trowes and es baptyst,	*Who; believes; baptized*
	Till endeles blys thai sall be broght,'	
	And allso: 'Who so trowes noght,	
	How Crist on mold toke our manhede,	*earth assumed a human nature*
	Thai sall be dampned withouten drede	*damned without doubt*
1815	And ever have bale withouten blys.'"	
	Than said the Pryor: "Tell me this:	
	Sen the Sarzyns and the Jewes	
	And the payens it noght trowes,	*pagans; believe*
	Whi God lates tham dwell so lang	*lets; remain*
1820	In thair thoght, sen thai trow wrang,	*believe wrongly*
	And sen thai will for na resoune	*argument*

Trow Cristes Incarnacyoune."   *Believe*
Than the voyce answerd him tyll:
"It es na questyoun of Godes will;
1825   And tharfor neven it noght me to   *mention*
To ask whi God dose so or so
Of thing that touches to His Godhede,   *Divinity*
Bot fande to do His will in dede.   *endeavor*
I wate noght whi tham lyf es lent,
1830   Bot if it be to this entent: *Unless*
That Cristen men may on tham fyght
In the fayth for to defend thair ryght;
For, on tham bataile for to bede,
May Cristen men encres thair mede,   *increase; reward*
1835   If faith be fully in thair fare."   *expedition*
And than the Pryor asked mare:
"Kan thou oght tell me, whilk manere of syn
Er used mast omang mankyn?"   *mankind*
The voyce answered on this wise:
1840   "Pryde and lychory and covatyse   *lechery; covetousness*
And usury, thir foure in fere   *these; together*
With thair braunches many and sere   *diverse*
That er full wlatsom day and nyght   *disgusting*
Bifor God and His aungels bryght.
1845   And thre syns er, if thai be done,
For whilk God will tak vengance sone:
Ane es, if man and woman here
Won samen, als thai wedded were,   *Live together*
And wandes noght thair will to wirk   *fear*
1850   Withouten the sacrament of Haly Kyrk,   *Holy Church*
Or if thai be wedded that tyde
And outher syn on outher syde   *either; either*
To breke thair spowsage in that space: *marriage*
To God this es a gret trispase.   *trespass*
1855   The tother syn es noght to say,   *The other*
Bot clerkes full kyndely knaw it may.
The thred syn es full evell thing,   *third*
That es manslaghter with maynsweryng."   *manslaughter; perjury*
Thus when all thir sawes war sayd   *these teachings*
1860   The woman to the Prior prayd,

That he wald spek the gast untyll,
So that he dyd hir no more ill
For the luf of God of myghtes mast.
The Pryor than said to the gast:

1865 "I conjure thee be God all ane   *command*
And bi His halows everilk ane,
If thou may schon, that thou sese   *believe; cease*
And lat thi wyf now lyf in pese
And persue hir no more with payne."

1870 Than the gast answerd ogayne:
"That may I noght for nanekyns nede,   *no kind of*
Bot scho lyf chaste in wydowhede   *Except if*
And allswa ger syng for us twa   *also has sung*
Thre hundereth messes withouten ma: *hundred; more*

1875 A hundreth of the Haly Gast sall be   *hundred*
Or els of the Haly Trinité,
And a hundreth of Our Lady
And of Requiem fyfty
And other fyfty als in fere   *together*

1880 Of Saint Peter, the apostell dere."
The woman herd thir wordes wele
And graunted to do ilk a dele,   *everything*
And went with gud devocyoune
Till all the freres of the toune

1885 And prestes and monkes of ilk abbay   *abbey*
And gert tham syng all on a day   *had them*
Thre hundreth messes gudely grayde   *performed*
On the covand bifore sayde.   *promise*
And so when that thai songen ware,

1890 The gast of Gy greved hir no mare.
Bot yhit the Pryor in that place
Unto the gast twa resons mase   *inquiries makes*
And asked, if he wist on what wyse   *knew in what way*
Or in whilk tyme Anticrist suld ryse

1895 And tak ogayn trew Cristen men.   *assail*
The gast on this wise answerd then
And said: "It falles noght unto me
To tell noght of Godes preveté.   *secret things*
It es na question us unto

1900   What so His will es for to do."
        The Prior said: "Me think ryght wele
        Thou heres my spekyng ilk a dele."
        The gast said: "Yha, for certayne."
        And sone the Pryor sayd ogayne:
1905   "Than has thou eres to thi hereyng,
        Forwhi thou ert a bodily thing
        And noght gastly, als thou has tald."
        The voyce answerd with wordes bald: *confident*
        "Haly Wryt schewes us this skyll: *explanation*
1910   The Spirit enspires whare it will,
        And His voyce wele may thou here,
        Bot thou may noght on na manere
        Witt what place that it comes fra
        Ne unto what place it sall ga."
1915   And, ryght als he thir wordes gan say,   *these*
        Sodainly he went oway,
        So that thai herd of him no mare
        In that tyme, whils thai war thare.
        And be than was tyme of evensange,   *by; evensong (vespers)*
1920   And the Prior bad ilk man gang,   *bade*
        In the name of God, whare thai wald be:
        "And, whare yhe com, in ilk contré,
        If yhe be asked of this case,
        Says the soth, ryght als it wase
1925   And als it es here proved in dede."
        And hastily than hame thai yhede.   *home; went*
        The Pryor than withouten faile
        The woman thus he gan counsaile,
        That scho suld kepe hir clene and chaste,
1930   Als scho was warned with the gaste.   *As*
        And als he bad aneother thinge,
        That ilk day a prest suld synge
        Contynuely thare in that place
        For Gy saule fro thethen to Pase.   *then to Easter*
1935   With full gud will the woman dyd
        Als the Pryor gan hir byd.
        A prest sho gat with full gud chere.
        Bot hir hows durst scho noght com nere;

	Scho was so dredand ay for dole.	*dreading always*
1940	And on the twelft day efter Yhole,	*Yule (Christmas)*
	That clerkes calles Epiphany,	
	Untyll the freres scho went in hy,	
	And tyll the Prior sone scho yhode,	*went*
	That had done hir so mykell gude.	*such great*
1945	And he ordaind with all his mayne	*determined; power*
	Untyll hir hows to wend ogayne	
	For to here and herken mare,	*hear; listen once more*
	If thai myght fynd that ferly fare.	*wonder done*
	He toke of other orders twa,	
1950	Of Austyns and Menours allswa,	*Augustinians; Franciscans also*
	So that thai war twenty freres	
	All samen outtane seculeres.	*together not counting diocesan priests*
	And samen so ogayne thai went	
	To Gyes hows with gud entent,	
1955	And in that hows said thai and he	
	"Placebo" with the "Diryge"	
	For his saule, that was husband thare,	
	Als he and his brether did are.	
	When thai had sayd in gud degré	
1960	Till "Requiescant in pace,"	
	Thai herd a voyce com tham besyde,	
	Als it did at that other tyde.	*time*
	Lyke a besom bi tham it went	*broom*
	That war swepand on a pavement.	*sweeping*
1965	Tharfor som of the folk war flayd,	*frightened*
	Bot till it sone the Pryor sayd:	
	"I conjure thee with mayn and mode	*strength and courage*
	In the vertu of Cristes blode,	
	In this stede at thou stand styll	
1970	And answer, what we say thee tyll."	
	And than the voyce with wordes meke,	
	Als a man that had bene seke,	*sick*
	Untyll the Pryor thus gan say:	*Unto*
	"Whi deres thou me thus ilk a day?	*trouble*
1975	It es noght lang sen I tald thee	
	What thing so thou wald ask of me,	
	What suld I now say to yhow here?"	

And than answerd aneother frere,
A divynour of gret clergy,   *wise man*
1980 And said: "Tell here till us in hy,
Whether that thou of payn be quytt,
Or els what payne thou suffers yhit."
The voyce answerd sone onane
And sayd: "Love God all His lane!   *grace*
1985 For swilk grace unto me es grayde   *conveyed*
Thurgh messes, that war for me sayde,
That fra this tyme now afterward
Am I past fra the payns hard
In comon Purgatory thare I was are.
1990 In that place sall I com no mare."
Untyll that voyce than said the frere:
"Tell us what penance has thou here,
Sen thou fra Purgatory es paste."   *passed*
The voyce answerd at the laste:
1995 "I suffer flawme of fyre full hate."   *flame; hot*
The frere said: "Tell us, if thou wate,   *know*
If anything amend thee may."
The voyce answerd and sayd: "Nay.
Me bus it suffer certaine days."   *I must*
2000 Yhit than the Prior to him says:
"Lo, how have I gederd here   *gathered*
Freres and other folk in fere   *together*
Of thi wordes to bere witnes
And of thir mervayls mare and les,
2005 That we may all this case declare
Bifor the pape, when we com thare.   *pope*
And tharfor tell us som mervaile
That we may trow withouten fayle."   *believe*
The voyce answerd to thir sawes: *these requests*
2010 "I am noght God, that wele thou knawes,
And mervayls falles to na man els
Bot unto Him and His aungels.
And nevertheless thus I yhow teche:
Bot if yhe better the pople preche   *Unless; people*
2015 Than yhe have done this tyme beforne,
Lightly may yhe be forlorne;   *lost*

And speke yhe sall mast specyally
Ogayns the syn of symony,   *simony*
Usur and manslaghter and maynsweryng,   *Usury; manslaughter; perjury*
2020 Avoutry and fals witnes beryng.   *Adultery; lying*
Thir syns, bot if the folk forsake,
I warn yhow God will vengeance take,
And warn it, whar for the prayere
Of myld Mary, His moder dere,
2025 And of His halows everilk ane
Grevouse vengance mond be tane   *Grievous; might; taken*
Full many tymes omang mankyn,
When thai use swilk outrage syn.   *commit such outrageous sin*
And yhe sall suffer the same payne,
2030 Bot if yhe preche fast thareogayne.   *Unless; hard thereagainst*
For syn es used now wele mare
Than any werkes of Godes lare.   *teaching*
That sall thai som tyme full sare rew."   *sorrowfully*
Than asked the Pryor, if he knew,
2035 How many papes suld be of Rome
Fra that tyme tyll the Day of Dome.   *Judgment*
The voyce said: "I kan tell nathing
What sall fall in tyme coming.
Tharfor thou may noght wit for me
2040 How many papes of Rome sall be
Ne what sall com ne what es gane.   *gone*
And tharfor may yhe now ilk ane,
Whare so yhe will, wende forth yhour way,
Bot for me luke fast that yhe pray   *look*
2045 And for all saules, that suffers payne.
For this I say yhow for certayne:
Haly Kyrk prays noght so fast
For Cristen saules, that hethen er past,   *hence; passed*
Als thai war won, ryght wele I ken   *used to*
2050 Ne no mare dose religiouse men.
Tharfor I rede thai mend tham sone,   *advise*
Or any evell be to tham done."   *Before*
Thir tales when he had tald tham tyll,   *These*
He sayd no mare, bot held him styll,
2055 And of him herd thai than no mare.

Tharfor all men that thare ware
Went and tald thir thinges ilk one   *these*
Playnly unto the Pape John
The twa and twenty, I understand.
2060 And at the Pasch next folowand   *following*
That same pape sent men of his
For to seke the soth of this.   *truth*
The hows of Gy oft sythes thai soght,   *many times*
Bot of the gast ne fand he noght,   *found*
2065 And thareby myght men witt full even
That he was went up intyll Heven,   *into*
Whare comforth es withouten care,
Als himself had said tham are.   *before*
Untyll that comforth Crist us ken
2070 Thurgh prayer of His moder! Amen.

Explanatory Notes to *The Gast of Gy*

Abbreviations: see Textual Notes.

1   *Saint Michael.* One of the three archangels (Michael, Gabriel, and Raphael), who were the special messengers of God. In Scripture he is the leader of the angels who will fight the dragon in the last days (Apocalypse 12:7), and, although not mentioned by name, he is traditionally considered the angel who stood guard at the gate of Eden to prevent Adam and Eve's return (Genesis 3:24). He is the guide in the tour of Hell in the *Apocalypse of St. Paul*, a late fourth-century non-canonical book which was influential in medieval vision literature.

2   *Saint Austyn.* St. Augustine, bishop of Hippo (354–430), is a Doctor of the Church — a learned teacher distinguished for interpretation of doctrine. He is also a Father of the Church, along with St. Gregory the Great, St. Ambrose, and St. Jerome — the most influential early Doctors. A prolific writer whose works include *Confessions, City of God, Enchiridion on Faith, Hope, and Charity*, and much more, he shaped the thinking of the Church for centuries, and was especially influential in the fourteenth century, when he is frequently cited by vernacular writers (Chaucer, Langland, Trevisa, Usk, Gower) as well as theologians like Bradwardine and Wyclif.

5   *clerkes.* Although "clerk" usually refers specifically to clerics in minor orders, it here refers to all learned men in religious life.

11   *Saint Paule.* St. Paul, author of the Epistles that comprise the largest segment of Christian Scripture, influenced Christian thought throughout the Middle Ages. His Epistles are frequently cited by St. Augustine and other Doctors of the Church as sound doctrine and reliable commentary on the rest of Scripture.

13–14   A loose translation of St. Paul's Epistle to the Romans 15:4. The idea that all writing, if properly interpreted, works for our spiritual instruction is a commonplace in the Middle Ages: see Augustine's *De Doctrina Christiana* 10, for example. Chaucer, at the conclusion of The Nun's Priest Tale, says:

For Seint Paul seith that al that writen is,
To oure doctrine it is ywrite, ywis. (*CT* VII[B²]3441–42)

Or, again, in the Retraction: "For oure book seith, 'Al that is writen is writen for oure doctrine,' and that is myn entente" (*CT* X[I]1083).

28   *withowten fabill.* Despite the proposition that all writing was, or could be, for our instruction, "fabill" is a particularly charged word. It was often used to identify fictions or illusory stories considered spiritually dangerous or misleading. Chaucer's Parson makes the distinction, explicitly referring to 1 Timothy 1:4, 4:7 and 2 Timothy 4:4:

Thou getest fable noon ytoold for me,
For Paul, that writeth unto Thymothee,
Repreveth hem that weyven soothfastnesse
And tellen fables and swich wrecchednesse. (*CT* X[I]31–34)

Although a fable can mean "a short fictitious narrative meant to carry a moral" (*MED*), it is much more often "a false statement intended to deceive; a fiction, untruth, falsehood, lie"; or "a fictitious or imaginative narrative or statement, especially one based on legend or myth" (*MED*).

31–42   These lines attempt to establish historicity by specific identification of time and place. In R, Gy dies on 20 November (*XII kalendes*, line 39) 1323. There are differences in other manuscripts, though all agree on the year except Q, which, erroneously, has 1333. In R, the Gast of Gy begins his haunting on the eighth day after his death (27 November). All MSS agree that his wife seeks out the Pryor three days after Christmas: 27 December, the feast of St. John the Evangelist.

37   *Alexty.* The name of the town, Alexty, is variable and confusing in the manuscripts. Alais (or Alés), in the Department of Gard, seems most likely.

38   *Bayoune.* I.e., Bayonne, though the city intended is almost certainly Avignon, which John XXII had made the seat of the Papacy in 1316. Avignon is, indeed, about thirty miles from Alais (Alexty).

48   The Gast of Gy's voice can be heard, but he is invisible. A pictorial representation of the scene found in MS Getty 31 shows the observers gathered around an empty space. Although some revenants appeared as spectral images, invisibility was more common, because of the incorporeality of the soul.

51   *rugged and rent.* It is unlikely that the body of Gy's wife is "distraught and torn," though she may have done herself some damage in her distress. More likely, *rugged* refers to her mental state, while *rent* suggests that she has torn her clothes ("rent her garments") in the classical manifestation of grief and perturbation.

54   *Eghtene.* The sense is "the eighth day in order," i.e., after a week.

56–57   The distinction between "good ghosts" and "fiends" was the object of much learned and popular speculation.

60–61   *freres . . . prechours.* I.e., Dominicans. Founded by St. Dominic in 1220, the Dominicans were one of the mendicant orders that propagated the doctrine of Purgatory most vigorously in the thirteenth and fourteenth centuries. A notably intellectual order, the order of both Albertus Magnus and Thomas Aquinas, they particularly opposed Pope John XXII's dubious position that the soul would remain in Purgatory until the Last Judgment.

63   *Pryor.* A prior is the chief officer, spiritual and administrative, of a Dominican establishment called a convent.

65   Gy died on 20 November and the "haunting" began on the eighth day (i.e., seven days later). Three days after Christmas, 27 December, she sought out the Dominican prior for help. (Medieval counting of duration, like the classical, included the first day in the numeration.)

75   *spyll.* The sense is that the ghost returns to that former place of rest to give audience to his agitated message. The bed is now "spoiled," "made desolate," "subverted," "deprived of its intended use" (*MED*).

97   *brether.* Friars were referred to as "brothers," emphasizing the communal basis of the mendicant orders.

104   *chapter bell.* The chapter bell summoned the friars to meet as a group, "in chapter."

114   After this line, other versions of the poem variously identify the disciplines of the two masters. See textual note.

134–36   It is essential that everyone involved, friars and mayor's men, receive the sacrament of Penance and receive the Eucharist before embarking on the mission, because the Pryor could not be sure whether they were about to encounter a benevolent spirit, as the Gast of Gy turns out to be, or a false or evil spirit, a fiend.

137   *Requiem.* I.e., Mass for the Dead. The name comes from the sentence *Requiem aeternam dona eis, Domine* (Eternal rest grant unto them, Lord.) This sentence also recurs throughout the *Officium defunctorum* (the Office of the Dead), which was part of the *Breviarium romanum* (the Roman Breviary), the compendium of prayers, mostly Psalms, required for daily recitation by members of mendicant orders and adapted to the liturgical season or a specific purpose, e.g., funerary. The use of the plural *eis* (them) in both the Requiem and the Office of the Dead is important in view of the later discussion in the poem about whether masses said for an individual also benefitted all the faithful departed.

141–42   *Howsell . . . howsyld.* The sacrament of the Eucharist (Holy Communion); the reception of the consecrated body and blood of Christ in the form of bread and wine.

146   *bost.* Any box or receptacle; here applied to a pyx, a vessel for carrying a consecrated Communion host, usually to the sick or dying.

155   The balanced construction in this line is a noteworthy feature of R. N usually provides a coordinating conjunction.

166   As the Pryor enters, he says *Pax huic domui* ("Peace be to this house"), the words that Jesus told the seventy-two disciples to say as they entered each house on their evangelical mission (Luke 10:5). The Latin is translated in the next two lines though *allway* is, strictly speaking, superfluous. The Pryor continues (lines 169–205) to say prayers appropriate to entering the house of one recently deceased.

171   *Vidi aquam.* The first words of the rite of sprinkling with holy water before Mass during Eastertide (from Easter Sunday to Pentecost). The prayer, a responsorial between priest and choir, is based on Ezechial 47:1, where Ezechial has a vision of waters pouring from under the Temple. Although the *Vidi aquam*, with its sprinkling of holy water, is an appropriate introductory prayer, it is out of season on December 27. The Pryor seems to be mounting a powerful introduction to the ceremonial prayers that follow.

Explanatory Notes

172   *Veni, Creator Spiritus.* The first words of one of the most popular hymns of the Middle Ages. It is an invocation of the Holy Spirit sung at the beginning of the Mass of the Holy Spirit and on other special occasions. The emphasis on the Holy Spirit is especially significant in view of the later discussion between the Gast of Gy and the Pryor about the special efficacy of the Mass of the Holy Spirit for souls in Purgatory (lines 817–902). It was included in various places in the recitation of the *Breviarium romanum* at the canonical hours, and dates from the ninth century.

173–74   *Colett . . . fidelium.* A Collect, or Oratio, is a short prayer consisting of an invocation, a petition, and a glorification of Christ or God. This Collect, *Deus, qui corda fidelium Sancti Spiritus illustracione docuisti* (O God, who didst instruct the hearts of the faithful by the light of the Holy Spirit), was assigned to the Mass of the Holy Spirit and fits well after the recitation of *Veni, Creator Spiritus.* The Holy Spirit remains prominent in the sequence of prayers.

176   *Asperges me.* The first words of the rite of sprinkling the congregation with holy water, usually before Mass, outside of Eastertide (when the *Vidi Aquam* was used). Like the *Vidi Aquam* it is a responsorial between priest and choir. The prayer is based in the Vulgate on Psalm 50:9. By using both the *Vidi Aquam* and the *Asperges*, the Pryor seems to be attempting an especially powerful invocation.

193   *Dominus vobiscum.* "The Lord be with you." A frequent phrase in many liturgies. The usual response, not given here, is *Et cum spiritu tuo* (And with your spirit).

197   *In principio.* "In the beginning," the first words of the Gospel according to St. John. The whole verse is: *In principio erat Verbum, et Verbum erat apud Deum, et Deus erat Verbum* (In the beginning was the Word, and the Word was with God, and the Word was God.) Traditionally, John 1:1–14 was recited at the end of the "Post-Communion," the last part of the Mass. The lines are an affirmation of Christ's Incarnation, which, like the Mass of the Holy Spirit, becomes prominent later in the poem (lines 447–56). The use of John 1:1 is also appropriate because it is the Evangelist's feast day.

202–05   These lines indicate that the Pryor recites the Office of the Dead (*Officium defunctorum*) from the Roman Breviary (*Breviarium romanum*). This liturgy was composed primarily of psalms, antiphons (short interspersed prayers from Psalms or elsewhere in Scripture), Collects (see explanatory note to lines 173–74), and responses appropriate to the canonical hours of Vespers, Matins, and Lauds. The canonical hours were prescribed times throughout the day: Matins (during the night), Lauds (just before

85

dawn), Prime (sunrise), Terce (mid-morning), Sext (noon), Nones (mid-afternoon), Vespers (sundown), and Compline (bedtime). They were required of all clergy and recited communally by religious orders of monks and friars. The prescribed prayers varied according to the liturgical season or some special purpose, such as prayers for the dead.

The Office of the Dead included the prayers and readings associated with Vespers (*Placebo* is the first word of the first antiphon for Vespers), Matins (*Dirige* is the first word in the prescribed Matins), and Lauds, followed by the seven Penitential Psalms (6, 31, 37, 50, 101, 129, and 142 in the Vulgate), a recitation of the Litany of the Saints, and concluding with the threefold invocation: *Agnus Dei, qui tollis peccata mundi, miserere nobis* ("Lamb of God, who takes away the sins of the world, have mercy on us"). The first half of this line is based on John 1:29, which itself is based on Isaias 53:7. In the Requiem Mass and in the Office of the Dead the second half of the line could be *dona eis requiem* (grant them rest). Some other variations were allowable. Thus, the Pryor and his two brothers effectively recite the Office of the Dead when they enter Gy's house.

208   *Als a child sayand: "Amen."* N expands to *als of* so as to mean "as of a child saying 'Amen.'" But R: *als* is clear: "Like a child saying 'Amen.'"

215   *was and es and sall be ay.* A thanksgiving (doxological) response common in Christian liturgy (*sicut erat in principio et nunc, et semper, et in saecula saeculorum*) that follows the priest's *Gloria Patri, et Filio, et Spiritui Sancto* (compare line 214). Here it serves as a precautionary warning against evil spirits. The English phrase is sometimes used by writers to indicate duration (e.g., Chaucer's *TC* 1.236–37).

224   *kynde.* A complex word that refers most generally to "the aggregate of inherent qualities or properties of persons" (*MED*). It can also refer to the "natural disposition or temperament of a person or animal," or even clan, parentage, or lineage (*MED*). Here, and in most places in the poem, it seems to indicate "intrinsic nature" or "natural capacity," that which is within the capacity of human nature.

235   *ill gast or a gud.* The poem returns to the familiar medieval distinction between good ghosts and demonic fiends or phantasms.

239–50 The Gast of Gy argues that, since Scripture says (Genesis 1:31) that all of God's creation is good, he is therefore a good ghost by nature (*kynde*, line 248) and only evil according to sinful deeds performed in life for which he is now making satisfaction.

Explanatory Notes

297–98   *For lawed folk . . . oft walkand.* The Pryor refers to the sightings by *lawed* (i.e., "uneducated") *folk* of evil men walking the land after death. Popular speculation and theological controversy both considered the question of whether the damned (as well as purgatorial spirits) had the power to return to earth. The orthodox answer was that it could occur only with God's permission for the instruction and benefit of the living.

331–34   *For ilk a man . . . or in Hell.* The Gast of Gy explains that penance for sins must be done on earth, in Purgatory, or in the endless pains of Hell. This section of the poem expounds an especially Dominican view on a controversial subject.

351–52   *Wa unto that man . . . whame sklaunder comes.* To give scandal is to perform an action that leads another towards spiritual destruction (Matthew 18:6–7).

377–83   *This ask I thee . . . sacramentes ilk ane.* The Pryor asks the crucial purgatorial question: how is it possible for a person to receive the last sacraments and still be evil after death. The Gast explains that, although the spirit is not evil by nature, there is a residue of guilt for which satisfaction must be made, even after sins have been forgiven, through penitential acts on earth or temporary suffering in Purgatory. Theologians distinguished between *culpa*, the guilt that could be absolved in the Sacrament of Penance, and *poena*, the retribution or satisfaction that still had to be made.

409–10   *And clerkes proves . . . reles us of a yher.* Although it is stated somewhat confusingly, the idea is that a day of penance done on earth will release the sinner from a year of suffering in Purgatory. Arithmetical correspondences came late in the development of the doctrine of Purgatory and were never universally agreed upon.

447–52   *Be Haly Wrytt . . . mayden myld of mode.* The Gast of Gy refers to statements by the Hebrew prophets that were taken by Christians to foretell the Incarnation of Christ (e.g., Isaias 7:14–15 and 9:6–7). A good source for a systematic cataloguing of such passages would be *The Bible of the Poor (Biblia Pauperum): A Facsimile and Edition of the British Library Blockbook C.9.d.2*, trans. with commentary by Albert C. Labriola and John W. Smeltz (Pittsburgh: Duquesne University Press, 1990). See the Latin transcription and English translation of the dozens of passages from the Hebrew Bible that are used as prefigurations of New Testament verses (pp. 55–139).

470–78   *It es na lyknes . . . what thing suld fall.* The Gast of Gy explains that prophets could speak of things they never saw because of a special gift of God to instruct the people. The question and answer are not compatible. The Pryor had asked whether the Gast knew who would be saved and who would be damned, and used the foreknowledge of the prophets as a reason why souls in Purgatory should know. The Pryor's analogy is weak, but the Gast simply responds to the question of the knowledge possessed by the prophets. The Gast does profess ignorance about the fate of other souls. Just what souls in Purgatory knew was a matter of disputatious conjecture.

475   *gyftes of the Haly Gaste.* The seven gifts of the Holy Spirit are *sapientia* ("wisdom"), *intellectus* ("understanding"), *consilium* ("counsel"), *fortitudo* ("might"), *scientia* ("knowledge"), *timor Domini* ("fear of God"), and *pietas* ("piety"). See Isaias 11:2 for the first six, to which the Vulgate added piety. According to Frère Lorens, in his *Somme le roi*, the gifts of the Holy Spirit "doth away and destroieth the seven deadly sins" (see Jeffrey, p. 307).

498–504   *Ryght in thi wordes . . . dampned had bene.* The Pryor objects that fiends (devils) sometimes have had knowledge of who has been saved and who has been damned. The Gast responds that souls in Purgatory do not know such things unless God or an angel tells them (quite a common view). The Pryor has switched his attention from previous knowledge, as in the example of the prophets, to present knowledge of who is saved and who is damned.

536–38   *Thare er Purgatoryes sere . . . aneother es.* The distinction between "comon" Purgatory (see line 556) and *departabill* (line 538) Purgatory was not universally accepted. Gregory the Great in his *Dialogues* has an *exemplum* involving a soul doing his purgation on earth. One common view was that Purgatory was experienced in two places — a common location, usually beneath the earth, and the place where the sin was committed. In such views, the soul generally was in common Purgatory by day and *departabill* Purgatory by night — just the reverse of the Gast's situation.

556–58   *comon Purgatori . . . In mydes of all the erth.* The location of a "common" Purgatory in the middle of the earth was an ancient tradition, perhaps borrowing from classical antiquity. That is where Dante places it, though he adds the mountain, another frequent image of Purgatory, and he has no "departabill" Purgatory. In *Sir Owain* and the whole tradition of St. Patrick's Purgatory, it is below ground and can be entered at Saints' Island (later at Station Island), Lough Derg, County Donegal. The important matter is that Purgatory was a place, not just a "state."

595–97   *Telle, if thou kan . . . when he es tane.* The experience of the soul immediately after death was a source of much controversy. The Gast proceeds to summarize how the saved are protected, the evil are condemned, and the middling are assigned to Purgatory, while angels and fiends hover. The roles of the angels and fiends vary in vision literature. There is no indication of gradations of punishment, merely various lengths of time. Views on these issues differed widely.

662   *clensyng fyre*. The Gast here distinguishes between "cleansing fire," which purifies the soul of the residuum of guilt for sins properly forgiven in the sacrament of Penance, and the "retributive fire" of Hell, reserved for the unrepentant. The distinction between purification and retribution was not definitively established until the Second Council of Lyons (1274).

663   *Cristes Passyon*. Christ's Passion is His suffering and death, recounted by all four Evangelists. His Passion made salvation possible after the Fall of Man, and it is through the merits of His Passion that man is redeemed, empowered to cooperate with Divine Grace. (See Matthew 26–27; Mark 14–15; Luke 22–23; John 18–19.)

676   *armoure gude*. See Ephesians 6:11–13: "Put you on the armour of God, that you may be able to stand against the deceits of the devil. For our wrestling is not against flesh and blood; but against principalities and powers, against the rulers of the world of this darkness, against the spirits of wickedness in the high places. Therefore take unto you the armour of God, that you may be able to resist in the evil day, and to stand in all things perfect."

713   *Mayden and moder*. A reference to the Virgin Birth, i.e., the idea that Mary conceived and bore Jesus without losing her virginity. The phrase is prominent in the hundreds of lyric poems on Mary. See, for example, *Middle English Marian Lyrics*, ed. Karen Saupe (Kalamazoo, MI: Medieval Institute Publications, 1998), Poem 3.49, 8.3, 9.2–3, 10.1, 11.2, 12.22, 13.17, 15.4, 16.19, 18.27, 29.26, 48.1, 50.50, 51.17, 55.2, 59.5, 61.1, 69.6, 70.1, 72.31, 73.5, 78.28, 87.1, 89.33–34, 90.1, 91.22. Compare Chaucer's *ABC*, line 49, and the prologue to The Prioress' Tale, *CT* VII(B²)467.

717   *emperys of Hell*. The idea of Mary as "empress of Hell," i.e., having dominion even over Hell, is probably derived from her traditional role as *Regina Coeli* ("Queen of Heaven"), the opening words of the Eastertide antiphon. In traditional iconography Mary was frequently portrayed trampling the serpent, probably based on a disputed reading in Jerome's Vulgate of Genesis 3:15. Medieval church authorities would have accepted Jerome's Marian interpretation of the verse.

728   *bede*. A word for prayer in that a true prayer makes a petition, i.e., asks for something (*beden*: *MED*). It is unlikely that this is a reference to a "bead," the means of counting prayers in the rosary, although there is a tradition that Mary gave the rosary to St.

Dominic to combat the Albigensian heresy, thus providing a special connection between Dominicans and the rosary.

731   *almusdede*. Almsgiving for the help of the poor and infirm was a common penitential act assigned as a means for a penitent to remove some of the guilt that remained after absolution. The practice of almsgiving as an act of charity has its source in Judaic tradition, but in the Middle Ages it had special prominence as a form of expiation for sin.

761–66   *On this wyse may gude prayere . . . unto clensyng fyre him bring*. The prayers of the saved have intercessory power with God on behalf of the souls in Purgatory. Thus, there is a reciprocal relationship between the living and the dead: to pray for the dead speeds their way to heaven where they can act as intercessors for the living and the souls in Purgatory. This doctrine depends upon the notion of the Communion of Saints, strongly espoused by St. Thomas Aquinas, according to which saved souls, souls in Purgatory, and the living are joined in a mutually beneficial union.

793–800   *For the grettest blys . . . war noght acordand thing*. The greatest joy of Heaven is the Beatific Vision, seeing God without intermediary in His "Godhead," that is, His Divine Essence. God, as the *Summum Bonum* (Greatest Good), is the goal of human existence; thus to see Him "face to face," as it were, is the ultimate gift of His grace.

828a   "Out of the abundance of the heart the mouth speaks." (Matthew 12:34; Luke 6:45). The line is translated in lines 829–30 of the poem. See textual note.

854a   "Whatsoever the Lord pleased, He hath done." (Psalm 134:6 in the Vulgate). The line is translated in lines 855–56 of the poem; see textual note. The latter half of the verse reads: "in Heaven, in earth, in the sea, and in all the deeps," which would include, presumably, Purgatory.

890–902   *Of Saint Spiritt thou sang . . . thou has the wrang*. That prayers for an individual are efficacious for all the departed is attested by the use of the plural *dona eis requiem* (grant them rest) in the Requiem Mass, the Mass of the Holy Spirit, and the Office of the Dead.

915–16   *with Jewes voyce / Was anely offyrd on the Croyce*. See Mark 15:34 and Matthew 27:46. The Gast's declaration of the details of the Mass declared "anely on a day" by priests (line 910) evokes St. Paul's observations that in the Eucharist the Passion is made present and plain in the eyes and hearts of all worshipers (see Galatians 3:1).

That the doctrine lives in the heart of the Gast of Gy is eloquently evident as he tells how Christ died and gave His spirit unto the Father for the salvation of humankind (lines 914–20). The point seems to be that the spirit of God dwells in the Gast of Gy even in Purgatory, regardless of whether the Pryor asks the right questions or not. His faith keeps him whole despite his trials.

921–22   *Ryght so the prest in ilk a Messe / Offers Criste.* The Gast of Gy's knowledge of the Bible, given his layman's status, seems almost proto-Wyclifite in its several allusions to the Gospels and the Epistles. But it is clear here that he values the sacraments of a conscientious priesthood, albeit in a kind of primitive way. The Pryor may be more subtle and academic in his inquisition into questions of Purgatory and who gets saved, but the Gast is the one guided by faith and its fundamental sensibilities.

941   *ryght resoune.* Right reason does not mean simply "correct" reason. It is the use of the ratiocinative power, under the direction of the will, to choose higher goals rather than lower. This distinction is made by many Doctors of the Church, notably St. Thomas Aquinas (*ST* 1–2.qu.76–77; 81–85; 94).

943   *Pater Noster.* The *Pater Noster* ("Our Father") has special importance as the prayer that Jesus taught his disciples (Matthew 6:9–13; Luke 11:3–4) and is incorporated into the Mass (the liturgy of the Eucharist).

954–58   *Haly Wryt witnes . . . dose here for thair mede.* The "speciall prayers and speciall dede" (line 957) are "suffrages," which could include masses, almsgiving, and penitential acts of all kinds. The doctrine, though pervasive and supported by St. Thomas Aquinas, only received definitive formulation at the Second Council of Lyons (1274) and more precisely by the Council of Trent (1545, 1563). It is tenuously based in Scripture (2 Machabees 12:46 and 1 Corinthians 3:13). See explanatory note to lines 447–52.

978   *sufferd foure yhere.* The Gast's statement that he had been assigned four years in Purgatory has an arithmetical specificity that is usually avoided in writings on Purgatory. The important point (lines 981–90) is that his sentence will be lessened by the "suffrages" of his cousin, the friar.

991–92   *I sall have penaunce in this place / No ferrer bot fra hethen to Passe.* That the Gast should know when he will be released from Purgatory is unusual if not unorthodox, though the correctness of his statement within the poem is soon validated in lines

999–1001, where we are told that the Pryor returned at Easter and found no sign of the Gast. See the explanatory note on "Pasch" for line 1013.

1008–09   *come never yhit in Heven. / Tharfor I may tell thee no mare.* The Gast's empirical response ("I can't talk about that since I haven't been there yet") reflects current philosophical investigations in England during the fourteenth century, particularly at Oxford. That the poet juxtaposes the Gast's empiricism with his Augustinian notion of seeing through faith locates him in a very English way within the culture for which the poem is written.

1012   *thus myne aungell to me tald.* After this line there is an interpolation in R of about 384 lines from *Cursor Mundi,* a compendious "history" from Creation to Doomsday. It was probably composed c. 1300 by an anonymous parish priest. Extremely popular, it survived in many versions of varying lengths. See textual note to this line.

1013   *To Pasch I suld in penance be.* The Gast reiterates what he said in line 992, that he will be in Purgatory until Easter. The repetition may be the result of scribal confusion because of the insertion of the long section from *Cursor Mundi* after line 1012.

        Pasch. "Pasch," sometimes "Passe," was used to refer both to Passover and Easter (*MED*). The use of the word for the two feasts derives from their proximity in the calendar and correspondences fashioned between the Old Law (Hebrew) and the New Law (Christian). The Gast here clearly means Easter.

1031   *The Office of the Ded.* See explanatory note to lines 202–05.

1046   *The seven Psalmes with the Letany.* The seven Penitential Psalms (Psalms 6, 31, 37, 50, 101, 129, and 142 in the Vulgate), followed by the Litany of the Saints, a Collect, and the *Agnus Dei,* conclude the Office of the Dead. See explanatory note to lines 202–05.

1050   *Ave.* The "Hail Mary," based on Elizabeth's words to Mary (Luke 1:42), achieved enormous importance with the increasing popularity of the cult of Mary in the fourteenth century.

1062–65   *me think that thair prayere . . . And the Crede, that the apostels purvayde.* To the *Pater Noster* and *Ave,* which have the authority of Scripture, the Pryor adds "The Apostles' Creed," which has limited Scriptural authority (Matthew 28:19) and is not found until St. Ambrose in the late fourth century. It is curious that the Psalms of David do not seem to have this kind of authority for the Pryor. It may be that their prescription as part of the Office of the Dead is already sufficient validation.

1092–95　*Tell me, what it avayls . . . for the ded es dyght.* When the Pryor questions the special efficacy of the Office of the Dead, the Gast gives an elaborate explanation of the value of each part of the Office with many numerological applications to other religious phenomena.

1094　*Placebo* includes five Psalms (114, 119, 120, 129, and 137 in the Vulgate); see line 1106. *Dirige* includes nine Psalms (5, 6, 7, 22, 24, 26, 39, 40, and 41 in the Vulgate), which correspond nicely with the nine orders of angels in the Gast's exposition.

1108　*antems.* An Anglicization of "antiphons," prayers said or sung between the Psalms.

1128　*Neghen orders.* Although throughout Scripture there are many references to angels (messengers of God), the idea of nine "choirs" of angels standing before the throne of God singing His praises is derived from Psalms 96:7, 102:20, 148:2, 5 in the Vulgate, and, especially, Daniel 7:9–10 and Matthew 18:10. The nine choirs, named by the Pseudo-Dionysius, are angels, archangels, virtues, powers, principalities, dominions, thrones, cherubim, and seraphim. The orthodox view is also expressed in St. Gregory the Great's (c. 540–604) *Dialogues* and by St. Thomas Aquinas (*ST* 1.qu.108).

1155　*Laudes.* Lauds in the Office of the Dead includes four true "Psalms": 50, 64, 62, 150. Between Psalms 62 and 150 is the "Canticle of Ezechias" (Isaias 38:10–14, 17–20). Canticles are frequently included in place of a true psalm in the five items under one of the canonical hours. Thus, in a loose sense, Lauds contains five so-called psalms to correspond to the five wits in line 1156.

1181–84　*Forwhi the saule dwelles als a stane . . . understandes als gud aungels.* These lines are a brief exposition of where man fits in the hierarchy of creation. He has existence like a stone, life like plants, sentience like a beast, and understanding like angels. The first Christian expression of this "chain of being" is in St. Augustine, *De libero arbitrio* 2.3.7. See textual note.

1187　*Benedictus.* The "Canticle of Zachary" (Luke 1:68–79). The Benedictus always concludes Lauds, and in Lauds for the Office of the Dead it follows Psalm 150.

1188　*Magnificat.* In Vespers in the Office of the Dead, after Psalm 137, the "Magnificat" is said. It is not a psalm but Mary's statement to Elizabeth concerning bearing Jesus

(Luke 1:46–55). The "Magnificat" was widely honored in the fourteenth century as a statement of how God would humble the mighty and exalt the humble. It was extended into secular romance, as a moral lesson, in poems like *Robert of Cisyle*.

1216–18 *Mi tyme es nere neghand me . . . To suffer payne in other place.* The Gast's need to return to common Purgatory at this point is not rationalized in the poem. Ordinarily, ghosts inhabited common Purgatory by day and "departabill" Purgatory by night, though in this poem the pattern seems reversed.

1226 *fyve joyes.* In Marian hymns, sometimes sung at the end of Compline, the five joys of Mary are the Annunciation, the Nativity, the Resurrection, the Ascension, and the Assumption. The hymn "Gaude, virgo, mater Christi" appears in Trinity College, Cambridge MS 323, where the Latin alternates with an English translation stanza by stanza. In the Thornton Manuscript (Lincoln Cathedral MS 91) the hymn is headed: "Another salutacioune till our lady of hir fyve Joyes." See Karen Saupe, *Middle English Marian Lyrics*, Poem 87.

1242 *sacrament of Godes Body.* The sacrament of God's Body, also called the Blessed Sacrament (line 1326), is the Eucharist, the reception of Christ's body and blood in the form of consecrated bread and wine, the central event of the Mass (the liturgy of the Eucharist).

1275–90 *And gude aungels war noght biforne . . . the devels may dere him noght.* The advice to priests in these lines echoes the subject of the 384 lines from *Cursor Mundi* intruded into this poem after line 1012.

1297 *Summe Sacerdos.* Here attributed to St. Augustine, this was more commonly identified as the "Prayer of St. Ambrose" (*PL* 17.751–64) and said before the beginning of Mass. In fact, it was more probably composed by John of Fecamp (d. 1076).

1382 *Scho wate hirself, als wele als I.* The Gast makes clear that he cannot confess for someone else, a point that the Pryor is slow to understand, perhaps because of his bias against women. But when, after the third attempt to get her to speak, the Pryor finally convinces her in the name of all that is holy (lines 1413–23), and, when the Gast explains further the circumstances, she finds her voice and asks of her husband whether there is hope for her salvation (lines 1467–71), whereupon he reassures her (lines 1473–75). She then voluntarily offers her prayers of gratitude to Jesus and Mary. Meanwhile, the Pryor suggests she give almsdeeds.

1426–29 *ane unkyndely syn . . . Of whilk we bath war schryven sone.* The Gast refers to a sin committed by him and his wife. The location of the commission of the sin is their bedroom, the appropriate place for a spirit to go when outside common Purgatory. The mutuality of the transgression suggests a sexual sin. The ascetic tradition that grew out of St. Paul, St. Augustine, and St. Jerome condemned sexuality even between husband and wife except when the primary intention was procreation. Compare Chaucer's Parson's Tale (*CT* X[I]858–59, 903–05), which is based in part on St. Jerome's *Adversus Jovinianum*, though the Parson grants the body its privileges and makes allowances for paying the debt and moderation. The Gast refers to the sin as unnatural, but that could include anything from infanticide to recreational sex.

1438–41 *God will it noght . . . we bath war schryven.* A sin confessed and forgiven in the sacrament of Penance need not be revealed to anyone else. The Gast's statement is an orthodox affirmation of absolute privacy with regard to absolved sins. Auricular confession, common in the early Church, revived in the twelfth century, and the obligation of secrecy was enjoined on the priest at the Fourth Lateran Council (1215), although it certainly was practiced long before.

1475 *Thou sall be saved.* The Gast's assertion that his wife will be saved is not presumptuous in that the sin in question has been forgiven. His mission merely relates to the penance necessary to satisfy for the guilt of the sin, preferably in this life, in order to avoid or minimize purgation.

1488 *the Pryor than gan him frayne.* The Pryor would have the Gast confide in the priest before speaking to his wife, since, he says, the priest is nearer to God than a woman is (lines 1493–94). But the Gast's answer that he loves his wife more, and that that is why he has gained permission from God to return to earth to warn his wife, is an authoritative response that gives precedence to personal relationships.

1541 *vertuse.* The plural of *vertu,* "a particular mental faculty or power of the soul necessary for thought, imagination" (*MED*).

1620–36 *His aungell demed his saule to dwell . . . fra now unto to morne at pryme.* The arithmetic of the passage is doubtful. The assignment of specific terms for purgatorial suffering was a matter of debate, and the two-hour delay, while prayers are offered to reduce the sentence, is idiosyncratic if not unique.

1623 *efter his dede.* "After his death" is the obvious sense, though the phrase might also mean "according to his deeds," which would be an applicable reading as well. Compare lines 1632–34 and 1638–39, where the Pauline notion of the efficacy of deeds is stressed.

1673   *grayde*. From *greithen*, "to arrange . . . salvation" (*MED*). Earthly time is seen as a preparation for the ultimate goal, salvation.

1675–78   *I se in ilk state . . . nane sall be dispraysed for me*. The Gast's assertion that no state of life is superior to any other fits the spiritual equality of all Christians, but is a peculiarly egalitarian point to make in view of ecclesiastical preference of virginity to marriage.

1710   *God dose nathing ogayns kynde*. The Pryor asserts that God does nothing against the law of Nature. In the subsequent lines the Gast explains that, as Creator, God has the power to suspend the laws of Nature as ordinarily observed, that is, to perform miracles. Thus, souls in Purgatory may experience the corporeal pain of fire as well as the spiritual pain of loss. The idea is traditional and expounded by St. Thomas Aquinas (*Summa contra Gentiles* 3.102).

1735–38   *Yhe weryed gastes . . . to the devell and his aungels*. Matthew 25:41: "Depart from me, you cursed, into everlasting fire, which was prepared for the devil and his angels."

1742–54   *Bi miracle ogayns kynde . . . Fra fyre and fra that kyndely dede*. The story of the three young men in the fiery furnace is related in Daniel 3. Sidrach, Misach, and Abdenago, refusing to bow down to Nabuchodonosor's golden idol, were cast into a fire, but walked around within it, praising God, without being consumed. The example is to prove the point that it is possible to dwell with fire but not be incinerated. Compare Chaucer's Second Nun's Tale (*CT* VIII[G]514–22). The motif is common in saints' lives.

1794   *trowed. Trow* means "believe," but may include the more fundamental sense of "have trust, be trustful, place one's confidence" (*MED*).

1810–11   *Wha trewly trowes . . . sall be broght*. Mark 16:16: "He that believeth and is baptized shall be saved." These lines provide perhaps the clearest example of the scribe's tendency to be inconsistent in number and/or tense from clause to clause. He rarely is inconsistent within a clause and, in such instances, I have corrected the text.

1812–15   *Who so trowes noght . . . have bale withouten blys*. Probably John 3:36: "He that believeth in the Son hath life everlasting; but he that believeth not the Son shall not see life, but the wrath of God abideth on him." The paraphrase, however, might also refer to John 5:34 or 6:40. The idea is recurrent in John's presentation of the importance of belief in Christ the Son.

1817–22 *Sen the Sarzyns and the Jewes . . . Cristes Incarnacyoune.* The Jews, in rejecting Christ, put themselves beyond the possibility of salvation from that point on, though some descriptions of the afterlife provide a place for the patriarchs of the Old Testament (the *Limbo Patrum*). *Saracins* can refer to Arabs, Turks, or Moslems, especially with regard to the Crusades (*MED*). Whoever is not encompassed by the above is incorporated into the most general term *pagens* (line 1818). Thus, the reference is to all those outside the Christian world who have rejected (or been unaware of) the divinity of Christ. It does not, of course, include Christian heretics who have denied the divinity of Christ, another category altogether.

1829–34 *whi tham lyf es lent . . . encres thair mede.* The Gast cannot see why God endures Jews, Muslims, and pagans except as an opportunity for Christians to win merit by fighting in the Crusades. Indulgences, remissions of time spent in Purgatory, were granted for participation in Crusades.

1840–58 *Pryde . . . maynsweryng.* The identification of the four most common sins and the three for which God will take vengeance quickly is odd in the way that it partially uses the seven deadly sins and partially diverges from them. Among the four most common sins are the deadly sins listed in line 1840 of *pryde* ("pride"), *lychory* ("lust"), and *covatyse* ("greed"), but *usury* (line 1841) is not one of the "deadly," or root, sins, but rather a form of *covatyse*. Among the three provoking vengeance, the first includes fornication and adultery (forms of lust); the second, the unspeakable sin, probably sodomy (a form of lust), may be a satirical jibe at clerics; the third is manslaughter with perjury (a form of anger combined with pride, since perjury involved pride). The more common way to generalize sin was according to the seven deadly sins as in Dante's *Purgatorio* and Chaucer's *Parson's Tale* (*CT* X[I]386–957). This poet clearly has special concerns, which his arrangement reflects.

1841 *usury.* Usury was the charging of any interest whatsoever on borrowed money. The doctrine was affirmed by the Fourth Lateran Council (1215) though it was civilly permitted to Jews since they were beyond the Christian community anyway.

1894 *Anticrist.* The Antichrist is the chief of God's enemies, referred to by this name in 1 John 2:18, 22; 4:3; 2 John 7. He has also been taken to be the inherent sin in the beasts of the Apocalypse. 2 John 7 specifically identifies the Antichrist with those who deny the Incarnation, a doctrine particularly important in this poem.

1898 *Godes preveté*. Those things that are known to God into which human beings should not inquire. There are some kinds of knowledge appropriate only to God, such as the underlying meaning of spiritual mysteries and Divine Providence, which it would be prideful for human beings to try to fathom.

1905–07 *eres to thi hereyng . . . als thou has tald*. The Pryor, in addressing the Gast's power to hear, is returning to an issue similar to the matter of the Gast's power to speak (lines 1519–22). It seems that the Pryor still wants to be sure that he is speaking to a true purgatorial spirit, not a demonic apparition.

1940 *Yhole*. I.e., Yule. Of Old English derivation, the word was used for Christmas as early as 900 (*The Old English Martyrology*) and 901 (*The Life of Aelfred*).

1941 *Epiphany*. The Feast of the Epiphany (January 6), sometimes called Little Christmas, was the day on which the three wise men honored the infant Jesus, signifying the incorporation of the Gentile world into the mission of the Messiah.

1949 *orders*. Religious orders were foundations of men or women who lived communally according to a rule, such as the Rule of St. Augustine or the Rule of St. Benedict. In general, orders were either monastic (monks) or mendicant (friars). Although communities of women (nuns) were formed, women could not be mendicants since this involved going out into the world to beg and preach.

1950 *Austyns*. Augustinian monks (or Canons Regular), who lived according to a rule attributed to St. Augustine of Hippo after his death.

   Menours. Franciscan friars; i.e., the Order of Friars Minor.

1952 *seculeres*. Ordained priests in the service of the diocese, not members of any religious order.

1960 *Requiescant in pace* ("May they rest in peace") is repeated throughout the Office of the Dead.

2018 *symony*. Simony is the purchase of any religious office or privilege, strictly and repeatedly forbidden by Church Councils. The name comes from Simon Magus, who attempted to buy office (Acts 8:18–24).

2035–36 *How many papes . . . tyll the Day of Dome*. The Pryor wants to know how many popes there will be before Judgment Day. At least since Apocalypse, the most popular kind of prophecy had to do with when the end of the world would come; early Christianity tended towards chiliasm. In the Middle Ages, questions about the "end times" were frequently posed in terms of how many popes there would be. The most famous prophecy on the subject was by St. Malachy (b. c. 1094 in Armagh) during the reign of Innocent II (d. 1143). St. Malachy predicted 112 subsequent popes. John Paul II, by the way, is the 110th.

2058–59 *Pape John . . . The twa and twenty*. After the death of Clement V in 1314, the College of Cardinals could not agree on a successor. In 1316, John XXII was elected. He moved the seat of the Papacy to Avignon, thus beginning the so-called "Babylonian Captivity," which lasted until 1367 under the reign of Urban V. John XXII died in 1334. The communication of the experiences of the Pryor to John XXII would have been very important to the Dominican Jean Gobi. John XXII had expressed the opinion, though not in a formal papal declaration, that souls were not assigned to Heaven, Hell, or Purgatory until the General Judgment at the end of the world. John's view was inimical to Dominicans and other mendicant orders, who preached that souls were assigned their place at the time of death or a few hours thereafter. Thus, according to their view, suffrages offered by the living could be immediately efficacious. This teaching may have been self-serving, since the mendicants derived income from suffrages. Nevertheless, even the monastic orders and diocesan authorities would have thought, by the early fourteenth century, that Pope John's opinions bordered on heresy.

Textual Notes to The Gast of Gy

I have based my text on the complete version in Bodleian Library MS Rawlinson Poet. 175 (**R**). Schleich's edition (**S**) uses R as a basis but is truly comparative and freely incorporates variations from Horstmann's edition (**H**) of British Library MS Cotton Tiberius E. vii (**N**). S also includes a Latin text (**L**) based on British Library MS Cotton Vespasian E. i (**D**) with variants from British Library MS Cotton Vespasian A. vi (**C**) and Berlin, Staatsbibliothek Preußischer Kulturbesitz MS Diez C (**A**). Except for a few illustrative examples, I have noted and incorporated only instances where S clearly improves R. I have noted Horstmann readings of N as **H, N**.

There are also three prose versions, one in Bodleian Library MS Eng. poet. A. 1 (*SC* 3939), the Vernon Manuscript (**V**), printed in the H edition of N, one in Oxford, Queens College MS 383 (**Q**), edited by R. H. Bowers (*The Gast of Gy*. Leipzig: B. Tauchnitz, 1938), and one in Gonville and Caius College, Cambridge MS 175 (fragmentary). One quatrain version exists, edited by Ed Eleazer (Ph.D. Dissertation: Florida State University, 1984) (**E**). The most significant manuscript of the quatrain version is Magdalene College, Cambridge MS Pepys 2125 (**P**).

I have expanded abbreviations and corrected obvious scribal errors without comment. In the notes as in the text, I have replaced Middle English graphemes with modern orthography unless the original grapheme is relevant to the explanation. Further manuscript and bibliographical information precedes the text of the poem.

17	*lede our lives.* R: *Trewly trow*; N: *lede thair liues*; S: *lede our lives.* I have accepted S because R rarely uses double formulas (*Trewly trow, mare and les*) in the same line and the sense of S fits line 18. S modification of N: *thair* to *our* fits the surrounding use of the first person.
22	*Of ded and of the Day.* S, following H, N: *Als in dede and the day.* Although I have not accepted this change, I mention it because R is much clumsier.
27–28	These lines are supplied by S, from H, N. Although perhaps not absolutely necessary, they gracefully complement the thought in lines 25–26 and 29–30, and may well have been a scribal omission in R.
29	*And so in world He will us wys.* So R. S, following H, N: *And so he will us wisely wys.* I have retained R, but note this variant to exemplify the kind of change S often makes based on H, N even though R is perfectly satisfactory.
30	After this line H, N has four additional lines, printed in S as a footnote:

> *Tharfore who so will lyke to lere*
> *A soth ensampill sall ye here;*
> *How it bifell byfor this day*
> *And therefore beres it wel away.*

S notes many such additional lines from H, N, but they are not necessary to R so I have not noted them subsequently.

38   *Bayoune.* So R. H correctly reads N as *ba* with the rest of the word obscured. V: *Bayon*; Q: *Bayone*; P: *avynon*; L: *auiniona*. Avynon is certainly correct. The introduction of variants of Bayonne may have resulted from an earlier Latin version that may attempt to place the story in Italy and confused identification of the city with Bologna.

46   *suede.* R: *psuede*, but there are two dots beneath the *p* to indicate deletion.

49   *And.* R: *bot*; S, following H, N: *and. And* makes more sense since it indicates a continuation rather than a movement away from the action. The R scribe may have been distracted by the *bot* that begins line 48.

    his. So R. S, following H, N: *hir* makes sense by pluralizing the pronoun, but R: *his* highlights that the room is Gy's, perhaps a better emphasis at this point.

    chaumber. R: *chumber*; N: *chamber*; S: *chaumber*. I have accepted S. The *MED* does not list *chumber* as a possible variant.

51   *oft.* So S, H, N. The *ft* are unclear in R, but *oft* is certainly correct in context.

73   *For.* R: *ffor.* R frequently doubles *f* at the beginning of a line.

106   *thai.* R: *he*; S, following H, N: *thai.* The plural pronoun is required by the grammar of the lines.

114   After this line S inserts two lines from H, N:

> *The tone maister of geomettri*
> *And the tother of philisophie.*

120   *men.* R: *man*, but the narrative needs the S, H, N plural: *men.* The mayor clearly does not send one man with the Pryor, and R does not characteristically use *man* as an unchanged plural.

122–23   These lines are supplied by S, from H, N. I have printed them because they fill out the sense without doing violence to the verse.

125–26   See textual note to lines 122–23.

129   *armed.* R: *arme*; S, H, N: *armed.* The grammar requires the past tense.

138   This line is difficult to read. I have accepted S.

149   *He and his forsayd brether twa.* R: *and his forsayd brether twa*; S, H, N: *he and the men and the maisters twa.* I have done less violence to R by simply inserting *He* at the beginning of the line.

150	*Unto.* R begins the line with *and*. I have followed S in removing *and*, because it is not clear what *and* is linking line 150 to.
166	Full lines of Latin that rhyme with adjacent English lines are numbered (see also lines 201–02, 1093–94, 1125–26). The Latin is translated in the immediately following lines.
178	*wonder.* R: *wonder.* The word is hard to read but undoubtedly correct in context.
191	*Gy.* So R. S, H, N: *his.* I have retained R because there are many examples in R of unchanged genitives: "God Son" (lines 857, 859, 863); "man saule" (line 754); "Son servyse" (line 741); "man syn" (line 920).
235–39	Here and at many subsequent places, the corresponding lines in N are unintelligible, thus reinforcing the selection of R as a base text.
236	*myld.* So R. S, H, N: *eger.* The mildness, patience, even compassion of the Gast's response suggests that *myld* is preferable to *eger* ("eager," but with a sense of sharpness and censure).
280	*Whase man.* So R. S, H, N: *Whilkmans.* I have retained R because the genitive in the relative adjective is grammatical.
285	*Than.* R: *that*; S, H, N: *than.* This change from R is necessary because the prior is indicating that his discourse follows on from what the Gast has just said.
303	*Gy.* Although the reference to "Gy" by the Gast of Gy himself seems odd, I have retained R and not substituted S, H, N: *mi bodi.*
321	*he.* So R. S, H, N: *it.* S apparently prefers to think of the body as impersonal, but the Gast's discussion of it seems to prefer the personal *he.*
328	*Gy.* So R. S, H, N: *Gyes bodi.* There is some merit in S, but I think the distinction between body and self is clear enough without the change.
375	*the sauwes.* R: *the saules.* S misreads R as *thir saules*, but the change to S, H, N: *sauwes* (sayings, truths) is necessary to the sense of the line.
428	*thai.* S, H, N: *he* is, strictly, correct, but I have retained R: *thai*, which is loosely correct. R is sometimes inconsistent in switching between singular and plural pronouns, but not to the point where they need to be "fixed."
446	*That.* R: *than*, but I have accepted S, H, N: *that.* The demonstrative makes more sense than the conjunction.
455	*tald thai.* R: *tald he*, but I have accepted S, H, N: *tald thai*, which is necessary to agree with "prophetes" (line 448).
461	*thinketh me.* R: *think me*; S, H, N: *thinkes me* is better, but I have preferred to change to the more common *thinketh.*
473	*The.* R: *and*; S, H, N: *the* is better because it makes clear that the Gast is proceeding to the *prophetes* as distinguished from the "sawles" (line 472). In addition, *and* makes an odd linkage with the preceding sentence.

497   *The Pryor than said.* So R. S, H, N: *than said the prior.* This phrase recurs and S almost always changes R to N, apparently for metrical reasons; I see no material advantage. The *P* in *Pryor* is capitalized in R in this line only.

567   *If.* R: *of;* but S, H, N: *if* provides the necessary conditional.

574   *gastly.* R: *gastily,* but I prefer S, H, N: *gastly* for consistency with line 575.

609   *fayne.* So R. S, H, N: *frayne. Frayne* makes sense: "to inquire about or ask something" (*MED*), but I have retained *fayne:* "desirous of, or eager for something" (*MED*).

653   *synned.* R: *synnes;* H, N: *sinned;* S: *synned.* I have accepted S because it provides the necessary past tense without otherwise changing R.

666   *dartes.* So R. S, H, N: *desaytes. desaytes* is possible: "deceit or treachery" (*MED*), but *dartes* seems more to the point in context: "an attack or assault, as of the Devil, of death, of hunger, etc." (*MED*).

674   *abaysed.* R: *abaysted;* H, N: *abaist;* S: *abaysed.* I have accepted S because it retains the meter while getting rid of the intrusive *t* in R, for which there is no precedent.

713   *Mayden and moder both am I.* R: *both mayden and moder am I;* H, N: *moder and mayden both am I;* S: *mayden and moder both am I.* The selective use of N by S (moving *both*) is a case in which the improvement is so marked as to be acceptable while retaining the R order of *mayden and moder.*

734   *penaunce.* R: *penaune,* but the *c* in S, following H, N: *penaunce* is clearly necessary.

735   *es.* R: *er;* but S, H, N: *es* is necessary to agree with *penaunce.*

740   *at.* So R. S, H, N: *that* is tempting, but the *MED* notes *at* as a variant for *that* and R uses the variant often.

750   *flesch.* So R. S changes to *fless* without explanation but apparently for rhyme. *MED* lists *fless* as a possible variant, but the imperfect rhyme at lines 801–02 inclines me to retain R.

758   *his.* R: *This,* but I prefer S, following H, N: *his,* because there is no previous reference to a specific *turment.*

759   *gastes.* R: *gast;* but I prefer S, following H, N: *gastes,* because there are multiple fiends in the scene.

801–02   Not a perfect rhyme in R, but see explanatory note to line 750.

828a   The line is clear in N. It is written in red ink in R and translated in lines 829–30. It appears in L, but not in V, P, Q, though all include a translation. The line is a quotation, with minor variations, of Vulgate Matthew 12:34 and Luke 6:45: *Ex abundantia enim cordis os loquitur.*

837–38   S, following H, N omits these lines from R, but they are consistent with the Gast's explanation even if awkward in construction.

842   *ofte.* R, S: *of;* H, N: *oft.* I have changed to *ofte,* which makes sense of the sentence and fits the meter.

851   *it.* R: *he,* but I have preferred S, H, N: *it* because the neuter is required for sense.

854a   Like line 828a, the Latin line is written in red ink; it is translated in lines 855–56. Its treatment in the other versions of the narrative is the same as line 828a. It is a quotation, with a minor variation, of Vulgate Psalm 134:6: *Omnia quae voluit Dominus fecit.* S is clearly right in placing the line after line 854 rather than two lines earlier as it is in R.

868   *used in foule.* S, H, N insertion of *in* is necessary to make sense with line 869.

876   *To the Thre.* S insertion of *the* before the mention of the Trinity is necessary even though it is present in neither R nor N.

887   *sungen.* R: *syngyng,* but I have accepted S, H, N: *sungen,* which corrects the grammar.

919   *For.* R: *in* is odd; I have accepted S, H, N: *for.*

922   *Criste.* R: *God;* S, H, N: *Criste.* I have accepted the change to *Criste* as more accurate to the liturgy.

1012   This line is from R, fol. 101va, line 40. As S noted, there follows in R an interpolation of approximately 384 lines from another poem. S transcribed, perfectly accurately, the first six lines:

> How oft sythe and on what manere
> This aw the prest to ken all clere
> With this word wha tham may thou myn
> What man it es at dose the syn
> That es whether it kar man be
> Woman or barn thrall or fre.

The 384 lines do not correspond to anything in N, L, V, Q, P. Max Kaluza (p. 34) identified them as corresponding to *Cursor Mundi* (ed. Richard Morris, EETS o.s. 101), lines 27162–67. Indeed, the whole interpolation, with some variations and a few omissions, is from the "Book of Penance" in *Cursor Mundi,* lines 27162–521 (directions to priests on how to hear confessions) and lines 28614–59 (a section on the importance of prayer, fasting, and almsgiving by the penitent). I have not included the lines because they intrude on the narrative of the Gast, even though they deal with a closely related subject. Oddly, the lines are certainly written by the R scribe in "hand," with linguistic characteristics such as *at* or *att* for *that* and the system of abbreviations. Although there are occasional large red capitals and some paragraph indications (none of either particularly significant) in R, there is no indication whatsoever of the beginning of the interpolation. The narrative of the Gast resumes in R at fol. 103vb, 29 (line 1013 of this edition).

1021   *be loved.* R lacks the *be,* which S, following H, N, properly inserts.

1033   *tham more than.* R lacks the *more,* which S, following H, N, properly inserts.

1039   *That.* R: *the;* S, following H, N, supplies the necessary conjunction: *that.*

1084   *us.* R lacks the *us,* which S, following H, N, properly inserts.

1108–09   These lines are inserted by S from H, N. They help make arithmetical sense of the
            devotions.

1115–24   S does not include these lines from R, probably because they are repetitive. They are,
            however, a continued application of the five psalms from the Placebo. (See
            explanatory note to lines 202–05.)

1126   At the end of this line in R there is a space and *Dirige*, capitalized, is repeated.

1150   *he.* R lacks *he*, which S, following H, N, properly inserts.

1165   *world.* R, S: *word*; H, N: *werld.* I have changed to *world.* It is clear from the rest of the
            line that the beginning of the world is intended, so I have simply supplied the *world*
            that R lacks.

1183   *tres.* R: *man*; S: *tres.* The substitution of *tres* (trees) for *man* makes sense in the
            presentation of the scale of being (see St. Augustine, *De Libero Arbitrio* 2.3.7)
            presented in lines 1181–84. Man shares "existence" with a "stane" (line 1181),
            "sentience" with a "best" (line 1182), "life" (i.e., plant life) with "tres" (line 1183),
            and "understanding" with "aungels" (line 1184). The use of *als tres* corresponds to
            the use of "cum arboribus" in L, which retains the more traditional hierarchical order
            of stone, tree, beast, angel. I have not tried to rearrange the lines in R to reflect this
            movement upward.

1227   *help.* R: *hel* is properly filled out to *help* by S, following H, N.

1261   *For.* S properly deletes the initial word in R: *and.*

1285   *fendes.* R: *fende*; S, H, N: *fendes.* The plural is necessary.

1329   *thou.* R: *that*; S, H, N: *thou.* The second person pronoun is necessary.

1334   *In.* Initial R: *that* is deleted by S, following H, N. It was probably miscopied by R from
            the beginning of line 1335.

1359   *The.* R: *Thee.*

1460   *me.* R: *men*, but S, following H, N: *me* must be correct because the Gast is explaining
            why God let him come to speak to the Pryor.

1526   *Withouten.* R: *with*; but S, following H, N: *withouten*, must be correct since the Gast
            is referring to the idea that a carpenter cannot work without his axe (his instrument
            of work).

1567   *The.* R: *that*; but S, following H, N: *the*, is better because the sentence does not call for
            a demonstrative.

1629   *oyres.* So R, S. H, N: *owres.* I have found no attestation elsewhere of *oyres.* The
            variants *ouris* and *owrys* appear in the *OED* and *MED.* Still, the meaning is clear,
            so I have let the oddity stand.

1858   *That es.* R: *ffor* (common doubling of initial *f*); S: *that es.* I have accepted S, even
            though it is based on a problematic reading of an initial *þ* in N.

1925   *proved.* R: *pued*; H, N: *proved.* Following S, I have assumed that the abbreviation
            mark for *ro* is missing and have printed *proved* as it is in N.

1943–44 The lines do not rhyme perfectly, but the same is true of lines 749–50 and 801–02, so there seems no reason to "improve" R.

2008 *we*. R: *thai*; but S, following H, N: *we*, is necessary for consistency of person.

2026 *Grevouse*. The first four letters are rubbed out, but the reading, as S agrees, is correct.

2030 *preche*. R: *prest*; but S, following H, N: *preche*, is necessary for the sense of the line.

2045 *for all saules*. R: *for all payns*; but S, following H, N: *saules*, must be accepted or the line is nonsense.

Sir Owain

Introduction

Sir Owain is the story of the successful penitential visit of the sinful knight Sir Owain to Purgatory and the Earthly Paradise by way of "St. Patrick's Purgatory" on Lough Derg, County Donegal, Ireland. Although much is obscure about the origins of St. Patrick's Purgatory as a place of entry into the next world, and much is debatable about the emergence of St. Patrick's Purgatory as a place of pilgrimage, this poem is a clear and vigorous version of Owain's journey, presented more in the form and manner of medieval metrical romance than of a didactic treatise or tract. The moral lessons remain clear, but that is not foreign to the medieval romances, which characteristically represent and celebrate an idea or ideal.

Ancient Irish legends associated the existence of an entry into the next world with the mission of St. Patrick (c. 389–c. 461) to convert the pagan Irish.[1] In these legends, the Irish would not accept St. Patrick's teachings unless a man was able to enter the next world and return again. Providentially, God appeared to St. Patrick on an island in Lough Derg, by means of a vision or a dream, led him into a wilderness, or barren place, pointed out a pit that was the entry to Purgatory, and assured St. Patrick that anyone who stayed a day and a night in the next world would be cleansed of his sins. Apparently, as a gesture of authenticating good faith, God left behind a book and a staff. The book was often taken to be the Book of Armagh, which was thought to be a relic of St. Patrick. Legend here conflicts with reality, since the clearly ninth-century Book of Armagh, preserved in Trinity College Dublin, is too late for the fifth-century saint, and does not contain the information about "Godes priveté," divine knowledge not available to or appropriate for human beings, which the legend mentions.[2] The staff may simply be a symbol of St. Patrick's

---

[1] See Michael Haren and Yolande de Pontfarcy, *The Medieval Pilgrimage to St Patrick's Purgatory*, pp. 7–43; Jean-Michael Picard, trans., *Saint Patrick's Purgatory: A Twelfth Century Tale of a Journey to the Other World*, intro. Yolande de Pontfarcy (Dublin: Four Courts Press, 1985), pp. 18–21; Shane Leslie, *St. Patrick's Purgatory: A Record from History and Literature*, pp. ix–xv.

[2] The Book of Armagh, compiled by a ninth-century scribe, contains the first surviving versions of two seventh-century Irish "Lives" of St. Patrick, one by Muirchu Macca Machteni and one by Tirechan, documents in Latin and English concerning the life of St. Patrick and the prerogatives of the See of Armagh, a Vulgate New Testament with various commentaries, and the "Life of St. Martin of Tours" (c. 316–67) by Sulpicius Severus (c. 360–420/425).

episcopal authority, but Giraldus Cambrensis (c. 1147–1216/20) associated it with St. Patrick's driving the snakes out of Ireland, and many legends assign the staff mysterious magical powers.

A second version of the origins of the entry says that St. Patrick drew a circle on the ground and cast a staff, already in his possession, into the middle of it, and a deep chasm opened up. A third version, apparently a more modest rationalization of the second, held that St. Patrick came upon a cave and experienced a vision of the next world within it. The first version, with its wealth of imaginative detail, was the most prominent down through the Middle Ages. In all versions, St. Patrick orders a church to be built over the site and gives it to the care of Augustinian Canons Regular (perhaps an anachronism, depending upon which dating of the origins of the Canons Regular one accepts).

The precise location of St. Patrick's Purgatory is unclear. There are two islands in Lough Derg: Station Island, the larger of the two, and Saints Island. Both comprised the site of a single Celtic monastic community and may have been located on the site of a still earlier pagan magical place. The location of the entry in legend seems to have been on Saints Island, though confusion of the two islands became common, and Saints Island seems to have been the preferred location through the Middle Ages. St. Malachy, archbishop of Armagh, did set up in the early 1130s on Saints Island a dependency of the Abbey of Saints Peter and Paul, Armagh, under the control of the Augustinians Canons Regular, who certainly had been established, by St. Norbert, by 1100. Eventually the Canons assumed authority over both islands until the site was taken over by the Franciscans in 1632.

It is at about the time of the arrival of the Augustinians in the early 1130s, despite the suggestions of Irish legends, that St. Patrick's Purgatory truly became a destination of pilgrimage and penitence. It remained so until its suppression by Pope Alexander VI in 1497. So powerful, however, had the site become that pilgrimages resumed in the sixteenth century, with Station Island assuming primacy, maybe because it did in fact have a likely cave. The attraction of the site has been enduring. The church on Station Island was destroyed, and later rebuilt, in 1632, 1701, and 1727. In 1931, an enormous new church was built and pilgrimages to the site continue to this day. Such was, and is, the power of St. Patrick's Purgatory.

Regardless of what one makes of Irish legends, the first recorded pilgrimage was in 1152. The tradition had been so firmly established by that time that the "Purgatory" became a ubiquitous object of theological and literary attention in the second half of the twelfth century, though the experiences of the pilgrims were probably less like that of Owain than that of Antonio Mannini in 1411, who recounts the bureaucracy of the necessary permissions and a penitential experience of a more familiar, mundane kind. Nevertheless, it is important to remember the mysterious potency of the story of St. Patrick's Purgatory in the mid to late twelfth century, when the religious reality of Purgatory far surpassed any question of geographical actuality.

The seminal literary document associated with the rebirth of Purgatory at this special place, and the document that first gives an account of Owain's journey, is the *Tractatus de Purgatorio Sancti Patricii* by H. of Sawtrey. Here we are on firmer historical ground, at least in the origins and transmission of the narrative, because the text exists and its genesis can be reconstructed from contemporary ecclesiastical sources, even if they are not always precise. What seems probable is that a Cistercian monk, Gilbert, was sent with several other monks in the late 1150s to establish a Benedictine dependency in Ireland, probably at Baltinglas. Unable to speak Irish, Gilbert was given the assistance of an interpreter, Owain, either a Cistercian monk or an assistant to the Cistercians. Owain, in the course of a two-and-a-half-year association with Gilbert, told him of his own marvelous visit to Purgatory at Lough Derg. Gilbert returned to England by 1159 to become abbot of Basingwerk and repeatedly recounted Owain's story. Gilbert told H. of Sawtrey (the H was expanded to Henricus by Matthew of Paris in the thirteenth century) the story of Owain's journey. Among those to whom Gilbert recounted the story was another H., Henry, abbot of Sartis, who urged Sawtrey (or Saltrey) to commit the narrative to writing. The *Tractatus* itself merely identifies the author, the first H., as a monk of Saltereia, but there was a Cistercian monastery at Saltrey in Huntingdonshire. The person addressed in the *Tractatus*, the second H., is identified as the abbot of Sartis, probably Henry of Wardon.

Although the *Tractatus* does not specify, the visit of Owain to Purgatory occurred, according to various sources, some time between 1146 and 1154: 1154 according to the *Chronicles* of Roger of Wendover (d. 1236), 1153 according to Matthew of Paris, or 1146–47 according to probabilities established by Robert Easting from the monastic records of abbacies. Henry of Saltrey did not in fact commit Gilbert's account of Owain's story to writing until some time later, perhaps 1179–81, or even later in 1189–90. The latter is the more traditional date; the former is persuasively argued by Easting, the most distinguished scholar on the subject.

The *Tractatus* is a serious Latin prose work which begins by establishing the authenticity of purgatorial doctrine by referring to St. Gregory the Great and St. Augustine, even citing Augustine's division of the afterlife into four parts: the *boni* (the saved), the *mali* (the damned), the *non valde mali* (the "not completely evil" in a middle state), and the *boni non valde* (the "not completely good" in another intermediate state). The invocation of the authority of St. Augustine is especially odd in that St. Augustine believed Purgatory to be a "state," and the *Tractatus*, by its very nature, identifies Purgatory as a place, with a very specific location. The tendency of commentators between St. Augustine and the *Tractatus* had been towards a "place," though the Church was not definitive on the topic even at the Council of Trent in the sixteenth century. Moreover, in the *Tractatus*, Purgatory seems in many ways to be the abode of the *non valde mali* and the Earthly Paradise seems to be the abode of the *boni non valde*. This is at odds with the idea in the *Tractatus* that souls, after purgation, move to the Earthly Paradise for an undetermined period of time before being allowed entry into Heaven. (The very idea of the Earthly Paradise as part of the afterlife was eventually rejected at the Second Council of Lyons in 1274, even as that council affirmed the doctrine of Purgatory as a matter of dogma.) Thus, the *Tractatus* is not here entirely self-consistent, but it remains a serious, generally orthodox didactic treatise.

Soundly, it draws on Hugh of St. Victor (c. 1078–1141) for much of its preface and many of the torments. More fancifully, it relies heavily on the apocalyptic, late-fourth-century *Apocalypse of*

St. Paul for its visions of the sufferings of the souls and the idea of the bridge over the river of Hell. The *Tractatus* did transmit important doctrinal opinions, among them that souls in Purgatory did not know how long they would be there, nor, indeed, did they know that they would eventually be saved. This is quite different from the Gast's certainty in *The Gast of Gy* (early fourteenth century) that he would be delivered from suffering at Easter; it is likewise different from the appealing comfort that some of the souls in Dante's *Purgatorio* take in knowing that they will eventually see the Beatific Vision.

Some of the opinions in the *Tractatus* are debatable, but much about Purgatory was debatable in the twelfth century. It does not assign souls to especially appropriate punishments as was so gloriously accomplished later in the *Divine Comedy*; it does not even consider specific sins at all in its presentation of Purgatory. It does, however, intersperse homilies and appeals to authority which embed the legend of Owain in a context that gives it greater theological weight. What is most important is that the *Tractatus*, in particular its central engaging account of the journey of Sir Owain, was an enormous hit. It survives, in whole or in part, in over one hundred and fifty manuscripts in Latin alone, including the *Chronicles* of Roger of Wendover, the *Speculum historiale* of Vincent of Beauvais (d. 1264), and an account by Henricus Salteriensis of *Purgatorio Sancti Patricii* in the *Patrologia Latina*, as collected and edited by Migne (*PL* 180.977–1004), and in over three hundred translations and adaptations in almost every European vernacular, ranging from a Sicilian version that adds King Arthur and transforms the mountain described in the *Tractatus* into Mount Etna to a lively version by Marie de France (fl. 1175–90), *Espurgatoire S. Patriz*. In addition, there are countless references to the story such as the description in the *Legenda aurea* of St. Patrick being led to the gates of Hell.

Four versions survive in Middle English: the stanzaic version printed here from the Auchinlick Manuscript; two fifteenth-century manuscripts of a version in couplets; the earliest English version in ten manuscripts of the *South English Legendary* (ranging up to 714 lines in length); and a quatrain fragment transcribed by Thomas Hearne from a fragment in MS Harley 4012, itself based on a *South English Legendary* version. Two other pieces, not connected to Owain, complete the Middle English corpus of works on St. Patrick's Purgatory: a short narrative of the journey of a certain Nicholas in the *Legenda aurea* and a prose account of the 1409 *Vision of William Staunton*, preserved in two fifteenth-century manuscripts. Nicholas' vision is rather more like Owain's; Staunton's is a more eclectic account.

To anyone who knows anything of the Middle English literature of St. Patrick's Purgatory, it may seem odd to give the title *Sir Owain* to an edition of this poem. Ordinarily it has been known simply as *St. Patrick's Purgatory* or *Owayne Miles*. However, the former seems too general and the latter is adopted from the running headings of the couplet version in MS Cotton Caligula A. ii. The title *Sir Owain* seems to me more precise, and consistent with what is by far the most common spelling of the knight's name in the Auchinleck stanzaic version.

The Middle English stanzaic poem is largely consistent with the narrative in the *Tractatus*, even though the English version probably derived from an Anglo-Norman intermediary rather than directly from any of the Latin versions. It does omit prefatory material and much of the interspersed didactic material, as is so often the case with fourteenth-century English adaptations of works from Latin and French. However, the structure of *Sir Owain* is essentially that of the *Tractatus*, especially with regard to the geography of Purgatory. In the English version, Sir Owain is changed from an Irish knight into an Englishman, a Northumbrian who has been in the service of King Stephen (r. 1135–54), and he is, probably following Roger of Wendover's version, guilty of serious sins. His visit to St. Patrick's Purgatory is to do penance for the evils in the life he has led.

Still, the overall structure does mirror the *Tractatus*. After securing the reluctant permission of the bishop and the prior, Owain undertakes fifteen days of prayer and fasting before beginning his journey. These are prescribed rituals before entry into the Purgatory common to virtually all versions and practiced in fact at the shrine. Owain is directed by the prior through a door towards a hall without walls where he will meet and receive instruction from thirteen, rather than the fifteen of the *Tractatus*, white-robed men, who look remarkably like otherworldly Augustinian Canons Regular, who normally wore a white habit. They remind Owain that he is in grave danger and that he must resist the temptations of the fiends, especially not to return without completing the journey, which would be disastrous. They do, however, give him the comfort that, if he is in serious difficulty, he need only repeat the name of God to be preserved. Owain proceeds and is quickly greeted by loud and gruesome fiends who immediately urge him to go back to the upper world.

The geography of the Purgatory proper follows the pattern of the *Tractatus*, despite a few differences in detail. First the fiends make a fire and throw Owain in, but he calls upon the Lord and the fire is put out. Then the fiends lead him to the first true scene of purgation, a field in a valley where wounded naked souls of both sexes are fastened face down with iron nails. Unlike the *Tractatus*, which does not associate souls with specific sins, *Sir Owain* identifies these souls as guilty of sloth, one of the seven deadly sins — not just laziness, but a slowness to a full commitment to the laws of God and the precepts of charity. Conversely, in the next area, the souls are bound face up and are tormented by dragons, newts, and snakes, and the hooks of the devils. *Sir Owain* adds to the *Tractatus* that these souls are guilty of gluttony, another of the seven deadly sins, and they rightly, in a detail unique to *Sir Owain*, accuse the knight of having committed this sin. They tempt him to return, but he calls upon God and proceeds.

In the next field, souls are hanging by various body parts, some immersed in fire, some on gridirons. These are thieves, backbiters, false swearers, and false witnesses; Owain may be guilty of such sins because he recognizes acquaintances in the group (a detail not in the *Tractatus*). Some notion of the punishment fitting the crime, also unique to *Sir Owain*, is apparent in the false swearers and witnesses hanging by their tongues, but the punishments are not consistently condign even within this field.

Owain next confronts the "wheel of fire," to which sinners are affixed, spinning rapidly. The sin here is identified as covetousness, and Owain is accused of such greed by the demons and bound to the wheel. While other souls are rotating in and out of fire and being burnt to powder, Owain utters the name of God and is again delivered. The fiends then bring Owain to a great mountain from which souls, some rising like sparks, are blasted by a cold wind into a hot and stinking river. He suffers this punishment, pointedly identified as the penalty for malice and spite, more completely than any other, but is again restored by calling God's name. The next torment is the house of fire and smoke. In a recurring motif, the devils tempt Owain to go back, but he perseveres and observes souls in molten baths up to various heights on their bodies. They are guilty of usury, not a deadly sin but a fundamental violation of charity. Though unnamed other sins also seem to be punished here, the demons accuse Owain of "money-lending," that is, usury. The poet of the English version seems to be drawing up a "bill of particulars" against the knight. Again he survives.

Then a blast of fire makes Owain think that he must be at the true pit of Hell. The demons throw him in, but he again is saved by saying the name of God, though he is somewhat the worse for purgatorial wear. The *Tractatus* identifies this pit as not really the true pit of Hell, but a demonic deceit, in that the true location of Hell will come later. *Sir Owain* makes no mention of this deceit, and true Hell does come later, but in some sense it is potentially a true Hell for Owain because it would have been permanent if he had not been rescued by calling upon God and, indeed, it is the place of those guilty of the most fundamental of all the deadly sins — pride. That Owain shows signs of suffering associates him with the sin and reminds us that he is, after all, not there like a distanced visionary, but flesh and blood, in a real place.

The horrors continue as beasts with sixty eyes and sixty hands, apparently significant of an indeterminately large number, seize the knight and threaten to throw him into a stinking, burning river — the most terrifying sight yet seen. Although the punishments so far have been loosely borrowed, through the *Tractatus*, from the *Apocalypse of St. Paul*, the bridge over this foul river is especially reminiscent of the *Apocalypse*. The bridge crosses the boiling river that covers true Hell. The poem emphasizes the source and the horror by referring to the "dominical" of St. Paul, apparently an admonitory Sunday reading, of uncertain substance, but likely based on the *Apocalypse*. Owain must cross the bridge as demons throw stones at him and fiends in the river wait to snatch him. The daunting bridge is high, narrow, and sharp as a razor. The devils again tempt him to give up and go back, but Owain proceeds and astonishingly does not find the bridge sharp or the crossing as perilous as he had feared. The bridge does not gradually become a broader road to salvation as in the *Tractatus*, but Owain's success is noteworthy and his purgation is complete.

At this point Owain reaches the Earthly Paradise and is given a cloth of gold that he puts on and is healed of the wounds he has incurred. It is striking that so gruesome are the purgatorial scenes that it easily goes unnoticed that almost all of the rest of the poem is devoted to the Earthly Paradise, an amount roughly equal to the number of lines devoted to the torments. It is important to keep in mind that the poet, like the author of the *Tractatus*, seems equally interested in Owain's ultimate visions of the glories of the fully purged. After great fear and suffering, consolation and celebration come. Owain enters a glittering world of flowers, gems, choirs, and birdsong and he beholds a procession of the saved who have not yet been admitted to their ultimate bliss in Heaven.

He is in the Garden of Eden, a place where we would all have lived were it not for the sin of Adam, which is emphasized during the tour that Owain is given by two archbishops. The knight sees "the tree of life," oddly described as the means of Adam's temptation, though scripturally Adam and Eve ate of "the tree of the knowledge of good and evil," and it was to keep them from "the tree of life" that God placed Michael at the gates to keep them out after their expulsion.

As the two archbishops explain the Earthly Paradise, a place of complete natural fulfillment where all of the senses are gratified, there is the only mention in the whole poem of the doctrine of suffrages — that the living can help the dead with prayers, masses, and almsgiving — a doctrine that became central to Dominican preaching on Purgatory from the thirteenth century. Although *Sir Owain* is a fourteenth-century poem it is here true to its twelfth-century Cistercian source which naturally emphasized personal penance more than suffrages. Nevertheless, the foregoing summary of the structure of the whole poem suggests that *Sir Owain* gradually becomes its own poem, especially in references to specific sins and accusations of Owain of particular offenses. The result is not entirely systematic, but it is significantly different and almost transforms the poem into a metrical romance.

It has become, in its abbreviation and its vitality, very much an English poem and Sir Owain is very much a doughty English knight who has been in the service of King Stephen. When he sets out on his journey, and more clearly as he proceeds, he is much more like a romance hero than a religious visionary. As in so many Arthurian romances, Owain is on a quest; he sets out to do something that is dangerous, difficult, and worthwhile in an encompassing world that would have him, despite adversity, succeed.

That this version of St. Patrick's Purgatory should take on rather the form of romance than of vision should not be surprising. It appears in the Auchinleck Manuscript, which was produced in a commercial London scriptorium between 1330 and 1340, for a popular audience. The dialect seems to be that of London, certainly of the East Midlands. True, *Sir Owain* is, in the manuscript, sandwiched between two religious works (*The Life of St. Catherine* and "The Desputisoun bitwen the Bodi and the Soul"), and the Auchinleck Manuscript has many religious pieces, but the manuscript is better known for its abundant inclusion of romances suited to a popular taste, many of them excellent, such as *Guy of Warwick, Floris and Blauncheflur, Bevis of Hamtoun, Amis and Amiloun*, and *Sir Orfeo*.

It is not, however, just the company the poem keeps that suggests that it is a didactic religious poem struggling to become a romance. The focus in *Sir Owain* is very much the knight and the adventures he experiences, even though the adventures are fashioned out of the stuff of religious tract. It is true that Sir Owain starts out as a sinful man, but that is not a disqualification for a romance hero; think only of *Sir Amadace*, whose hero must painstakingly regain his kingdom because he has been negligent in his religious life, or Sir Gowther, who has raped nuns, incinerated a convent, abducted wives, and murdered men, women, and children by the score, only, after extended penance, to become a saint. Sir Owain is faced with the fundamental religious challenge: to reform his life and achieve salvation. That his desire to undertake the rigors of St. Patrick's

Sir Owain

Purgatory is unmotivated within the poem is quite like the kind of "vertical motivation" characteristic of romance: the hero is moved to action not as much by psychological or religious introspection as by what the narrative needs in order to demonstrate its courtly or moral ideals.

Perhaps most persuasively, the story has a happy ending, a prime requisite of romance, and the narrator, though he allows, even insists, that we be frightened for Owain's sake, as well as our own, never lets us believe that Owain will be anything but successful. The trials may be difficult but the happy outcome is assured. Visions all, in some way, have a happy ending, but they tend to be admonitory. *Sir Owain* is decidedly a narrative in which the questing hero, because of his innate characteristics and the way in which those characteristics suit the values of the world in which he lives, is tested, but ultimately successful. When Owain undertakes his adventures, it is less a matter of the blinding insight of the visionary than the recovery of that from which he has been dispossessed. In this case, of course, it is the ultimate dispossession and consequently the ultimate recovery — Christian redemption — but the circumstances are reminiscent of romance losses and recoveries as early as *Havelok*. Havelok's recovery is primarily secular, while Owain's is spiritual, and even the magic talisman with which Owain is provided, firmly in the tradition of romance, is appropriately spiritual — the name of God.

It is not that Owain's success is necessarily permanent or secure; he is not guaranteed a long and happy life issuing in assured salvation as some romance heroes are. In some respects, Sir Owain is more like Redcrosse in Book 1 of Spenser's *Faerie Queene*. Not that Redcrosse was a sinner, except in the sense that everyone is a sinner, but he does have to return to the fray after slaying the dragon: even after purificatory and enlightening tests, Christian life must still be lived, and this is very much the situation of Owain; but, for reasons that make sense best in the world of romance, Owain, like Redcrosse, will live out his life in a world that is ultimately on his side. He is not given the assurance, or rather we are not given it, of a long and happy life like Sir Orfeo or Sir Cleges, but the familiar "reprieve of romance" puts him in a morally privileged and optimistic position.

Much else about *Sir Owain* suggests that it is at least on the borderline of romance. As a man of flesh and blood, who suffers during his journey, Owain experiences formidable trials, but we are not truly worried. We almost rejoice in them because the narrator will not let us suspect anything other than eventual success. The structure of the narrative makes it unthinkable that Owain actually will be destroyed or fall into the pit of Hell. The narrator ensures that this is a possibility we never entertain even as we observe pain and trial. It just does not feel like a story that will end in anything but eventual vindication and triumph.

The poem feels like a romance in other ways, besides its presentation of a struggling hero within a universe that rewards the kind of person he is or wishes to be. On a very basic level, the verse form is of the tail-rhyme stanza: six lines comprised of two tetrameters, a trimeter, two tetrameters, and a trimeter, rhyming AABCCB. The form was so commonly used in popular romance that Chaucer employed a version of it to parody romances gone bad in his Tale of Sir Thopas. In *Sir Owain* this familiar romance verse form is well-managed; the narrator's willingness to let the story flow beyond the ends of individual stanzas allows for a fluidity if not felicity. Moreover, the narrator's relationship with the audience is very much like the "confidential" relationship that is characteristic of romance. We are, we feel, all in this together. The narrator, for example, often reminds us that his story is based on antecedents, not in the ponderous citations of tract, but in the relatively informal manner of romance: "As it seyt [says] in the storie" (line 144), or "As it seyt in this rime" (line 174). Similarly, the narrator addresses us with direct exhortations: "Jhesu ous thider bring!" ("May Jesus bring us there," line 156); "For Godes love, bewar therbi!" (line 425); and "Ich man bewar therbi!" (line 570). The narrator even calls for our attention in the manner of romance:

Now herknes to mi talking:	*listen*
Ichil thou tel of other thing,	*I will*
Yif ye it wil yhere. (lines 166–68)	*If; hear*

Although the opening lines are missing, it would not be hard to imagine it beginning: "Listeth, lordes, in good entent . . ." (*CT* VII[B²]712).

In addition, the demons in Purgatory, though they are gruesome, threatening, and continually putting Owain in danger of damnation, often express themselves with a grim but amusing irony that relieves the unrelenting gloom and fire of orthodox Purgatory:

And seyd he was comen with flesche and fel	*said they; flesh and skin*
To fechen him the joie of Helle	*fetch him to*
Withouten ani ending. (lines 322–24)	

and:

Hem schal sone com a bevereche,	*To them; drink*
That schal nought thenche hem gode. (lines 545–46)	*think*

and:

This ben our foules in our caghe,	*birds; cage*
And this is our courtelage	*garden*
And our castel tour. (lines 643–45)	

All of this rings of romance rather than tract.

Even the bridge over the river of Hell that Owain must cross to reach the Earthly Paradise, firmly based though it is in the *Tractatus*, seems more like the bridge that Lancelot crosses in Chrétien de Troyes than it does like a passage over the infernal. Though unscathed, unlike Lancelot, Owain faces a romance-like challenge. And when he arrives in the Earthly Paradise, although the doctrine is, again, directly from the *Tractatus*, the world bears similarities to the unearthly otherworlds that are entered by Orfeo and Sir Cleges. He sees a procession, not of maidens, but of all human estates (though a heavy emphasis is, perhaps appropriately, placed on the clergy). More striking even are the catalogues of flowers and gems, which are appropriate to the terrestrial paradise, but sound more like the catalogues in the *Alliterative* and *Stanzaic Mortes* and in countless other romance descriptions of ideal beauty.

The archbishops who instruct Owain do explain matters of doctrine concerning the nature of the fate of the souls in Purgatory and the Earthly Paradise, but their affirmation of suffrages — sound doctrine, though rather an odd Dominican concession in this essentially Cistercian view of the afterlife — is rather in the mode of romance guidance to the hero than doctrinal exegesis. Even when true in substance to his ultimate source, this narrator has the capacity to make us feel that we are in a romance.

It is, however, in the shape of Owain's whole experience that the poem seems to have transformed Owain from a visionary or pilgrim. A good, if misguided, English knight sets out, body and soul, to face dangers that his world presents but he is prepared for. The ideals in *Sir Owain* seem, quite appropriately, the four cardinal moral virtues: prudence, justice, fortitude, and temperance. These are the virtues in which he has found himself lacking and these are the virtues he embodies as he suffers and triumphs in a world that will not let him fail in his quest for Redemption. The job is not complete; that comes only with eternal salvation, but Owain has brought himself into accord with the ideals, and is armed with the virtues, that are rewarded in the world in which he lives. Tract has become romance.

Select Bibliography

Manuscript

National Library of Scotland Advocates' MS 19.2.1 (Auchinleck), fols. 25r–31v. [c. 1330–40]

Editions

Easting, Robert, ed. *St Patrick's Purgatory*. EETS o.s. 298. Oxford: Oxford University Press, 1991.

Kölbing, Eugen, ed. "Zwei mittelenglische Bearbeitungen der Sage von St. Patrik's Purgatorium." *Englische Studien* 1 (1877), 57–121.

Introduction

Laing, David, and William B. D. D. Turnbull, eds. *Owain Miles and Other Inedited Fragments of Ancient English Poetry*. Edinburgh: [s.n.], 1837.

The Auchinleck Manuscript. National Library of Scotland Advocates' MS 19.2.1. Facsimile with an introduction by Derek Pearsall and I. C. Cunningham. London: The Scolar Press, 1977.

Commentary

Curtayne, Alice. *Lough Derg: St. Patrick's Purgatory*. Monaghan, Ireland: R & S Printers, 1962.

Easting, Robert. "The Date and Dedication of the *Tractatus de Purgatorio Sancti Patricii*." *Speculum* 53 (1978), 778–83.

————. "Owein at St. Patrick's Purgatory." *Medium Ævum* 55 (1986), 159–75.

————. "Purgatory and the Earthly Paradise in the *Tractatus de purgatorio Sancti Patricii*." *Citeaux* 37 (1986), 23–48.

————. "The Middle English 'Hearne Fragment' of *St. Patrick's Purgatory*." *Notes and Queries* 35 (1988), 436–37.

————, ed. *St. Patrick's Purgatory*. Pp. i–xciii.

Haren, Michael, and Yolande de Pontfarcy. *The Medieval Pilgrimage to St Patrick's Purgatory: Lough Derg and the European Tradition*. Enniskillen: Clogher Historical Society, 1988.

Leslie, Shane. *St. Patrick's Purgatory: A Record from History and Literature*. London: Burns, Oates and Washbourne, 1932.

McGuinness, Joseph. *St Patrick's Purgatory, Lough Derg*. Dublin: Columba Press, 2000.

McKenna, J. E. *Lough Derg: Ireland's National Pilgrimage*. Dublin: Catholic Truth Society of Ireland, 1928.

O'Connor, Daniel. *St. Patrick's Purgatory, Lough Derg*. London: Burns and Oates, 1895.

Seymour, St. John Drelincourt. *Irish Visions of the Other World: A Contribution to the Study of Mediæval Visions*. New York: Macmillan, 1930.

Wright, Thomas. *St. Patrick's Purgatory: An Essay on the Legends of Purgatory, Hell, and Paradise, Current during the Middle Ages.* London: John Russell Smith, 1864.

Sir Owain

[The first thirty-two lines of the poem are lost. They would have probably called for the attention of the audience and given a brief introduction of St. Patrick and his mission to the pagan Irish.]

1

. . . .
. . . .
And lived in dedeli sinne. *deadly*
Seyn Patrike hadde rewthe *St. Patrick; pity*
5 Of hir misbileve and untrewthe, *their false belief; error*
That thai weren inne. *they were in*

2

Oft he proved sarmoun to make, *attempted sermon*
That thai schuld to God take *should take to God*
And do after his rede. *follow; advice*
10 Thai were fulfild of felonie; *full of crime*
Thai no held it bot ribaudie *They held it but foolishness*
Of nothing that he sede. *Everything he said*

3

And al thai seyd commounliche, *they all said commonly*
That non of hem wold sikerliche *none of them would surely*
15 Do bi his techeing, *Abide by his teaching*
Bot yif he dede that sum man *Unless; caused some man*
Into Helle went than, *then*
To bring hem tiding *them tidings*

4

Of the pain and of the wo
20 The soulen suffri evermo, *souls suffer forever*
Thai that ben therinne; *They who are therein*
And elles thai seyd, that nolden hye *Otherwise; would not quickly (i.e., soon)*

	Of her misdede nought repenti,	*their sins not repent*
	No her folies blinne.	*Nor their follies (i.e., sins) cease*

5

25	When Sein Patrike herd this,	*Saint*
	Michel he card forsothe, ywis,	*Greatly he cared truly, indeed*
	And sore he gan desmay.	*sorely; became dismayed*
	Oft he was in afliccioun,	*suffering*
	In fasting and in orisoun,	*prayer*
30	Jhesu Crist to pray,	

6

	That He him schuld grace sende,	
	Hou he might rathest wende	*most quickly lead*
	Out of the fendes bond,	*fiend's control*
	And do hem com to amendement	*cause them to*
35	And leve on God omnipotent,	*believe*
	The folk of Yrlond.	

7

	And als he was in holy chirche,	*while*
	Godes werkes for to wirche,	*work*
	And made his praier,	
40	And bad for that ich thing,	*prayed; very thing*
	Sone he fel on slepeing	*fell asleep*
	Toforn his auter.	*Before; altar*

8

	In his chapel he slepe wel swete.	*slept quite sweetly (i.e., comfortably)*
	Of fele thinges him gan mete	*many; began to dream*
45	That was in Heven blis.	*Paradise*
	As he slepe, forsothe him thought	*slept, truly it seemed to him*
	That Jhesu, that ous dere bought,	*us dearly bought (i.e., redeemed)*
	To him com, ywis,	*came, indeed*

9

	And gaf him a bok that nas nought lite:	*gave; book; was not little*
50	Ther nis no clerk that swiche can write,	*is no learned man; such*
	No never no schal be;	

It speketh of al maner godspelle,   *It spoke of all manner [of] gospels*
Of Heven and erthe and of Helle,
Of Godes priveté.   *secret knowledge*

10

55   More him thought, that God him gaf   *Further he thought; gave*
In his hond a wel feir staf,   *beautiful staff*
In slepe ther he lay;   *sleep where*
And Godes Staf, ich understond,   *God's Staff*
Men clepeth that staf in Yrlond   *call*
60   Yete to this ich day.   *Yet; very*

11

When God him this gif hadde,   *had given*
Him thought that He him ladde   *He thought; led*
Thennes be the way ful right   *Thence by*
Into an gret desert;   *great open space*
65   Ther was an hole michel apert,   *Where; quite open*
That griseliche was of sight.   *gruesome*

12

Rounde it was about and blak;   *black*
In alle the warld no was his mack,   *world; its match*
So griselich entring.   *gruesome to enter*
70   When that Patrike yseye that sight,   *saw*
Swithe sore he was aflight   *Full sorely; afflicted*
In his slepeing.   *sleep*

13

Tho God almighten him schewed and seyd,   *Then; almighty; explained; said*
Who that hadde don sinful dede   *Whoever; deeds*
75   Ogaines Godes lawe,   *Against*
And wold him therof repenti,   *would; repent*
And take penaunce hastily,
And his foliis withdrawe,   *sins (follies) withdraw from*

14

So schuld in this ich hole   *very [same] hole*
80   A parti of penaunce thole   *portion; endure*

For his misdede;
A night and a day be herinne,
And al him schuld be forgive his sinne,
And the better spede.   *fare*

15

85 And yif he ben of gode creaunce,   *if; faith*
Gode and poure withouten dotaunce,   *Good; blameless without uncertainty*
And stedfast of bileve,   *steadfast; belief*
He no schuld nought be therin ful long,
That he ne schal se the paines strong   *see*
90 Ac non no schal him greve   *But none shall; trouble*

16

In wiche the soules ben ydo,   *what [to] the souls is done*
That have deserved to com therto,
In this world ywis;   *indeed*
And also than sen he may   *then see*
95 That ich joie that lasteth ay,   *very joy; forever*
That is in Paradis.

17

When Jhesu had yseyd al out,   *explained*
And yschewed al about   *showed*
With wel milde chere,   *full gracious manner*
100 God, that bought ous dere in Heven,   *bought us dearly (i.e., redeemed)*
Fram Him he went with milde steven,   *sound*
And Patrike bileft there.   *left*

18

When Seyn Patrike o slepe he woke,   *of*
Gode token he fond and up hem toke   *Good signs he found; them took*
105 Of his swevening.   *dreaming*
Bok and staf ther he fond,   *Book; staff; found*
And tok hem up in his hond,   *took them; hand*
And thonked Heven king.   *thanked*

124

19

	He kneld and held up his hond,	*knelt; hand*
110	And thonked Jhesu Cristes sond	*Jesus Christ's messenger*
	That He him hadde ysent,	*him had sent*
	Wharthurth he might understond	*Through which*
	To turn that folk of Yrlond	*[How] to*
	To com to amendement.	

20

115	In that stede withouten lett	*place without delay*
	A fair abbay he lete sett	*abbey; had built*
	Withouten ani dueling,	*Without any delay*
	In the name of Godes glorie,	
	Seyn Peter and Our Levedy,	*Saint; Lady*
120	For to rede and sing.	*To chant and sing [praises]*

21

	Seyn Patrike maked the abbay:	*made; abbey*
	That wite wele men of the cuntray,	*knew; country*
	That non is that yliche.	*none; like*
	Regles is that abbay name;	*abbey's*
125	Ther is solas, gle, and game	*solace, joy; delight*
	With pover and eke with riche.	*poor; also*

22

	White chanounes he sett therate	*canons; established there*
	To serve God, arliche and late,	*early*
	And holy men to be.	
130	That ich boke and that staf,	*very book; staff*
	That God Seyn Patrike gaf,	*gave*
	Yete ther man may se.	*Still; see*

23

	In the est ende of the abbay	*east*
	Ther is that hole, forsothe to say,	*truth to say*
135	That griseliche is of sight,	*gruesome*
	With gode ston wal al abouten,	*good stone walls all around*
	With locke and keye the gate to louken,	*lock*
	Patrike lete it dighte.	*had it built*

24

That ich stede, siker ye be,	*same place, sure be you*
140 Is ycleped the right entré	*called; very entrance*
Of Patrikes Purgatorie:	
For in that time that this bifelle,	*occurred*
Mani a man went into Helle,	
As it seyt in the storie,	*says*

25

145 And suffred pein for her trespas,	*pain; their trespasses*
And com ogain thurth Godes gras,	*returned again through; grace*
And seyd alle and some,	*said every one of them*
That thai hadde sen sikerliche	*seen surely*
The paines of Helle apertliche,	*clearly*
150 When thai were out ycome.	*had come out*

26

And also thai seyd with heye,	*said with haste*
Apertliche the joies thai seye	*Clearly; joys; saw*
Of angels singing	
To God almighti and to His:	
155 That is the joie of Paradys;	*joy; Paradise*
Jhesu ous thider bring!	*May Jesus bring us there!*

27

When alle the folk of Yrlond	
The joies gan understond,	*began to*
That Seyn Patrike hem sede,	*them told*
160 To him thai com everichon,	*they came every one*
And were ycristned in fonston,	*baptized; baptismal font*
And leten her misdede.	*forgiven; sins*

28

And thus thai bicom, lasse and more,	*became, all of them*
Cristen men thurth Godes lore,	*Christian; through; teaching*
165 Thurth Patrikes preier.	*prayers*
Now herknes to mi talking:	*listen*
Ichil thou tel of other thing,	*I will*
Yif ye it wil yhere.	*If; hear*

29

Bi Stevenes day, the king ful right,

170 That Inglond stabled and dight
Wel wiselich in his time,
In Northumberland was a knight,
A douhti man and swithe wight,
As it seyt in this rime.

In the time of Stephen
stabilized; ordered
wisely

doughty; mighty person
says; poem (rhyme)

30

175 Oweyn he hight, withouten les,
In cuntré ther he born wes,
As ye may yhere.
Wel michel he couthe of batayle,
And swithe sinful he was saunfayle

180 Ogain his Creatour.

was named, without lies
country where; was
hear
Very much; understood; battle
quite; without doubt
Against; Creator

31

On a day he him bithought
Of the sinne he hadde ywrought,
And sore him gan adrede,
And thought he wold thurth Godes grace

185 Ben yschrive of his trispas,
And leten his misdede.

One day; thought to himself
sins; done
sorely; began to dread
would through
Be shriven; trespass
leave; misdeeds

32

And when he hadde thus gode creaunce,
He com, as it bifel a chaunce,
To the bischop of Yrlond,

190 Ther he lay in that abbay,
Ther was that hole, forsothe to say,
Penaunce to take an hond.

good faith
came, as it happened
bishop
Where
Where; truth to tell
To undertake Penance

33

To the bischop he biknewe his sinne,
And prayd him, for Godes winne,

195 That he him schuld schrive,
And legge on him penaunce sore.
He wold sinne, he seyd, no more,
Never eft in his live.

revealed
salvation
should shrive
lay; severe
would
again; life

34

200 The bischop therof was ful blithe, *happy*
And for his sinne blamed him swithe, *rebuked; at once*
That he him hadde ytold,
And seyd he most penaunce take, *must*
Yif he wald his sinne forsake, *If; would*
Hard and manifold. *Serious; many kinds*

35

205 Than answerd the knight Owayn,
"Don ichil," he seyd, "ful feyn, *I will do; quite eagerly*
What God me wil sende.
Thei thou me wost comandy *Even if; would command*
Into Patrikes Purgatori,
210 Thider ichil wende." *Thither I will go.*

36

The bischop seyd, "Nay, Owain, frende! *friend*
That ich way schaltow nought wende," *shall you not go*
And told him of the pine, *pain*
And bede him lete be that mischaunce, *bade; avoid; adversity*
215 And "Take," he seyd, "sum other penaunce,
To amende thee of sinnes thine."

37

For nought the bischop couthe say, *could*
The knight nold nought leten his way, *would not give up*
His soule to amende.
220 Than ladde he him into holy chirche, *Then led*
Godes werkes for to wirche, *to work*
And the right lawe him kende. *true law; teach*

38

Fiften days in afliccioun, *Fifteen; suffering*
In fasting and in orisoun *prayer*
225 He was, withouten lesing. *lying*
Than the priour with processioun, *Then; prior*
With croice and with gonfanoun, *cross; banner*
To the hole he gan him bring.

39

The priour seyd, "Knight Oweyn,
230   Her is thi gate to go ful gain,
Wende right even forth;   *Go directly forward*
And when thou a while ygon hast,   *have gone*
Light of day thou al forlast,   *completely lost*
Ac hold thee even north.   *But; directly*

40

235   "Thus thou schalt under erthe gon;   *earth go*
Than thou schalt finde sone anon   *soon*
A wel gret feld aplight,   *field assuredly*
And therin an halle of ston,   *a hall of stone*
Swiche in world no wot Y non;   *Such; I know of none*
240   Sumdele ther is of light.   *A little bit*

41

"Namore lightnesse nis ther yfounde   *No more; is not; found*
Than the sonne goth to grounde   *Than when the sun moves low*
In winter sikerly.   *surely*
Into the halle thou schalt go,
245   And duelle ther tille ther com mo,   *remain; until; more*
That schul thee solaci.   *Who shall you comfort*

42

"Thritten men ther schul come,   *Thirteen; shall*
Godes seriaunce alle and some,   *servants every one*
As it seyt in the stori;   *says*
250   And hye thee schul conseily   *quickly [they] shall counsel you*
Hou thou schalt thee conteyni   *sustain yourself*
The way thurth Purgatori."   *through*

43

Than the priour and his covent   *convent*
Bitaught him God, and forth hy went;   *Commended him to; he*
255   The gate thai schet anon.   *shut*
The knight his way hath sone ynome,   *taken*
That into the feld he was ycome   *[So] that; field; come*
Ther was the halle of ston.   *Where*

44

260

The halle was ful selly dight,   *wondrously constructed*
Swiche can make no ertheliche wight;   *Such; earthly creature*
The pilers stode wide.   *pillars stood far apart*
The knight wonderd that he fond   *found*
Swiche an halle in that lond,   *Such*
And open in ich side.   *on each*

45

265

And when he hadde long stond therout,   *stood outside*
And devised al about,   *examined*
In he went thare.   *there*
Thritten men ther come,   *Thirteen men*
Wisemen thai war of dome,   *judgment*

270

And white abite thai bere,   *habit they wore*

46

And al her crounes wer newe schorn;   *crowns [of their heads] were newly shorn*
Her most maister yede biforn   *Their chief master went in front*
And salud the knight.   *greeted*
Adoun he sat, so seyt the boke,   *Down; says*

275

And knight Owain to him he toke,
And told him resoun right.   *reason true*

47

"Ichil thee conseyl, leve brother,   *I will counsel you, dear brother*
As ichave don mani another   *I have done*
That han ywent this way,   *have gone*

280

That thou ben of gode creaunce,   *faith*
Certeyn and poure withouten dotaunce   *true; uncertainty*
To God thi trewe fay;   *true source of doctrine*

48

"For thou schalt se, when we ben ago,   *are gone*
A thousend fendes and wele mo,   *fiends; many more*

285

To bring thee into pine.   *pain*
Ac loke wele, bise thee so,   *But look well, ponder you so*
And thou anithing bi hem do,   *If; with them*
Thi soule thou schalt tine.   *lose*

49

"Have God in thine hert,

290 And thenk opon His woundes smert,   *think; painful*

That He suffred thee fore.   *for you*

And bot thou do as Y thee telle,   *unless*

Bodi and soule thou gos to Helle,   *you go*

And evermore forlore.   *And [are] lost forever*

50

295 "Nempne Godes heighe name,   *Call out; high*

And thai may do thee no schame,   *disgrace*

For nought that may bifalle,"   *occur*

And when thai hadde conseyld the knight,   *counseled*

No lenge bileve he no might,   *No longer remain*

300 Bot went out of the halle.

51

He and alle his fellawered   *company*

Bitaught him God, and forth thai yede   *Entrusted him to God; went*

With ful mild chere.   *gracious manner*

Owein bileft ther in drede,   *left*

305 To God he gan to clepi and grede,   *call; cry out*

And maked his preier.   *prayers*

52

And sone therafter sikerly   *certainly*

He gan to here a reweful cri;   *began to hear; rueful cry*

He was aferd ful sore: *frightened; keenly*

310 Thei alle the warld falle schold,   *Though; world*

Fram the firmament to the mold,   *earth*

No might have ben no more.

53

And when of the cri was passed the drede,   *cry; dread*

Ther com in a grete ferrede   *company*

315 Of fendes fifti score   *fiends fifty*

About the knight into the halle.

Lothly thinges thai weren alle,   *Loathsome*

Behinde and eke bifore.   *also*

54

320

And the knight thai yeden abouten,   *went about*
And grenned on him her foule touten,   *growled; their foul arses*
And drof him to hetheing,   *pursued; with abuse*
And seyd he was comen with flesche and fel   *said they; flesh and skin*
To fechen him the joie of Helle   *fetch him [to]*
Withouten ani ending.

55

325

The most maister fende of alle   *master fiend*
Adoun on knes he gan to falle,   *knees*
And seyd, "Welcome, Owein!
Thou art ycomen to suffri pine   *suffer pain*
To amende thee of sinnes tine,   *damnable*

330

Ac alle gett thee no gain,   *But; get you no profit*

56

"For thou schalt have pine anough,   *pain enough*
Hard, strong, and ful tough,
For thi dedli sinne.   *deadly*
No haddestow never more meschaunce   *Never had you; bad experience*

335

Than thou schal have in our daunce,
When we schul play biginne."

57

"Ac no for than," the fendes sede,   *But; fiends said*
"Yif thou wilt do bi our rede,   *If; by; advice*
For thou art ous leve and dere,   *to us beloved; precious*

340

We schul thee bring with fine amour   *perfect love*
Ther thou com in fram the priour,   *Where*
With our felawes yfere;   *fellows gathered together*

58

"And elles we schul thee teche here,   *otherwise; you teach*
That thou has served ous mani yer

345

In pride and lecherie;   *lust*
For we thee have so long yknawe,   *known*
To thee we schul our hokes thrawe,   *Into you; hooks thrust*
Alle our compeynie."   *company*

59

	He seyd he nold withouten feyle:	*would not; fail*
350	"Ac Y forsake your conseyle;	*But I; counsel*
	Mi penaunce ichil take."	*I will*
	And when the fendes yherd this,	*had heard*
	Amidward the halle ywis	*In the middle*
	A grete fer thai gun make.	*fire; began to make*

60

355	Fet and hond thai bounde him hard,	*Feet and hands*
	And casten him amidward.	*cast; in the midst*
	He cleped to our Dright;	*called; Lord*
	Anon the fer oway was weved,	*At once; fire away; quenched*
	Cole no spark ther nas bileved,	*Coal nor; was not left*
360	Thurth grace of God almight.	*Through*

61

	And when the knight yseighe this,	*had seen*
	Michel the balder he was ywis	*Much more confident; indeed*
	And wele gan understond,	
	And thought wele in his memorie,	
365	It was the fendes trecherie,	*treachery*
	His hert forto fond.	*tempt*

62

	The fendes went out of the halle,	
	The knight thai ladde with hem alle	*led*
	Intil an uncouthe lond.	*Into; uncivilized land*
370	Ther no was no maner wele,	*no kind of comfort*
	Bot hunger, thrust, and chele;	*Only; thirst; cold*
	No tre no seighe he stond,	*tree; saw; stand*

63

	Bot a cold winde that blewe there,	*blew*
	That unnethe ani man might yhere,	*scarcely; hear*
375	And perced thurth his side.	*pierced through*
	The fendes han the knight ynome	*taken*
	So long that thai ben ycome	
	Into a valay wide.	*valley*

133

64

Tho wende the knight he hadde yfounde — *Then thought; found*

380 The deppest pit in Helle grounde. — *deepest*

When he com neighe the stede, — *near; place*

He loked up sone anon;

Strong it was forther to gon, — *Hard; further to go*

He herd schriche and grede. — *shrieking; lamentation*

65

385 He seighe ther ligge ful a feld — *saw; lay; field*

Of men and wimen that wern aqueld, — *women; were destroyed*

Naked with mani a wounde.

Toward the erthe thai lay develing, — *sprawling*

"Allas! Allas!" was her brocking, — *calls of distress*

390 With iren bendes ybounde; — *iron bands bound*

66

And gun to scriche and to wayly, — *began to shriek; wail*

And crid, "Allas! Merci, merci! — *cried*

Merci, God almight!"

Merci nas ther non, forsothe, — *was not*

395 Bot sorwe of hert and grinding of tothe: — *teeth*

That was a griseli sight. — *gruesome*

67

That ich sorwe and that reuthe — *very sorrow; regret*

Is for the foule sinne of slewthe, — *sloth*

As it seyt in the stori. — *says*

400 Who that is slowe in Godes servise — *sluggish*

Of that pain hem may agrise, — *they may dread*

To legge in Purgatori. — *lie*

68

This was the first pain aplight — *in fact*

That thai dede Owain the knight: — *did to*

405 Thai greved him swithe sore. — *troubled; very sorely*

Alle that pain he hath overschaken; — *passed by*

Until another thai han him taken, — *To*

Ther he seighe sorwe more — *Where; saw sorrow*

69

Of men and wimen that ther lay,   *women*
410   That crid, "Allas!" and "Waileway!"   *cried*
For her wicked lore.   *their; conduct*
Thilche soules lay upward,   *These*
As the other hadde ly donward,
That Y told of bifore,

70

415   And were thurth fet and hond and heved   *through feet and hands and head*
With iren nailes gloweand red   *iron nails glowing*
To the erthe ynayled that tide.   *nailed at that time*
Owain seighe sitt on hem there   *saw sit; them*
Lothli dragouns alle o fer,   *Loathsome; on fire*
420   In herd is nought to hide.   *In public nothing can be hidden*

71

On sum sete todes blake,   *sat toads black*
Euetes, neddren, and the snake,   *Newts, adders*
That frete hem bac and side.   *bit them [in the] back*
This is the pain of glotoni: *gluttony*
425   For Godes love, bewar therbi!
It rinneth al to wide.   *runs all too widely*

72

Yete him thought a pain strong   *And then*
Of a cold winde blewe hem among,   *them*
That com out of the sky;
430   So bitter and so cold it blewe,
That alle the soules it overthrewe   *knocked over*
That lay in Purgatori.

73

The fendes lopen on hem thare,   *leapt; them there*
And with her hokes hem al totere,   *their hooks them tore up*
435   And loude thai gun to crie.   *began to cry*
Who that is licchoure in this liif,   *lecher; life*
Be it man other be it wiif,   *wife (i.e., woman)*
That schal ben his bayli.   *country (dwelling place)*

74

The fendes seyd to the knight,

440   "Thou hast ben strong lichoure aplight,   *lecher indeed*

And strong glotoun also: *glutton*

Into this pain thou schalt be dight,   *placed*

Bot thou take the way ful right   *Unless; right away*

Ogain ther thou com fro."   *Back where*

75

445   Owain seyd, "Nay, Satan!

Yete forthermar ichil gan,   *Still further I will go*

Thurth grace of God almight."   *Through*

The fendes wald him have hent: *would; seized*

He cleped to God omnipotent,   *called*

450   And thai lorn al her might.   *lost*

76

Thai ladde him forther into a stede   *led; further; place*

Ther men never gode no dede,   *Where men; did*

Bot schame and vilanie.   *shame; villainy*

Herkneth now, and ben in pes!   *Listen; be in peace!*

455   In the ferth feld it wes,   *fourth field; was*

Al ful of turmentrie.   *torment*

77

Sum bi the fet wer honging,   *feet; hanging*

With iren hokes al brening,   *iron hooks; burning*

And sum bi the swere,   *neck*

460   And sum bi wombe and sum bi rigge,   *belly; back*

Al otherwise than Y can sigge,   *say*

In divers manere.   *various ways*

78

And sum in forneise wern ydon,   *furnace; placed*

With molten ledde and quic brunston   *lead; caustic brimstone*

465   Boiland above the fer,   *Boiling; fire*

And sum bi the tong hing,   *tongue hung*

"Allas!" was ever her brocking,   *calls of distress*

And no nother preiere.   *no other prayer*

79

	And sum on grediris layen there,	*gridirons lay*
470	Al glowand ogains the fer,	*glowing upon; fire*
	That Owain wele yknewe,	*recognized*
	That whilom were of his queyntaunce,	*at some time; acquaintance*
	That suffred ther her penaunce:	
	Tho chaunged al his hewe!	*Then; color*

80

475	A wilde fer hem thurthout went,	*fire them throughout*
	Alle that it oftok it brent,	*overtook; burned*
	Ten thousend soules and mo.	*more*
	Tho that henge bi fet and swere,	*Those; feet; neck*
	That were theves and theves fere,	*thieves; companions*
480	And wrought man wel wo.	*caused; woe*

81

	And tho that henge bi the tong,	*those; hung*
	That "Allas!" ever song,	*sang*
	And so loude crid,	*cried*
	That wer bacbiters in her live:	*backbiters; lives*
485	Bewar therbi, man and wive,	*Beware; wife (i.e., woman)*
	That lef beth for to chide.	*Who are eager to scold (complain)*

82

	Alle the stedes the knight com bi	*places*
	Were the paines of Purgatori	
	For her werkes wrong.	*their works*
490	Whoso is lef on the halidom swere,	*willing to; relics swear*
	Or ani fals witnes bere,	*false witness bear*
	Ther ben her peynes strong.	

83

	Owain anon him biwent	*went*
	And seighe where a whele trent,	*saw; wheel turned*
495	That griseliche were of sight;	*gruesome*
	Michel it was, about it wond,	*Great; moved*
	And brend right as it were a brond;	*burned; brand*
	With hokes it was ydight.	*hooks; fitted out*

Sir Owain

84

500 An hundred thousand soules and mo
Opon the whele were honging tho,
The fendes thertil ourn.
The stori seyt of Owain the knight,
That no soule knowe he no might,
So fast thai gun it tourn.

85

505 Out of the erthe com a lighting
Of a blo fer al brening,
That stank foule withalle,
And about the whele it went,
And the soules it forbrent
510 To poudre swithe smal.

86

That whele, that renneth in this wise,
Is for the sinne of covaitise,
That regnes now overal.
The coveytous man hath never anough
515 Of gold, of silver, no of plough,
Til deth him do doun falle.

87

The fendes seyd to the knight,
"Thou hast ben covaitise aplight,
To win lond and lede;
520 Opon this whele thou schalt be dight,
Bot yif thou take the way ful right
Intil thin owhen thede."

88

Her conseyl he hath forsaken.
The fendes han the knight forth taken,
525 And bounde him swithe hard
Opon the whele that arn about,
And so lothly gan to rout,
And cast him amidward.

wheel; hanging
thereto arranged
says
recognize
made it turn

came lightning
blue (i.e., livid) fire; burning
burnt up
powder very fine

runs in this way
covetousness
reigns; completely
covetous; enough
land
Until death makes him fall down

covetous indeed
land; nation
placed
Unless; immediately
Unto your own country

Their counsel
very
turned
hideously; bellow
in the midst

89

Tho the hokes him torent,   *Then; hooks; tore*

530 And the wild fer him tobrent.   *fire; burned fiercely*

On Jhesu Crist he thought,

Fram that whele an angel him bare,   *bore*

And al the fendes that were thare

No might him do right nought.

90

535 Thai ladde him forther with gret pain,

Til thai com to a mounteyn   *mountain*

That was as rede as blod,   *red; blood*

And men and wimen theron stode;   *women; stood*

Him thought, it nas for non gode,   *He thought; was not*

540 For thai cride as thai were wode.   *cried; crazy*

91

The fendes seyd to the knight than,

"Thou hast wonder of thilche man   *these men*

That make so dreri mode: *woeful mood*

For thai deserved Godes wreche,   *God's vengeance*

545 Hem schal sone com a bevereche   *[To] them; drink*

That schal nought thenche hem gode."   *intend*

92

No hadde he no rather that word yseyd,   *sooner; said*

As it is in the stori leyd,   *told (recorded)*

Ther com a windes blast,

550 That fende and soule and knight up went

Almest into the firmament,   *Almost*

And sethen adon him cast   *afterwards down*

93

Into a stinkand river,   *stinking*

That under the mounteyn ran o fer,   *mountain; of fire*

555 As quarel of alblast,   *missile of a siege engine*

And cold it was as ani ise   *any ice*

The pain may no man devise,   *describe*

That him was wrought in hast.   *in haste*

94

Seyn Owain in the water was dreynt,	*drenched*
560 And wex therin so mad and feynt,	*grew; faint*
That neighe he was forlore;	*nearly; lost*
Sone so he on God might thenchen ought,	*As soon as; think at all*
Out of the water he was ybrought,	
And to the lond ybore.	*borne*

95

565 That ich pain, ich understond,	*very*
Is for bothe nithe and ond,	*malice; spite*
That was so wick liif;	*wicked life*
Ond was the windes blast	*Fierce*
That into the stinking water him cast:	
570 Ich man bewar therbi!	

96

Forth thai ladde him swithe withalle,	*led; quickly*
Til thai com to an halle,	
He no seighe never er non swiche.	*saw; before; such*
Out of the halle com an hete,	*heat*
575 That the knight bigan to swete,	*sweat*
He seighe so foule a smiche.	*saw; smoke*

97

Tho stint he forther for to gon.	*Then stopped; to go*
The fendes it aperceived anon,	*realized*
And were therof ful fawe.	*livid*
580 "Turn ogain," thai gun to crie,	
"Or thou schalt wel sone dye,	
Bot thou be withdrawe."	*taken out*

98

And when he com to the halle dore,	*door*
He no hadde never sen bifore	
585 Halvendel the care.	*A half part of; pain*
The halle was ful of turmentri:	*torments*
Tho that were in that bayly	*Those; fortress*
Of blis thai were ful bare,	*bare*

140

99

For al was the halle grounde
590   Ful of pittes that were rounde,   *pits*
And were ful yfilt   *filled*
To the brerdes, gret and smal,   *rims*
Of bras and coper and other metal,   *brass; copper*
And quic bronston ymelt;   *caustic brimstone molten*

100

595   And men and wimen theron stode,
And schrist and crid, as thai wer wode,   *shrieked; cried; crazy*
For her dedeli sinne;   *deadly*
Sum to the navel wode,   *waded*
And sum to the brestes yode,   *breasts went*
600   And sum to the chin.

101

Ich man after his misgilt   *Each; sin*
In that pein was ypilt,   *pain; thrust*
To have that strong hete;   *heat*
And sum bere bagges about her swere   *bore bags (i.e., pouches); necks*
605   Of pens gloweand al of fer,   *coins glowing all on fire*
And swiche mete ther thai ete: *such meat; ate*

102

That were gavelers in her liif.   *usurers*
Bewar therbi, bothe man and wiif,
Swiche sinne that ye lete.   *permit*
610   And mani soules ther yede uprightes,   *stood upright*
With fals misours and fals wightes,   *sinners; creatures*
That fendes opon sete.   *set upon*

103

The fendes to the knight sede,   *said*
"Thou most bathi in this lede   *bathe; area*
615   Ar than thou hennes go;   *Before; hence*
For thine okering and for thi sinne   *money-lending*
A parti thou most be wasche herinne,   *period of time; washed*
O cours or to."   *A cycle or two*

104

620

Owain drad that turment, *dreaded*
And cleped to God omnipotent, *called*
And His moder Marie. *mother*
Yborn he was out of the halle, *Borne*
Fram the paines and the fendes alle,
Tho he so loude gan crie. *Then*

105

625

Anon the knight was war ther, *aware*
Whare sprang out a flaumme o fer, *flame of fire*
That was stark and store; *strong; fierce*
Out the erthe the fer aros.
Tho the knight wel sore agros, *Then; sorely terrified*

630

As cole and piche it fore. *coal; pitch it spewed*

106

Of seven maner colours the fer out went,
The soules therin it forbrent; *burned up*
Sum was yalu and grene, *yellow; green*
Sum was blac and sum was blo; *black; blue*

635

Tho that were therin hem was ful wo, *Those*
And sum as nadder on to sene. *as if one saw an adder*

107

The fende hath the knight ynome, *fiends; taken*
And to the pit thai weren ycome,
And seyd thus in her spelle, *their spiel*

640

"Now, Owain, thou might solas make, *solace*
For thou schalt with our felawes schake *fellows hurry*
Into the pit of Helle.

108

"This ben our foules in our caghe, *birds; cage*
And this is our courtelage *garden*

645

And our castel tour;
Tho that ben herin ybrought, *Those*
Sir knight, hou trowestow ought, *do you believe at all*
That hem is anithing sour? *That they are at all agonized*

109

	"Now turn ogain or to late,	*back before too late*
650	Ar we thee put in at Helle gate;	*Before*
	Out no schaltow never winne,	*shall you*
	For no noise no for no crie,	
	No for no clepeing to Marie,	*calling*
	No for no maner ginne."	*contrivance*

110

655	Her conseil the knight forsoke.	*counsel*
	The fendes him nom, so seith the boke,	*took*
	And bounde him swithe fast.	*fully*
	Into that ich wicke prisoun,	*wicked*
	Stinckand and derk, fer adoun,	*Stinking; dark, far*
660	Amidward thai him cast.	*Amidst*

111

	Ever the nether that thai him cast	*deeper*
	The hatter the fer on him last;	*hotter*
	Tho him gan sore smert.	*Then; be pained*
	He cleped to God omnipotent,	*called*
665	To help him out of that turment,	
	With gode wille and stedefast hert.	*good*

112

	Out of the pit he was yborn,	*carried*
	And elles he hadde ben forlorn	*otherwise; lost*
	To his ending day.	
670	That is the pine, that ich of rede,	*pain; tell of*
	Is for the foule sinne of prede,	*pride*
	That schal lasten ay.	*forever*

113

	Biside the pit he seighe and herd	*saw; heard*
	Hou God almighten him had ywerd;	*protected*
675	His clothes wer al torent.	*torn*
	Forther couthe he no way,	*could*
	Ther him thought a divers cuntray;	*strange country*
	His bodi was al forbrent.	*burned badly*

114

	Tho chaunged Owain rode and hewe;	*Then; face and complexion*
680	Fendes he seighe, ac non he no knewe,	*saw, but*
	In that divers lond;	*strange*
	Sum sexti eighen bere,	*sixty eyes bore*
	That lotheliche and griseliche were,	*loathsome; gruesome*
	And sum hadde sexti hond.	*sixty hands*

115

685	Thai seyd, "Thou schalt nought ben alon,	
	Thou schalt haven ous to mon,	*attend to*
	To teche thee newe lawes,	
	As thou hast ylernd ere,	*learned before*
	In the stede ther thou were	*place*
690	Amonges our felawes."	

116

	The fendes han the knight ynome;	*taken*
	To a stinkand water thai ben ycome.	*stinking*
	He no seighe never er non swiche.	*saw; before; such*
	It stank fouler than ani hounde,	*hound*
695	And mani mile it was to the grounde,	
	And was as swart as piche.	*black as pitch*

117

	And Owain seighe therover ligge	*lay*
	A swithe strong, naru brigge.	*very; narrow bridge*
	The fendes seyd tho,	*then*
700	"Lo, sir knight, sestow this?	*do you see*
	This is the brigge of Paradis,	
	Here over thou most go;	*must*

118

	"And we thee schul with stones throwe,	
	And the winde thee schal over blowe,	
705	And wirche thee ful wo.	*inflict misery on you*
	Thou no schalt, for al this midnerd,	*for all the world*
	Bot yif thou falle amidwerd	*Avoid falling in the middle*
	To our felawes mo.	*other fellows*

144

119

"And when thou art adoun yfalle,   *fallen*

710 Than schal com our felawes alle,

And with her hokes thee hede.   *behead*

We schul thee teche a newe play

Thou hast served ous mani a day

And into Helle thee lede."

120

715 Owain biheld the brigge smert,   *bridge painful*

The water therunder, blac and swert,   *black; dark*

And sore him gan to drede.   *sorely; dread*

For of o thing he tok yeme: *one; notice*

Never mot in sonne beme   *motes; sun beams*

720 Thicker than the fendes yede.   *came*

121

The brigge was as heighe as a tour,   *high; tower*

And as scharpe as a rasour,   *sharp; razor*

And naru it was also;   *narrow*

And the water that ther ran under

725 Brend o lighting and of thonder,   *Burned of lightning; thunder*

That thought him michel wo.   *Which he thought [a] great difficulty (misfortune)*

122

Ther nis no clerk may write with ynke,   *is no; ink*

No no man no may bithinke,   *imagine*

No no maister devine,   *master figure out*

730 That is ymade, forsothe ywis,

Under the brigge of Paradis,

Halvendel the pine.   *One half of; pain*

123

So the dominical ous telle,   *(see note)*

There is the pure entré of Helle: *entry*

735 Sein Poule berth witnesse.   *Saint Paul bears*

Whoso falleth of the brigge adoun,   *off (from)*

Of him nis no redempcioun,

Noither more no lesse.   *Neither*

124

The fendes seyd to the knight tho,   *then*

740 "Over this brigge might thou nought go,

For noneskines nede.   *For any need at all*

Fle periil, sorwe, and wo,   *Flee peril*

And to that stede, ther thou com fro   *place*

Wel fair we schul thee lede."   *lead*

125

745 Owain anon him gan bithenche   *consider*

Fram hou mani of the fendes wrenche   *wiles*

God him saved hadde.

He sett his fot opon the brigge,

No feld he no scharp egge,   *felt; edge*

750 No nothing him no drad.   *dreaded*

126

When the fendes yseighe tho,   *saw then*

That he was more than half ygo,   *gone*

Loude thai gun to crie,

"Allas, allas, that he was born!

755 This ich knight we have forlorn   *lost*

Out of our baylie."   *prison*

127

When he was of the brigge ywent,   *gone*

He thonked God omnipotent,

And His moder Marie,

760 That him hadde swiche grace ysent,

He was deliverd fro her turment,   *from their*

Intil a better baylie.   *Unto; keep*

128

A cloth of gold him was ybrought,

In what maner he nist nought,   *did not know*

765 Tho God him hadde ysent.

That cloth he dede on him there,   *That clothing he put on*

And alle woundes hole were,   *healed*

That er then was forbrent.   *earlier; burned*

129

He thonked God in Trinité,

770 And loked forther and gan yse   *see*

As it were a ston wal.   *stone wall*

He biheld about, fer and neighe,   *far and near*

Non ende theron he no seighe,

O red gold it schon al.   *Of; shone*

130

775 Forthermore he gan yse   *see*

A gate, non fairer might be

In this world ywrought;

Tre no stel nas theron non,   *Wood nor steel was not*

Bot rede gold and precious ston,

780 And al God made of nought:

131

Jaspers, topes, and cristal,   *topaz; crystal*

Margarites and coral,   *Pearls*

And riche saferstones,   *sapphires*

Ribes and salidoines,   *Rubies; celadon*

785 Onicles and causteloines,   *Onyx; chalcedony*

And diamaunce for the nones.   *diamonds indeed*

132

In tabernacles thai wer ywrought,   *sanctuaries*

Richer might it be nought,

With pilers gent and small;   *columns beautiful; delicate*

790 Arches ybent with charbukelston,   *curved; carbuncle*

Knottes of rede gold theropon,

And pinacles of cristal.

133

Bi as miche as our Saveour

Is queinter than goldsmithe other paintour,   *more skillful; or*

795 That woneth in ani lond,   *lives*

So fare the gates of Paradis   *far*

Er richer ywrought, forsothe ywis,   *Are*

As ye may understond.

134

	The gates bi hemselve undede.	*opened*
800	Swiche a smal com out of that stede	*smell; place*
	As it al baume were;	*balm*
	And of that ich swetenisse	*sweetness*
	The knight tok so gret strengthe ywis,	*truly*
	As ye may fortheward here,	

135

805	That him thought he might wel,	
	More bi a thousand del,	*times*
	Suffri pain and wo,	
	And turn ogain siker aplight,	*firmly assured*
	And ogain alle fendes fight,	*against*
810	Ther he er com fro.	*Where; earlier; from*

136

	The knight yode the gate ner,	*went; near*
	And seighe ther com with milde chere	*in gracious manner*
	Wel mani processioun,	*many [in] procession*
	With tapers and chaundelers of gold;	*candles; candle-holders*
815	Non fairer no might ben on mold,	*earth*
	And croices and goinfainoun.	*crosses; banners*

137

	Popes with gret dignité,	
	And cardinals gret plenté,	
	Kinges and quenes ther were,	
820	Knightes, abbotes, and priours,	
	Monkes, chanouns, and Frere Prechours,	*canons; Friar Preachers (i.e., Dominicans)*
	And bischopes that croices bere;	

138

	Frere Menours and Jacobins,	*Friars Minor (i.e., Franciscans); Dominicans*
	Frere Carmes and Frere Austines,	*Carmelites; Augustinian Friars*
825	And nonnes white and blake;	*nuns*
	Al maner religioun	*religious*
	Ther yede in that processioun,	*went*
	That order hadde ytake.	*religious orders had taken*

139

The order of wedlake com also,   *wedlock*
830   Men and wimen mani mo,   *more*
And thonked Godes grace
That hath the knight swiche grace ysent,
He was deliverd from the fendes turment,
Quic man into that plas.   *Living*

140

835   And when thai hadde made this melody,
Tuay com out of her compeynie,   *Two; company*
Palmes of gold thai bere.   *bore*
To the knight thai ben ycome
Bituix hem tuay thai han him nome,   *Between; two; taken*
840   And erchebischopes it were.   *archbishops*

141

Up and doun thai ladde the knight,   *led*
And schewed him joies of more might,   *power*
And miche melodye.   *much*
Mirie were her carols there,   *Merry*
845   Non foles among hem nere,   *There were no sins among them*
Bot joie and menstracie.   *minstrelsy*

142

Thai yede on carol al bi line,   *went; in a line*
Her joie may no man devine,   *understand*
Of God thai speke and song;   *spoke; sang*
850   And angels yeden hem to gy,   *went; guide*
With harpe and fithel and sautry,   *fiddle; psaltery (i.e., stringed instrument)*
And belles miri rong   *merrily rang*

143

No may ther no man caroly inne,   *carol (i.e., sing)*
Bot that he be clene of sinne,   *Unless*
855   And leten alle foly.   *leave*
Now God, for Thine woundes alle,
Graunt ous caroly in that halle,   *Let us sing*
And His moder Marie!

144

860

This ich joie, as ye may se,   *very*
Is for love and charité
Ogain God and mankinne.   *Towards*
Who that lat erthely love be,   *leaves behind earthly love*
And loveth God in Trinité,
He may caroly therinne.   *sing*

145

865

Other joies he seighe anough:
Heighe tres with mani a bough,
Theron sat foules of heven,   *birds*
And breke her notes with miri gle,   *trilled; merry glee*
Burdoun and mene gret plenté,   *Bass; melody*
870   And hautain with heighe steven.   *treble; loud sound*

146

Him thought wele with that foules song   *birds'*
He might wele live theramong
Til the worldes ende.
Ther he seighe that tre of liif   *life*
875   Wharthurth that Adam and his wiif   *Whereby*
To Helle gun wende.   *went*

147

Fair were her erbers with floures,   *gardens*
Rose and lili, divers colours,
Primrol and paruink,   *Primrose; periwinkle*
880   Mint, fetherfoy, and eglentere,   *chrysanthemum; briar rose*
Colombin and mo ther were   *Columbine*
Than ani man mai bithenke.   *imagine*

148

It beth erbes of other maner   *There are plants of other kinds*
Than ani in erthe groweth here,
885   Tho that is lest of priis.   *Those that are least of value*
Evermore thai grene springeth,
For winter no somer it no clingeth,   *summer; shrivels*
And swetter than licorice.   *sweeter*

149

Ther beth the welles in that stede,	*wells*
890 The water is swetter than ani mede,	*sweeter; beverage*
Ac on ther is of priis,	*But one; value*
Swiche that Seynt Owain seighe tho,	*Such; then*
That foure stremes urn fro	*streams flow from*
Out of Paradis.	

150

895 Pison men clepeth that o strem,	*Phison; one*
That is of swithe bright lem,	*gleaming*
Gold is therin yfounde.	
Gihon men clepeth that other ywis,	*second*
That is of miche more priis	*value*
900 Of stones in the grounde.	

151

The thridde strem is Eufrates,	*third*
Forsothe to telle, withouten les,	*Truth to tell, without lies*
That rinneth swithe right.	*quickly forth*
The ferth strem is Tigris;	*fourth stream*
905 In the world is make nis	*none other*
Of stones swithe bright.	

152

Who loveth to live in clenesse,	
He schal have that ich blisse,	
And se that semly sight.	*pleasing*
910 And more he ther yseighe	*saw*
Under Godes glorie an heighe:	*on high*
Yblisced be His might!	*Blessed*

153

Sum soule he seyghe woni bi selve,	*saw stay alone*
And sum bi ten and bi tuelve,	*twelve*
915 And everich com til other;	*to the others*
And when thai com togiders ywis,	*together*
Alle thai made miche blis	*much*
As soster doth with the brother.	*sister*

154

Sum he seighe gon in rede scarlet,
920 And sum in pourper wele ysett,   *purple; attired*
And sum in sikelatoun;   *silk woven with gold*
As the prest ate Masse wereth,
Tonicles and aubes on hem thai bereth,   *Vestments; albs*
And sum gold bete al doun.   *hammered gold*

155

925 The knight wele in alle thing
Knewe bi her clotheing   *their*
In what state that thai were,   *status*
And what dedes thai hadde ydo,
Tho that were yclothed so,   *Those*
930 While thai were mannes fere.   *among mankind*

156

Ichil you tel a fair semblaunce,   *I will; comparison*
That is a gode acordaunce   *That accords well*
Bi the sterres clere: *stars bright*
Sum ster is brighter on to se
935 Than is bisides other thre,   *three others*
And of more pouwere.

157

In this maner ydelt it is,   *dealt*
Bi the joies of Paradis:
Thai no have nought al yliche;   *alike*
940 The soule that hath joie lest,   *least*
Him thenketh he hath aldermest,   *believes; most of all*
And holt him also riche.   *holds; as*

158

The bischopes ogain to him come,   *back to*
Bituen hem tuay thai him nome,   *Between; two; took*
945 And ladde him up and doun,   *led*
And seyd, "Brother, God, herd He be!   *God, be He praised*
Fulfild is thi volenté,   *desire*
Now herken our resoun.   *listen; explanation*

152

159

"Thou hast yse with eighen thine   *seen; eyes*

950   Bothe the joies and the pine: *pain*

Yherd be Godes grace!   *Praised*

We wil thee tel bi our comun dome,   *common judgment*

What way it was that thou bicome,

Er thou hennes pas.   *hence pass*

160

955   "That lond that is so ful of sorwe,

Bothe an aven and a morwe,   *evening and morning*

That thou thus com bi

(Thou suffredes pain and wo,

And other soules mani mo)

960   Men clepeth it Purgatori.

161

"And this lond that is so wide,   *broad*

And so michel and so side,   *great; spacious*

And is ful of blis,

That thou hast now in ybe,

965   And mani joies here yse,

Paradis is cleped ywis.   *called*

162

"Ther mai no man comen here

Til that he be spourged there,   *cleansed*

And ymade al clene.

970   Than cometh thai hider." The bischop sede,

"Into the joie we schul hem lede,

Sumwhile bi tuelve and tene.   *At some time; twelve; ten*

163

"And sum ben so hard ybounde,   *bound*

Thai nite never hou long stounde   *do not know; time*

975   Thai schul suffri that hete;   *heat*

Bot yif her frendes do godenisse,   *friends*

Yif mete, or do sing Messe,   *If appropriate; have Mass sung*

That thai han in erthe ylete,   *arranged for*

164

        "Other ani other almosdede,   *Or; almsdeed*
980   Alle the better hem may spede   *hasten*
        Out of her missays,   *misery*
        And com into this Paradis,
        Ther joie and blis ever is,   *Where*
        And libbe here al in pays.   *live; peace*

165

985   "As hye cometh out of Purgatori,   *quickly*
        So passe we up to Godes glori,
        That is the heighe riche,   *high kingdom*
        That is Paradis celestien;   *celestial*
        Therin com bot Cristen men: *only Christian*
990   No joie nis that yliche.   *like*

166

        "When we comen out of the fer
        Of Purgatori, ar we com her,   *before*
        We no may nought anon right.   *right away*
        Til we han her long ybe,
995   We may nought Godes face yse,
        No in that stede alight.   *place stay*

167

        "The child that was yborn tonight,
        Er the soule be hider ydight,   *Before; here placed*
        The pain schal overflé.   *pass over*
1000 Strong and hevi is it than,   *heavy*
        Here to com the old man,
        That long in sinne hath be."

168

        Forth thai went til thai seighe
        A mounteyn that was swithe heighe,   *extremely high*
1005 Ther was al gamen and gle.   *playing; glee*
        So long thai hadde the way ynome,   *taken*
        That to the cop thai weren ycome,   *summit*
        The joies forto se.

169

Ther was al maner foulen song,   *all kinds of birds'*

1010 Michel joie was hem among,

And evermore schal be;

Ther is more joie in a foules mouthe,   *bird's*

Than here in harp, fithel, or crouthe, *fiddle; croud (i.e., stringed instrument)*

Bi lond other bi se.   *By land or by sea*

170

1015 That lond, that is so honestly,

Is ycleped Paradis terestri,   *called; terrestrial*

That is in erthe here;

That other is Paradis, Godes riche: *kingdom*

Thilke joie hath non yliche,   *That; like*

1020 And is above the aire.

171

In that, that is in erthe here,

Was Owain, that Y spac of here,   *I spoke*

Swiche that les Adam;   *Which; lost*

For, hadde Adam yhold him stille,   *firmly*

1025 And wrought after Godes wille

As he ogain him nam,   *against him took up*

172

He no his ofspring nevermo   *offspring*

Out of that joie no schuld have go;

Bot for he brac it so sone,   *broke*

1030 With pike and spade in diche to delve,   *ditch*

To help his wiif and himselve,

God made him miche to done.   *much*

173

God was with him so wroth,

That he no left him no cloth,   *clothing*

1035 Bot a lef of a tre,   *leaf*

And al naked yede and stode.   *went; stood*

Loke man, yif hye ner wode,   *Look; if you are not mad*

At swiche a conseil to be.   *counsel*

174

Tho com an angel with a swerd o fer,   *Then; sword of fire*

1040   And with a stern loke and chere,   *countenance*

And made hem sore aferd;   *afraid*

In erthe to ben in sorwe and wo,

Therwhile thai lived evermo,

He drof hem to midnerd.   *drove; earth*

175

1045   And when he dyed to Helle he nam,   *traveled*

And al that ever of him cam,

Til Godes Sone was born,

And suffred pain and Passioun,

And brought him out of that prisoun,

1050   And elles were al forlorn.   *lost*

176

Hereof speketh David in the Sauter,   *Psalter*

Of a thing that toucheth here,   *is relevant here*

Of God in Trinité,

Opon men, that ben in gret honour,

1055   And honoureth nought her Creatour

Of so heighe dignité.

177

Alle that ben of Adames kinne,   *kin*

Th[at here in erthe have don sinne,]

S . . . .

1060   O . . . .

H . . . .

A . . . .

178

. . . .

. . . .

1065   . . . .

. . . .

. . . .

. . . .

179

Th . . . .
1070 B . . . .
In the paine of Purgatori;
And bot he have the better chaunce,
At Domesday he is in balaunce   *Judgment Day*
Ogaines God in glorie.   *With regard to*

180

1075 The bischopes the knight hete   *commanded*
To tellen hem, that he no lete,   *leave out*
Whether Heven were white or biis,   *gray*
Blewe or rede, yalu or grene.   *Blue; yellow*
The knight seyd, "Withouten wene,   *doubt*
1080 Y schal say min aviis.   *opinion*

181

"Me thenketh it is a thousandfold
Brighter than ever was ani gold,
Bi sight opon to se."
"Ya," seyd the bischop to the knight
1085 "That ich stede, that is so bright,   *very place*
Nis bot the entré.   *entry*

182

"And ich day ate gate o sithe   *one time*
Ous cometh a mele to make ous blithe,   *To us; meal; glad*
That is to our biheve: *benefit*
1090 A swete smal of al gode,   *piece*
It is our soule fode.   *food*
Abide, thou schalt ous leve."   *believe*

183

Anon the knight was war there,   *aware*
Whare sprong out a flaumbe of fer,   *flame of fire*
1095 Fram Heven gate it fel.
The knight thought, al fer and neighe,   *far and near*
Ther over al Paradis it fleighe,   *flew*
And gaf so swete a smal.   *gave; smell*

184

The Holy Gost in fourme o fer   *form of fire*
1100   Opon the knight light ther,   *alighted*
In that ich place;
Thurth vertu of that ich light
He les ther al his erthelich might,
And thonked Godes grace.

185

1105   Thus the bischop to him sede,
"God fet ous ich day with His brede,   *feeds; bread*
Ac we no have noure neighe   *But; nowhere near*
So grete likeing of His grace,   *Such a great enjoyment*
No swiche a sight opon His face,
1110   As tho that ben on heighe.   *those; high*

186

The soules that beth at Godes fest,   *feast*
Thilche joie schal ever lest   *last*
Withouten ani ende.
Now thou most bi our comoun dome,   *judgment*
1115   That ich way that thou bicome,
Ogain thou most wende.   *Back; must go*

187

Now kepe thee wele fram dedli sinne,   *well; deadly sin*
That thou never com therinne,
For nonskines nede.   *For no reason at all*
1120   When thou art ded, thou schalt wende
Into the joie that hath non ende;
Angels schul thee lede."   *lead*

188

Tho wepe Seynt Owain swithe sore,   *Then*
And prayd hem for Godes ore,   *pardon*
1125   That he most ther duelle;   *might; remain*
That he no seighe nevermore,
As he hadde do bifore,
The strong paines of Helle.

189

Of that praier gat he no gain

1130 He nam his leve and went ogain,   *took his leave; back*

Thei him were swithe wo.   *Though*

Fendes he seighe ten thousand last,

Thay flowe fram him as quarel of alblast,   *fled; like a missile from a catapult*

That he er com fro.

190

1135 No nere than a quarel might flé,   *stone; flee*

No fende no might him here no se,   *hear; see*

For al this warld to winne;

And when that he com to the halle,

The thritten men he fond alle,

1140 Ogaines him therinne.   *Facing towards*

191

Alle thai held up her hond,

And thonked Jhesu Cristes sond   *help*

A thousaned times and mo,

And bad him heighe, that he no wond,   *hurry; wander*

1145 That he wer up in Yrlond,   *might be*

As swithe as he might go.   *quickly*

192

And as ich finde in this stori,

The priour of the Purgatori   *[To] the prior*

Com tokening that night,   *Came with a premonition*

1150 That Owain hadde overcomen his sorwe,

And schuld com up on the morwe,

Thurth grace of God almight.

193

Than the priour with processioun,

Wih croice and with goinfainoun,   *cross; banner*

1155 To the hole he went ful right,

Ther that knight Owain in wende.   *traveled*

As a bright fere that brende,   *fire; burned*

Thai seighe a lem of light,   *gleam*

159

194

1160
And right amiddes that ich light
Com up Owain, Godes knight.
Tho wist thai wele bi than,
That Owain hadde ben in Paradis,
And in Purgatori ywis,
And that he was holy man.

195

1165
Thai ladde him into holi chirche,
Godes werkes forto wirche.   *works to do*
His praiers he gan make,
And at the ende on the fiften day,
The knight anon, forsothe to say,
1170
Scrippe and burdoun gan take.   *Pilgrim's bag and staff*

196

That ich holy stede he sought,   *place*
Ther Jhesus Crist ous dere bought
Opon the Rode tre,   *Cross*
And ther He ros fram ded to live
1175
Thurth vertu of his woundes five:
Yblisced mot He be!

197

And Bedlem, ther that God was born   *Bethlehem*
Of Mari His moder, as flour of thorn,   *flower*
And ther He stighe to Heven;   *arose*
1180
And sethen into Yrlond he come,
And monkes abite undernome,   *habit assumed*
And lived there yeres seven.

198

And when he deyd, he went ywis
Into the heighe joie of Paradis,
1185
Thurth help of Godes grace.
Now God, for Seynt Owain's love,

Sir Owain

Graunt ous Heven blis above
Bifor His swete face! Amen.
    Explicit

Explanatory Notes to Sir Owain

Abbreviations: see Textual Notes.

In order to maintain consistency with other editions of *Sir Owain* and with citation practices in secondary criticism about the poem, this edition includes stanza numbers. The explanatory and textual notes, following METS format, are, however, listed by line number.

1–2   The first two lines of this stanza and probably the five preceding stanzas are missing. E explains the excision from the preceding folio of A that would have caused the loss (p. xxii) and prints in a note (pp. 155–56) the first 36 lines of the Anglo-Norman version of the poem.

11–12   *Thai no held it . . . that he sede.* The sense of these lines is that the Irish understood (held) everything he said to be "foolishness concerning nothing."

13–24   *al thai seyd commounliche . . . No her folies blinne.* The Irish say they will all be convinced if a man visits Hell and returns with information about the pain suffered there. This is a bit inconsistent with the primarily purgatorial experience to which the poem turns.

20   *suffri.* The use of an *i* ending for the third person plural present indicative is unusual even in descendants of Class 2 Old English weak verbs. One would expect *-ith*. The use of the *i* or *y* ending for the infinitive, though ordinarily a Southern dialect characteristic (occasionally on the borders of the Southwest Midland), is common throughout: see 23, 76, 208, 246, 250, 251, 305, 328, 391, 614, 807, 853, 857, 864, and 975.

43–102   St. Patrick has a dream vision in which Jesus comes to him. He gives St. Patrick a heavy book, apparently more comprehensive than Scripture, because it includes *Godes priveté* (line 54), those matters which are properly the knowledge of God alone and usually not to be enquired into by man. In addition, Patrick is given *Godes Staf* (line 58), a symbol of episcopal authority. He is shown an entry way into

Purgatory and told that, if a penitent spends a night and a day, he will be forgiven and have a vision of Paradise. When St. Patrick awakes, the book and staff remain with him.

47   *dere bought.* Redemption is, etymologically, a "buying back." The theological idea is frequently rendered as a process whereby Christ *dere bought* ("dearly bought") us.

49   *bok.* It is tempting to see the book as the ninth-century Book of Armagh, often taken to be a relic of St. Patrick. This book, however, seems to contain more comprehensive information about "Godes priveté" (line 54) than does the Book of Armagh, which is preserved in Trinity College Dublin (MS 52). Indeed, the Book of Armagh contains documents related to St. Patrick, so the book cannot be the Book of Armagh as we know it, but a good deal of confusion surrounds such artifacts in the fourteenth century.

54   *Godes priveté.* Since men are ordinarily not to know *Godes priveté*, the book is a powerful gift to St. Patrick.

58   *Godes Staf.* The *Staf*, "a bishop's staff, crosier" (*MED*), is clearly a sign of episcopal authority granted by God. *Godes Staf* may have a special meaning with regard to St. Patrick. It is mentioned by Giraldus Cambrensis (c. 1147–1216/1220) in connection with St. Patrick's expulsion of the snakes from Ireland, and it appears in many other Patrician legends. That it was a real object is attested by its being seized from the archbishop of Armagh in 1177 and lodged in London, where it was probably burned in 1538. For an interesting bibliography, see E, p. 196.

64   *gret desert.* A *desert* was "a barren area, wooded or arid" (*MED*). The location is on Saints' Island in Lough Derg, County Donegal. The site of the entry was later redefined as Station Island (Lough Derg), which remains a site of penitential pilgrimage. See Introduction for greater detail.

82–83   *A night and a day . . . be forgive his sinne.* The idea that a day and a night, preceded and followed by prayer and fasting, would forgive sins and satisfy purgatorial punishment was traditional. The inclusion of a view of the "Earthly Paradise" was less common in visions of the hereafter. The foreground of the poem switches to the purgatorial rather than the infernal at this point.

119   *Peter*. A: *patrike* is clearly not possible. I have followed E in substituting *Peter* because of the foundation of Sts. Peter and Paul's, Armagh. Around 1130 the Augustinian Canons Regular of the Abbey of Sts. Peter and Paul, Armagh, were given authority over a dependent priory on Saints' Island.

120   *rede*. More than simply "read"; it is a liturgical observance: "To read aloud or chant during a church service" (*MED*).

124   *Regles*. There is confusion in the manuscripts of various versions of the poem about whether the name *Regles* is derived from the Irish *reicles* (a small church or monastic cell) or from Latin *regula* (rule of a religious order). Regardless, it is clear that the *Regles* in A is a monastic establishment and becomes the repository of the book and the staff (lines 130–32).

127   *White chanounes*. E identifies these as Premonstratensian Canons, founded by St. Norbert at Prémontré in 1120, and called "white" because of their habit. They lived according to the Rule of St. Augustine (St. Augustine appeared to St. Norbert) with some Cistercian influence probably because of St. Norbert's friendship with St. Bernard of Clairvaux, the founder of the Cistercians. Premonstratensians were extremely austere and propagated the doctrine of Purgatory from their inception. There is, however, no certainty that the canons were Premonstratensian. Other Canons Regular of St. Augustine had existed for some time and generally wore white habits.

143   *went into Helle*. The meaning is clearly "visited Hell," but some confusion about the use of the terms Purgatory and Hell exists. Purgatorial visions often represented souls as suffering infernal pains, sometimes less severe, but only for a limited time.

144   *storie*. No specific source may be intended. The poem frequently makes such references to a vague source of a sort much more common in romance than in devotional literature. See Introduction for comment on similarities with romance including formulas of the sort noted below at lines 147 and 163, as well as more substantive narrative techniques.

147   *alle and some*. A line-filling formula more common in romance than in devotional literature.

154   *His*. The word is mysterious, but seems intended since it rhymes with "Paradys" (line 155). A word seems to be missing or implied, such as *His [own]*.

156   *Jhesu ous thider bring.* This is the first of a number of pious ejaculations that the narrator sprinkles though the poem.

163   *lasse and more.* A line-filling formula, like "alle and some" (line 147), more common in romance. See also "withouten les" (line 175) and "forsothe to say" (line 191).

166   *Now herknes.* This address directly to the reader is another feature rather characteristic of romance.

169   *Stevenes.* King Stephen (r. 1135–54). It is unusual to think of him as a wise king. His contemporary, Henry of Huntingdon (c. 1080–1160), characterized Stephen's reign as a period of civil and political disorder largely the result of Stephen's weakness and indecisiveness. See Henry, archdeacon of Huntingdon, *Historia Anglorum: The History of the English People*, ed. and trans. Diana Greenway (Oxford: Clarendon Press, 1996), pp. 698–777. Huntingdon's view has never been seriously challenged.

189   *the bischop of Yrlond.* The bishop is, of course, not St. Patrick, since the story has moved to the twelfth century. The prior of the abbey becomes Owain's main interlocuter.

192   *Penaunce to take.* Sir Owain asks to receive the sacrament of Penance, which would forgive his sins but still leave purgatorial satisfaction to be accomplished. The reception of Penance and the Eucharist, as well as a fifteen-day period of prayer and fasting, were required of all fictional visitors to St. Patrick's Purgatory and all pilgrims to the geographical site.

200   *blamed.* "Rebuked" or "convicted," but not in a legal sense. Rather it is a recognition of Owain's self-admitted sinfulness, a holding accountable.

211   *Nay, Owain, frende.* The bishop acts according to the tradition in trying to dissuade Owain.

226   *priour with processioun.* At this point the prior becomes the master of ceremonies and leads the determined Owain to the entry hole. It was traditionally the prior's duty, as well as the bishop's, to try to dissuade penitents from this extreme and dangerous journey, but the prior does not do so in this version.

247   *Thritten men.* The *Tractatus* has fifteen men.

253	*the priour and his covent. Priour* and *covent* are more characteristically Dominican terms, though Augustinians and Cistercians used them with regard to dependencies as opposed to primary establishments.

253   *the priour and his covent. Priour* and *covent* are more characteristically Dominican terms, though Augustinians and Cistercians used them with regard to dependencies as opposed to primary establishments.

271   *newe schorn.* Their heads were freshly shaved with the tonsure of religious orders.

276   *resoun right.* "Right reason" is reason informed by the will's selection of higher rather than lower goals. (St. Thomas Aquinas, *ST* 1.qu.94)

293   *thou gos to Helle.* Owain's experience is purgatorial, but he is warned that he is in danger of falling into Hell.

329   *tine.* This seems to be derived from the verb *tinen,* "to perish spiritually" (*MED*); thus it means sin's damnation or damnation by sin.

340   *fine amour. Amour* is "love between the sexes" (*MED*), and *fine amour* is usually reserved for "courtly love," characteristic of romance, especially French romance; but in a moral sense *fine* can also mean "pure, true, genuine, perfect, faithful, unwavering" (*MED fin* adj.6).

345   *pride and lecherie.* Pride and lust are two of the seven deadly sins, the root sins that are the source of all others. Although Dante constructed his *Purgatory* around the seven deadly sins, no such systematic presentation appears in this poem. Other deadly sins — greed, sloth, and gluttony — are mentioned but they are not schematically arranged. Anger and envy seem to be missing except implicitly.

385–90   The situation of the suffering souls here is reminiscent of Dante, though it is not shaped into a systematic allegory. Dantean condign punishments are especially notable also at stanzas 69, 70, 71, and 77.

398   *slewthe.* Sloth is one of the deadly, or source, sins. The Middle English variant used at line 400, "slowe," aptly emphasizes the basic failing involved in the sin — a slowness to act, particularly with regard to spiritual obligations.

403–05   *This was the first pain . . . greved him swithe sore.* The verb *dede* (line 404) refers to his seeing this "first pain" of Purgatory rather than experiencing it. Owain has already been cast upon the fire in the hall. Here he begins his observation of the torments.

420   *In herd.* "In public." The point is that there is no way to hide from the torments.

479   *theves and theves fere.* Although the connection is not explicitly made, thieves and their companions are guilty of the deadly sin of greed or covetousness. "Covaitise" is mentioned specifically at line 512.

484   *bacbiters.* Although backbiting is not, by itself, a deadly sin, it flows from the deadly sins of anger and envy. Thus, the effects of all the deadly sins seem to be acknowledged even if the poem is not arranged around them.

493–516   The wheel of punishment, rather than of fortune, seems Dantean in its imaginativeness, but the relation between punishment and sin is not as clear as in Dante.

515   *plough.* "A unit of land measure" (*MED*), thus the greed is for gold, silver, and land.

604–07   In medieval art, usurers and misers are frequently represented as wearing a pouch (of coins) around their necks. E (p. 174) has many examples. Also, in Dante's *Inferno*, XVII, 52–57, usurers gaze down into the pouches around their neck. This section of *Sir Owain* (stanzas 99–103) is rather Dantean in the way punishment fits the crime.

611   *misours.* E (p. 298) suggests that *misours* is an early form of *misers* not found in the *MED* and first found in the *OED* c. 1560. The generality of *wightes* later in the line suggests that perhaps *misours* here is also general, a combination of *mis* ("sin, sinfulness . . ." *MED*) with *-our* as an agentive suffix, thus yielding "sinners" or "evildoers."

618   *cours.* "A sequence of periods, stages, or events" (*MED*), thus some indeterminate measurement of time periods.

631   *seven maner colours.* The significance of the seven colors is not clear. E (p. 175) suggests a relation to the seven seals of Hell mentioned in the thirteenth-century early Middle English "Vision of St. Paul," but the circumstances here are quite different. Only four colors are mentioned. The number seven may be a numerological convention, but the fires likely are from the "Vision of St. Paul," 23:1–2.

671   *sinne of prede.* Pride was the chief of the seven deadly sins. Just as the presentation of the deadly sins here is not systematic, pride is not given an especially prominent place as it was in Dante, Langland, Spenser, and many others. See Morton Bloomfield, *The Seven Deadly Sins: An Introduction to the History of a Religious*

Explanatory Notes

Concept, with Special Reference to Medieval English Literature (East Lansing, MI: Michigan State College Press, 1952).

682–84   *Sum sexti eighen bere . . . sum hadde sexti hond.* Owain had been dealing with "fiends," largely undescribed physically. Here, just before coming to the bridge, the fiends become loathsome beasts, some with sixty eyes and some with sixty hands. The number sixty may have simply implied many. See S. J. Tucker, "Sixty as an Indefinite Number in Middle English," *Review of English Studies* 25 (1949), 152–53.

697–756   The narrow bridge to Paradise crosses over true Hell and is the last danger to be faced. This bridge appeared in the fourth-century *Apocalypse of St. Paul* and became a staple of the medieval literature of Purgatory. It is prominent in the Middle English version of Paul's Apocalypse, "The Vision of St. Paul," and perhaps surfaced in altered form in secular literature in Chrétien's *Lancelot. Sir Owain* borrows or shares many features of the Middle English "Vision," including the seven-colored fire and many of the specific punishments. Both Middle English poems, however, are in fact borrowing from the fourth-century *Apocalypse*, a vision of Hell whose influence is ubiquitous in the medieval literature of Purgatory.

706–08   *Thou no schalt . . . To our felawes mo.* There is a verb missing in this sentence, perhaps "cross" or "pass over." The sense is: "you will not cross, for all middle-earth, without falling down towards our fellows." E (p. 178) comes to much the same conclusion.

733   *dominical.* The term is conjectured from an obscure abbreviation in A (see textual note). The *MED* cites the word in *The Eleven Pains of Hell* (also called *The Vision of St. Paul*), from Laud Miscellany 108 (Bodleian), with the sense "noun: ? a book containing the liturgy for Sunday." That the *Owain*-poet cites "Sein Poule" ("St. Paul" — line 735) as his authority helps to substantiate this meaning. Regardless, the dominical here is a source of information about the true Hell that Owain must pass over by means of the bridge that St. Paul mentions.

775 ff.   Having escaped the fiends and passed over the treacherous bridge, Owain finds himself at the entry to Paradise. It is, however, not true Heaven, "the celestial Paradise," but the earthly or "terrestrial" Paradise. In the early Church and through the Middle Ages, the Earthly Paradise was, in the first instance, the Garden of Eden, from which Adam and Eve were expelled after the Fall. It was a place of abundant beauty and gratification befitting the prelapsarian state of Adam and Eve. Many

people searched for it, unsuccessfully, and learned opinion was that, for one reason or another, it was inaccessible. The terrestrial Paradise took on an additional meaning in controversy and poetry about the places of the afterlife. By some it was considered the temporary abode of the saved until the Last Judgment. By others it was taken to be a stage in the movement to the celestial Paradise after purgation had been completed. Dante's presentation, *Purgatory* 27–32, was the most elaborate and theologically complex, but many treatments of Purgatory describe, often with beautiful details of gems, flowers, and birdsong, this place of joy that immediately preceded true, celestial Paradise.

781–822   The catalogue of gems on the door is a familiar poetic figuration of the beauty and value of the terrestrial Paradise. Catalogues (of gems, flowers, birds, weapons, etc.) were a stock decorative feature of Middle English verse, especially the romances. The stones mentioned include jaspers, sapphires, chalcedony, and topaz, all foundation stones of the New Jerusalem (Apocalypse 21:19–20).

784   *salidoines.* "A fabulous stone of two kinds, said to be found in the stomach of a swallow" (*MED*). The term, usually "celadon," is listed under *celidoine* with many spelling variations.

785   *causteloines.* "Some kind of precious stone; ? chalcedony" (*MED*). The term is listed under *calcedoine*. According to the *OED*, it is "transparent or translucent."

786   *for the nones.* The phrase functions as an intensifier.

787   *tabernacles.* "A canopied niche or recess in a wall, pillar, etc., designed to contain an image" (*MED*). Other definitions associate the term with the portable Hebrew sanctuary, the dwelling place of God, the repository for the Eucharist, and reliquaries. Thus, in context it is architectural and in resonance it is spiritual.

790   *charbukelston.* The *OED* records that carbuncles were said to give off light or glow in the dark.

793–94   *our Saveour . . . paintour.* God, as the Creator of the world, was frequently described as the greatest of all artists or makers.

813   *mani processioun.* Although I have not followed E in inserting *in*, clearly one single procession is intended.

817–28   These stanzas provide a dignified catalogue of the higher orders of the clergy and laity. Although the list is a bit haphazard, it incorporates the aristocracy, the ecclesiastical hierarchy, monks, friars, and nuns.

820   *abbotes, and priours.* Although the titles were sometimes used loosely, an abbot was the chief religious and administrative officer of a monastery. A prior was the chief officer of a conventual establishment of friars, especially Dominicans, but sometimes applied to the head of a dependent monastic establishment.

821   *chanouns.* Canons regular were priests who lived communally, ordinarily at a collegiate church, according to some religious rule. Their role was often to devote their lives to saying masses for the dead.

       Frere Prechours. Dominicans. They were especially distinguished for their preaching, notably about Purgatory, and their learning, counting among their number Albertus Magnus and Thomas Aquinas.

823   *Frere Menours.* Franciscans, technically the Order of Friars Minor (O.F.M.), counting among their number St. Bonaventure, Roger Bacon, Duns Scotus, and William of Ockham.

       Jacobins. Dominicans, so called because of their first establishment in Northern France (1218) on the Rue St. Jacques in Paris. Thus, the Dominicans are mentioned twice in this catalogue, either by accident or design.

824   *Frere Carmes* (Carmelites) and *Frere Austines* (Augustinians) comprise, with the Dominicans and Franciscans, the four great mendicant orders.

825   *nonnes white and blake.* The habits of nuns, white or black, could apply to many, almost all, of the religious orders of women.

828   *order.* To take "orders," whether as a monk, a friar, or a nun, meant to live according to some religious rule, such as that of St. Augustine or St. Benedict, though orders could simply refer to the hierarchical stations in life.

829   *order of wedlake.* It is noteworthy that the poet should list wedlock as an order, suggesting that it is an honored way of life guided by spiritual principles.

851   *fithel.* "Fiddle," the most popular stringed instrument of the Middle Ages. It had three

to five strings, was rectangular with rounded sides, and was about the size of a modern viola (*Dictionary of the Middle Ages*).

sautry. "Psaltery," a stringed instrument, essentially a resonator with ten or more strings supported by bridges at each end (*Dictionary of the Middle Ages*). The *OED* notes that it resembled a dulcimer and was plucked with the fingers or a plectrum.

868   *breke her notes.* Henry Holland Carter defines the phrase as "To begin to sing," that is, to break out in song. See *A Dictionary of Middle English Musical Terms*, p. 52.

869–70   Carter, *Musical Terms*, provides the following definitions for vocal music. *Burdoun* (line 869) refers to "the recurring refrain, in a low, usually bass, tone, which is sung or sounded with a melody of a higher pitch" (p. 57), *mene* (line 869) signifies "the middle part, whether instrumental or vocal" (p. 278), while *hautain* (line 870) means "high in range or volume" (p. 200).

874–76   As E notes, this clearly sets the scene as "the Earthly and not the Celestial Paradise" (p. 185). The reference to *that tre of liif* (line 874) as the means by which Adam and Eve went to Hell is unusual. The original sin was the eating of the fruit of the tree of the knowledge of good and evil (Genesis 2:17). Adam and Eve were expelled from the Garden of Eden so that they would not eat of the tree of life and become immortal (Genesis 3:22–24).

877–82   A decorative catalogue of flowers. Flowers, like birds and gems, were particularly characteristic of the Earthly Paradise.

883–88   The description of perpetual summer echoes the characterizations of medieval "otherworlds" generally associated with fairies. The pleasantness here, however, is of an orthodox spiritual character suitable to the Earthly Paradise.

895   *Pison.* Although the first letter of this line in A may be *d*, the intention must be *p*, thus *Pison.* The first of the four rivers of Eden was Phison (Genesis 2:11).

898   *Gihon.* A: *fison* must be *Gihon*, or something quite like it. St. Jerome's Vulgate says "Geon" (Genesis 2:13), and the two other rivers (Genesis 2:14) are the "Tigris" (line 904) and "Eufrates" (line 901).

931–42   Although not clearly scriptural, the idea of gradations of bliss in Heaven was the recurrent teaching of the fathers and doctors of the early Church. It was not, however, defined as dogma until the Council of Florence in the early fifteenth century.

973–84   The souls in Purgatory in this poem do not know how long they are going to be there. In *The Gast of Gy*, the Gast knows that he will be released by Easter. Although there was controversy about what the souls in Purgatory knew, the belief that suffrages (masses, prayers, almsgiving) could shorten the length of purgation was consistent and central to the doctrine.

985–1020 The distinction between the "terrestrial" and "celestial" Paradise is made clear in these lines.

1013   *crouthe*. A stringed musical instrument identified by the *MED* as Celtic and Middle Eastern.

1021–32   Although opinion was somewhat divided, it was broadly held that Adam and Eve would have remained in Eden if they had not sinned. Although they would not have been immortal, they would not have suffered the pains of earthly existence. After death, like the Old Testament patriarchs, they presumably went to that "Hell" (*limbus Patrum*), while waiting for the Resurrection of Christ.

1045–50   Adam and all his descendants had to await Redemption by Christ in "Hell." Thus, there are at least two places called Hell. The idea of Christ's "descent into Hell," is based on tenuous interpretations of Matthew 27:52–53, Luke 23:43, 1 Peter 3:18–12, and Ephesians 4:9. The notion appears in the Apostles' Creed by the fifth century. The "harrowing of Hell," Christ's descent to "Hell" to release the virtuous who had died before the Redemption, was popular in the Middle Ages, supported by the apocryphal *Book of Nicodemus* and perpetuated by Aelfric's *Homilies*, Bede's *Ecclesiastical History*, and the mystery plays. The story is well summarized in *Cursor Mundi*.

1048   *Passioun*. The Passion of Christ is His suffering and death described in Matthew 26–27, Mark 14–15, Luke 22–23, and John 18–19.

1057–70   The missing lines probably stated that all of the descendants of Adam required Redemption and were in some intermediate place or state until that time. They probably also indicated that individual sin after baptism required penance and satisfaction.

1087–92   The bishop's speeches recall both the manna that sustained the Israelites during their flight from captivity (Exodus 16:13–20) and reception of the sacrament of the Eucharist.

1105–1110 See explanatory note to 1087–92.

1148   *The priour. To* must be assumed at the beginning of this line since *the priour* must be in the dative case for the line to make sense.

1168   *on the fiften day.* Owain performs the traditional fifteen days of prayer and fasting following his return from Purgatory.

1170   *Scrippe and burdoun.* "A pilgrim's wallet" and "a pilgrim's staff" (*MED*). The appurtenances of medieval pilgrims included a cape over a loose frock and a broad-brimmed hat. Over their breasts they wore a pouch (*scrippe*) to hold food, money, relics, and whatever. They carried a staff (*burdoun*) made of two sticks tightly wrapped together. The traditional dress is well-described in the romance *The Squyr of Low Degre.*

Textual Notes to Sir Owain

The basis of my text is National Library of Scotland MS Advocates' 19.2.1, the Auchinleck Manuscript (**A**), which is the only non-fragmentary source extant of the quatrain version. Easting's edition (**E**), entitled *St. Patrick's Purgatory*, includes, in addition, two couplet versions, the English prose *Vision of William Staunton* and the Latin *Tractatus Sancti Patricii*. Easting provides extensive commentary on these versions as well as relations to versions in other languages. Easting uses the title *Owayne Miles* because that title appears at the head of the couplet version in British Library MS Cotton Caligula A. ii, while the quatrain version in the Auchinleck Manuscript is literally acephalous. I have preferred to entitle the quatrain version *Sir Owain* because it is the spelling that appears twenty-three times in the quatrain version. No other spelling appears more than twice.

I have accepted readings from E only when they seem necessary for the coherence or intelligibility of the narrative. I have compared these changes to Kölbing's edition and subsequent addenda (**K**) and Zupitza's (*Zeitschrift für deutsches Altertum* 10.247–57) corrections (**Z**) to Kölbing. The Auchinleck Manuscript is generally quite clear even in the Scolar Press facsimile. The manuscript does have many places where the scribe has corrected an error by writing over it, but these are easy to decipher and I have accepted them, usually without comment. I have also expanded abbreviations without comment. In the notes as in the text, I have replaced Middle English graphemes with modern orthography unless the original grapheme is relevant to the explanation. Further manuscript and bibliographical details precede the text of the poem.

Missing lines:	Approximately 32 lines are missing at the beginning of the poem. Apparently a miniature on the folio preceding where *Sir Owain* begins was excised. (See E, p. xxi.) Easting provides the roughly corresponding lines from the Anglo-Norman version in his notes.
5	*untrewthe*. So K, E. A: *untrewe*. A's reading is not attested in the *MED* and K, E preserve the rhyme with line 4.
16	*sum man*. A: *no man* (though a bit unclear). E's emendation makes sense of the sentence.
22	*thai*. Inserted above the line in A.

28   *afliccioun*. A: *afliccoun*; E: *afflicioun*. A's reading is not attested in the *MED*, which offers no examples of *afliccoun* as a variant. *Afliccioun* provides a closer rhyme to *orisoun* (line 29), though the *affliccoun/orysoun* rhyme recurs in A, line 223. But both "affliccoun" and "orysoun" in this later stanza rhyme with "processioun"; thus my emendation to *afliccioun* here and in line 223. N.b., Robert Mannyng's *Handlynge Synne*, where "afflycccyouns" (line 310) is rymed with "orysouns" (line 309); the rhyme there sounds right through metathesis.

36   *Yrlond*. So K, E. A: *Yrluod*. A is clearly in error.

83   *schuld be forgive*. Z, E insert *be*, which makes the line appropriately passive.

87   *stedfast of bileve*. Z, E insert *of*, an important clarification.

112   *Wharthurth*. So A. K reads *thurch* throughout, but A's *thurth*, though a less common spelling, is clearly correct.

119   *Peter*. So E. A: *patrike*. I have accepted E's emendation. See explanatory note.

152   *seye*. A: *seiȝe*. I have followed the rhyme with "heye" (line 151), though elsewhere I have transcribed "seighe" (line 773).

172   *Northumberland*. A: *Norþhumberland*. There is no need to double the *h*.

174   *As*. So K, E. A: *At*. The change to *As* makes the line intelligible.

175   *Oweyn*. A: *Uweyn*; E: *Oweyne*. Although there is variation in the spelling of the hero's name, I have accepted E's emendation because elsewhere the name always begins with *O*.

223   *afliccioun*. A: *afliccoun*. See textual note to line 28.

267   *thare*. So A. As E notes, *there* would improve the rhyme with line 270, but the difference does not seem great enough to intrude on A.

292   *do as Y*. A: *do y*. K, E insertion of *as* repairs the grammar.

296   *do thee*. A: *doþe doþe*, with the second excised.

416   *gloweand*. Corrected from *groweand* in A.

419   *dragouns*. A: *dragrouns*. K, E's correction of an obvious slip.

425   The scribe of A, normally very consistent, marks the stanza break after this line, though clearly it should come after the next line.

427   *strong*. *r* is inserted above the line in A.

433   *thare*. So A, E. K: *there*. I agree with E's retention of A; it is consistent with line 267, where, in fact, K does not make the change.

440   *lichoure*. The *ho* in *lichoure* is partially obscured, but I agree with K, E reading of *ho*.

455   *the*. Inserted above the line in A.

499   *and*. Inserted above the line in A.

520   *thou schalt*. A: *he schal*. K, E: *thou shalt*. The change to the second person is necessary for the sense of the passage.

524   *forth*. The *þ* is added above the line in A.

552   *sethen.* A: *seþþen.* There is no need to double the *th* in transcription. So, too, in line 1180.

641   *schake.* The *ch* is added above the line in A.

642   *the.* Inserted above the line in A.

643   *foules.* The *s* is added above the line in A.

683   *were.* A: *we.* I have accepted K, E's correction on the basis of rhyme.

703   *with.* Corrected from *wis* in A.

708   *felawes.* A: *fewes.* I have accepted K, E's correction.

733   *dominical.* So K, E. A: *dmcl.* Although the stroke over the *m* is similar to the abbreviation mark for *m, n,* or *e,* there is no way to make sense of the word orthographically. See explanatory note.

743   E reads A as *cou* and changes to *thou* (*þou*), but I agree with K that the scribe of A has already made this correction.

746   *fendes.* Although the first *e* of *fendes* is obliterated, there is no doubt about the whole word.

762   *better.* A: *beiter.* The A form is not cited in *MED* as a variant of *better.*

794   *goldsmithe.* A: *goldsmitþe.* The scribe of this part of A frequently combines *t* and *þ* where either *th* or *þ* would do, as he does in the A version of *Amis and Amiloun.* (See Bliss, p. 658.)

803   *ywis.* The *y* is inserted above the line in A.

813   *processioun.* So A. E inserts *in* before *processioun,* but I agree with K that it is not necessary.

817   *dignité.* A: *dingnite.* Clearly a scribal slip.

830   *mo.* An *r* is canceled before *mo* in A.

853   *may.* Corrected from *man* in A.

884   *groweth here.* E notes correctly that the second half of this line is partially obscured, though legible, because of a piece of paper placed in A to repair the damage caused by the excision of a miniature on fol. 31v.

891   *is.* Inserted above the line in A.

895   *Pison.* A: *dison.* E is clearly correct about the name of the river, though A clearly reads *dison.*

898   *Gihon.* A: *fison.* Again E is correct about the name of the river. See explanatory note.

912   *be.* K, E have properly inserted the *be,* which is missing in A.

927   *were.* A: *weren.* I have accepted E's emendation, which is grammatically possible and repairs the rhyme with line 930.

930   *While.* A: *Whise.* K, E's emendation makes sense, and some alteration is clearly necessary.

938   *Paradis.* A: *parabis*; K, E *paradis* is obviously necessary; K does not indicate that this is a change from A.

956	K, E read A: *Bothe auen and a morwe*. K leaves *auen* as a variant of *of even*. E changes to: *Bothe an euen and a morwe*.
970	*sede*. Second *e* inserted above the line in A.
988	*celestien*. Corrected from *celestian* in A.
993	*may*. Corrected from *mar* in A.
1016	*Is*. Corrected from *þis* in A.
1018	*other*. Corrected from *oner* in A.
1044	*midnerd*. So A. K incorrectly reads *miduerd*. The word in A is a derivative of Old English *middangeard* (*MED*). It seems to refer to the extra-paradisal world.
1058–70	These lines are lost in A. E: "The excision of the miniature at the head of 'The deputisoun bituen the bodi and the soule' has caused the loss of most of thirteen lines." The miniature was on fol. 31v. The initial *th* (*Þ*) of line 1058 is legible, as are the upper parts of *have don s* in this line. The K, E reading of the whole line is from Laing and Turnbull's early transcription (1837). The initial letters are legible in succeeding lines: 1059 *s*, 1060 *o*, and 1070 *b*. Laing and Turnbull were apparently able also to see initial letters at lines 1061: *h*; 1062: *a*; and 1069: *Þ*.
1180	*sethen*. A: *seþþen*. See textual note to line 552.

The Vision of Tundale

Introduction

Few critics have commented on *The Vision of Tundale*, and even fewer have found any merit. From its earliest versions, in prose or verse, in whatever language, commentators have disparaged the narrative as structurally chaotic, dramatically pointless, and doctrinally slender. To the Middle English poetic version in particular one might add linguistically repetitive and rhythmically pedestrian. Why, then, was the narrative so well received for over three hundred years? Why was it, with *Sir Owain*, one of the two most popular religious narratives of the Middle Ages? Why was it so highly regarded until Dante seized the laurels? It may be that recent readers have not found in the narrative what they expected. *The Vision of Tundale* is very much its own self. That it has seemed formless or wandering or insubstantial may simply reflect that the narrative is not what its critics, learned in the traditions of religious narrative, thought *The Vision of Tundale* ought to be.

The Latin original was written by Marcus, an Irish Benedictine monk from Cashel, recently arrived from Ireland at the influential Cistercian establishment of St. James in Regensburg. According to its dedication, it was a story brought from Ireland, written down at the behest of a certain Abbess G. Within the tract's own introduction it is dated by the author as 1149, a date open to quibbles, but certainly close and having the advantage of Marcus' authority. In a German translation later in the century by a Bavarian priest, Alber, the Abbess G. is more specifically identified as Gisela, and indeed there was an Abbess Gisela of the Benedictine convent of nuns in Regensburg at about the right time. Alber, who says that he made his translation into German in order to make this admirable work more accessible was the first of a long line of translators and adaptors, who included the Cisterian Helinand of Froidmont (d. 1235) in his *Chronicon*. Helinand shortened Marcus' version, removing many of the specifically Celtic references made by the very Irish Marcus, though so integral were St. Patrick and other Irish religious and legendary figures that they survived in Helinand and subsequent versions. Helinand's version seems to have been the source for St. Vincent of Beauvais' Tundale in his *Speculum historiale*, written some time between 1244 and 1254. Both Helinand and St. Vincent relate the story under the year 1149. Although many versions followed (there are over 150 Latin manuscripts and the story was at the last reckoning adapted into thirteen vernaculars), the St. Vincent version seems to have been the primary source of the English poetic version found in five fifteenth-century manuscripts.

In all renderings of the narrative the structure and the dogma are consistent with Marcus' original, and these are the fundamental matters which seem to trouble recent readers most. The structure is, indeed, problematic. It is, metaphorically, as if *The Vision of Drythelm*, Bede's influential story of a vision in his *Ecclesiastical History* (731), recorded under the year 696, were exploded and Marcus put it back together again, without the instructions, and with many extra pieces acquired notably from works such as the *Apocalypse of St. Paul*, a late fourth-century apocryphon accessible throughout the Middle Ages in a series of Latin redactions, for scenes of torment; from *The Vision of Wetti* (824) for particularly sexual punishments; and from many other visions, popular in narrative and in sermons from the time of St. Gregory's *Dialogues* (593–94), all enlivened by Celtic elements apparently introduced by Marcus himself. Each of the elements taken from existing versions would fit within the Cistercian traditions of meditation, sermons, and reading as part of their spirituality, but the combination of them in this poem seems bizarre.

The Vision of Drythelm is an orderly account of a good man, who dies but revives the next morning and provides his distraught wife with an account of what occurred while he was "dead." A shining angel first shows Drythelm the horrors of purgatorial punishments of fire and ice, but warns him that this is not the worst. In a darker place, Drythelm sees the more severe infernal punishments at the mouth of Hell, with damned spirits who bob up and down in globes of fire, though the depths of Hell lie still further beyond. The fiends try to seize Drythelm, but the angel returns, gradually taking form from a shining star, and guides Drythelm to a place of joy and light, in which Drythelm longs to stay. The angel, however, informs him that the souls in this happy place are not yet fully saved, but awaiting entry to Heaven itself, of which Drythelm gets a glimpse but is not allowed to enter. Some of this sounds very much like Tundale's experiences, but *The Vision of Drythelm* is concise and compact. Its tight narrative includes the four states of the afterlife according to St. Augustine: the state of purgation for the *mali non valde* (sinful souls who undergo a severe purgative experience), the *mali* (the damned), the *non valde boni* (sinners in a place of beauty, who have either completed purgation or were guilty of lesser faults, but are not quite ready for entry to Heaven), and the *boni* (the saved). The vision contains details present in *Tundale*, but the narrative is clear and straightforward. *The Vision of Tundale* is an eclectic representation that preserves the four groups, but changes emphases, adds a wealth of detail, and ambles through the afterlife in a more circuitous, divagating fashion. It is not that *The Vision of Tundale* is amorphous; in fact, in some ways it is the most precise and detailed fictional account of the Christian afterlife before Dante, and may even have been read by him. Rather it is that *The Vision of Tundale* moves through the afterlife according to its own logic.

The Middle English version replaces Marcus' references to the Irish Church and his location of the story in Cork with a formulaic call for attention that could be part of any number of contemporary narratives. In both versions Tundale is identified as a serious sinner; unlike the good Drythelm and most other visionaries, he is guilty of the eight deadly sins: pride, covetousness, lust, anger, gluttony, envy, sloth, and the particularly Irish addition to the traditional seven, treachery. It is amidst callous behavior towards a debtor that the story begins. Tundale, generously invited to stay to dinner by his aggrieved debtor, is stricken with a violent fit that results rapidly in his apparent death. It is hard to see how one could ignore the drama of this beginning; unexpected and vivid, it is a powerful demonstration of the scriptural admonition: "Watch ye therefore, because

Introduction

you know not the day nor the hour. . ." (Matthew 25:13). His soul, parted from his apparently dead body, finds itself in a dark and grim place that causes an immediate regret that will deserve more attention in the discussion below of Tundale's character as visionary.

Tundale's guardian angel emerges from a star and accuses Tundale of ignoring him during life. Tundale readily and fearfully admits his guilt and the journey begins. In the Advocates' Manuscript version, printed here, Tundale's experiences are divided into ten Passus (literally "paces," but a common division of parts in medieval narrative); seven Gaudia, "joys"; and a *Reversio Anime*, a section in which Tundale's soul returns to his body, he reports his experiences, and promises to reform. Although the other Middle English manuscripts do not have these divisions, they accurately segment Tundale's experience, although sometimes, especially in the Gaudia, the distinctions between parts are not precise.

The Passus, however, are a rather neatly arranged catalogue of sins:

I: In this prologue Tundale is threatened and abused by fiends and comforted by the angel.

II: The murderers are melted and re-formed in the fires of a stinking pit. As the poem proceeds, *The Vision of Tundale* is distinctive in the way it associates specific places with specific sins.

III: The thieves and deceivers are swept back and forth between fire and ice.

IV: The proud are in a pit of fire and brimstone over which is suspended a narrow bridge that can be traversed only by someone as humble as the pilgrim priest who makes his way across. So far, the angel has been explicit about the sin, but the punishments have not been noticeably suitable to one sin rather than another. Here the punishment fits the crime.

V: The covetous must enter the gaping maw of Acheron to be tormented with fire and ice. There is some appropriateness in the greedy mouth of Acheron, but this section is more striking in that it is the first place where Tundale must actually undergo punishment rather than simply be a terrified observer. Perhaps appropriately to the sin, he is bitten by lions, adders, and snakes within the belly of Acheron.

VI: Robbers, and more particularly the sacrilegious, who have defiled holy ground are in a fiery lake full of beasts. The punishment is not especially appropriate, but the angel makes clear that there are gradations of suffering, a point not always noted in visions. Across the lake is a bridge — long, narrow, and sharp — which Tundale, again suffering in his own person, must cross. That he must lead a wild cow across the bridge is a part of his particular transgression: he had stolen his neighbor's cow and, though he had returned it, his intention had been sinful. It is hard to avoid the comedy in this scene, perhaps a remnant of Irish legend, even within the gruesome circumstances.

VII: Those guilty of sexual sins are tormented within an oven-like house. The souls, again not without some grim comedy, are hacked into bits by fiends, with devices ranging from weapons to farm implements, and then re-formed and hacked up again. Once more Tundale must suffer the punishment, but, as after each such torment, he is restored by his guardian angel. Here we see specific attention to genitals, appropriate to the sin; among the sinners are men of religion and, for the first time in the poem, Tundale recognizes some of the sufferers.

VIII: Lustful clergy and religious who have broken their vows are swallowed by a great bird and infested with vermin that creep in and out of their bodies. The torment seems to fit the carnality and again Tundale must suffer.

IX: In this Passus, what has earned the sinners their places in Vulcan's forges does not appear to be any particular type of sin, but rather the sheer number of sins they have committed. In the smithy of Vulcan they are tossed back and forth between infernal blacksmiths, who beat them with hammers on fiery forges. Again Tundale must suffer, because he has been a perpetrator of many and various sins.

X: The last Passus is devoted to Hell itself and Satan. Although it has been suggested in IX that the tormented so far are in a purgatorial rather than infernal state, it becomes clear that in II through IX the sinners have not yet been judged and have no idea whether or when they might finish purgation; both Heaven and Hell are still possibilities, and they have no knowledge of the duration of their fate. In Passus X we have those who have already been judged and are certainly and eternally lost. The Passus culminates in a long description of the prideful archfiend and corrupter of mankind — Lucifer, who inflicts horrendous pains and is simultaneously tortured by the pains he inflicts, even as he is bound fast until the Last Judgment so that he will not cast the world into chaos. Pain here is horrendous and eternal, and, for the second time in the poem, Tundale ruefully recognizes some individuals he knows. But the Passus is dominated by the huge, black, and horrible vision of Satan, the author of all evil.

This schematic summary has been provided to show in detail something of the structure of the ten Passus as a whole as well as some of the features that are distinctive in Marcus', and thereby his successors', vision of the afterlife. Specific locations are designated for specific sins, an element so unusual that some have thought it influential on Dante. Tundale, despite the fact that he is there only in spirit not in body, must himself suffer for five of them; Marcus ignores the problem of an incorporeal soul suffering physical punishments in favor of directly involving Tundale in the horrors he observes. The presentation of the suffering sinners has not been climactic throughout the truly purgatorial parts in which sinners suffer but have not yet been finally judged. Perhaps the lack of dramatic climax has caused some disappointment with the poem, though, taken as a whole, the punishments are at least comprehensive. There is, however, beginning in Passus IX and mounting through the whole of Passus X, a climactic movement in the ultimate horrors of true Hell and the elaborate portrait of Satan. Finally, Marcus recognizes some souls, both among those not yet judged in Passus VII and among the damned — a small gesture in the direction Dante took more extensively and dramatically.

The poem could be over, but Marcus proceeds to show us better worlds in the seven Gaudia. This continuation is not unique to *The Vision of Tundale*; indeed it is almost a traditional part of visions of the afterlife such as Drythelm. It is rather the way that Marcus moves from the ten Passus to the Gaudia, especially the first two Gaudia, that is distinctive and has caused most consternation about the structure of the narrative. After the climactic movement of the ten Passus towards Satan and true Hell, Marcus backtracks in the first two Gaudia to a more tolerable Purgatory.

In Gaudium I are souls who, although in a much more pleasant place than anywhere in the ten Passus, suffer hunger and thirst. More strikingly, these souls know that they will eventually be saved, but they are not yet wholly without pain. Marcus is embarking on an Augustinian view of the afterlife, which, because of its placement after Lucifer and Hell, is structurally odd. These souls, as in the Augustinian tradition, are specifically called *mali non valde*, though the precision of Marcus' Latin is somewhat obscured in the language of the Middle English version:

> All leved they well in honesté,   *lived*
> Yet grevyd they God in sum parté. (lines 1519–20)

Gaudium II presents the Augustinian *non valde boni*, again rendered less obviously in the Middle English:

> Thawye they ben clansyn of all ylle,   *Though*
> Here mot thei abydon Goddus wylle. (lines 1567–68)

These souls include the Irish kings Cantaber (Conor O'Brien), Donatus (Donough MacCarthy), and the renowned Cormake (Cormac MacCarthy), who is especially well known to Tundale. All of them apparently must still suffer, but the pains of Cormake are particularly striking and vivid.

The remaining Gaudia move through a kind of Earthly Paradise to Heaven. Gaudia III–VI present an increasingly beautiful set of locations, decorated in more and more ornate ways for the virtuous of many sorts, including the chaste married, martyrs, virgins, virtuous clergy, and those who have founded and supported churches and religious orders. The region never specifically becomes the Earthly Paradise or the Garden of Eden, but references, especially to the fall of Adam, make clear that this is what it is. The beauties, in singing choirs, flowers, gems, and splendid pavilions, make it hard to believe that we are not in Heaven itself. It must be granted that Marcus finds it hard to sustain a dramatic progression through stages of this Paradise, straining to find a vocabulary that will sustain a sense of ever greater glory and gratification. However, by assertion if not by dramatic representation, it becomes clear that the joys increase as Tundale proceeds. And all of these souls are aware that at some indeterminate time, unknown to them, they are assured of salvation.

In Gaudium VII, devoted to a view of Heaven, the angel and Tundale climb to the top of the most magnificent wall of all, in a land of magnificent walls, composed of precious gems and mortared with gold. From here they see the whole of creation, not only the earthly and purgatorial, but Heaven itself. Improbably, Tundale sees the nine orders of angels that perpetually praise God and even more improbably, he has a glimpse of the Trinity. It remains only for Tundale, after a cordial greeting by Renodan (St. Ruadan, the patron saint of Lorrha in County Tipperary, perhaps Marcus' place of birth), to meet St. Patrick, the patriarch of the Irish Catholic Church and epitome of active holiness for an Irish narrator, and the four bishops who "reformed," that is, Romanized, the Irish Church in the first half of the twelfth century, and to see the empty seat reserved, apparently, for St. Bernard of Clairvaux, the greatest Cistercian of them all. Nothing is left but for Tundale to return to his body and live his life in conformity with the profound lessons he has learned.

Critical objections have been made, with some justification, to the static quality of Gaudia III–VI, but it is harder, in Latin or Middle English, to find a vocabulary for the increasingly glorious than for the increasingly horrific. It may also be that we have, retroactively, the supreme vision of Dante standing in our way. It has also been objected that the climax with the Irish saints would be very much beside the point to an English audience in the fourteenth or fifteenth century. Here again, there is some justice in the criticism, though the scene is handled with an economy and sense of ultimacy that transcends ethnic unfamiliarity. The most serious criticism, however, is that there is a structural discontinuity between the Passus and the Gaudia: the former move through gruesome descriptions of souls who are purged without even the assurance of salvation and issue in a staggering infernal vision of Lucifer; the latter begin with mildly suffering souls and lead to the Beatific Vision. *Tundale*, it is suggested, seems like two different visions with a radical disruption in between. It is as if the author tried at the beginning of the Gaudia to incorporate the Augustinian categories more explicitly. The result, for the structure of the whole poem, is that the vision begins with the *non valde mali* and proceeds to the *mali*, then reverts to the *boni non valde* and proceeds to the *boni*.

This final criticism must be acknowledged, but for the reader it may not be devastating and may even be a virtue if one does not insist that linear narrative is the only or the best kind. It may not be that the structure is chaotic, but that Marcus, and his inheritors so widely admired by a variety of audiences, has taken advantage of one kind of climax in the Passus and another in the Gaudia and that far from being clumsy or incompatible, they enhance each other in a way that is consistent with a monastic, especially a Cistercian spirituality. The audience is asked to balance two types of meditation, one of horror and one of hope, both representative of ultimate spiritualities. The Passus lead from torment to hopelessness; the Gaudia lead from a milder suffering to bliss. Both are true visions and to balance them against each other, even at the expense of linear narrative, is to represent quite dramatically the contrasts between eternal destinations.

If the structure of the whole has not been received generously, neither has the character of Tundale, who has been seen to have lost the distinctive characteristics of his sinful life and become a bland and undifferentiated traveler to the next world. Here again, I would defend the *Tundale* poet. It would be just as unthinkable to have him remain a miscreant as it would for him to react more variously to the spectacles provided him. In the Passus, he suffers and we have a sympathy for him impossible for other visionaries. Upon "dying" and finding himself alone in a bleak place, he immediately and sympathetically recognizes the error of his ways. He is intriguing because he sometimes seems not the sinner we began with, but a professed religious, being instructed in the afterlife. Those instances may be authorial lapses.[1] If they are a flaw, they are a welcome flaw that adds variety to the sometimes dreary role that a visionary is called upon to play. Regardless, Tundale is a participant-observer and, at a few crucial places, engages in dialogue with his angel or listens attentively to instruction that the angel provides, but those are more appropriate to the consideration of the theology of the narrative below, where it becomes clearer that we care about Tundale, and ought to.

Even if this poem is oddly, even clumsily, structured and Tundale has, for the most part, the blandness of the visionary, though his role is enhanced by the need actually to suffer along the way, it is not accurate to say that it is slender on doctrine. It is not a theological narrative, but it is imbued with doctrine that is fundamental to the idea of Purgatory. *Tundale* does not argue refinements on the doctrine of Purgatory. For example, it mentions but does not inquire into what the souls know, how long they will be purged, when salvation will ultimately come. It does not even seem to worry, in an analytic way, about having two classes of purgatorial souls — those who suffer unjudged and those who know they are saved. Nor does it quail at Tundale's seeing the Trinity when he is not truly dead. These are all taken for granted, mentioned, but rather as a matter of fact than a matter of contention. Most important in this regard, the story does not seem to be interested in the doctrine of suffrages, which became so important in purgatorial literature. Indeed, the only mention of suffrages is as a discouragement by the demons who first greet Tundale.

"All the gud that in tho erthe is,	*good; the earth*
Nor all the matens ne all the masse	*matins; masses*
Myght not help thee from the peyn of hell." (lines 211–13)	*pain*

Their assertion that suffrages will now do him no good must, of course, in context be taken to suggest that suffrages can do good, but this aspect of purgatorial teaching is not what Marcus, or those who transmitted his narrative, were interested in. Suffrages were to become prominent soon after Marcus' work, when the doctrine of Purgatory became more the property of the Dominicans than the Cistercians. For Dominican scholars and preaching friars, suffrages had a special potency, but that focus is different from what seems to have been most important to the Cistercians in their uses of Purgatory as part of their meditative spirituality.

That difference is highlighted by the doctrine that is central to the theology and spirituality of Purgatory in *Tundale*: God's justice and mercy. That doctrine, which pervades the poem and gives it its spiritual vitality and compassion, is raised early, if obliquely, by the fiends who greet and torment Tundale immediately after his death. They emphasize that Tundale deserves to suffer. When they taunt him with what he deserves, they echo the scriptural counsel: "For what doth it

---

[1] See St. John Drelincourt Seymour, "Studies in the *Vision of Tundal*," p. 88. I find it hard to agree with Seymour that they are intentional or forgetful lapses into autobiography by Marcus.

profit a man, if he gain the whole world, and suffer the loss of his own soul?"[2] Tundale's earthly power has abandoned him to what, in reality, he merits. Likewise, when the infernal fiends at the gates of Hell in Passus IX threaten Tundale, they emphasize what Tundale deserves:

> For thi wykkydnes and thi foly
> In fyr to brenne art thu worthy. (lines 1213–14)

Even Tundale's guardian angel, in his first address to the soul, chastises Tundale for his guilt in not having paid attention to his urgings to live a better life and thereby not have to fear a deserved horrible eternity (lines 239–44).

It is important that Tundale is not wholly passive and the angel does more than lead him, identify the sins, and indicate when Tundale's special guilt makes it necessary for him to suffer a particular torment. The most important location in which the angel provides the advice which is fundamental to this vision of Purgatory is in Passus VII. There Tundale, viewing the horrors of punishment, questions God's mercy by alluding to Scripture:

> "Wher his the word that wryton was
> That Goddus mercy schuld passe all thyng?
> Here see Y therof no tokenyng." (lines 812–14)   *sign*

Tundale is echoing Latin Vulgate Psalm 32:5, which the scribe quotes in Latin after line 814. The long response of the angel is a dissertation on the nature and profundity of God's mercy. He begins by asserting:

> "Allthauff God be full of myght and mercy,   *Although*
> Ryghtwessnes behowyth Hym to do therby.   *Justice requires*
> But He forgevyth more wykkydnes,   *forgives*
> Thenne He findeth ryghtwesnes.   *righteousness*
> Tho peynus that thu haddus wer but lyght.
> Grettur thu schuldyst have tholud with ryght." (lines 817–22)   *suffered*

The angel has succinctly stated the necessary interconnection between God's justice and mercy. He continues by asking (lines 826–29), why, without the threat of punishment, would man do God's will? But the main burden of his discourse is that all human beings, even babies, deserve, by justice, punishment by God; it is only the benevolence of God's mercy that makes salvation, or even alleviation, possible. In addition, granted the difference between what we deserve and what God's mercy makes possible, it behooves us to do penance on earth and live according to God's

---

[2] Matthew 16:26; see also Mark 8:36; Luke 9:25.

will. Later the angel expands on this point in answering Tundale's question about why the wicked prosper, while the good on earth are often deprived (lines 1446–52); he explains that discomfort on earth may help human beings to struggle and live more in accord with divine will (lines 1453–60). That suffering on earth is desirable is a corollary of the doctrine of divine justice and mercy, especially in view of the fact that God tempers with mercy the retributive justice that we all deserve. Thus, it is better to suffer on earth than to have to face even a merciful reckoning after death. Penitence on earth is preferable in view of what we all deserve according to a strict interpretation of God's justice. However, even purgatorial punishment in all its horrors is a manifestation of the operation of God's mercy. Purgatory becomes the "doctrine of the second chance," a powerful manifestation of God's prevailing mercy.

Much later than Marcus, Dante inscribed over the gates of Hell:

> Justice moved my high maker.[3]

This is a hard saying, but Dante could have equally as well introduced Purgatory by announcing it as the demonstration of God's mercy. That is the doctrine that underlies all of the pain in *The Vision of Tundale's* Hell and Purgatory, and the incomplete joy of the first two Gaudia, and even the waiting in Gaudia III–VI.

The angel's speech on justice and mercy is central to the whole narrative. Once one sees clearly what we get in contrast with what we deserve, the merciful solace that runs throughout the narrative becomes clearer. If one has not noticed before, one can see how the poem's demonstration of justice is repeatedly moderated by the pervasive recognition of how justice is tempered with mercy. As early as the preface, the narrator makes the fundamental doctrine clear. Tundale is a sinner:

> Yett nold not God is sowle tyne   *would not; his soul harm*
> For He hit boghthe from Hell pyne,   *it bought; Hell's pain*
> For His mersy passud all thynge. (lines 37–39)   *mercy surpassed*

Long before Tundale's complaint in Passus VII, the narrator has assured us of the theological basis of all that we will see. In the act of Redemption, God demonstrated and made effective the doctrine that informs even the most gruesome aspects of the poem. After Tundale dies, the first recognition he has is that he must now rely on God's mercy and his angel soon comforts him:

> But Goddus mercy schall thee save. (line 257)   *God's*

---

[3] Dante Alighieri, *The Divine Comedy*, trans. Charles S. Singleton, Bollingen Series 80, 3 vols. (Princeton: Princeton University Press, 1970–75), 1.3.4.

The angelic reassurance may destroy suspense, though the descriptions of the torments that come tend to preserve our unease, but mercy is a theme that recurs perpetually: in the fact that Tundale is allowed not to suffer in Passus II; in the angel's comfort upon their approach to Lucifer; in the explanation of why Cantaber and Donatus are not damned; and repeatedly in casual assertions throughout the journey. The doctrinal substance of *The Vision of Tundale* lies not in theological disputes about the refinements of the nature of Purgatory, but in its horrifying, though ultimately exalting, recognition of our dependence upon God's mercy in a universe where we would deserve even worse than what we see. In such a context, Tundale's *Reversio Anime* becomes not only a logical consequence of his journey, but an ultimate manifestation of the narrative's central consolation, the mercy of God.

Thus, it may be that the concatenation of horrors issuing in beatitude, presented in the context of the prevailing mercy of God, was the combination of elements responsible for the sustained popularity of the narrative in the Middle Ages. This is not to say that the narrative's twelfth-century audience saw exactly the same horrors and comforts that its fifteenth-century audience did, any more than it is to say that our perspective is the same as either. What in the twelfth century was an appropriate stimulus for Cistercian meditation and edification may be quite different from the sources of the narrative's popularity in the later Middle Ages. The Middle English version seems rather to rely on a more popular taste for the grotesque and horrific, mediated by eventual consolation, rather than on Cistercian spirituality. That four of the five manuscripts of the Middle English version include a large number of romances, including *Sir Gowther, Sir Isumbras, Sir Amadas, Guy of Warwick, Sir Eglamour*, and *Sir Launfal*, may argue that interest in Tundale was consistent with a more general interest in stories of adventure.

Yet the perdurance of Tundale into the fifteenth century seems more than that. Yes, the fascination of the grotesque seems a likely attraction, but the integral affirmation of God's mercy seems likely to have been as comforting to a more popular and secular, though still religious, audience. The version in which they received the story admittedly is not graceful verse, though the story flows more rhythmically if one emphasizes its verse form simply as a four-stress line rather than as strict octosyllabics. Still, the power of the poem seems to reside largely in characteristics intrinsic to the narrative. The fifteenth century may have revelled more in the gory descriptions than Cistercian predecessors did. And the story may have been altered in its effect by the partial skepticism implied by the scribe at the end of the English poem:

> Be it trwe, or be it fals,   *true*
> Hyt is as the coopy was. (lines 2382–83)   *copy*

That is to say, a fifteenth-century audience may have seen fiction where a twelfth-century audience saw history. Nevertheless, even if catering to a different taste for the descriptions and a different sense of the poem's verisimilitude, the demonstration of God's tempering of justice with mercy must have contributed to the later audience's pleasure and solace.

Introduction

No one would mistake *The Vision of Tundale* for the *Divine Comedy*, in which Dante endowed the matter of the afterlife not only with rare linguistic excellence but also with a metaphoric universality that transcends all ages. But there are many layers of quality between the sublimity of Dante and the banality of trivial descriptions. *The Vision of Tundale* is somewhere in between and deserves our attention more than as simply a document in literary history.

Select Bibliography

Manuscripts

National Library of Scotland MS Advocates' 19.3.1, fols. 98r–157v. [c. 1425–1450]

British Library MS Cotton Caligula A. ii, fols. 95v–107v. [c. 1400–1450]

British Library MS Royal 17.B.xliii, fols. 150r–184v. [c. 1400–1450]

Bodleian Library MS Ashmole 1491 (*SC* 7656), five leaves at the end of the book; fragmentary. [c. 1400–1450]

MS Takamiya 32 (*olim* Penrose 10, *olim* Penrose 6, *olim* Delamere), fols. 166v–75v. Presumably in a private collection. Photographic copies are available at the Library of the University of Chicago and at the British Library: Facs. 405 (16). [Fifteenth century]

Editions

Gardiner, Eileen, ed. "The Vision of Tundale: A Critical Edition of the Middle English Text." Ph.D. Dissertation: Fordham University, 1980. *DAI* 40.12A (1980), p. 6266A.

Mearns, Rodney, ed. *Visio Tnugdali: The Vision of Tundale.* Heidelberg: C. Winter, 1985.

Turnbull, William B. D. D., ed. *The Visions of Tundale, together with Metrical Moralizations and Other Fragments of Early Poetry.* Edinburgh: Thomas G. Stevenson, 1843.

Wagner, Albrecht, ed. *Tundale: Das mittelenglische gedicht über die Vision des Tundalus.* Halle: Max Niemeyer, 1893.

Commentary

Gardiner, Eileen. "The Translation into Middle English of the *Vision of Tundale*." *Manuscripta* 24 (1980), 14–19.

————. "A Solution to the Problem of Dating in the *Vision of Tundale*." *Medium Ævum* 51 (1982), 86–91.

Hines, Leo James. "The *Vision of Tundale*: A Study of the Middle English Poem." Ph.D. Dissertation: University of Wisconsin-Madison, 1968. *DAI* 29.6A (1968), p. 1869A.

Marshall, J. C. Douglas. "Three Problems in *The Vision of Tundale*." *Medium Ævum* 44 (1975), 14–22.

Seymour, St. John Drelincourt. *Irish Visions of the Otherworld: A Contribution to the Study of Mediæval Visions.* New York: Macmillan, 1930.

————. "Studies in the *Vision of Tundal*." *Proceedings of the Royal Irish Academy* 37.4, Sec. C (January 1926), 87–106.

The Vision of Tundale

	Jesu Cryst, lord of myghttus most,	*greatest power*
	Fader and Son and Holy Gost,	*Father; Ghost*
	Grant hem alle Thi blessyng	*them*
	That lystenyght me to my endyng.	*listen till my conclusion*
5	Yf ye that her ben awhyle dwell,	*a while abide*
	Seche a sampull Y wyll yow telle,	*example*
	That he that woll hit undurstand,	
	In hart he schall be full dredand	*heart; greatly fearful*
	For hys synnus, yf he woll drede	*sins; fear*
10	And clanse hym her of his mysdede.	*cleanse him here; misdeeds*
	In Yrlond byfyll sumtyme this case	*Ireland; occurred once upon a time*
	Sethyn God dyeyd and from deythe arase.	*After; died; death arose*
	Aftyr that tyme, as ye may here,	
	A thowsand and a hondryt yere	*hundred years*
15	And nyn wyntur and fourty,	*nine winters*
	As it hys wretyn in tho story,	*is written in the*
	I woll yow tell what befell than	*happened then*
	In Yrlond of a rych man;	
	Tundale was is right name.	*his proper*
20	He was a man of wykud fame.	*wicked reputation*
	He was ryche ynow of ryches,	*enough*
	But he was poore of all gudnesse.	
	He was ay full of trychery,	*always; treachery*
	Of pride, of yre, and of envy.	*anger*
25	Lechery was all his play,	
	And gloteny he loved ay.	*gluttony; always*
	He was full of covetyse	*covetousness (avarice)*
	And ever slouthe in Goddus servyse.	*slothful; God's service*
	Nou warkus of mercy wold he worch;	*No works; work (perform)*
30	He lovyd never God, ne Holy Chyrch.	*loved; nor Holy Church*
	With hym was never no charyté;	*charity*
	He was a mon withowton pyté.	*man without pity (compassion)*
	He loved well jogelars and lyers.	*deceivers (entertainers); liars*

	He mayntyniod ay mysdoers.	*abetted always miscreants*
35	He lovyd ay contakt and stryve.	*always dissension; strife*
	Ther was non holdyn wors on lyf.	*considered*
	Yett nold not God is sowle tyne,	*would not; his soul harm*
	For He hit boghthe from Hell pyne,	*it bought (redeemed); Hell's pain*
	For His mersy passud all thynge.	*mercy surpassed*
40	But Tundale had an hard warnyng,	*severe*
	For as he in his transyng lay,	*trance (unconsciousness)*
	His sowle was in a dredeful way.	
	Ther hit saw mony an howge payn,	*many a huge pain*
	Ar hit come to the body agayn.	*Before it came*
45	In Purgatory and in Helle	
	As he saw, he cowthe well telle.	*could*
	But how he had a hard fytt,	*severe fit*
	Yf ye woll here, ye may whytt.	*will hear; understand*
	Tundale had frendys full mony,	*friends very many*
50	But he was full of trichery.	*treachery*
	Of his maners mony had dred,	*behavior many had dread*
	For he was lythur in word and dede.	*evil*
	Throw ocur wold he sylver leyn;	*usury; silver lend*
	For nyne schyllyng he wold have ten.	*nine shillings*
55	For frystyng wold he ocur take,	*delaying would; usury*
	And nothyng leyn for Goddus sake.	*give [to the poor]*
	When he sold his marchandyse,	*merchandise*
	He sold ay derur than ryghtfull prise.	*always dearer; proper price*
	He wold gyve dayes for his best,	*allow days for his own benefit*
60	But he sold the derur for the fryst.	*dearer; delay*
	Tundale, he went upon a day	
	To a mon to ascon his pay	*man; demand*
	For thre horsus that he had sold,	*three horses*
	For the whych the penys wer untold.	*pence (money); unpaid*
65	That mon hym prayd of respite	*requested a delay*
	Unto a day the deyt to quytte	*For a certain time; debt; repay*
	And proferud hym sykurnes by othe.	*offered him security; oath*
	Anon he grucchud and waxyt wrothe	*At once he grumbled and became angry*
	For he had not evon tho pay,	*exactly the payment*
70	But thratte hym fast and made gret deray.	*threatened him vigorously; great uproar*
	But Tundale was bothe quynte and whys;	*clever; wise*
	He sette the horsus to full hye prise	*set the horses at a very high price*

192

For he had no pay in honde.	*Because; payment in hand*
To hym the mon in scripture hym bonde.	*The man gave him his bond in writing*
75 The mon spake to hym curtesly	*man spoke; courteously*
And broghtte hym owt of is malycoly.	*And brought him out of his anger*
He sobort his hart that was so greyt	*calmed; heart; great*
And made Tundale dwell at tho meytt.	*invited; stay to dinner*
And when he was seytt and servyd well,	*seated and served*
80 A greytt evyl he began to fele.	*A great illness he began to feel*
At the fyrst mossel soo syttand	*first morsel while sitting*
He myght not well lefte up his hond.	*could; lift; hand*
He cryed lowde and changyt chere,	*cried loud; changed expression*
As he had felud dethe nere.	*As if; felt death near*
85 To the weyf of the howse than callud he,	*wife; house; called*
"Leve dame," he seyd, "for charyté	*Dear lady; for charity*
Loke me my sparthe wher that he stande,	*Find; battle ax wherever it is*
That Y broghtt with me in my hande,	*I brought*
And helpe me now hethon awey,	*hence away*
90 For Y hope to dye this same day.	*I expect to die*
So harde with evyll am Y tane	*severely; illness; taken*
That strenthe in me fell Y nane.	*strength; feel I none*
For now my hart so febull Y fele,	*heart; feeble; I feel*
Y am but dede, Y wot full wele.	*I am surely dead, I know full well*
95 A Jesu Cryst, Y aske Thee mercy,	
For can I now non odur remedy."	*know I; other*
Ryght as he schuld ryse of that stede,	*Just as he was about to rise from that place*
Anon in the flore he fell don dedde.	*Instantly on; floor; down dead*
Tho that wer his frendys by sybbe	*Those who were; friends; kinship*
100 Herd of that cause that hym bytydde.	*Heard; experience; befell him*
Thei comyn to hym with hart sore	*They came; heart sad*
And saw Tundale lygge dedde in the flore.	*lying dead*
For hym wer the bellus yronge	*bells rung*
And "Placebo" and "Dyrge" sone ysonge.	*sung*
105 All his cloths wer of hym tane.	*clothes; taken*
He lay cold dedde as any stan,	*stone*
But of the lyft syde of Tundale	*left*
Was sumwat warme the veyne corale,	*somewhat; median vein*
Wherfor sum hyld hym not all dedde;	*believed him not fully dead*
110 Forwhy thei flytte hym not fro that sted.	*Therefore; moved; place*
But styll as a dedde mon ther he lay	

	From mydday of that Wenusday	*midday; Wednesday*
	Tyl the Setturday aftur the none;	*Until; Saturday; noon*
	By than wyst Tundale what he had done,	*then knew*
115	Then he lay dedde, as ye han hard,	*have heard*
	But herus now how is sowle fard.	*hear; his soul fared*
	Wen Tundale fell don sodenly,	*When; down suddenly*
	The gost departyd sone from the body.	*spirit parted immediately*
	As sone as the body was dedde,	
120	Tho sowle was sone in a darke sted.	*The soul; dark place*
	Full wrechudly hit stod allone;	*wretchedly; it stood alone*
	Hit weput sore and made gret mone.	*It wept sorely; lamented greatly*
	He wend to a byn dampnyd ay to payne	*thought [himself] to have been damned forever*
	And never a com to tho body agayne	*to come; the*
125	For the synnus that the body dyd,	*sins*
	That myght nether be layned nor hydde.	*neither; concealed; hidden*
	He had lever then al mydylerde	*rather; than all the world*
	Ha ben agayne, so was he ferd	*To have been [alive] again; frightened*
	But he sawe mony a hydwys payne	*saw many a hideous pain*
130	Or he come to the body agayne,	*Before; again*
	But sum had more and sum had lasse,	*some [souls]; less*
	As tho story beyrthe wyttnesse.	*the; bears witness*

I Passus

	As the gost stod in gret dowte,	*spirit stood; great confusion*
	He saw comyng a full loddly rowte	*terrifying rabble*
135	Of fowle fendys ay grennyng,	*foul fiends ever baring their teeth*
	And as wyld wolfus thei cam rampyng.	*wolves; leaping*
	He wold a flown from that syght,	*would have fled*
	But he wyst never whydur he myght.	*knew; whither*
	Thes fowle fendys cam to hym ther.	*These foul fiends came*
140	The sowle for ferd made drury chyr,	*soul; fear; woeful countenance*
	And that was full lytull wondor;	*little wonder*
	He went to a byn ryvon asondur.	*thought [himself] to have been ripped open*
	Thei wer so loghtly on to loke,	*They were; horrible to look at*
	Hym thoghtte the eyrthe undur hym schoke,	*He thought; earth; shook*
145	Her bodys wer bothe black and fowle;	*Their*
	Full gryssly con thei on hym gowle.	*terribly began they; howl*

Her ynee wer brode and brannyng as fyr;   *eyes; wide; burning; fire*

All thei wer full off angur and yre.   *they; anger; ire (wrath)*

Her mowthus wer wyde; thei gapud fast.   *mouths; wide; gaped open*

150 The fyre owt of her mowthus thei cast.   *fire out; mouths*

Thei wer full of fyr within.

Her lyppus honget byneythe her chyne.   *lips hung beneath their chins*

Her tethe wer long, tho throtus wyde,   *Their teeth; the throats*

Her tongus honged owt full syde.   *Their tongues hung out at great length*

155 On fete and hondus thei had gret nayles,   *feet; hands; great nails*

And grette hornes and atteryng taylys.   *great horns; poisonous tails*

Her naylys wer kene as grondon styll;   *Their nails; sharp; ground steel*

Scharpur thyng myght no mon fyll.   *Sharper; man feel*

Of hem cam the fowlest stynk   *From them came*

160 That any erthyly mon myght thynk.   *earthly man*

With her naylys in that plas   *their nails; place*

Ychon cracched other in the face.   *each one scratched*

Thei faghtton ycheon with odur and stryvon,   *They fought each; other; brawled*

And ychon odur all toryvon.   *each other; tore to pieces*

165 Hit was a wondur grysely syght   *It; wondrously gruesome*

To see how thei weryn all ydyght.   *they were; shaped*

In tho word was no mon alive   *the world; man*

That cowthe so grysely a syghth dyscryve.   *could so gruesome a sight describe*

Full grymly thei on hym staryd,   *most fiercely; stared*

170 And all atonus thei cryd and rored   *at once; cried; roared*

And seyd, "Gow abowte we yond wykyd gost   *Let us go to yonder wicked spirit*

That hathe ey don owre cownsel most   *Who has always done our counsel most*

And syng we hym a song of deyd,   *death*

For he hathe wroght aftur owre red."   *done according to our advice*

175 Thei umlapud the soule abowte   *surrounded; about*

And creidon and mad an hugy schowt   *cried; made; great shout*

And seyd, "Thu synfull wrecchyd wyght,   *You; wretched creature*

In Hell a styd is for thee dyght,   *place; prepared*

For thu art now owre owne fere.   *companion*

180 Thu art deythus doghttur dere.   *death's daughter dear*

And soo to fyr withowttyn ende   *without*

And to darknes art thu frend,   *friend*

And to all lyght art thu foo;   *foe*

Therfor, with us schalt thu goo.

185 This his thi felyschyp, thu caytyff,   *is your fellowship; caitiff (wretch)*

195

	That thu chase to thee in thi lyffe;	*chose; life*
	Therfor, with us schald thu wende	*shall; go*
	To dwell in Hell withowton ende.	
	Thu hast ybyn bothe fals and fykyll,	*been; false; fickle*
190	And thu hast seyd fals sclandur mykyll;	*said; slander great*
	Thu lovedyst stryft nyght and day,	*loved strife*
	And thu and we lovyd ay.	*loved always*
	Thu hast ylovyd myche lechery,	*much*
	And myche thu hast usud voutry,	*much; committed adultery*
195	Pryde, envy, and covetys,	*covetousness (greed)*
	Gloteny with all odur vys.	*Gluttony; other vice*
	Why wolddust not thu leyve thi trichery	*would; leave; treachery*
	Whyle thu levedust and was myghty?	*lived; mighty*
	Wher his now all thi vanyté,	*Where is; vanity*
200	Thi ryches, and thi grette mayné?	*great power*
	Wher is thi pompe and thi pryde?	
	Thi wyckydnes may thu not hyde.	
	Wer is thi streynthe and thi myght	*Where; strength*
	And thi harneys soo gayly dyght?	*armor; fancily fashioned*
205	Wher is thi gold and thi tresour?	*treasure*
	Wher is thi catell and thi stor,	*property; possessions*
	That thu wendyst schuld never thee fayll,	*thought; fail*
	And now may all hit not thee avayle?	*avail*
	Thu lovyst neyver God, nor Holy Chyrch,	*loved*
210	Noo warkys of mercy woldyst worch.	*No works; would work (perform)*
	All the gud that in tho erthe is,	*good; the earth*
	Nor all the matens ne all the masse	*matins; masses*
	Myght not help thee from the peyn of Hell	*pain*
	For eyvermore therin to dwell.	
215	That wykkyd thought that was in thi brest,	*wicked; breast*
	Woldyst thu never schowe it to no preste.	*Would; make known; priest*
	Wreche, thu thar not calle nor crye.	*Wretch; there did not call*
	Thu wendust with us withowton mercy."	*traveled*
	Ther the gost stod. Hit was darke as nyght	
220	But sone he saw a sterre full bryght.	*soon; star; full bright*
	Tundale fast that sterre beheld.	*intently; star*
	Full wyll comfortud he hym feld.	*Very well comforted; felt*
	Throw tho vertu of his creatur	*Through the power; creator*
	He hopeyd to geyte sum socur.	*hoped; get some comfort*

225	That was the angell to beton is bale
	The whych was emer of Tundale.
	The angell sone with Tundale mett,
	And full mekely he hym grette.
	He spake to hym with myldde chere:
230	"Tundale," he seyd, "wat dost thu here?"
	When Tundale herd hym his name call
	And saw hym bryght schynyng withall,
	He was fayn and began to crie
	And seyd, "Swete fader, mercy!
235	These fowle fendys for my mysdede
	To tho fyr of Hell thei wold me lede."
	Then onsweryd tho angell bryght
	And seyd to the drefull wyght,
	"Fader and lord thu callust me now.
240	Why woldyst thu not er to me bow?
	Y was thi yemer evon and moron,
	Seython thu was of thi modur boron.
	Thu woldyst neyver to me take tent,
	Nor to non of myn thu woldest not sent."
245	Tundale seyd, and sykyd sore:
	"Lord, Y saw thee never before,
	Nor never myght Y here thee lowde nor styll,
	Therfor, wyst Y not of thi wyll."
	The angell that was of gret might
250	Chasyd won that was a fowle wyght.
	Of all that fowle company
	Ther semed non soo uggly.
	"Tundale," he seyd, "this is he
	That thu dyddest know and not me.
255	Aftur hym thu hast alwey wroght
	But in me trystys thu ryght noght.
	But Goddus mercy schall thee save,
	Allthaff thu servydyst non to have.
	Bot Y woll welle that thu wytte,
260	Thee behovyt fyrst an hard fyght."
	Than was Tundale full glad.
	But he was aftur full hard bystad,
	For he saw peynus greyt and strong.

Glosses: *remedy his misery; guardian [angel]; soon; met; graciously; greeted; gentle manner; what do; heard; shining; glad; Sweet father; misdeeds; the fire; would; lead; answered the; frightened creature; call; earlier; I; guardian evening and morning; Since; mother born; would; pay attention; none of mine; assent (be guided); sighed sorely; hear you loud or quiet; knew I; will; power; Chased one; foul creature; seemed; ugly; did know; Following him; always worked; trusted you not at all; God's; Although; deserve; want greatly; understand; must do; later severely afflicted; pains great*

	And sum of hem was he among.	*them*
265	Well he cowthe tell yche a peyn	*could report; each pain*
	When he come to the body ageyn.	*again*
	Tundale therowt the angell hym drowgh,	*out of there; drew*
	For hym thoght he had drede ynow.	*it seemed to him; dread enough*
	When that thei saw, tho fendys felle,	*When they; the fiends cruel*
270	That he schuld not goo with hem to Hell,	*them*
	Thei began to rore and crye	*roar*
	And sclanderyd then God allmyghty	*slandered*
	And seyd, "Thu art not tru justyce.	*true*
	Thu art fals and unryghtwysse.	*unjust*
275	Thu seydust Thu schuldust reward sone	*said; should; straightaway*
☞	Ylke mon aftur that he hathe done.	*Each man according to (see note)*
	Tundale is owrus with skyll and ryght,	*ours; reason*
	For he hathe sarvyd hus day and nyght,	*served us*
	Full wykydly has he levyd longe.	*lived*
280	Yf we leyf hym, Thu dost hus wronge."	*lose; us*
	Thei rorud and crydon, so wer thei woo	*roared and cried; grieved*
	That Tundale schuld wend hem froo.	*go; from*
	Ychon faght and with odur dyd stryve	*Each fought; other did struggle*
	And with her naylys her chekus dyd ryve.	*their nails; cheeks; tear*
285	So fowle a stynke, as thei cast than,	*foul a smell; gave off*
	Feld never before yrthely man.	*Felt; earthly*
	Then seyd the angell to hym at the last,	
	"Tundale, com forthe and folow me fast."	*closely*
	Then seyd he and sykud full sore,	*sighed very sadly*
290	"Lord, than seyst thu never me more.	*will see*
	Yf Y goo behind thee, then am Y schent,	*doomed*
	Thes fendys from thee wold me hent	*These; will; snatch*
	And leyd me with hom to Hell peyn,	*lead; them; pain*
	Then getust thu me never ageyn."	*get*
295	Then seyd the angell, "Have no drede.	*dread*
	Thei mey no wyse from me thee lede.	*may no way; lead*
	As mony, as thee thynkuth, semyth here,	*many; it seems to you, appear*
	Yet ar ther mo with naylys full nere.	*are; more; near*
	Whylus that God is with us bathe,	*While; both*
300	Thei may never do hus skathe,	*us harm*
	But thu may rede to fende thee with,	*consult to defend yourself*
☞	In the profecy of Davyd,	*prophecy; David (see note)*

	That ther schall fall of thi lyft syde	*on; left*
	A thowsand fendys in short tyde	*time*
305	And of thi ryght syde semand	*appearing*
	Schall fall also ten thowsand.	
	And non of hem schall com to thee,	*them*
	Bot with thi eyn thu schalt hom see.	*eyes; them*
	Thu schalt ysee, or we too twyne,	*see, before we two part*
310	What peynus fallyth for dyverse synne."	*pains befall; various*

II Passus

	When the angell had told his tale,	
	Throw an entré he lad Tundale,	*Through; entry; led*
	That was darke; they had no lyght,	
	But only of the angell bryght.	
315	Thei saw a depe dale full marke,	*deep dale very dark*
	Of that Tundale was full yrke.	*troubled*
	When he hit saw, he uggod sore.	*shuddered violently*
	A delfull dwellyng saw he thore.	*doleful; there*
	That depe dale fast he beheld.	*deep; intently*
320	A fowle stenke therof he feld.	*foul stench; sensed*
	Alle the grond, that ther was semand,	*ground; visible*
	Was full of glowyng colis brennand.	*coals burning*
	Over the colys yron lay,	*coals; iron*
	Red glowand hit semud ay.	*glowing it seemed always*
325	Fowr cubytus thyk hit was,	*Four cubits thick it*
	Tho heyte of the fuyr dyd throw pas.	*The heat; fire; go beyond*
	That yron was bothe large and brad.	*broad*
	For full strong payn was hit mad.	*made*
	The heyte of the yron was more	*heat; iron*
330	Then all the fuyr that was thore.	*fire; there*
	That fyr was ever ylyche brannyng	*always alike burning*
	And ever mor stronglyke stynkyng.	*more strongly*
	Of that fyr com more stynk	
	Then any erthely mon myght thynk.	
335	And that was peyn to hym more	
	Then all that he saw or he com thore.	*Than; before he came there*
	Apon that yron, as hit was seyd,	*Upon; set (determined)*

	Fendus with the sowlus wer layd.	*Fiends; souls*
	And in that stynke dyd thei brenne than	*burn*
340	And wer molton as wax in a pan.	*melted; cauldron*
	Thei ronnen throw fyr and yron bothe,	*ran through fire*
	As hit wer wax throw a clothe	*As if it; through*
	Thei weron gederud and molton agayn;	*re-formed (gathered); melted*
	And fro thes therin to new payn.	*from*
345	Then seyd the angell to Tundale.	
	"Her may thu see mykyll bale.	*great woe*
	For every mon is dight this payn	*assigned*
	That fadur or modur has yslayn,	*father; mother; slain*
	Or any odur throw cursyd red,	*other; advice*
350	Or ben asentyd to any monus ded.	*acquiesced; man's death*
	Of this geyte thei never reles,	*get; release*
	For this peyn schall never ses.	*cease*
	In odur peyn yet schall thei be	*other pain*
	Then this that thow may herre see.	*Than; here*
355	But of this peyn schall thu not fele,	*feel*
	And yett thu hast deservyd hit full welle."	*Unless*

III Passus

	Thei passyd forth from that peyn	
	And comyn to a greyt montteyn	*great mountain*
	That was bothe gret and hye.	*large; high*
360	Theron he hard a delfoll crye.	*heard; doleful*
	Alle that ton syde was semand	*that one side; seeming [to be]*
	Full of smoke and fyr brennand;	*burning*
	That was bothe darke and wan	*dim*
	And stank of pyche and brymston.	*pitch; brimstone*
365	On that todur syde, myght he know,	*that other side*
	Gret was the forst and snow,	*frost*
	And therwith gret wyndus blast,	*winds*
	And odur stormus that folowyn fast.	*other storms; follow immediately*
	He saw ther mony fendys felle	*many evil fiends*
370	And herd hom loghtly rorre and yelle.	*heard them angrily roar*
	Thei hadon forkys and tongus in hand	*had forks; tongs*
	And gret brochys of yron glowand	*skewers; glowing*

200

	With hom thei drowyn and putton ful sore	*With which; pulled; pushed*
	The wrecchyd sowlys that ther wore.	*were*
375	Owt of that fyr thei conne hom drawe	*began them drag*
	And putton hom into the cold snowe,	*pushed them*
	And seython into the fyr agayne	*afterwards*
	Thei putton hom into odur peyne.	*put them; other pain*
	Her peyn was turnod mony folde,	*Their; turned (alternated) many times*
380	Now in hotte, now in cold.	
	Then seyd the angell, that was soo bryght,	
	"This peyn is for thefus dyght	*thieves designed*
	And for hom that robry makus	*robbery commits*
	Or agayn mennus wyll her guddus takus	*against men's will their goods take*
385	Or throw falsehed any mon bygylys	*falsehood; beguiles*
	Or wynnyght mennus gude with wykyd wylys."	*win men's goods; wiles*
	When thei hadon seyn that wykyd turment,	*seen*
	Furdurmore yette thei went.	*Further on still*

IV Passus

	The angell ay before con pas,	*always; ahead proceeded*
390	And Tundale aftur that sore aferd was,	*because of; afraid*
	Thei hyldon ey forthe the way	*held always forward*
	Tyll thei come to anothur valay,	*valley*
	That was bothe dyppe and marke.	*deep; dark*
	Of that syght was the sowle yrke.	*troubled*
395	In erthe myght non deppur be.	*deeper*
	To the grond thei myght not see.	*bottom*
	A swowyng of hem thei hard therin	*groaning; them they heard*
	And of cryyng a delfull dyn.	*doleful din*
	Owt of that pytte he feld comand	*pit; sensed coming*
400	A fowle smoke that was stynkand	*stinking*
	Bothe of pycche and of brynston,	*pitch; brimstone*
	And therin sowlys brent, mony won.	*souls burned, many a one*
	That peyn hym thoght well more semand	*seeming*
	Then all the peynus that he byforyn fand.	*pains; before found*
405	That peyn passyd all odur peynus.	
	That pyt stod betwene two monteynus.	*pit stood between; mountains*
	Over that pyt he saw a bryge	*bridge*

201

	Fro tho ton to tho todur lygge,	*From the one to the other lie*
	That was of a thowsand steppus in leynthe to rede	*steps; count*
410	And scarsly of won fotte in brede.	*scarcely; one foot; breadth*
	All quakyng that brygge ever was,	*quaking (shaking); bridge*
	Ther myght no mon over hyt passe,	
	Leryd nor lewyd, maydon ne wyff,	*Learned; unlearned, maiden; wife*
	But holy men of parfyt lyff.	*Except; perfect life*
415	Mony sowlys he saw don falle	*down*
	Of that brygge that was so smalle.	*Off*
	He saw non that brygge myght passe,	
	But a prest that a palmer was.	*priest; pilgrim*
	A palme in his hond he had,	*palm; hand*
420	And in a slaveyn he was clad.	*pilgrim's cloak*
	Ryght as he on erthe had gon,	*Just*
	He passyd over be hymselve alon.	
	Then seyd the sowle to that angell tho,	
	"Y was never er soo wo.	*before*
425	Wo is me; Y not hom to passe,	*I do not know [how] to pass over them (i.e., the steps)*
	So sor adred never er Y wasse."	*sorely fearful; was*
	The angell seyd to Tundale ryght,	
	"Drede thee noght her of this syght.	*here*
	This payn schalt thu schape full well,	*escape*
430	But odur peyn schalt thu fell.	*other pain; feel*
	This peyn is ordeynyd full grevos	*ordained; grievous*
	For prowd men and bostus."	*boasters*
	The angell toke hym be the hond swythe	*by the hand firmly*
	And lad hym over, than was he blythe.	*led; happy*

V Passus

435	Yette went thei foryt bothe togeydur,	*Still; forth*
	But tho sowle wyst never wydur,	*knew; whither*
	Be a longe wey of greyt merknes,	*By; way; darkness*
	As the story beryth wyttenes.	*bears witness*
	Thei passyd that and com to lyght,	
440	But he saw then an hogy syght.	*huge (fearsome)*
	He saw a best that was more to knaw	*beast; larger (lit., more to know)*
	Then all tho monteynus that thei saw,	

	And his ynee semyd yette more	*eyes seemed; larger*
	And bradder then the valeyys wore.	*broader than; valleys were*
445	In all his mowthe, that was so wyde,	
	Nyne thowsand armyd in myght ryde,	*armed [men]*
	Betwene his toskys, that were so longe,	*tusks*
	Too greyt gyandys he saw honge.	*Two great giants; hung*
	The hed of the ton hyng donward	*head of the one hung downward*
450	And tho todur is hed stod upward.	*the other his head*
	In myddys his mowthe stodon on yche syde	*the middle; stood; each*
	Too pylers to hold hyt up wyde.	*Two pillars*
	Tho pylers weron sette on serewyse.	*apart*
	In his mowthe wer thre partyse,	*three parts*
455	As thre gret yatys that opon stode.	*gates; open stood*
	Gret flamus of fyr owt of hym yode,	*flames; went*
	And therwith come also fowle a stynke,	
	As tong myght tell or hert thynke.	*tongue; heart*
	Thei hard ther a dylfull dyn	*heard; doleful din*
460	Of mony thowsand sowlys withyn.	
	Gowlyng and gretyng thei hard within among.	*Howling; lamentation; heard*
	"Welaway" was ever her song.	*their*
	Lowd thei hard hem crye and yell;	*Loud they heard*
	Hor sorow myght no tong tell.	*Their*
465	Befor that bestys mowthe was sene	
	Mony thowsandus of fendys kene,	*cruel*
	That hyed hem with myght and mayne	*hastened; might and main*
	Tho wrecchyd sowlys to dryve to payne.	*Those*
	With brennyng baelys thei hem dong	*rods; beat*
470	And with hem droffe to peynus strong.	*drove*
	When Tundale had that best yseen	*beast*
	And tho wykyd gostys, that wer so kene,	*spirits; cruel*
	Tundale spake full delfully,	*sorrowfully*
	When he hard that hydos crie,	*heard; hideous*
475	And seyd than to that angell bryght,	
	"What bytokenyth this hydos syght?"	*means; hideous*
	The angell onswerud hym anon.	*answered*
	"This best is callud Akyron,	*beast; Acheron*
	And ther throw byhovyth thee to wend,	*must (it is fitting for); go*
480	Yff we schull goo owre way to the end.	
	Non from this peyn may passe quyte,	*entirely*

	But cleyne men of lyffe parfyte.	*pure; life perfect*
	This hogy best, as Y thee kenne	*huge beast; teach*
	His sette to swolo covetows men	*Is; swallow covetous*
485	That in erthe makyght hit prowd and towghe	*came to be; hard*
	And never wenon to have ynowghe,	*believed; enough*
	But evur coveton more and more	*always coveted*
	And that hor sowlys forthynkon sore.	*their souls repent*
	In tho profecy hit is wryton thus,	*prophecy; written*
☞	That a best schall swolewo the covetows.	*swallow (see note)*
491	So muche thurst hathe that best	*great thirst*
	That all the watur most and lest	*waters*
	That evur ran est or west	*east*
	Myght not stanche the bestys thurst.	*stanch*
495	Therfor, this payne is redy ydyght,	*prepared*
	Namely for yche a covetows wyght	
	That wenon never ynow to have,	*thought; enough*
	Ne holden hom payd, nor vochensaffe	*felt satisfied with*
	That God hom sent of His grace.	*What*
500	Therfor thei schen say, 'Alas! Alas!'	*must say*
	For ay the more that thei han free,	*always; have to themselves*
	Tho more covetows a mon may hem see.	
	The gyandys, that thu syst with ee,	*giants; see with [your] eyes*
	Hongyng betwene his toskus so hye,	*tusks so high*
505	Goddys law wold thei not knowe,	*acknowledge*
	But thei wer trew in hor owne lawe.	*to their own*
	Of whom tho namus wer callud thus:	*the names*
	That ton hyght Forcusno and that toder Conallus."	*That one is named; that other*
	"Alas," quod that sowle, "suche peyn have thay,	
510	Whedur thei schull never thennus away."	*Whither; thence*
	Quod the angell, "Thee falon no glee;	*You feel*
	And in erthe seche hast thu ybe."	*For; such; been*
	When he had seyd thus, ther thei yode,	*went*
	And byfor the best bothe thei stode,	*before*
515	But that was agayn Tundaleis wylle.	*against*
	The angell vaneschyd and he stod stylle.	*vanished*
	No wondur was thaw he had drede.	*though*
	The fowle fendys comyn gud spede,	*good speed (quickly)*
	Thei token hym and bowndyn hym fast,	*bound; tightly*
520	Withynne that best thei connen hym cast.	*beast; began to cast him*

	Awhyle within he most dwell.	*must*
	Ther was he beyton with fendys fell,	*beaten by; cruel*
	With kene lyonus that on hym gnowe	*savage lions; gnawed*
	And dragonus that hym al todrowe.	*dragons; pulled apart*
525	With eddrys and snakus full of venym	*adders; snakes; venom*
	He was all todrawyn yche lym.	*torn to pieces each limb*
	Now he was in fyr brennand,	*burning*
	Now in yse fast fresand.	*ice; intensely freezing*
	The terys of hys ynee two,	*tears; eyes*
530	Thei brendon as fyr. Hym was full wo.	*burned*
	Strong stynke he feld of brymston.	*sensed of brimstone*
	He was in peynus mony won.	*pains many a one*
	With his nalys in angur and stryfe	*nails*
	Hys owne chekus he con al toryfe.	*cheeks; began to tear to bits*
535	Of yche synne that evur he dudde	*each; did*
	He was upbraydud. Ther was non hudde.	*reproached; none hidden*
	In grett wanhope was he ay.	*despair; always*
	He went nevur to have passyd away.	*thought*
	But sone he come owt of that peyne.	
540	He wyst not how. He was full fayne.	*knew; glad*
	Ryght now was he in full grett dowt,	*perplexity*
	And anon aftur was he withowt.	*outside*
	He lay awhyly as he wer deed,	*a while as [if] he were dead*
	And sone aftur he stod up in that sted.	*place*
545	As he hym dressyd so syttande,	*raised up; sitting*
	He saw the angell byforyn hym stand.	*in front of*
	He had comfort than of that lyght,	
	When he saw thys angell bryght.	
	The angell twoched sone Tundale	*touched*
550	And gaff hym strynthe. Than was he hale.	*gave; strength; well*
	Then lovyd he God of His grace	
	With terys sore gretand in that place.	*tears; moaning*
	He thus passyd that turment,	*torment*
	But fordurmore bothe thei went.	*further on*

VI Passus

555	Anodur wey thei to con take,	*those two took*
	Tyll thei com to an hydous lake.	*hideous*
	That lake mad an hydous dynne	*noise*
	Throw wawys of watur that weron withyne.	*waves*
	Tho wawys of that watur roos as hye	*rose as high*
560	As any mon myght with is ee ysee.	*his eyes see*
	Therin wer howgy bestys and fell	*huge; cruel*
	That hydously con crye and yell.	*did cry*
	Her ynee wer brode and brandon bryght,	*eyes; burned*
	As brannyng lampus don on nyght.	*burning lamps do*
565	On yche a syde thei waytud ay	*waited*
	To swolow sowlys that was ther pray.	*swallow*
	Over that lake then saw thei lygge	*lie*
	A wondur long, narow brygge,	*narrow bridge*
	Too myle of leynthe that was semand	*Two miles; length; seeming*
570	And scarsly of the bred of a hand,	*breadth*
	Of scharpe pykys of yron and stell.	*spikes; steel*
	Hit was grevows for to fele.	*grievous*
	Ther myght non passe by that brygge thare,	
	But yeff her feet wer hyrt sare.	*Without their; hurt sorely*
575	The hydous bestys in that lake	
	Drew nerre the brygge her pray to take	*nearer; their prey*
	Of sowles that fell of that brygge don.	*off; down*
	To swolow hem thei wer ay bon.	*always ready*
	Cryyng and yelling and gowling yfere,	*growling together*
580	Tho noyse was wonder dredfull to here.	
	These hydous bestus wer wondur grette;	
	The sowlys that fell wer her mette.	*their food*
	Tundale saw the bestys all	
	And fyr owt of her mowthe walle.	*welled*
585	The fyr that he saw from hem faulland	*falling*
	Made the watur all hotte walland.	*boiling*
	He saw won stond on the brygge	*one*
	With a burden of corne on is rygge	*grain; his back*
	Gretand with a dylfull crye	*Moaning; doleful*
590	And pleynud his synne full pytuysly.	*bewailed; piteously*
	The pykys his fett pykud full sore.	*spikes; feet pricked*

	He dredyd the bestys mykyll mor	*dreaded; much more*
	That hym to slee wer ay bowne,	*ready*
	Yef that he had falle of the brygge don.	*If; off*
595	Tundale askyd the angell bryght,	
	"What meneghth that hydous syght?"	*means*
	The angell onswerud thus agayn,	
	"For hym is ordeynyd this payn	*ordained*
	That robbyght men of hor ryches	*robbed; their*
600	Or any gudys that herys is,	*goods; theirs*
	Lewd or leryd, or Holy Kyrke,	*Unlearned; learned; Church*
	Or any wrong to hem woll wyrk.	*work (do)*
	But sum haght more peyn and sum lase	*have; less*
	All aftur that her synnus his.	*All according to their sins*
605	Sum reckys not wat thei deyre	*care not what; injure*
	And woll not a kyrke forbeyre.	*refrain from destroying a church*
	Sum ar fekul and sum unleylle.	*fickle; unfaithful*
	Sum woll robbe and sum wol stell	*rob; steal*
	Thyng that to Holy Chyrche fallys;	*belongs*
610	Sacrileggi that men callys	*Sacrilege; call*
	Thei that done wronge or vylony	*villainy*
	Within that sted of seyntwary,	*place of sanctuary*
	Or within the sted of relegyon	*place of religion*
	Maketh any dystruccioun,	*destruction*
615	All schull thei here turmentyd be	*tormented*
	In this peyn that thu may see.	
	And he that thu syst on the brygge stand,	*see*
	With tho schevus so sore gretand,	*sheaves; moaning*
	Fro Holy Chyrch he hom stale,	*them stole*
620	For thei wer teythe told by tale.	*tithes counted up*
	Therfor, byes he hem full dere	*pays; dearly*
	That dede throw peyn that he haght here.	*deed; has here*
	Over the brygge schalt thu wend nowe	*travel*
	And with thee lede a wyld cowe.	*lead; cow*
625	Loke thu lede her warly	*Be careful to lead; warily*
	And bewar she fall not by,	
	For wen thu art passyd thi peyn,	*when*
	Thu delyvur hur me agayn.	
	Thee behovys to lede huyr over alle,	*You must (it behooves you); her*
630	For that thu thi gossypus cow stale."	*friend's; stole*

207

	Than spake Tundale with drury chere,	*dreary mood*
	"A mercy, Y aske my lord dere.	
	If all Y toke hur agaynus his wyll,	*Even though; against*
	He had hur agayn, as hit was skyll."	*as it turned out*
635	"That was soght," quod that angell,	*so*
	"For thu myghttust not from hym hur stell.	*keep away*
	And for he had is cow agayn,	
	Thu schalt have the lesse payn.	
	Yche wyckyd dede, more or lesse,	
640	Schall be ponnysched aftur the trespass,	*punished; according to*
	But God allmyghty lykusse noght	*likes not*
	Nowdur ell dede, nor evyll thoght."	*Neither ill deed*
	As Tundale stod that was ylle lykand,	*ill liking*
	The wylde cow was broght to is hande.	
645	Maygrey is chekys hym byhovyth nede	*Despite everything; must*
	To take the cow and forthe here lede.	
	Hym thoght hit was to hym gret payne,	
	But he myght not be ther agayn.	
	He dud the angell commandment.	*did*
650	By the hornes the cow he hent.	*grabbed*
	He cheryschyd the cow all that he myght,	*took good care of*
	And to the brygge he leduth hor ryght.	*her*
	When he on the brygge was,	
	The cow wold not forthur pas.	*further go*
655	He saw the bestys in the lake	
	Draw nerre the brygge her pray to take.	*their prey*
	That cow had ner fall over that tyde	*nearly; [at] that time*
	And Tundale on that todur syde.	*that other*
	He was wonderly sor aferd than	*afraid*
660	Of gret myscheffe. Up than thei wan.	*went*
	Thei passydon forthe, that thoght hym hard,	*passed*
	Tyll thei come to the mydwarde,	*middle*
	Odur wylye he abovyn, odur wyle the cow;	*Some times; other times*
	Bothe the hadon sorow ynow.	*They both; enough*
665	Then mette thei hym that bare the corne	*bore; grain*
	Ther went thei bothe. Thei hadon ben lorne,	*Where; lost*
	So narow then the brygge was	
	That nowdur myght for othur pas.	*neither*
	To hom bothe hit was grette peyn,	

670	For nowdur myght ther turne ageyn.	
	Nor nowdur dorst for all myddylerd	*dared; the world*
	Loke byhynd hym, so wer thei ferd.	*afraid*
	The scharpe pykys that thei on yede	*spikes; went*
	Made hor feet sore to blede,	*their; bleed*
675	So that hor blod ran don that tyde	*[at] that time*
	Into that watur on eydur syde.	*either*
	He prayd Tundale of mercy	
	That he wold lette hym passe by.	
	He seyd, "Certus Y ne may,	*Certainly*
680	For Y may not passe for thee away."	
	Thei wepton sore. Gret dele ther was,	*wept; distress*
	For nowdur myght lette odur pas.	*neither; other pass*
	As Tundale stod with the cow in honde,	
	He saw the angell byfor hym stond.	
685	The angell broght hym from that wo	
	And bad hym, "Lette the cow goo."	
	And seyd, "Be of gud comford now,	*comfort*
	For thu schalt no more lede the cow."	
	Tundale schewyd his fett, that thei wer sore,	*showed*
690	And seyd, "Lord, Y may goo no more."	
	Then seyd the angell, that hym ladde,	*led*
	"Thynke how sore thi feett bledde,	
	Therfor dredfull is thi way	
	And full grevous, soghth to say."	*truth to say*
695	Then towchyd he the feet of Tundale,	*touched*
	And as tyd was he all hale.	*quickly; healed*
	Then seyd Tundale, "A blessyd be thu,	
	That I am delivered from peyn now."	
	The angell seyd, "Thow schalt sone ywytte,	*know*
700	A grett peyn abydus hus yette.	*waits for us*
	Fro that sted woll Y thee not save,	*place*
	That is full and more woll have.	
	And thydur now behovyth thee.	*to there now [it] behooves you [to go]*
	Ageynes that may thu not bee."	*Against*

209

VII Passus

705	Tundale went forght, as the boke says,	*forth*
	Throw wyldernys and darke ways.	*wilderness*
	He saw an hows hym agayn	*house in front of him*
	Was more than any montayn.	
	As an ovon that hows was mad,	*Like; oven*
710	But the mowthe therof was wyd and brad.	*wide; broad*
	Owt at the mowthe the fure brast,	*fire burst*
	And fowle stynkyng lye com owt fast.	*fire*
	The lye was bothe grett and thro	*dangerous*
	And start a thowsand fote therfro.	*reached*
715	The sowlys withhowten that brene to noght,	*outside; burn to nothing*
	That wykyd gostys thydur had broght.	*thither*
	When Tundale had sen that syght,	
	He spake to that angell bryght:	
	"Now goo we to a delfull stedde.	*sorrowful place*
720	Yondur Y holde the yatys of dedde.	*behold; gates of death*
	Who schall delyver me from that sore?	
	Y wene to be ther forevermore."	*know (expect)*
	Then seyd the angell gud,	
	"Thu schalt be delyvyred from that styd."	*place*
725	"Gret myght he hathe of Goddus grace	
	That may delyver me from that plas."	
	The angelle sone hym answerd,	
	"Tundale," he seyd, "be noght aferd.	
	Withynne yonde hows byhovyth thee to wend,	*yonder house [it] behooves you to go*
730	But yonde lye schall thee not schend."	*fire; destroy*
	When Tundale com that hows nere	
	He saw mony a fowle bocchere,	*butcher*
	Evyn in the mydward the fyre thei stond	
	And scharp tolys in her hond.	*tools; their hands*
735	Summe hade syculus, knyvus, and saws,	*sickles; knives*
	Summe had twybyll, brodax, and nawgeres,	*pickaxes; broad axes; augers*
	Cultorus, sythus, kene wytall,	*Coulters (plowshares), scythes, sharp withall*
	Spytyll forkus the sowlys to fall.	*Pitchforks*
	Thei wer full lodly on to loke.	*loathsome*
740	Summe had swerdys and summe hoke,	*swords; hooks*
	Summe gret axes in here hond	*their hands*

	That semyd full scharpe bytond.	*honed*
	Of that syght had he gret wondur,	
	How thei smyton the sowlus insondur.	*smote; apart*
745	Summe stroke of the hed, somme the thyes,	*off; thighs*
	Summe armus, summe leggus by the kneys,	*arms; legs; knees*
	Summe the bodyes in gobedys small,	*chunks (gobbets)*
	Yette kevered the sowlys togedur all.	*recovered*
	And ever thei smoton hem to gobbetus ageyn.	
750	This thoght Tundale a full grette peyn.	
	Then seyd Tundale to the angell tho,	
	"Lord, delyver me from this woo.	
	Y beseche yow that Y mey passe this care,	
	For sweche a peyn saw Y never are,	*before*
755	And all odur turmentus that ben schyll,	*will be*
	I woll suffur at yowre wyll."	
	Then seyd the angell to Tundale thus,	
	"This peyn thee thenke full hydous,	
	But in this peyn byhovus thee to bee	*[it] behooves you*
760	And eke in more that schalt thu see."	*also*
	Of that peyn he thoght more aw	*awe*
	Then of all tho peynus that ever he saw.	
	But sone theraftur he saw thare	
	A peyn that he thoght mare:	*more*
765	He saw an hydous hwond dwell	*hound*
	Withinne that hows that was full fell.	
	Of that hound grette drede he had.	
	Tundale was never so adrad.	*afraid*
	Wen he had seyn that syght,	
770	He bysoght of that angell bryght	*besought*
	That he wold lett hym away steyl,	*sneak*
	That he com not in that fowle Hell.	
	But the angell wold not for nothyng	
	Grant hym hys askyng.	
775	The wykyd gostys that wer within	
	Abowt hym com with gret dynne,	*noise*
	With hor tolys and with her geyre,	*tools; equipment*
	That he saw hom byfore beyre.	*bear*
	Among hom thei tokyn Tundale	*took*
780	And hewyd hym in gobettus smale.	*hewed*

He myght not dye for that peyn,
For he was sone hole ageyn. — *whole*
The most maystur of that hows hyght — *great master; was named*
Preston; that was his name ryght.
785 He saw and hard wyle he was thare — *heard while*
Gowlyng and gretyng and mykyll care. — *Howling; lamentation; great grief*
The lye that he saw withowtton passe — *fire*
Wastyd all that theryn was. — *Destroyed*
Ther was full delfull noyse and crie
790 And hongur for glotenye, — *hunger*
That all the sowlys that therin wer
Myght not stanche the appetyt there. — *satisfy*
Tundale saw theryn allsoo
Men and wemen that wer full woo,
795 That peynud wer in her prevytys — *private parts*
And all tognawyn bytwene hor kneys. — *gnawed; their thighs*
He saw within that dongeon
Mony men of relygeon — *Many*
That full wer of fowle vermyn — *vermin*
800 Bothe withowttyn and withyn.
Strong vermyn on hem he saw,
And on every lym beton and gnaw. — *bite*
Tundale knew summe ther full wyll
That worthy wer that peyn to fele.
805 But he com sone owt of that peyn.
He wyst never how. Than was he fayn. — *knew; glad*
Then stodde Tundale in a darke stede, — *place*
That was callyd the cawdoron of drede. — *cauldron of dread*
As he satte, his syght was dym:
810 He saw his angell byfor hym.
He seyd to the angyll, "Alas!
Wher his the word that wryton was
That Goddus mercy schuld passe all thyng?
☞ Here see Y therof no tokenyng." — *sign (see note)*
815 Then answeryd the angyll and seyd anon,
"That word desseyves mony a mon. — *misleads*
Allthauff God be full of myght and mercy, — *Although*
Ryghtwessnes behowyth Hym to do therby. — *Justice requires*
But He forgevyth more wykkydnes, — *forgives*

212

820	Thenne He findeth ryghtwesnes.	*righteousness*
	Tho peynus that thu haddus wer but lyght.	
	Grettur thu schuldyst have tholud with ryght."	*suffered*
	Tundale than began to knele	*kneel*
	And thonked God He schappud so wele.	*created*
825	Then sayd the angell to Tundale,	
	"Wherto schuld any mon geff tale,	*Why; give heed*
	Yf God schuld ay forgeffe hym sone	*forgive*
	All tho synnus that he had done	
	Withowttyn any peyn to fele?	
830	Thenne nedyd a mon nevur to do wele.	*needed*
	But thei that ar wykyd and synfull kyd	*known*
	And no penans in body dyd,	*penance*
	God takyth on hem no venjans,	*vengeance*
	Yf thei hadon any repentans.	*repentance*
835	Throw His mercy ar thei save.	
	But yette the sowle som peyn schalt have.	
	Oftontymes from mony a wyght	
	Guddus, that han to hom be dyght,	*Goods; assigned*
	Fro hym God hom hathe ytake	
840	And dothe here his peynus slake,	*pains lessen*
	For insted of peyn is worldus catell,	*possessions (are taken)*
	Yf that a mon thonke God of all yll.	*thank; ill*
	So schall ther sowlys have lasse peyn	
	Wen dethe to grond hathe hom slayn,	*When*
845	And the seyner from all peyn wende	*sooner*
	To the blysse withowtten ende.	
	But in the world is non, Y wene,	*I believe*
	Be he of synne nevur so clene,	
	Noght a chyld, for sothe to say,	*Not even*
850	That was boron and deed today	*born; died*
	Have peyn and drede he schall ryght well,	
	Thaw he schull not hom sore fele.	*Though*
	To love more God he woll be fayn	*eager*
	That soo may schape suche payn,	*escape*
855	As the mon that dampnyd is	
	To Hell for his wykkydnes.	
	He schall suche joy in Hevyn ysee	
	That more icy myght nevur bee.	*comfort*

	That schall greve hym more the syght	*grieve*
860	Then all the peyn that in Hell is dyght,	*established*
	When he may see that grette blysse	
	That he schall forever mysse.	*miss*
	But the prest that tho palmer was,	*pilgrim*
	That thu saw ovur the brygge pas,	
865	He saw all the peynus stronge,	
	But non of hem was he among,	
	For he lovede God almyghty ay	
	And servyd Hym well to his pay.	*reward*
	Goddes joy may he not mysse,	
870	For he hathe a trone of blysse."	*throne*
	When the angyll had thys told	
	To make Tundale the more bold,	
	The angell lad hym yett furdurmare,	
	Tundale folowyd with myckyll care	

Passus VIII

875	A wondur hydous best thei saw,	
	Of whom Tundale had grett aw.	*awe*
	That best was bothe felle and kene	*cruel*
	And more than he had evur ysene.	
	Two grett wyngys that wer blacke	*wings*
880	Stod on eydur syde on his backe.	*either*
	Two fett with naylys of yron and stell	*feet*
	He had, that weron full scharpe to fell.	*feel*
	He had a long nekke and a smalle,	*slender*
	But the hed was grett withall.	
885	The eyn wer brode in his hed	*eyes*
	And all wer brannand as fyr red.	
	His mowthe was wyd and syde-lyppud;	*wide-lipped*
	Hys snowt was with yron typpud	*nose; tipped*
	Fyr, that myght nevur slakyd bee,	*extinguished*
890	Owt of is mowthe com gret plentee.	
	That best sat evyn in mydward	
	A lake, that was froson full hard.	*frozen*
	That lake was full of gret yse.	*ice*

	Ther had sowlys full gret angwysse.	*anguish*
895	That best was bothe fell and gredy	*cruel; greedy*
	And swollod tho sowlys that wer redy,	*swallowed*
	And when the sowlys wer theryn,	
	Ther wer thei peynod for her syn.	*pained*
	In strong fyr ther brand thei ay,	
900	Too thei wer ner wastud away,	*Till; wasted*
	And than ycast fro that peyn	*cast*
	Tyll thei wer covert agayn.	*recovered*
	Then wax thei blacke and bloo	*grew; blue*
	For sorow and care and muche woo.	
905	As wemen doght bothe meke and mylde,	
	When thei ben in berying of chylde,	*bearing*
	Thei playnod hem and seydon, "Alas!"	*complained (bewailed)*
	Harde wer hor peynus for hor trespas.	
	For strong bytyng thei had withyn	
910	With wood edderys and odur vermyn	*wild adders*
	That was withynne hem gnawyng ay,	
	As thei among snakys lay.	*snakes*
	When thei her tymys myght know and see,	*times*
	Thei made hem sorow then gaynyd no glee.	
915	Thei made suche dylle sothe to telle,	*dole*
	That noyse of hem nygh fylled Hell.	*nearly*
	So dylfull a noyse was never hard	*heard*
	Of men and wemen, so thei fard.	*fared*
	But her tyme behovys hem to kepe,	*their; [they are] obliged*
920	When the edders schulld owt of hem crepe,	*adders; creep*
	Noght only throw prevy place,	*private*
	But throw ylke a lym maketh her trace.	*each limb*
	Throw hed and feyt, backe and syde,	*feet*
	Throw armus and leggys thei con glyde.	*began to glide*
925	Throw wombe and brest thei wer crepand	*creeping*
	And throw ylk a joynt that thei fand.	*found*
	Thei crepud owt all attonus.	*crept; at once*
	Thei sparud neydur flesse nor bwonus.	*neither flesh; bones*
	Tho eddres wer full gret and longe	
930	With hedys of yron that wer full stronge.	*heads*
	Thei had mowthys of fyr glowand	*glowing*
	And glowand tongus owt schetand.	*sticking*

215

	Her taylys wer full of smale broddys	*picks*
	As wether hokys wer the oddes.	*shepherds' crooks; points*
935	Whan the vermyn wold have owt crepon	
	At the holys that thei made opon,	*holes; open*
	Thei myght not wyn owt hor taylys,	
	Soo fast hyldon the crokyd naylys.	*held; crooked*
	Thei turnyd her hedys in agayne thar	
940	Throw ylke a joynt thei madon full bare.	
	Thei fretud hom within and hem gnew,	*chewed; gnawed*
	And all her bowell they owt drew.	*bowel*
	Thei smyton her hedds owt and yn;	*stuck; heads*
	Her taylys thei myght not owt wyn.	*get out*
945	When tho hokys thay hom ageyns tyt,	*back pulled*
	Thei turnedyn ageyn and toke ther bytt.	
	Fro hed to fotte ay was gnawyng,	
	Scrattyng, fretyng, fleyng, and styngyng.	*Scratching, eating, flaying*
	To Hevon the noyse myght have ben harde,	*Heaven; heard*
950	So hydously thei crydon and sowle fared.	*fared*
	The sowlys thei crydon for grett angwis	*anguish*
	And pleyndon gretly ther folys.	*lamented; sins (follies)*
	Thei wer not lyveryt of hor payn,	*delivered*
	For hit was newed ay agayn.	*renewed*
955	Tundale seyd to the angyll bryght,	
	"Lord, this is a dredfull syght.	
	Me thynkyght this peyn well more	
	Then all tho peyn that Y saw before."	
	Then onsweryd the angell ageyn	
960	And seyd, "Tundale, this peyn	
	Ys ordeynyd for men of relygyon	
	That kepud not well hor professyon;	*kept; their vows*
	For monkus, channons, prestus, and clerkus,	*monks, canons, priests; clerks*
	And for odur men and wemen of Holy Kyrke	
965	That delytus hor bodys yn lechery	*delight*
	Or in any odur maner of foly,	
	And dothe not as ther ordyr wyll,	*order requires*
	But ledus hor lyffe aftur ther wyll.	*lead their lives*
	Thei schull have the same evermore	
970	If thei amend hom not or thei goo before.	
	And for the same thow hast bene,	

This schalt thu thole, that thu hast sene."   *suffer*
When the angyll had seyd thus,
The fendys, that wer full hydeous,
975   Within the best Tundale thei ladde,
And ther was he within full hard bestad.   *beset*
Therin was he peynyd full long,
Brennyng in fyr that was full stronge.
Seththyn the best hym owt kest,   *Afterwards; cast*
980   Then was he swollod as he wold brest.   *swollen; burst*
All full of edders than he was,
And non of hem myght from odur passe.
But wen he shuld delyvered be,
Then he myght the angyll ysee
985   With mylde chere befor hym dyd stond.
He towched Tundale with hys hond
And delyvured hym of that bale.   *harm*
Then seyd the angyll to Tundale,
"Com furdurmore and folow me,
990   For more peyn byhovyth thee to se."
Fordurmore thei went than,
But Tundale thoght hit no gam.   *game (pleasure)*
Thei come into a wey full derke.
Of that way was Tundale yrke,   *troubled*
995   For ther was no more lyght,
But that at come of the angyll bryght.
That way was strayt and longlastand   *straight; longlasting*
And worst of all that Tundale fand.   *found*
Afrontte unnethe thei myght passe   *Forward scarcely they might not pass*
1000   So narow of steppus don that was,   *steps down*
As thei had come from a hye hyll
Don into a deppe dongyll.   *deep valley*
The more that Tundale folowyd ay,
The lengur hym thoght was that way.
1005   Tundale feld a stynkyng ayre;   *sensed; air*
Then of his lyffe he was in speyr.   *despair*
Then he sykud and wept full sore,   *sighed*
And seyd to the angyll thore,   *at that time*
"Lord, wydur schalt this way wend?
1010   Me thenkyth this way hasse non ende."   *has*

217

Then onsward the angyll fre   *courteous*
And seyd, "Y wyll telle thee
How this way lythe and into what sted.   *lies*
This is the way that lyght to the dedde."   *leads*
1015 Then seyd Tundale, "How may this be?
In boke we may wryton ysee
That the way that schall to the deythe lede
☞   Ys bothe large and mykyll of brede.   *great of breadth (see note)*
Thys is now a narow way
1020 That thu us ledust, and longe to asay."   *assay*
Then seyd the angyll, "Wyll Y wate   *Well I know*
That the boke spekys not of this gate,
But of the way of unclannes,   *impurity*
Of fleschely lust that dedly is.
1025 Be that way men lyghtly wende   *By*
To the dethe withowttyn ende."

IX Passus

Then went thei forghthe and furdurmore   *forth*
By that darke way that they in wore.
They come to a depe dongyll.   *valley*
1030 Of that syght lykyd hym full yll.
That dongyll full of smytheus stood,   *forges*
And smythus abowtte hom yode   *blacksmiths; went*
With grett homerus in hor hond   *hammers*
And gret tongus hoote glowand.   *tongs*
1035 The smythus wer grymly on to loke.   *forges; terrifying*
Owt of hor mowthus com grett smoke.
These smythus wer full of sowlys within   *forges*
That wepton and madyn grett dyn.
In grett fyres thei con hom cast   *proceeded to throw them*
1040 And sethen with homerus leydon on fast.   *then; hammers laid on*
The master of that smythy was bold.
Vlkane was is name hold.   *forge*
                                                                   Vulcan
"Lo yond," quod the angyll, "with is gyn   *his devising*
Hathe made mony a mon do syn.
1045 Wherfor with hym aftur thare dede,   *death*

218

Thei schull be peynod with hym in this stede." *tortured; place*
Then asked Tundale, "Lord fre,
Schall Y among yond fendys be,
As odur that han servyd well,
1050 So grett peynus for to fell?" *feel*
Then seyd the angyll sone,
"Tundale," he seyd, "thu hast so done
That thee behovyth to thole this turment." *suffer*
And then to the smythy he went. *forge*
1055 The turmentowrus com rennand *tormenters; running*
With furgons and with tongus glowand. *pokers; tongs*
Betwene hom hent thei Tundale thar *seized*
And laddyn hym to muche care.
Tundale had thei with hom than
1060 And leyt the angyll stond alan. *alone*
Into that smythy thei hym caste, *forge*
In myddys the fyr as hem liked best.
With gret balyws at hym thei blew, *bellows*
As hit wer as yron ymulton new. *melted*
1065 Tundale bygan to brenne yche lym,
But thowsandus thei brend with hym.
Sum of hom thei madyn nesche, *flaccid*
As is the watur that is fresche.
Sum wer molton as molton ledde,
1070 Sum as yron glowyng redde.
Thei cast attonus full smartly *at once*
A thowsand sowlys full peteusly. *piteously*
With yron homorus thei stode
And leyde on hem as thei wer wode. *laid on; crazy*
1075 A thowsand sowlys togedur thei dong *beat*
In a pott full wonderly long,
As men schull tempore yron and stell, *temper*
And that was a grysly peyn to fele.
That turment most thei long dre, *undergo*
1080 But yett myght thei not fully dye.
These turmentowrys wer fowle and blake. *tormenters*
Ylke onto odur in cownsell spake *counsel*
What peynus thei myght the sowlys wyrke; *work*
Of wykkyd labourus thei wer not yrke. *tired*

219

1085	Yet thei dud hom more peyn.	
	Thei smyton hom all insondor ageyn.	
	Odur smythus wer ther that tyde	*blacksmiths*
	Of anothur smythy ther besyde.	*forge*
	Thei seyd, "Habbuth yowr wel her yowr pay.	*You have had; enjoyment*
1090	Kest ye hom hydour, lett us asay."	*Cast; assay*
	Thai lepedon and roredyn and criedon fast	*leapt*
	And bad tho sowlys to hom kast.	
	And so thei dedyn with greyt talent,	
	And odur smythus thei con hom hent	*blacksmiths proceeded to seize them*
1095	With hokys and tongus hootte glowand,	*glowing hot tongs*
	That thei hyldon in hor hand.	*held in their hands*
	Hom thoght thei wer not smythyd ynoghe,	*beaten enough*
	Up and don the develes hom droghe,	*pulled*
	And in strong fyr thei brendon hom ay,	
1100	Tyll thei wer nye brand away.	*nearly*
	But sone then aftur was Tundale	
	Delyvered owt of that greyt bale	
	Ageyns that grysly smythys wylle.	*gruesome blacksmith's*
	But all tho todur sowlys lafton stylle.	*the other; left*
1105	When Tundale com owt of that payn,	
	He was sone kevered ageyn.	*recovered*
	Sone the angyllys voys he hard.	
	The angyll asked hym how he fard.	
	"Tundale," he seyd, "now may thu see	
1110	Werof thi synnus servyd thee.	*In what way*
	Thee behowyt to have a gret angwys	*deserve*
	For thi delytes and thi folys.	
	These that thu art delyvered froo,	*from*
	Wer ordeynyd the peyn for to doo,	
1115	For with that same company	
	Foluyddyn thee yn thi foly."	*Followed*
	Tundale stod and cowthe noght say,	*could*
	For his wytte was ner away.	
	Then seyd the angyll as he stood,	
1120	"Looke thu be of comford gud.	
	Yf all that thu have had tene	*suffering*
	In sum peyn that thu hast sene,	
	Grettur peynus yett schalt thu see	

	Heraftur that abydus thee.	*waits for*
1125	Fro hem schalt thu schap full well,	*escape*
	But thee byhovyth sum to fell.	*you are obliged to feel some*
	Thu schalt see or we wende	
	Sowlys in peyn withowttyn ende.	
	Hor mysdedys hom dampnyd has;	*Their; them damned*
1130	Therfor her song is ay 'Alas.'	
	But odur that soghton Goddys mercy	
	Passon that peyn well sycurly."	*Pass; safely*
	When the angyll had this sayd,	
	His hond upon Tundale he layd.	
1135	Then was he hoole and feld no soor;	*whole; felt*
	Yett went they furthe furdurmore.	

X Passus

	As the angyll and he went in company,	
	Ther com a cold all sodenly.	
	Suche a cold Tundale feld	
1140	That his lymes myght hym not weld.	*control*
	He was ner froson to dedde.	
	Strong darkenes was in that stedde.	
	Then was Tundale full ferd,	
	For more peyn never he hade.	
1145	For drede of peyn full sore he qwoke.	*quaked*
	Hym thoght his hedde all toschoke.	*shook*
	All his peyn byforyn, hym thoght,	
	So muche as that grevyd hym noght.	*grieved*
	Then he spake to tho angyll sone	
1150	And seyd, "Lord, what have Y done?	
	Y am so combret fott and hond	*numbed*
	That Y may not upryght stond."	
	Then the angyll hym not onsweryd.	
	Then wept Tundale and was ferd.	
1155	He myght not steron lythe nor lym.	*stir joint; limb*
	The angyll went away from hym.	
	When he myght not the angyll see,	
	Dele he made that was pyté.	*Dole*

     He went forthe ay furdurmare.
1160 To Helle the way lay evyn thare.
     A deelfull criye he hard sone
     Of sowlys that wer in peyn don,
     That dampnyd wer in peyn endles
     For hor synne and hor wykkydnes.
1165 He hard a strong noyse of thondur;
     To here that dyn hit was grett wondur.
     Noo hart myght thenke, nor no tong telle
     How hydous was the noyse of Helle.
     Then was that sowle in grett dowtte.   *anxiety*
1170 He lokyd in every syde abowtte.
     Ever whan come that hydous dyn,
     He lokyd to have be takyn in.
     Butt he saw hym besyde
     A deppe putt muckyll and wyde.   *deep pit great*
1175 Owt of that pyt he saw comand   *pit; coming*
     A grett flam of fyr all stynkand.
     Suche a stynke com of that hole
     That he myght not long hit thole;   *endure*
     Owt of that dyke ther ros evon   *ditch*
1180 A pylar that ner raght to Hevon.   *pillar; nearly reached*
     All brannand that pylar was
     With lye abowtte as a compas.   *fire; circumference*
     He saw fendys and sowlys flye
     On that pylar bothe low and hye.
1185 Thei flow ay up and don fast,
     As sparkelys of fyr thoro wyndus blast.   *sparks; through wind's*
     And when the sowlys wer brent to askus all,   *ashes*
     In myddys the dyke they con falle.
     They keverdyn that and wer broyght agayn;   *recovered*
1190 On this wyse was ever newyd hor payn.
     Tundale had lever than all myddelerd   *rather*
     Have turned ageyn, soo was he ferd.   *back*
     But ageyn myght he not goo,
     Ne styr hys lymus to nor froo.
1195 As he was clomsyd, styll he stod.   *enfeebled*
     He was so ferd he was ney wod.   *nearly mad*
     With hymselffe he began to stryve

And his owne chekys all toryve.
He grevdde, he gowlyd, hym was full woo;
1200 For he myght not ageyn goo.
"Alas," he seyd, "what is tho best red?   *advice*
For now Y wot, Y am but dedde."
Tho wykyd gostus, as thei flow
Abowt the peler in that low,   *pillar; fire*
1205 Thei hardon that gowlyng and that crye;   *heard; yowling*
Thei come to hym full hastyly.
Brennand hokys with hom thei broght;
To turment sowlys wer thei wroght.
Thei gretton hym, that sowle that meyné,   *greeted; group*
1210 "Kaytyfe, wealand myght thu bee.   *Wretch; surrounded*
Thu metust well with us at home;   *meet*
Tell us now fro wennus thu come.   *whence*
For thi wykkydnes and thi foly
In fyr to brenne art thu worthy,
1215 For thu come in noo peyn yet to fele.
Here in Hell fyr we woll the kele,   *cool*
For now with us schalt thu wende
And dwell in Hell withowtyn ende.
Of owre maneres we schull thee kenne.   *customs; teach*
1220 Withowt kelyng schalt thu brenne,   *cooling*
Evermore to brenne in fyr reed,
For thu schalt never passe this steed.   *place*
Thee tharre not thynke, on no wysse,   *must; way*
Too be delyvered of this angwysse
1225 In darknes schalt thu ever bee,
For lyghtnes schalt thu never see,
Trust thu not helpe to have,
For noo mercy schall thee save.
Wrechyd gost, we schull thee lede
1230 To Hell gatys for thi mysdede,
For in thi lyffe thu bare thee ylle
And wroghttust all ageyn Goddus wyll.
Wherfor we wyll thee with us bere
Too Satanas owre mastere,
1235 That lythe depe in tho pytt of Helle,   *lies*
And with hym schalt thu ther dwelle.

He gaffe thee full evyll reyd, *advice*
That broght thee heddur to this steyd. *hither*
Ovur late to com woll hym falle *Too late*
1240 To delyver thee from us alle.
But now sykyr may thu bee *certain*
That thu schalt nevur more hym see."
The wykkyd gostus togedyr spake
And seyd, "This sowle wolle we take.
1245 To Satanas cast we hym, that grymly groonus. *groans*
He schalle hym swolow all attoonus."
They brawneschedyn hym and manast fast *threatened; menaced hard*
To Sathanas that sowle to cast.
Ther he lay depe in Helle pytte.
1250 Thydour they saydon thei wold hym flytte. *thrust*
A hydous noyse the fendys made.
Hor eyn wer brannand and brade; *Their eyes; burning; broad*
As brennand lampus glowand they ware. *lamps*
Full grymly con they on hym stare.
1255 Hor teyt wer blacke, scharpe, and long. *Their teeth*
With tuskus both grett and strong,
Her bodyus wer lyke dragonys;
Hor tayles wer lyke schorpyonys. *scorpions*
They had naylys on her krocus, *crooks*
1260 That wer lyke ankyr hokys *anchor hooks*
As they wer made all of stele; *steel*
The poyntus wer full scharpe to fele.
They had wyngus long and brade;
As backe wyngus wer thei made. *bat's wings*
1265 Whedur they wold, low or hye,
With hor wyngus myght they flye.
They grennyd on hym and bleryd here yye. *snarled; stuck out their eyes*
That wondur hit was that he dyd not dye.
Then com the angyll that hym ladde;
1270 Tho fendys than fast away fledde.
"Tundale," he seyd, "thu wer full radde. *frightened*
Now may thu make joy and be glad.
Thow was the sone of peyn full ryght, *son*
And now thu art the sone of lyght. *son*
1275 For now forward sycur thu bee; *safe*

224

Goddus marcy schall helpe thee.

God hathe thee grantyd, thu mayst be feyn, *glad*

That thu schalt fele noo more payn,

But Y woll well that thu wette *know*

1280 Moo peynus schalt thu see yette.

Com foryt with me smertly; *forth; quickly*

Y schall thee schew thi most enmy *greatest enemy*

To monkynd that ever was,

That tysus al men to trespas." *entices*

1285 A lytull furdurmore they yode, *went*

And sone at Hell gatus thei stode.

Ther Tundale saw a greyt pytte,

That all this world myght not hit dytte. *fill up*

"Com hydour," quod the angyll bryght.

1290 "Thu schalt here see an hydous syght.

Stond ner this pytte, and loke adon.

Thu schalt see her an hydous demon.

That pytte is ay darke as nyght

And ever schall be withowttyn lyght.

1295 Bothe fendys and sowlys, that therin is,

Thu schalt see bothe more and lesse.

And Satanas, that lythe bound in Helle grond,

Thu schalt hym see in a lytull stond. *while*

But they schall soo ywrekyd bee *compelled*

1300 That non of hem schall see thee."

Tundale than to the pytte wentt

Throw the angyll commandmentte.

He lokyd don with grett aw.

Sathanas at the grond he saw.

1305 So ugly was that loghtly wyght *loathsome*

Nevur ar was seyn so hydous a syght. *before*

And so orybly he fard, *horribly*

And such dull he saw ther and hard, *dole; heard*

That yeffe a mon had varely *if; truly*

1310 An hundryd hedys on won body

And as mony mowthus withall,

As to yche hed schuld falle, *belong*

And yche a mowthe above the chyn

Had an hundryd tongys within,

1315	And ylke a tong cowthe all the wytte	*each; knew; learning*
	That all men have that lyvythe yette,	
	All wer not ynow to tell	*enough*
	The peyn that he saw in the pytte of Hell.	
	But Tundale toke full gud kepe	*paid close attention*
1320	On Satanas, that lay soo depe,	
	And avysede hym of that syght	*considered*
	On what maner he myght dyscrivyn hit aryght.	*describe*
	He cowthe not wetton, he was so grym,	*tell*
	In what maner he myght dyscryvyn hym.	
1325	Hym thoght he was as grett to know	*horrible*
	As any best that ever he saw.	
	His body was bothe brood and thykke,	
	And as blakke as ever was pykke.	*pitch*
	So blakk was non, as hym semyd than.	
1330	Hym thoght he had the schappe of a mon.	*shape*
	He was bothe grett and strong	
	And of an hundryt cubytes long.	*cubits*
	Twenty cubytes was he brad,	
	And ten of thyknes was he mad.	
1335	And when he gaput, or when he gonus,	*gapes; opens his mouth wide*
	A thowsand sowlys he swoluwys attonus.	*at once*
	Byfor and behynd hym was kende	*seen*
	On his body a thowsand hande.	
	And on ylke a honde was ther seyn	
1340	Twenty fyngrys with nayles keyn,	*sharp*
	And ylke a fyngur semud than	*finger seemed*
	The leynthe of an hundryt sponne	*span*
	And ten sponne abowt of thyknes;	
	Ylke a fyngur was no les.	
1345	Hys nayles semyd of yron strong.	
	Full scharpe they wer and full long,	
	Lengur than evur was spere of werre,	*war*
	That armyd men wer wont to berre.	
	Mony teght he had that was so wondur.	*teeth*
1350	With hom he gnew sowlys insondur.	*gnawed*
	He had a muche long snowt,	*nose*
	That was ful large and brod abowt.	
	And hys mowthe was full wyde	

With hongyng lyppus on eyther syde.   *hanging lips*
1355   Hys tayle was greyt and of gret lenthe,
And in hit had he full gret strynthe.
With scharpe hokys that in is tayle stykythe
The sowlys therwith sore he prekydthe.   *pricked*
Apon a gredyron full hot glowand   *gridiron*
1360   That fowle fende was ay lyggand.   *lying*
Brennand colys lay ay undur,   *coals*
But they wer dym, and that was wondur,
Many fendys as gloand folus,   *fiery imps*
With balys blowyng ay at tho colys.   *bellows*
1365   So many a sowle abowt hym flow,
In myddys the fyr and in the low,   *flame*
That Tundale had full gret farly   *wonder*
How the world myght bryng forthe so many.
Satanas, that is soo grym,
1370   Lay ther bondon yche a lym.   *bound*
With yron cheynus gret and strong   *chains*
On that gredyron that was so long.
As Tundale thoght, the cheynus was
Lappud abowt with walland bras   *Surrounded; boiling brass*
1375   And the sowlys that he hent   *seized*
With hys hondes wer all torent.   *torn to pieces*
He thrast hom insondur, as men dos
Grapbys, thrastyng owt the wos.   *Grapes, pressing; juice*
When he had grond hom alle
1380   Into the fyr he lette hom falle.
And yeyt they kevered all ageyn,   *recovered*
And ever putte to new peyn.
Tundale hard and saw allsoo
How Satanas gronod for woo,   *groaned*
1385   Forwhy that he was bond so fast.   *Because*
At ylke a sykyng he con owt cast
A thowsand sowlys; from hym they flow
Owt at his mowthe into the low.   *flame*
They wer sone scateryd wyde   *scattered*
1390   Abowt hym ther on ylke a syde.
But that peyn was not ynow.
When he ageyn his ande drow,   *breath*

227

	Alle the sowlys he cast owt,	
	That wer yscateryd rond abowt,	
1395	He swalowyd hom ageyn ychon	
	With smoke of pycche and of brymston.	
	The sowlys that passyd owt of hys hond	
	Fellon into the fyr and brand.	
	When thei ageyn keveryd wor,	*recovered were*
1400	With his tayle he smot hom sore.	
	Thus peynyd he tho sowlys and dud hom woo	
	And hymselfe was peynyd allsoo.	
	The more peyn that he thare wroght	
	To tho sowlys that thydur were broght,	
1405	The more peyn his owne was,	
	And fro that peyn may he not passe.	
	The angyll seyd to Tundale,	
	"Here may thu see muche bale.	
	Satanas," he seyd, "this ugly wyght	
1410	That semyth soo muche unto thy syght,	
	He was the furst creature	*first*
	That God made aftur His fygure.	*likeness*
	Fro Hevon throw pryd he fell adon	
	Hydour into this depe donjon.	*dungeon*
1415	Here ys he bounde, as thu may see,	
	And schall tyll Domusday bee.	*Doomsday (Judgment Day)*
	For yeffe they faylyd, that hym schuld hold,	
	Heyvon and erthe trobull he wold.	*trouble*
	Of tho that thu mayst see with hym,	
1420	Sum they ar of Adames kyn	
	And odur angells, as Y thee telle,	
	That owt of Hevon with hym felle.	
	Ther ys neydur sowle ne fend,	
	But they ar dampnyd withowttyn ende.	
1425	And mony mo hydur schulle come	
	Or that hyt bee the Day of Dome,	*Judgment Day*
	That forsakyth Goddus law	
	And Hys warkys wyll not know,	*works*
	Bothe lewyd men and clarkys,	*clerks*
1430	That lovyth synne and cursyd warkys.	
	Thesse sowlys, that thu hast here yseyn,	

228

In all the peynus they have beyn.
Now ar they cast on this manere
To Satanas to thole peyne here.   *endure*
1435   And whosoo is broght to thys kare   *grief*
☞   Schall dwelle therin forevermare.   *(see note)*
Men that ar of muche myght,
That don to pore men wrong and unryght,
And woll algate fulfylle hor wyll,   *always*
1440   Whedur hyt be gud or ylle,
And streyn the pore, that ar lesse,   *distress*
Thei aron prynces of wykydnes.   *are*
In strong turment schull thei bee
With fendys, that have of hom posté."   *over them power*
1445   Tundale seyd to the angyll sone,
"Syr, Goddus wylle behovys to be don,   *must*
But o thyng wolld Y fayne lere.   *like to learn*
Why gevyth not God suche power
Too all they that aron hold gud men,
1450   That throw ryght wollyn odur ken,   *through good others will learn*
As He dothe wykkyd men tylle
That evermore wykkydnes wyll fullefyll?"
The angyll seyd that, "Sumtyme lettus   *allows*
The wykkydnes of suggettus   *subjects*
1455   That wolle not be reulyd welle,   *ruled*
Therfor gret peynus behovus hom to fele,
And for sumtyme God wolle noght
That the gud men of this world wer broght
To over muche worldys guddus havyng,
1460   Lest here tyme of gudnes thei wold lesyng.   *lose*
Thes fowle kaytyf, for all his myght,   *This foul wretch*
His not callyd prynse of ryght,
But hys men mey hym calle
Cheffe of markenes and pryncypalle   *Chief; darkness; principal*
1465   All theys peynus that thu hast sene,
To reckyn hom all bedene,   *together*
That ordeynyd ben for monnus mysse,   *man's sin*
Ar but lytyll to the regard of thys."   *with regard to*
"Sartus," quod Tundale, "ye say well.   *Surely*
1470   Y have more dred now as Y fele,

229

Of this syght and more awe
Then of all the peyn that evur Y sawe.
Therfore, Y pray yow that ye me lede
Fro this syght and fro thys drede.
1475   Sum felows have Y here ysee
That sumtyme with me prevey have bee.   *close*
Now is hor wonnyng here full depe;   *dwelling*
Y cleyn forsake hor felyschepe.
And to that had Y ben worthy
1480   Ner that Jesu on me had mercy;   *Unless*
To that same peyn schuld Y have goo
And dwellyd therin forevur and oo."   *always*
This worde the angyll hard, that ther stood,
And spake to hym with myld mod,
1485   "A blessyd sowle Y may thee calle,
For thu art passyd thy peynus all.
And all the syghttus that thee have deyred,   *suffered*
Therof now thar thee never be aferd.
Thu hast now seyn in sorow and stryffe
1490   Men that wer of wykyd lyffe.
And now schalt thu see that blysse
That God hathe holy choson for Hys,
And therfor glad may thu be.
Cum now forthe and folow me."

Primum Gaudium

1495   Tundale dyd hys commandment
And with the angyll forthe he went.
Sone wax hit bryght as the day,   *grew*
And the darkenes was sone away,
And the drede that Tundale hadde
1500   Was awey; than was he glad.
Sone he thonkyd God of Hys grace
And folowyd forthe the angylls trace.
By that they hadon gon a lytull stonde.
They saw a walle was feyr and rounde.   *fair*
1505   Full hye hit was, as Tundale thoght;

But sone within the angyll hym broght.
Men and wemen saw he thare
That semud full of sorow and care,
For they had bothe hongur and thurst
1510 And grett travell withowttyn rest.   *travail*
Gret cold they hadon alsoo,
That dudde hom sorow and made hom woo.
Hem wantedyn clothys and foode;   *They lacked*
As dowmpe bestys, nakyd they yode.   *dumb; went*
1515 Her penanse was hard to see,
But lyght they had grett plenté.
"Thys folke," quod the angyll, "aryn all save,
But penance yett behovys hom to have.
All leved they well in honesté,   *lived*
1520 Yette grevyd they God in sum parté.
Honestely and well wold they leve,
But ovur lytull gud wold they geve,
Nowdur to clothe nor to fede
The powre men that had gret nede.
1525 Therfor wolle God sumtyme that they had peyn,
Thoro wykyd stormus of wynd and reyn,   *rain*
And throw greyt hongur and thurst
But aftur He woll that they com to rest."
The angyll wold noo more say,
1530 But went forght fast upon his way,   *forth*
And Tundale folowd aftur fast.
They come to a gate at the last.
That gate was openyd hom ageyn,
And in they went. Tundale was fayn.   *glad*
1535 A feld was ther of feyr flowrys   *field; fair*
And hewyd aftur all kyn colowrys.   *hued; kind of colors*
Of how com a swete smylle,   *smell*
Swettur than any tong may telle.
That plase was soo clere and soo bryght
1540 Tundale was joyfull of that syght;
Full clerly ther schon the sonne
That well was hym that ther myght wonne.   *live*
Mony feyr treus in that place stood   *trees*
With all kynnus fruyt that was gud.   *types of*

231

1545	That Tundale hard ther ay amonge	
	Full swet noyse of fowlys song.	*birds'*
	Full mekyl folke ther was seen	*many folk*
	That of all kynne syn wer mad clene	*kind of sin*
	And delyvered owt of all kyn peyn.	
1550	They wer joyfull and full feyn.	
	In myddys that plase was a welle,	
	The feyryst that any mon might of telle.	
	From that ran mony stremus sere	*streams various*
	Of watur, that was both feyre and clere.	
1555	Tundale thoght ther joy ynooghe.	*enough*
	He spake to the angyll and looghe.	*laughed*
	"Lord," he seyd, "here is greyt solace.	
	Leyt us never wynde from this place."	*depart*
	The angyll seyd, "Hit beys not soo.	*It may not be so*
1560	Furdurmore behovus hus to goo.	*us*
	The sowlys that thu syst here within	*see*
	Han ben in peyn for hor syn,	
	But they ar clansyd throw Goddus grace	
	And dwellon here now in this place.	
1565	But yett hennus may they noghyt	*hence*
	To the blysse of Hevon to be broght.	
	Thawye they ben clansyn of all ylle,	*Though*
	Here mot thei abydon Goddus wylle.	*await*
	The well that thu hast seyn here,	
1570	With the watur that spryngus soo clere,	
	Ys callyd be scylle the well of lyfe.	*by reason*
	The name of that welle is full ryfe.	*well-known*
	Whosoo drynkyth of hit ryght weyll,	
	Hongur schall he never yfeyll.	
1575	Ne thrust schall he neyvermare,	*thirst*
	But lykyng have withowttyn care.	*pleasure*
	Yeffe he wer old, withowttyn peyn	
	Hyt wold make hym yong ageyn."	

II Gaudium

	Yett fordurmore the angyll yede,	*went*
1580	And Tundale folowyd with gud spede.	
	Sone then aftur, as they went,	
	He beheld and toke gud tent	*paid attention*
	Tyll a plas wer they schuld passe,	
	Wer mony a lewde mon wasse.	*ordinary man*
1585	Tundale hade seyn sum of hom are	*before*
	And knew full weyll what thei ware.	
	Among hom too kynggus saw hee,	*two kings*
	That wer sumtyme of greyt posté.	*power*
	Tho whyle they lewyd on bon and blod,	*lived in bone and blood*
1590	Bothe they wer men of truthe full gudd.	
	The ton of hom Cantaber hyght;	*The one of them; was called*
	That todur was callyd Donatus ryght.	*The other*
	Then Tundale spake to the angyll free,	
	"Lord," he seyd, "what may thys bee?	
1595	These too kynggus, that Y see here,	
	They wer men of greyt powere.	
	They wer bothe stowt and kene.	*staunch; brave*
	In hom was lytull mercy aseen.	*them*
	Aydur of hem hatyd odur,	*Each; hated the other*
1600	As cursyd Caym and his brodur.	
	Sertus, syr, me thenkyth ferly,	*Certainly; a wonder*
	How they myght be so worthyly	
	To come to thys joyfull stedde.	
	Me thynkyght they wer worthy to be dedde."	
1605	The angyll thoght hyt gret nede	
	To bryng hym owt of that drede	
	And seyd, "Thu schald wytte why	
	That God of hom hathe marcy.	
	Byfor hor deythe ther fylle suche schanse	*chance*
1610	That they had verey repentanse.	*true repentance*
	For Cantaber, when he felle seke,	
	To God con he hys hart meke.	*he was able to make his heart receptive*
	He made a vow with delfull cry	
	To yeld hymselfe to God allmyghtty	
1615	And all hys lyffe in penans to bee	

When he wore hole and had posté.   *healthy; power*
Donatus was in a preson strong;   *prison*
Beefor hys dethe ther was he long.
All hys guddus gaffe he away   *goods gave*
1620 To pore men for hym to pray.
In grett pevertté was he withstadde,   *poverty; placed*
And in preson hys lyffe he ladde.
Yeffe all they wer kynggys of myghtt,   *Even though*
Yette they dyodon in povertté dyghtt.   *died; set*
1625 Therfor God wold not hom forsake,
But to Hys blysse He wold hom take.
Of all hor synnus they con hom scryve,   *confess*
Therfor marcy behovus hom have."   *mercy*
Full mekyll joy saw Tundale thare,
1630 But yett went they bothe furdurmare.
They saw an halle was rychely dyght;   *decorated*
Tundale saw never so feyr a syght.
The wallys semyd gold of that hows
Full well ysett with stonus full precyous.   *stones; precious*
1635 The rofe semyd of carbunkyll ston.   *roof; carbuncle*
Dorrus nor wyndows was ther non,   *Doors*
But mony entrys and thei wer wyde,   *entries*
That stodon ay opon on every syde,
For all tho that wold in passe
1640 Was non lattyd that ther was.   *prevented*
Hyt semyd as bryght, bothe far and ner,
As evur was sonne that schon here,
Large and round were the wonys.   *rooms*
The flore was paved with precyous stonus.
1645 The halle was withowtton post.   *column*
Hyt semyd an hows of gret cost.
Hyt schon within and withowtte.
Tundale lokyd over all abowtte.
He saw a seyt ryche aparalyt,   *seat richly adorned*
1650 Of red gold fynly ennamelyd   *finely decorated*
Clothus of gold and sylke gret plenté
Saw he ysprad apon that seytté.   *spread; seat*
He saw sytte on that seytt
Kyng Cormake, that was full greytt.

1655	Hys clothyng was of ryche hew.	
	Tundale full well that kyng knew.	
	Meche pepull to hym soghtt,	
	And ryche gefftus they hym broghtt.	*gifts*
	Befor hym stodde they full gladde,	
1660	And muche joy of hym thei made.	
	Tundale stood ner and toke gud kepe,	*paid attention*
	And byheld that grett worchepe	
	Tho men to Kyng Cormake thus dydde,	
	That sumtyme was hys lord kydde.	*known*
1665	For he was sumtyme with hym of meyné,	*company*
	Therfore farly of that syght had hee.	*wonder*
	Prestus and deykenus come ther mony;	*Priests; deacons*
	Befor hym a greyt company	
	All revescyd, as they schuld syng Mas	*vested; Mass*
1670	With ryche clothus of holynes.	
	That halle was seytte, within and withowtte,	
	With greytt rychesse all abowtte,	
	With cowpus and chalys rychely dyghtt,	*cups; chalices*
	With sensowrys of selver and gold bryghtt,	*censers; silver*
1675	With basseynus of gold fayr and seemly,	*basins*
	And with tabyllys peyntyd rychely.	*tables*
	Tundale thoght, yeffe he had no mare	
	But that joy, thatt he saw thare,	
	He had of joy greytt plentté,	
1680	So greyt murthe and joy ther saw hee.	
	They knelyd befor that kyng alle,	
	Tho folke that comyn into the halle,	
	And seyd, "Weyll is thee on yche a syde,	
	And weyll thee mott evur betyde.	
1685	For tho warkys of thi hondys free	
	We have now presented here to thee."	
	Then spake Tundale to the angyll bryght,	
	For he was amerveld of that syght,	*amazed*
	And seyd, "Of all tho that Y here see,	
1690	Non hym servyd in lege posté,	*as a vassal*
	Therfor grett farly have Y here	*wonder*
	That they hym worscheppe on this manere."	
	Then answerd the angyll curtesly	

And seyd to hym, "Well wott Y
1695 That of all tho that thu may see
Was nevur non of hys meyné,   *company*
But sum wer pore pylgrimus kyd   *known*
Too whom oft hys charyté he dyd,
And sum wer men of Holy Chyrche,
1700 To hold hom was he nevur yrke.   *support; unwilling*
Therfor wold God, full of myght,
That hyt be yold throw hor hondus ryght."[1]
"Syr," quod Tundale, "haght he no turment   *had*
Sothen that he owt of the world went?"   *Since*
1705 Then answerd the angyll ageyn
And seyd, "He sufforyd mony a peyn,
And in more turment schall he bee.
Thu schalt abyde and the sothe ysee."
Anon the hows wax darke as nyght,   *grew*
1710 That before was clere and bryght.
And all the men that therin wer,
They laft hor servyse and dyd no more.
The kyng turnyd then from hys seyt.
He grevde, he gowlyd, hys dull was gret.   *wailed; dole (sorrow)*
1715 Tundale folowyd aftur sone
To wytte wat schuld be with hym ydone.   *know*
He saw mony men sytte kneland,   *kneeling*
With hor hondys up to God prayand,   *praying*
And seyd, "Gud lord, and Thi wyll hit bee,
1720 Have mercy on hym and pyté."
Then saw he hym in gret bareyt   *distress*
And in a fyr to the navylle yseytt   *navel*
And above from the navyll upward
Clothed with an hayre scharpe and hard.   *hairshirt*
1725 "This peyn," quod the angyll, "behovyth hym to have
Yche a day onus, as God vochesave,   *once; grants*
Forwhy he kept hym not clene   *Because; pure*
Fro that tyme that he weddyd had bene,
And also he breke hys othe   *broke; oath*

---

[1] *That it (i.e., fealty) be yielded by their right hands*

1730	That he had made to wedlocke bothe.	
	Yche day by ryght he brent schall bee,	
	Sette unto the navyll, as thu myght see,	
	And forwhy that he commandyd to sloo	*because; to be killed*
	An erle that he hatyd as his foo,	*earl*
1735	That was slayn for hatered	
	Besyde Seynt Patrycke in that sted.	*place*
	Therfor he tholuth, as thu wottus wele,	*suffers; understand*
	This hayre that is full hard to fele,	*hairshirt*
	That grevys hym wher the knottus lyes	
1740	And dothe hym full grett angwys.	
	Of all odur peyn is he qwytte	
	Save of these too, as thu mayst wytte."	*two*
	Then seyd Tundale anon ryght thus,	
	"How longe schall he suffor thys?"	
1745	The angyll seyd, "Ilke a day owrys three	*hours*
	This grett peyn sufferyn schall hee,	
	And the space of won and twenty owrys	
	He schall have joy and gret honowrys."	
	And with that the angyll went furdurmore	
1750	Too odur blyssys that was thore.	*there*

III Gaudium

	Sone they saw thro syght of yye	*eye*
	A wall that was wondur hye,	
	All of bryght sylver all to see,	
	But hit had no yatys nor entré.	
1755	Within that wall they wer sone togedur,	
	But he west not how they com thydur.	
	Ther they fwond a full delyttabull place	*found; delightful*
	That was fulle of murthe and solace.	
	Tundale lokyd abowtte hym thanne	
1760	And saw mony a mon and woman	
	Synggand ay so muryly	*Singing*
	And makand joy and melody.	*making*
	Ther they honowryd God allweldand	*all-ruling*
	And pleydon and song to not cessand,	*played; ceasing*

237

1765	"Blysse be to God of myghttus most,	
	Fadur and Son and Holy Gost."	
	Hor clothus wer precyows and new,	
	As whytte as snow that ever dyd snew.	*snowed*
	They wer joyfull and blythe ynogh	*happy*
1770	And song and made myrthe and logh.	*laughed*
	They lovyd God in Trynité,	
	Nott cessand of that solemnyté,	*ceasing; celebration*
	And ay as they wer syngand	*always*
	Her vocys was ever acordant,	*voices; harmonious*
1775	As melodyes of musyk clere,	
	That full delectabull was to here.	
	Ther was gret swetnes and lykyng	
	And joy and murthe withowttyn sesynge,	*ceasing*
	Honesté, beawtté, and clennes,	*beauty; purity*
1780	And helthe withowttyn sekenes.	*sickness*
	They weron all off wylle free	
	In parfyte love and charyté.	
	The swette savour that ther was	*savor*
	All the swetnes of eyrthe dud it passe.	
1785	"This joy," quod the angyll bryght,	
	"Hathe God ordeynyd for weddyd men ryght	
	That levon in cleyne maryage	*pure*
	And keputhe hor bodys from owttrage,	*keep; outrage*
	And for hom that hor guddys gevyn	
1790	Too the pore that in myscheff levyn,	*distress*
	And for hom that techon dylygenly	*teach*
	Hor sogettus to lovyn God allmyghty	*subjects*
	And chastyn hom aftur hor myght	*chastise*
	When they don wrong and lyffe not right,	
1795	And for hom that Holy Chyrche honowrys	
	And mayntenyth hom and sockors.	*succors*
	For thoo that don wylle schall at gret Dom here	*well; Judgment*
	The voys of God that woll say, 'Com neer	
	My Fadur, blessyd chyldyr free,	*children*
1800	And receyve My kyndam with Mee	*kingdom*
	Ordeynyd and dyght for man	
	Seythyn the tyme that the word began.'"	
	Tundale prayd with gud wylle	

The angell that he myght dwell stylle.

1805   The angell gaff hym noo onswer,
For he wold not doo hys prayer.

IV Gaudium

Furdurmore yett then went thay,
Withowttyn travayll or peyn, her way,   *travail*
And ylkon, as they went abowte,
1810   Come to Tundale and to hym dyd lowtte   *bow*
And haylsyd hym and callyd hym ryght   *greeted*
By hys name, as he hyght.
They made gret joy at is metyng,
For they wer fayn of his commyng
1815   And thonkyd God allmyghtty,
That hym delyvered thoro Hys mercy,
And seydon. "Honour and lovyng myght bee
To the Lord of blys and pyté,   *bliss and pity (compassion)*
That wold not the deythe of synfull men,   *does not want*
1820   But that they turne and leve ageyn;   *Unless; live*
And throw Is mercy wold ordeyn   *His*
Too delyver this sowle from Helle peyn
And wold bryng hym thus gracyously
Among this holy company."

V Gaudium

1825   The angell and Tundale yett furdur went,
And Tundale lokyd and toke gud tent.
They saw a walle, as they schuld passe,
Well herre than that todur wasse;   *higher*
That wall semyd to Tundale syghtt
1830   As hyt wer all of gold bryght,
That was schynand and more clere
Than ever was gold in this world here.
Tundale thoght more joy of that walle
To behold, that bryght metalle,

239

1835	Then hym thoght of the solemnyté	*celebration*
	And of the joy that he had see.	
	Within that wall come they sone,	
	As they hadon erward done.	*before*
	Tundale beheld that place thare.	
1840	So fayr a plas saw he never are,	*before*
	Ne he, ne noo eyrthely mon,	*Neither he, nor any earthly man*
	As that was, that he saw anon.	
	Therin saw he, as hym thoght	
	Mony a trone all of gold wroght	*throne*
1845	And of precyous stonus seer,	*various*
	That wer sette ther on dyverse manere.	
	With ryche clothus wer they kevered ychon,	*covered*
	So ryche was ther, eyr never see he non.	
	Holy men and wemen bothe	
1850	Saten in hom, clad in ryche clothe.	
	He saw abowt hom in that tyde	
	Fayr honourmentys on yche a syde.	*ornaments*
	All that he saw wer full bryghtt.	
	Tundale saw never suche a syght.	
1855	Ne noo hert myght thynke of eyrthely man	
	Soo fayr a syghtte, as saw he than.	
	Tho greytt bryghtnes of Goddus face	
	Schon among hom in that place.	
	That bryghtnes schon more cleer	
1860	Then ever schon any sonne here.	
	Allwey hit was fayr and schyre	*shining*
	And semyd as hyt had ben gold wyr.	*wire*
	Crownus on hor heddus they had ychon	
	Of gold with mony a prescyous ston,	
1865	Of grett vertu and dyvers colowrys.	*value; various colors*
	They semyd all kyngys and emperowrys.	
	Soo feyr crownus, as ther was seen,	
	In this world weron kyng ne qwene.	
	Lectornes he saw befor hem stande	*Lecterns*
1870	Of gold, and bokys on hem lyggande,	*books; lying*
	And all the lettornes that he saw thare	*lecterns*
	Wer made of gold, bothe lasse and mare.	
	They song all ther with myld chere,	

"Aleluya" with vocys soo clere.

1875 Hym thoght they song so swete and clene
Hyt passyd all the joyes that he had seen,
And soo mykyll joy had he of that
That all odur joyes he forgatte.
"These men," quod the angell bryght.

1880 "Ar holy men that God loyvyd ryght,
That for Goddus love wer buxum   *ready*
In eyrthe to thole martyrdum,   *suffer martyrdom*
And that waschyd hor stolys in the blod   *washed their robes*
Of the lombe wyt myld mod,   *lamb*

1885 And had laft the world all holely
For to sarve God allmyghty
And to kepe hor boddys ay fre
Fro lechery to chastyté.
And they lovyd soburnes ay   *sobriety*

1890 And wold not lye, but sothe to say.   *truth*
Therfor they ar to God full dere,
As hys darlyngys that bee thus here."
Among all that joy and solas
Tundale lokyd and saw a plas

1895 Full of pavelons schynand;   *pavilions*
Soo fayr wer never non seyn in land.   *seen*
They wer keveryd with purpull and grys,
That wer full ryche and grett of pryse,
The whylk was oversette and dyght   *which; covered; decorated*

1900 With besantes of gold and selver bryght,   *coins*
And all odur thyngus of beawté
That hart myght thynke or eyne myght see.
The cordys therof wer bryght and new.   *binding cords*
They wer of sylke and of rych hew.

1905 They wer all with sylver twynud   *entwined*
And freyt with gold, that bryght scheynod.   *fretted; shone*
On tho cordys wer instrumentus seer   *instruments various*
Of musykys that hadon swette sond and clere,   *music; sound*
Orgons, symbals, and tympanys,   *Organs, cymbals; drums*

1910 And harpus that ronge all at onys;   *harps; once*
They geve a full delectabull sond,
Bothe trebull and meyne and burdown,   *treble; mean; bass*

And odur instrumentus full mony
That madon a full swette melody.

1915 All maner of musyk was ther hard thanne.
Soo muche in eyrthe hard never no manne,
Not by an hundrythe thowsand part,
As this was to any monnus regarde.
Within the ryche pavelons, whyte schynande, *pavilions*
1920 Ay mekyll folke wer syngande *many folk*
Full swetly with a mery stevon, *sound*
With all maner of musyk accordant eyvon. *harmonious*
So muche myrthe as thei made within,
No wordlyche wytte may ymagyn. *worldly*
1925 Tundale thoght that all the blys
That evur he had seyn was not to thys.
Then spake the angyll with myld chere
Unto that sowle on thys manere.
"These folke," he seyd, "that murthe makyth thus,
1930 They wer gud relygyous,
As frerus, monkys, nonnus, and channonus,
That welle heldon hor proffessyonnus. *vows*
The wyche to God wer beysy ay, *busy*
Too serve hym bothe nyght and dey,
1935 Bothe blythelyche and with gud wyll *happily*
Hys commandementys to fullfylle,
And lovyd ay God in hor lyfe here
And to Hym ever obeydyand were, *obedient*
And putte hom with clene conscyons *conscience*
1940 Undur the rewle of obeedyons, *obedience*
And to chast lyfe hom toke
And all hor fleschely wyll forsoke.
Thei hyldon sylens withowtton jangelyng *kept silence; chattering*
And best lovyd God over all thyng."
1945 "Syr," seyd Tundale, "Y pray thee
Lett hus goo nerre, that Y may see *nearer*
The swete semland and feyr chere
Of the mury songus so schyll and clere." *resonant*
Then seyd the angell so feyr and bright,
1950 "Hereof thu schalt have a syght
Of hem, as thu hast mee besoghtte,

Butt entré to hom getust thu noght.   *them*
The syghtt," he seyd, "of the Trinyté
Schall not be schewyd unto thee.
1955   But this Y wolle thee schewe, that Y have hight.   *promised*
Thu schalt be unknowyn of that syght.   *ignorant*
For all they in worlde here,
That have bee borne and children were,
That throw Godus grace have ben gud in levyng,
1960   Ar now ordeynyd suche lykyng   *pleasure*
That here they schulle dwell ever for sothe
With all halows and with angells bothe;   *saints*
That in hor lyffe ay chast have bene
And levyd wylle, as vergynes clene,   *virgins*
1965   Thei schall ever thus joyfull bee,
For they seen ever God in Hys see."   *seat*

VI Gaudium

They went then forthe and fordurmore
By a fayr way that they in wore.
Full greyt plenté then saw thay
1970   Of men and wemmen by that way
That semyd all as angells bryght;
Soo feyr they semyd to hor syght.
Ther was soo swete savour and smyll,   *smell*
That noo hart myght thenke, ne tong telle,
1975   And swete voyse and melody
Was among that company
That made Tundale forgette clene
All odur joyes that he had seyn.
For all maner instrumentys seer   *diverse*
1980   Of musyk that wer swete and clere
Gaffe ther sown and wer ryngand   *sound*
Withhowttyn towchyng of monnus hand.
And the vocys of spyrytus thare   *spirits*
Passyd all joyes that ther ware
1985   And made joy and wer gladde
And non of hom travell hadde   *travail*

243

	Hor lyppus wer not mevand,	*lips; moving*
	Ne made no contynanse with hand.	*gesture*
	The instrumentys rong ther full schryll,	*clearly*
1990	And noo travaylle was don thertyll.	
	All maner of sownd was therin,	
	That hart myght thynke or ymagyn.	
	Fro tho fyrmament above hor hedde	
	Com mony bryght beymus into that sted,	*beams*
1995	Fro the wyche hyng chynus of dyvers fold	*chains*
	Schynand full bryght of fyn gold.	
	They hongyd full thycke on ylke a party	*each part*
	And annamelyd wondur rychely.	*decorated*
	All wer they joynyd and fastenyd ryght	
2000	In yardys of selver full gayly dyght,	*rods*
	That hongud up full hye in the eyre.	*air*
	Ther was noo eyrthely lyght never soo feyre.	
	Among them hong greyt plenté	
	Of ryche jowellys and of greyt beawtté,	*jewels*
2005	Fyollys and cowpus of greytt prysse,	*Bowls; cups; price*
	Symbals of sylver and flowre delyce	*Chimes (Cymbals); fleur-de-lis*
	With bellys of gold that mery rong,	
	And angellys flewyn ay among	
	With whyngus of gold schynand bryght.	*wings*
2010	Noo eyrthely mon saw ever seche syght	
	As the angels that flewyn in the eyre	
	Among the beymus that wer soo feyre.	
	Ther was suche joy melody and ryngyng,	*joyous*
	And suche murthe and such syngyng	
2015	And suche a syghtt of rychesse,	
	That all this world might hit not gesse,	
	Nor all the wyttus that ever wer sey	*wits*
	Cowthe hyt never halfe dyscry.	*describe*
	Tundale ever grett delyte had	
2020	Of that myrthe and joye that was soo glad,	
	That he wold never have gon away,	
	But ther have ydwellyd forever and ay.	
	Then spake the angell with myld mod	
	Unto Tundale ther he stode.	
2025	"Cum now," he seyd, "hedur to mee."	

Anon he come and saw a tree,
That wonderly mykyll was and hye.
Suche on saw he never with yye.   *a one*
Grett and hye that tre was,
2030   And brod and round all of compas,
Chargytt on yche a syde full evon   *Laden*
With all kyn frytte that mon myght nemon,   *kinds of fruit; name*
That full delycyous was to fele,
With all kyn flowres that savoryd wele,
2035   Of dyverse kynd and seer hew: *various*
Sum wyte, sum reede, sum yolow, sum blew.
And all maner erbys of vartu   *herbs (plants); power*
And of every spyce of valew,   *value*
That feyr was and swette smylland,   *smelling*
2040   Growyd ther and wer floryschand.
Mony fowlys of dyverse colowrys   *birds*
Seyt among tho fruyt and the flowrys
On the branchus syngant so meryly
And madon dyverse melody,
2045   Ylkeon of hom on hys best manere.   *Each one*
That song was joyfull for to here.
Tundale lystenyd fast and logh   *attentively; laughed*
And thoght that was joy ynoghe.
He saw undur that ylke tree,
2050   Wonand in cellys, gret plenté   *Living; cells*
Of men and wemen schynand bryght
As gold, with all ryches dyght.   *arrayed*
They loved God with gret talent   *desire*
Of the gyftus that He had hem sent.   *For the gifts*
2055   Ychon had on hys hed a crowne
Off gold that was of semyly faschyon,
All sett abowtte on seyrwyse   *in various ways*
With precyous stonus of full gret prise,
And septurus in ther hand they had.   *scepters*
2060   With gold they wer full rychely clad,
With bryght clothus of ryche hew,
As they wer kyngys crownyd new.
So rychely as they wer dyght   *arrayed*
Was never eyrthely mon of myght.

2065 Than spake the angell as swythe   *earnestly*
   To Tundale, that was bothe glad and blythe, *pleased*
   And seyd, "Thys tree, that thu myght see,
   To all Holy Chyrche may lykkynyd bee.
   And tho folke, that thu seyste here dwelle
2070 Undur tho tree in her scelle,   *cells*
   Tho ar men that throw devocyon
   Made howssus of relygyon   *houses*
   And susteynyd well Goddus servyse
   And fowndyd chyrchys and chantryse *founded; chantries*
2075 And mayntened the state of clargy   *clergy*
   And feffud Holy Chyrche rychely, *endowed (see note)*
   Bothe in londys and in rentys,
   With feyr and worchepfull honowrmentys *valuable ornaments*
   As they that the world forsoke
2080 And to clene relygyon hom toke;
   Therfor they ar, as thu myght see,
   All reynyng in won fraternyté   *reigning; one*
   And ay schull have rest and pes.
   And joy and blys that never schall ses." *cease*

VII Gaudium

2085 Noo lengur ther they stoode,
   But furdurmore yett thei yood.   *went*
   They saw anodur feyr wall stand
   Of greyt heyght, full bryght schynand.
   Passe that todur wer feyr ther they had ben, *Passing that other*
2090 But non so feyr as that was seen.
   Tundale beehyld hyt and abadde *hesitated*
   And avysud hym wharof hyt was made. *considered; how*
   Hee saw this wall, as hym thoght,
   All of precyous stonus wroght.
2095 Hit semyd that the stonus brand,
   So wer they of red-gold schynand.
   The stonus wer full whyte and clere;
   What stonus they wor ye schall here:
   Crystall that was white and clere, *crystal*

2100	Berell, cresolyte, and saphere,	*Beryl, chrysolite; sapphire*
	Emeraudus, dyamondus that men desyres,	*Emeralds, diamonds*
	Iacyntus, smaragdynes, and rubyes,	*Zircons, emeralds; rubies*
	Emastyce and charbokull allsoo,	*Bloodstones; carbuncle*
	Omacles and tapaces and odur moo.	*Onyx; topaz*
2105	Strong stonus of dyverse hew,	
	Suche saw he never, ne knew.	
	Thcn spake the angell so feyr and free,	
	"Tundale," he seyd, "cum up and see."	
	They clombon bothe up on that wall	
2110	And lokyd don and seyyn over all.	
	The greyt joy that they saw thare	
	Semyd a thowsand fold mare	
	Then all the joy that they had seyn	
	Ther, as they befour had beyn.	
2115	For noo wytte myght tell of monnus mowthe,	
	Passe he all the wytte of the world cowthe,	*Surpass*
	Ne hart myght thynke, ne eyr yhere,	*ear*
	Ne ee see wer hee never soo clere,	*eye*
	The joy that ther was and the blysse,	
2120	That God had ordeynyd for all Hysse.	
	They saw ther, as the story doghthe tell,	
	The nyne ordyrs of angell.	
	They schon as bryght as the sonne,	
	And holy spyrytus among hom wonne.	*lived*
2125	Prevey wordys they hard than,	*Secret*
	That fallyth to be schewyd to no man.	
	Then seyd the angell on this manere,	
	"Tundale, opon thyn eyrus and here,	*open; ears; hear*
	And that thu herust, thu not foryete,	*what you hear; forget*
2130	For in thi mynd loke thu hyt sett:	
	God, that ys withowttyn ende,	
	Wolle turne to thee and be thi frend.	
	Now see that here ys joy and blys,	
	That they that here aron schull never mysse."	
2135	Over that yett sew they moore	
	Among the angelles that ther wore.	
	They seen the Holy Trynyté,	
	God syttyng in Hys majesté.	

	They beheld fast His swette face,	
2140	That schon so bryght over all that place.	
	All the angells that ther were	
	Renne to behold Hys face so clere,	*Ran*
	For the bryghtnes and the bewté,	*beauty*
	That they in Hys face myght see,	
2145	Was seyvon sythus bryghttur to syght	*seven times*
	Then ever schon sonne, that was soo lyght;	
	The whyche syght is foode to angelles	
	And lyffe to spyrytus that ther dwelles.	
	In the styd wher they stode,	
2150	They saw all, bothe evyll and gud,	
	All the joy and the peyn beneythen	*beneath*
	That they had beforon yseyyene.	*seen*
	They saw allsoo all the world brad	
	And all the creaturys that God had mad.	
2155	Ther saw they the ordur, here as wee wonne,	*in which we live*
	In a bryght bem of the sonne.	*beam*
	Ther may nothyng in this world bee	
	Soo sotyll, nor so prevé,	*subtle; secret*
	But that he may see a party	*part*
2160	That hathe seyn God allmyghtty.	
	Tho eene that have seen Hym	
	Mow never be made blynd nor dym.	*May*
	Bot they had suche power and myght,	
	Ther they stodon on the walle bryght,	
2165	That they myght see at a syght clere	
	All thyng that was bothe far and nere.	
	Alle that was behynd hom at that tyde,	
	Byfor hom and on ylke a syde,	
	All at onus, in that bryght place	
2170	Was schewyd ther befor her face.	
	Of thyngys that Tundale had knowyng thare	
	Hyt was myster to have noo mare.	*needful*
	He knew wat thyng that he wold	
	Withowttyn any boke to be told.	
2175	As Tundale stod, he saw com thanne	
	Won that hyght Renodan	*One*
	That made joy and glad chere	

	And grett hym on fayr manere	*greeted*
	And toke hym in hys armus lovely	
2180	And schewyd hym love and curtesy.	
	And seyd as they stod togedur,	
	"Son, blessyd be thi comyng hydur.	
	Fro this tyme forward thu may have lykyng	*comfort*
	In the world to have gud endyng.	
2185	Y was sumtyme thy patron free	
	Too whom thu schulldust boxum bee.	*courteous*
	Thu art holdyn, as thu wost welle,	*bound*
	Too me namly on kneus to knele."	*knees to kneel*
	And when he had seyd thes wordys thare,	
2190	Hee lafft hys speche and spake noo mare.	
	Tundale loked with blythe chere	*happy*
	On ylke a syde, bothe farre and nere.	
	He saw Seynt Patryk of Yrland	
	Commyng in a bryght tyre schynand	*attire*
2195	And mony a byschop nobely dyghtt,	*dressed*
	Then had he grett joy of that syght.	
	They wer full of joy and lykyng	
	Withowttyn dele or any sykyng.	*sadness; sighing*
	Among that blessydfull company	
2200	He saw ther fowre byschopus namly	*bishops*
	That he knew be syght of semland,	*appearance*
	Whan he was in tho world dwelland.	
	They wer gud men and lyved with ryght,	
	And won of hom Celestyen hyght,	
2205	That was archebyschop of Armake	*Armagh*
	And muche gud dedde for Goddus sake.	
	And anodur hyght Malachye,	
	That come aftur hym full gracyouslye,	
	That Pwope Celestyen of hys grace	*Pope*
2210	Mad archebyschop of that place.	
	In hys lyfe he gaffe with hart glad	*gave*
	Too pore men all that he had.	
	He mad colagys and chyrchys mony,	*colleges*
	That nomburd wer to fowre and fowrty,	*numbered*
2215	Namely for men of relygyon	
	Too sarve God with devocyon.	

	He feffyd hem and ynoogh hem gaffe	*donated; enough; gave*
	All that was nedfull hom to hafe,	*have*
	Save that aght to hymselfe only,	*Except what was necessary to himself only*
2220	Hee laft hym noght to lyve by.	
	The thrydde of hom that he knew than	
	Hyght Crystyne, that was an holy man,	
	That was sumtyme byschop of Lyons	
	And lord of mony possessyons,	
2225	But hee was ay meke in hert,	
	Symplyst of wyll and povert.	*poor*
	He was Malachynus owne brodur;	
	Aydur of hom loved well oodur.	
	The fowrte of hom, that he ther knew,	
2230	Hyght Neomon, that was full trew	
	And ryghtwyse whyle he levyd bodyly,	*just*
	That sumtyme was byschop of Clemy	
	And passud all the todur thre	
	Of wytte and wysdam in his degré.	
2235	Tundale saw besyde hom stand	
	A sege, that was full bryght schynand,	*seat*
	But hyt was voyde wen he saw hyt,	*void (empty)*
	For he saw non therin sytte.	
	He beheld fast that sege soo bryght	*seat*
2240	And askyd for whom hyt was ydyght.	*prepared*
	Then spak Malachye and seyd	
	"Thys sege is ordeynud and purveyd	*seat; ordained; prepared*
	For won of owre bredur dere,	*brothers*
	Wen he commthe schall sytton here,	
2245	The whyche is yette in the world levand.	*living*
	Ay tyll he com hyt schall voyde stand."	
	Tundale had delyte greytt	
	Of the syghtt of that fayr seytt,	
	And as he stod joyfull and blythe	*happy*
2250	Then com the angell to hym full swythe	*quickly*
	And spake to hym with blythe chere,	
	"Tundale," he seyd, "how lykuth thee here?	
	Thu hast mony a feyre syght seyn.	
	In dyverse places ther thu hast beyn."	
2255	"That have Y lord," he seyd, "and loogh,	

Y have seyn joy ynoogh.
Dere lord, Y pray thee of thy grace
Leyt me not owt of thys place.
For Y wold never owt of this place wende,   *go*
2260 But dwell here withowttyn ende."
"Thu spekyst," quod the angell, "all in veyn.   *in vain*
Thu schalt turne to the body ageyn.
That thu hast seyyn, hold in thy thoght;
And thatt thu hast hard, foryete hyt noght."   *what*
2265 When he had seyd on thys manere,
Then wept Tundale and made sory chere
And seyd, "Lord, what have Y done
That Y schall turne ageyn so sone
To my body full of wrechydnes
2270 And leyve all this joy, that here is?"
The angell onswerd on thys manere
And seyd that, "Ther may non dwelle here,
But holy vyrgyns that have bene
Chast and kept hor bodys clene,
2275 And for the love of God allmyghty
Have forsake the world all holely,
And to God ar gevyn fro all ylle   *delivered*
With all her thoghttus and all her wyll.
But suche a thoghtte and wyll was no in thee
2280 When thu wast in thi nowne posté.   *your own power*
To God wold thu not the bowe,
Ne my conseyle wold thu not know.
To dwelle here art thu not worthy.
But turne agayn to thy body,
2285 And of fylthe make thee clene,
And fro syn henforward thu thee absteyne.
My helpe thu schalt have and my consell,
So that thu schalt not of Hevyn fayll."
When the angell had seyd thys,
2290 Tundale turnyd from all that blysse.

Reversio Anime

	As hys sowle wox all hevy	*grew; heavy*
	And feld hyt chargyd with hys body,	*burdened*
	He oponyd hys eene then and saw	*eyes*
	And hys lymes to hym con draw.	
2295	And or he spake anythyng,	
	He lyfte up a greyt sykyng.	*raised; sighing*
	They that hym saw and stodon by	
	Wer astoneyd and had farly.	*astonished; wonder*
	And tho that lovyd hym wer full fayn	
2300	That he was turnyd to the lyfe ageyn.	
	He dressyd hym up all sykande	*lifted*
	And weptt and made hevy semlande	*heavy appearance*
	And seyde thus with a grette crye,	
	"Lord Jesu Cryst, Thy marcé!	*mercy*
2305	Worse than Y am," quod he than,	
	"Was never noo boron of woman.	
	But now wylys that Y have space,	*while*
	Y wolle amend with help and grace	
	Off God, that for us tholyd pyne;	*suffered pain*
2310	Y hoope He wolle not my sowle tyne."	*harm*
	He spake to hymselfe and seyd, "Kaytyff,	*Wretch*
	Why hast thu levyd so wykd lyff?	
	Hy have ben," he seyd, "a wyckyd man."	*I*
	Full sore hym tenyd at hymselfe than.	*accused*
2315	He bethoght hym of all the tyme,	
	Of the greyt syghttus that he had syen.	
	Therfor hyt semyd be hys contynance	*countenance*
	That for hys synne he had repentance.	
	All had they ferly that by hym stode	*wonder*
2320	That he soo well had turnyd hys mood,	
	For that he was sumtyme soo fell,	*cruel*
	As ye before have hard me tell,	
	Won of hom, that stod hym next,	*One*
	Askyd hym yf he wold have a preste,	
2325	For to schryve hym of all the foly	*shrive; sin (folly)*
	And to hosull hym with Goddus body.	*give the Eucharist*
	Then answerd he ageyn.	

"Yee," he seyd, "Y wold full feyn
That the prest come to me

2330 To here my schryft in prevyté   *confession; privacy*
And to howsull me; then wer Y saffe.   *safe*
Y pray yow do me a prest to haffe,
And Goddus body that Y may take,
For all my synnus Y woll forsake."

2335 The prest come sone, for he was soght,
And Goddus body with hym he broght.
When Tundale was schrevon and made redy,   *shriven*
He receyvyd the ost full mekely.   *[Communion] host*
Then spake Tundale with hert free,

2340 "Lord," he seyd, "lovyd mot Thu bee,
For Thy marcy and Thi gudnes
Passus all mennys wykkydnes.
Passe hyt be muche and grevus soore,
Thy grace and Thi mercy is meche more."

2345 Mony a mon and also wemen
Wer geydoryd abowt hym then.   *gathered*
He told hom wer he had yben,
And wat he hard had and seyn;   *heard*
And wat he had feld was in his thoght,

2350 He held in mynde and forgeet hit noght;
And he warnyd ylke a man that peyn wold drede
Too amend hom here, or that they yeede.   *before; died (went)*
He cownseld hom to bee holy
And bad hom leyve hor greyt foly

2355 And turne hom to God allmyghtty,
Servyng Hym evermore devowtly.
He prechyd the wordys of God tharc,
That never was prechyd among hem are,
And hom that synfull wer he told

2360 He repreved hem as Goddus lawe wold;   *reproved*
And comfordud gud men, that wer clene,
Throw the joy that he had seyn.
And whyles he levyd synnus he fledde
And all hys lyffe in holynes ledde.

2365 He made to the world noo countynance,
But he levyd ever in peynanse.

He gaffe all hys gud away
Too pore men for hym to pray.
Noo worldys gud more wold he have,
2370 But levyd as long as God vochedsave.   *permitted*
And at the last wen he schuld hennus pas,
When that Goddus swete wylle was,
The sowle departyt from the body
And yoode to God allmyghty,   *went*
2375 In Hevon evermore to dwell.
Ther more joy is than tong may tell.
Too that joy He hus bring
That made Hevyn, eyrthe and all thyng.
Ylkon of yow that have hard mee
2380 Seythe "Amen" for charytee.

Explicit Tundale, quod Hyheg.   *Here ends; says Heeg*
Be it trwe, or be it fals,   *true*
Hyt is as the coopy was.   *copy*

Explanatory Notes to The Vision of Tundale

Abbreviations: see Textual Notes.

11   *In Yrlond byfyll.* Marcus, the author of the original Latin version, was an Irish monk. Ireland is an appropriate location because of its tradition of mythological "otherworlds" and because many visions of the Christian afterlife are associated with Ireland from at least the time of the *Ecclesiastical History* (731) of Bede, who narrated "The Vision of Furseus" under the year 633.

16   *in tho story.* The reference to a source, which recurs throughout the poem, is appropriate in that the story ultimately comes from Marcus' Latin prose *Tractatus*, though the immediate source of this version of the poem is not certain. In any case, the reference to a source is a common way of establishing "authority" in both religious and secular literature. N.b., the A scribe frequently writes *tho* for the definite article "the" as well as the demonstrative pronoun "those"; e.g., lines 489, 507, etc.

23–28   *full of trychery . . . And ever slouthe.* The poet lists the seven "deadly sins": pride, anger, envy, lust (lechery), gluttony, greed (covetousness), and sloth. These are the seven root sins, the dispositions, sinful in themselves, which underlie all other sins. St. Gregory the Great (c. 540–604) referred to them as "capital sins" because they lead to others. They were often used as a means for the examination of conscience, especially before auricular confession, which revived in the twelfth century. They are the basis of the structure of Dante's *Purgatorio* and Gower's *Confessio Amantis*, are crucial to Chaucer's Parson's Tale, and *Piers Plowman* B.5, and are frequently cited in penitential literature. See Morton W. Bloomfield, *The Seven Deadly Sins: An Introduction to the History of a Religious Concept, with Special Reference to Medieval English Literature* (East Lansing: Michigan State College Press, 1952). Line 23, however, in the original Latin version lists an eighth deadly sin "treachery," which the early Irish Church added to the traditional seven.

29   *warkus of mercy wold he worch.* Besides avoiding sin, it was required, or at least strongly counseled, that the Christian perform works of mercy. According to Church tradition, there are seven spiritual and seven corporal works of mercy. The spiritual

255

works are to instruct the ignorant, counsel the doubtful, admonish sinners, bear wrongs patiently, forgive offenses willingly, comfort the afflicted, and pray for the living and the dead; the corporal works are to feed the hungry, give drink to the thirsty, clothe the naked, harbor the harborless, visit the sick, ransom the captive, and bury the dead. The corporal works are loosely based on scriptual passages: the first six on Matthew 25:31–46, the seventh on Tobias 1:17–19. The spiritual works seem simply to be generally drawn from scriptural ideas. However, both groups of works of mercy are listed and explained in many highly popular fourteenth-century manuals of religious instruction, such as the *Speculum Vitae*, the *Speculum Christiani*, and the *Prick of Conscience*. They also appear often in graphic form in the fourteenth century.

31   *charyté*. The Christian's primary duty is charity, the love which is central to the Christian message. Of the three theological virtues (faith, hope, and charity), it is called the greatest by St. Paul (1 Corinthians 13:13) because it will last into eternity. The importance of charity has many other scriptural bases, such as Luke 10:25–27; 2 Corinthians 9; Galatians 6:6–10. The goal of charity is pure love of God for His own sake, but that love is manifested in works of mercy.

38   *boghthe*. A common medieval usage for "redeem" based on the etymological meaning of "redemption": "to buy back" (*redemptare*).

40–44   Tundale's soul separates from his body. This is the most common mode in vision literature. It differs from narratives like *Sir Owain* and the *Divine Comedy*, in which the visionary enters the next world body and soul.

45   *Purgatory*. The narrator promises that Tundale will see both Purgatory and Hell, though most of what he sees seems infernal except for the suggestion that early release is sometimes possible and the fact that Tundale himself is undergoing a kind of purgation.

53   *leyn*. Usury, the taking of any interest on loans at all, was formally forbidden by the Fourth Lateran Council (1215), though it had long been condemned by the early Church. It is punished in Dante's *Inferno* 17, is prominent in *Sir Owain*, stanzas 96–103, and was a frequent subject in medieval art. The word *leyn*, thus, may simply mean "to lend," though the *MED* lists one meaning of the verb *lenden* as "to allow (a longer time) for repayment of a loan."

76   *malycoly.* Melancholy is "one of the four humors, black bile" (*MED*). When out of balance with the other humors (yellow bile, phlegm, and blood), black bile was thought to cause melancholy, sadness, and ill will. The *MED* also defines it as "anger, rage, hatred" and "sorrow, gloom, anxiety."

103   *bellus yronge.* In addition to tolling the hours of the day, especially the canonical hours of prayer, church bells were rung to call Christians to worship, to recognize other significant events, and especially to note the death of a parishioner.

104   *"Placebo" and "Dyrge."* Placebo is the first word of the first antiphon for Vespers in the Office of the Dead (*Officium defunctorum*). *Dirige* is the first word of Matins in the same liturgy. The Office of the Dead included psalms and short prayers appropriate to the canonical hours of Vespers, Matins, and Lauds, along with a recitation of the seven Penitential Psalms (6, 31, 37, 50, 101, 129, and 142 in the Vulgate) and a litany. The Office was recited at the time of death and, usually, on commemorative dates after the death, e.g., a month, a year, etc. For a more complete explanation of the canonical hours, see *The Gast of Gy*, explanatory note to lines 202–05.

108   *veyne corale.* The "vena cephalica" or "median vein" (*MED*). The median vein runs through the arm and into other veins which eventually join with the jugular vein. Thus, the warmth on the left side of Tundale's body suggests that the venous system is still functional.

113   *none. MED* lists this word as "the canonical hour of nones; thus three o'clock p.m." and "midday, the period about 12:00 noon." Both uses existed, though I prefer the latter for symmetry with line 112.

118   *gost departyd.* Although Tundale's soul has left his body, he has some "bodily" form since he suffers some physical punishments during his journey.

123   *wend to a byn.* Compare C line 181: *He wend to have be.* See also C line 200, which repeats the phrase. A often uses *a* as an abbreviated form of *hav* or *han* (e.g., lines 124 and 137); and *byn* as a participial form of the verb *to be* in lines 142 and 189. The idiom is repeated in line 142.

127   *mydylerde.* Besides "the earth," the word could refer to "worldly things as opposed to divine or spiritual" (*MED*). It is implied in phrases like "for all the world."

133   The poem is divided by A into an introductory section, ten *passus*, seven *gaudia*, and the *reversio anime* (change or turning of the spirit or heart.) The beginning of the first passus is actually marked in the margin at line 135: *j passus*, but, because it makes more sense, I have moved it to follow line 132, as G does. A passus, etymologically a pace or step, is "a section, division, or canto of a story or poem" (*OED*). Passus are usually more regular in length than in *The Vision of Tundale*. Since the passus in this poem correspond with moving on to another segment of Hell, it may be that A, the only scribe to use these divisions, had in mind *passus* in a different etymological sense: suffering.

134–36   *a full loddly rowte . . . as wyld wolfus thei cam rampyng.* These are clearly infernal demons, denizens of Hell. The vision at this point is of Hell, though the effect on Tundale is educational and purgatorial.

159   *fowlest stynk.* The poet repeatedly emphasizes the stench. Hell is a place of pain not just by fire (and ice) but through all of the senses.

199–218   *Wher his now . . . withowton mercy.* Using a variant of the *ubi sunt* trope ("where are . . ."), the fiends taunt Tundale with the transience of worldly riches that have no use after death. They refer to the fact that Tundale has not received the sacrament of Penance (lines 215–16) and therefore deserves Hell for his sins. They are literally correct, though Tundale is in fact being given a second chance. Finally, they assert that suffrages, in this case masses and prayers for the dead, will do him no good. Suffrages also included other works such as fasting and almsgiving on behalf of the dead. The efficacy of suffrages was an important part of the doctrine of Purgatory, as in *The Gast of Gy, Sir Owain*, and many works of fiction and theological instruction especially from the twelfth century. Aquinas' view was especially prominent, based on his notion on the doctrine of the Communion of Saints — the essential unity of the saved, the living, and the suffering souls in Purgatory.

226   *emer.* Guardian. Travellers to the next world characteristically have guides, providing the possibility for didactic dialogue. The guides included St. Michael (*The Apocalypse of St. Paul*, fourth century), St. Nicholas (*The Monk of Eynsham*, late twelfth century), St. John (*The Vision of Thurkill*, early thirteenth century), but from *The Vision of Drythelm* (Bede, *Ecclesiastical History*, 731) and *The Vision of Wetti*, early ninth century, the guide was usually a "guardian angel," an angel especially assigned for the protection of an individual. Although the idea of a "guardian angel" was never defined as dogma by the Church, it has a venerable history. It was

variously based on Matthew 10:10 and the apocryphal Book of Tobias, but taken seriously by St. Jerome, St. John Chrysostom, Aquinas, and Duns Scotus.

237   *bryght*. A common adjective for angels in works such as *The Vision of Drythelm*, *The Gast of Gy*, and many others.

276   ☞ **Latin Note:** After line 276, A has, boxed in red: *Uniquique secundum opus suum, etc.* ("For thyself renderest to a man according to his work" — Psalm 61:13 in the Vulgate). The verse is paraphrased in the poem at lines 275–76.

302   ☞ **Latin Note:** After line 302, A has, boxed in red: *Cadent a latere tuo mille et decem millia a dextris tuis, ad te autem non appropinquabit* ("Though a thousand fall at thy side, and ten thousand at thy right hand, naught shall come nigh to thee" — Psalm 90:7 in the Vulgate). The verse is paraphrased in the poem at lines 303–07.

325   *cubytus*. "A measure of length (orig. the distance from the elbow to the top of the middle finger); usually, eighteen inches" (*MED*).

337   *seyd*. *MED* gives *seyd* as a form of *set(ten)*, but does not cite this passage. Perhaps the word is a form of *seien* (*MED* v. 14), meaning "commanded," "prescribed," or, as my gloss suggests, "determined." "Set" makes the best sense, however.

355–56   *But of this peyn . . . yett thu hast deservyd hit*. The angel assures Tundale that he will not experience this particular torment, though later he does suffer physically, an experience shared by Furseus in his vision (seventh century) but by few other visionaries. The travelers ordinarily suffer emotionally or psychologically like Sir Owain.

364   *pyche*. Pitch, that is "wood tar, especially as a means of torture in hell" (*MED*). The *OED* expands: "A tenacious resinous substance, hard when cold, becoming a thick viscid semi-liquid when heated."

             brymston. "The mineral sulphur," perhaps more pertinently "burning sulphur" (*MED*).

407–10   *he saw a bryge . . . won fotte in brede*. The narrow bridge between two mountains recalls bridges over Hell in *The Apocalypse of St. Paul* (late fourth century), *The Vision of Sinniulf* by St. Gregory of Tours (538–93), *Sir Owain*, and other poems about the next world. It is a common "test" motif, perhaps dating to antiquity. In *The*

Apocalypse of St. Paul and its thirteenth-century early Middle English version, "The Vision of St. Paul," the bridge crosses all of Hell. In *Sir Owain* it leads to the "terrestrial paradise." Tundale's narrow bridge is only one foot wide and 1,000 steps long. It is perilous, for he sees souls falling off it into the fire below and only the holy palmer (pilgrim) is seen to traverse it safely.

453   *serewyse.* The word can mean "in a diverse way, variously" (*MED*), but in context the adverbial use of *sere* seems more probable: "physically apart; asunder," or "individually, separately" (*MED*).

469   *baelys.* Specifically "a bundle of sticks used in flogging" (*MED*).

478   *Akyron.* Acheron. In Homer and elsewhere in Greek antiquity, Acheron was the main river of the underworld. In Latin and Hellenistic poetry, Acheron came to be the underworld itself (*OCD*). The appearance of Acheron as a demonic character calls to mind the beasts, like Geryon (*Inferno* 16–17), that Dante puts in his Hell.

490   ☞ **Latin Note:** After line 490, A has, boxed in red: *Absorbebit flumen et non mirabitur et habebit fiduciam, quod influat Jordanus in os eius. Amen.* ("Behold, he will drink up a river, and not wonder: and he trusteth that the Jordan may run into his mouth" — Job 40:18 in the Vulgate). A corresponding idea is expressed in lines 491–94, in which Satan replaces the behemoth of Job.

508   *Forcusno . . . Conallus.* Forcusno and Conallus appear in Marcus' original Latin version as Fergusius and Conallus. Only A mentions them, suggesting that he was the only scribe with access to Marcus' original as opposed to the slightly shortened versions of Helinand and St. Vincent of Beauvais (M, p. 61). Fergusius and Conallus are the Latinized names of Fergus mac Roich and Conall Cearnach, prominent pagan characters in the Irish Ulster Cycle and cohorts of the famous Cúchulain. For Fergus, see *The Tain, from the Irish epic Táin Bó Cuailnge*, trans. Thomas Kinsella (Oxford: Oxford University Press, 2002), and for Conall, see the particularly amusing *Fled Bricrenn*, "Bricriu's Feast," translated in *The Celtic Heroic Age: Literary Sources for Ancient Celtic Europe and Early Ireland and Wales*, ed. John T. Koch in collaboration with John Carey, third ed. (Andover, MA: Celtic Studies Publications, 2000), pp. 76–105.

568   *A wondur long, narow brygge. The Vision of Tundale* uniquely includes a second bridge, this one over a lake full of souls. It is even narrower, a hand's breadth, than the first bridge, and crossing it is a man, who stole from the Church, bearing a burden

of grain. This is the bridge over which Tundale must lead the "wild cow." It is curious that the man and Tundale are going in opposite directions, thus causing a traffic jam (lines 665 ff.) from which Tundale is saved only by the angel's intercession, thus allowing him to stop leading the cow (lines 683–88). The description is long and amusing, even comic.

588   After this line R explains that the man has stolen the grain from his neighbor's field.

603–04   *But sum haght more peyn and sum lase / All aftur that her synnus his*. Although robbers have been mentioned before, this is the first specific reference in the poem to degrees of punishment related to the severity of the sin, a traditional early Christian concept clearly manifested in Dante, but rare as a literary trope before the fourteenth century.

610   *Sacrileggi*. A sacrilege is any sin against religion, but more strictly was applied to abuse of a sacred person (clergy), place (church), or thing (e.g., liturgical vessels.) It could manifest itself in striking a priest or unchastity by the priest himself, in the violation of a holy place or use of a holy place for secular purposes. Thus, it could range from theft from or desecration of a church to the action of a priest administering the sacraments while in a state of sin.

612   *seyntwary*. "A holy or sacred place; a place dedicated to God." More specifically, it could mean, besides the church itself, "a churchyard; a burial ground, a cemetery" or "land owned by or under the jurisdiction of the church" (*MED*). In ecclesiastical usage it often designated the part of a church, set off from the rest, where the priest actually said Mass and the sacred vessels were kept.

620   *teythe*. Tithes, one-tenth of income due the Church for its own support and for charity. Tithing is mentioned in various contexts in the Hebrew Scriptures as early as Genesis 14:20 and 28:22, but it was not common in the early Christian Church. It was first enjoined by the Council of Macon (585). At first it was one-tenth of profit from land, but was extended to any kind of earned income (bequests were generally exempt). Tithes were at first paid to the bishop, but by the twelfth century were generally paid directly to the parish priest. Failure to pay tithes was a serious offense and could result in charges being brought in an ecclesiastical court with the possibility of excommunication.

706   *wyldernys.* "Wild, uninhabited, or uncultivated territory; trackless, desolate land . . . a desert" or, by extension, "a state of ruin or desolation, the condition of devastation" (*MED*).

735–38   In these lines, which are in none of the other MSS, A provides the fiends with a remarkable catalogue of farm implements as instruments of torture.

784   *Preston.* In C, P, R: *Pystryne*; in B: *Pistroun.* The Latin has Fistrinus. I know of no one who has identified this figure under any of these spellings.

814   ☞ **Latin Note:** After line 814, A has, boxed in red: *Misericordia plena est terra, etc.* ("The earth is full of his kindness" — Psalm 32:5 in the Vulgate). The verse is a response to Tundale's questioning of God's mercy in lines 811–14.

836–46   *the sowle som peyn schalt have . . . To the blysse withowtten ende.* The angel describes some kind of purgatorial experience, since he is referring to souls which will pass from pain to salvation, even though such souls do not seem to have a separate, distinct location.

888   *snowt.* "A human nose . . . used derisively" because the primary meaning was "The snout of a swine, boar, rhinoceros, dog, dragon, etc." (*MED*).

909–54   The invasion of the bodies of the damned by biting adders is mentioned in *The Apocalypse of St. Paul* (late fourth century) and in many later visions. The presentation in this poem is particularly gruesome and specially applied to corrupt clergy (lines 960–62).

967   *ordyr.* A religious order, as of monks or friars, bound to some rule of life such as that of St. Augustine or St. Benedict.

971–72   *for the same thow hast bene, / This schalt thu thole.* Once again Tundale must suffer physically. This is odd in context since the punishment has been assigned to corrupt clergy and particularly lines 945–46 seem to associate Tundale with this group. It is possible that here, and in a few places later, the scribe has preserved an oddity in Marcus whereby there is some confusion, intentional or not, of the vicious, worldly Tundale with the monk-author.

1002   *dongyll.* This is a very unusual word. In the *MED* it is spelled "dingle," with no examples or cross-references, and defined as "a deep dell or hollow." The *OED* says a bit more under "dingle": "A single example meaning 'deep hollow, abyss' is known in the 13th century; otherwise the word appears to be only dialectal in use till the 17th century." The only example given is from *Sawles Warde* (1240). The *OED* defines the probably related word "gill" as "A deep rocky cleft or ravine, usually wooded and forming the course of a stream," the earliest example being from *The Destruccion of Troy* (1400). Regardless of the paucity of examples, the meanings in the *MED* and *OED* seem to fit the context in the poem.

1018 ☞ **Latin Note:** After line 1018, A has, boxed in red: *lata est via que ducit ad mortem* ("for wide is the gate and broad the way that leadeth to destruction" — Matthew 7:13). The verse is paraphrased in lines 1017–18.

1042 *Vlkane*. Vulcan, the "ancient Roman god of destructive, devouring fire," who was "highly admired, secretly feared" (*OCD*). From Greek antiquity, his counterpart, Hephaestos, was a blacksmith. This conflation of the Greek and Roman gods fits the hellish context perfectly.

1223 *Thee tharre not thynke*. "No thought must come to you." The construction is apparently an unusual dative of agency, analogous to "me thinks," in which the subject is acted upon, and is thus in an oblique case.

1296 *more and lesse*. A common medieval line-filling formula here meaning "completely."

1305–60 An extended description of Satan, who simultaneously punishes and is punished. The idea of Satan was developed in the early Church out of a long tradition in antiquity and a variety of comments in Hebrew Scripture (e.g., Isaias 14:12–15). Literally, Satan means "the accuser." He is the author of all evil. The notion of the fall of Satan was developed in the early Church from texts such as Apocalypse 12:4–11 and Jude 1:6, but more elaborately in the apocryphal Book of Enoch. The fall of Satan and the other rebellious angels was taken seriously by Church Fathers and Doctors including Augustine and especially Aquinas, who asserted (*ST* 1.qu.63a6) that Satan's sin must have been pride, wanting to be "as God." In this poem, as in the tradition of vision literature including Dante, Satan is in the deepest pit of Hell suffering the greatest torments.

1342 *sponne*. "A unit of length variously reckoned as corresponding to the distance from the tip of the thumb to the top of the middle or the little finger when the hand is fully extended . . . a hand's breadth" (*MED*).

1363   *gloand folus.* I.e., "fiery imps." See *MED fol* n 2: "an impious person, a sinner, a rascal."

1411–12   *the furst creature / That God made.* The Middle English suggests that God created Satan before all other creatures, which is consistent with the sequence of creation in all of the drama cycles. In *Cursor Mundi*'s account of creation we are told that humankind was created to fill the gap left by Satan and the other fallen angels. Compare Gower, *Confessio Amantis* 8.21–34. (See Russell A. Peck's discussion in *Confessio Amantis*, vol. 1 [Kalamazoo: Medieval Institute Publications, 2000], p. 226.) Augustine discusses the point in his *Enchiridion on Faith, Hope and Charity*, ch. 29, "The Restored Part of Humanity Shall, In Accordance with the Promises of God, Succeed to the Place Which The Rebellious Angels Lost." See also Augustine, *De civitate Dei*, Book 22, ch. 1. Marcus says: *Hic est Lucifer, principium creaturarum Dei* ("Here is Lucifer, the principal of God's creatures"), and may simply be suggesting the eminence of Lucifer before his fall, though *principium* probably means "first."

1436   ☞ **Latin Note:** After line 1436, A has, boxed in red: *Potentes tormenta paciuntur* ("The mighty shall be mightily tormented" — Wisdom 6:7). The sense of the verse is developed in lines 1437–44.

1495–1502 Tundale and the angel have entered the "terrestrial Paradise," the Garden of Eden. Most in the Middle Ages believed that the Garden of Eden had a physical location and many searched for it. Augustine and Aquinas saw it both as the literal place where Adam and Eve lived and fell and, figuratively, as a place of spiritual rest and beauty. It was sometimes considered a stage in the movement from Purgatory to Paradise. For some it was considered a beautiful and tranquil place where the saved, or those who had completed purgation, waited until the Day of Judgment, Doomsday, for admission to Heaven. By the time of *The Vision of Tundale*, the general view was that it was a transitional abode, as in *The Gast of Gy*, and that the saved went to Heaven after purgation, if necessary, was completed. Indeed, suggestions by Pope John XXII that it was a holding place until Judgment Day were considered potentially heretical. A place of sweet-smelling air, flowers, gems, and song, the prime literary example is in Dante's *Purgatorio* 27–32.

1504–28   *The Vision of Tundale* has a kind of vestibule to the terrestrial Paradise in which there is a mild form of punishment for those who, though shriven of their sins and saved, did not perform works of mercy during their lives. It is interesting that although their pain is temporary and not great, they are punished not for violation of

264

a commandment or the commission of a deadly sin, but for failure to perform a "counsel of perfection."

1535–46	The sweet air, the flowers, the light, and the birdsong are all staples of poems which include a terrestrial paradise. Lacking at this point are the catalogues of birds, gems, and flowers that are usually incorporated, even in secular romances. Some skeletal catalogues appear later in the poem at lines 1907–14 and 2099–104.
1551	*welle*. The well, a place of refreshment, even a "fountain of youth," has waters flowing from it. Contrary to expectation, it is not the source of the four rivers of Eden (Genesis 2:11–14). It is more reminiscent of the River Lethe, the river of forgetfulness (a kind of renewal) in Dante, *Purgatorio* 28.25–33.
1561–68	The souls have undergone some kind of purgation and merit salvation, but they must wait until God admits them to Heaven. A does not make it clear when that will be.
1584	*lewde mon*. A "lewed man" was "a member of the laity, layman, non-cleric" (*MED*).
1591	*Cantaber*. Conchobar, Conor O'Brien, the king of Thurmond. Conchobar was a friend of King Cormake. In 1138, however, Cormake was killed by Conchobar's brother, Cormake's father-in-law. For the whole story, see M, pp. 31–36.
1592	*Donatus*. Donough McCarthy, king of Munster from 1127, was the brother of Cormake.
1600	*Caym*. Cain, who killed his brother Abel (Genesis 4), was a symbol of murderous wrath and envy.
1607–10	The angel is careful to explain that the kings repented before death. This is necessary to justify their placement in the earthly Paradise, but it also reinforces the point that repentance always remains available even to great sinners.
1620	In the description of the moral rehabilitation of Donatus, A mentions that Donatus gave money to have prayers said for him. This is an example of a suffrage, an especially important part of Dominican teaching from the late twelfth century, but very prominent as an idea in this secularized version of a Benedictine Latin tract.
1635	*carbunkyll ston*. Carbuncle, which, according to the *OED*, was said to shine in the dark. See line 2103.

1654   *Kyng Cormake.* Cormac MacCarthy, king of Munster (1124), dethroned by Turlough O'Connor in 1127. He was murdered in 1138 in his own home, reportedly by some kind of treachery, the eighth of the Irish deadly sins. See explanatory note to lines 23–28. See also G (pp. 316–17), who thinks that the Teampuill Chormaic, which Cormac built, may be the model for the magnificat structure in which Tundale finds him. Cormac was generous to the Irish Benedictine foundation at Regensburg where Marcus, the author of the Latin original, lived. On the relevant Irish history, see M, pp. 31–36.

1667   *deykenus.* Deacons, members of minor orders; by the time of the composition of the Middle English poem the deaconate was generally a stage in the progress towards major orders (the priesthood) rather than a permanent office.

1673   *chalys.* A chalice is a vessel, usually of gold or silver, used to hold the water and wine that will become the body and blood of Christ at the Consecration of the Mass. Chalices were often highly ornamented with precious stones.

1674   *sensowrys.* Censers, the receptacles, often made of precious metals, in which incense was burned in many Church liturgies.

1706–48   Cormake, although saved, must still suffer because of the gravity of his sins. Much about this passage is odd. It is unusual that anyone who has entered the terrestrial Paradise must still suffer pain. Also, when Tundale asks how long Cormake will suffer, the angel gives the strangely specific answer of three hours a day rather than an ultimate duration before the end of suffering. Cormake's position is awkward in that he lived at a time, during the reforms of the early twelfth century, when marriage laws from the Roman Church were being imposed on the Irish. He was reputed to have ordered a murder that would have been mortally sinful under either disposition, and this is duly noted, but his punishments seem to be primarily for lechery.

1724   *hayre.* A hairshirt. "A shirt made of haircloth, worn next to the skin by ascetics and penitents" (*OED*). "A penitential garment woven from the hair of mountain goats or camels" (*MED*). The practice was usually monastic and was often discouraged by the Church as an egoistic excess, though when Thomas à Becket died he was found to be wearing one.

1736   *Besyde Seynt Patrycke.* This refers to a church, not the saint. G (p. 317) identifies it as probably the metropolitan church of Cashel.

Explanatory Notes

1759 ff. There follows a traditional description of the singing of hymns and carols in the joy of the terrestrial Paradise. Interestingly, in *The Vision of Tundale* it is specifically the abode of souls who have lived righteously in marriage, souls who have performed works of mercy, and good rulers (lines 1785–96).

1798–1802 This passage paraphrases Christ's invitation to the virtuous to enter Heaven (Matthew 25:24). It also suggests that the souls will be in the terrestrial Paradise until Doomsday, the day of the Last Judgment, when the world ends.

1838 *erward.* "At or during some earlier time in the past, on a former occasion, formerly, previously" (*MED*).

1897 *grys.* "A gray fur; probably from the back of the Russian gray squirrel in winter; also a piece of fur made from such skins" (*MED*).

1900 *besantes.* "A golden coin of Byzantium; any of several similar coins minted in Western Europe" or "a bezant used as an ornament" (*MED*).

1909 *Orgons.* Probably a large church organ, which might have had as many as 400 pipes, rather than the portable organ or any wind instrument. See Henry Holland Carter, *A Dictionary of Middle English Musical Terms*, pp. 337–41.

    symbals. "A set, or one of a set, of two concave plates of brass or bronze, which emit a clashing, metallic sound when struck together" (Carter, p. 110). *OED* lists the possibility of "castanets" or a "chime," but the clanging sound of cymbals seems more appropriate to the exuberant circumstances.

    tympanys. "A general name for the drum" (Carter, p. 532). *OED* additionally suggests "any kind of stringed instrument," but gives only one example. The more common meaning seems to fit the boisterous joy of the context.

1910 *harpus.* A true harp had "eight to eighteen strings of twisted hair, gut, or wire," but the term also was used loosely as the equivalent of other stringed instruments like the "lyre, lute, cithers, etc." (Carter, p. 185).

1912 *trebull and meyne and burdown.* The *trebull* (usually called a *hautein*) is the highest part in a three-part vocal or instrumental composition, with *meyne* and *burdoun* as the middle and lower parts (Carter, pp. 200, 278, 510).

1931   *frerus, monkys, nonnus, and channonus.* A is more specific than the other MSS. Friars were members of mendicant orders (Dominicans, Carmelites, Franciscans, Augustinians), who lived a communal life at "convents" but spent most of their time begging and preaching (and, especially in the case of the Dominicans, studying). Monks lived in cloister, separated from the world, and followed a "rule" such as that of St. Augustine or St. Benedict. Canons were members of religious orders (canons regular) or served communally in a cathedral or major church (canons secular); many groups of canons established endowed communities (chantries) devoted to suffrages in the form of masses and prayers for the dead.

2006   *flowre delyce.* Fleur-de-lis. Although it is a "flowering plant of the genus Iris," in this context of elegant embellishment it seems more likely "a representation on a coin, a spoon, etc." (*MED*).

2057   *seyrwyse.* Here, as opposed to line 453, the phrase seems to have its more usual meaning of "in a diverse way, variously" (*MED*).

2074   *chantryse.* Chapels at which canons prayed for the dead; they usually were endowed by benefactors seeking suffrages. They could be free-standing or associated with a neighboring church. They became increasingly popular in the thirteenth century both as a locus of suffrages and as a means of benefaction.

2076   *feffud.* This verb, from the feudal vocabulary of enfiefment, meant "to put (a person, a religious foundation) in possession of a feudal estate held in heritable tenure" and "to endow, furnish with anything by way of a gift" (*MED*). Thus, the souls here have given generously to the Church. See also line 2217, where the verb is used of St. Malachy's endowment and support of churches and colleges in addition to his charity to the poor.

2099–2104 A catalogue of gems characteristic of descriptions of the terrestrial Paradise and of otherworldly descriptions in romance. There is some scriptural basis in Apocalypse 21:19–20.

2100   *cresolyte.* Chrysolite. "A name formerly given to several different gems of a green color, such as zircon, tourmaline, topaz, and amatite" (*OED*). The catalogue of gems has some apparent overlapping and vagueness.

2102   *Iacyntus.* "A reddish orange variety of zircon" (*OED*). "A precious stone of blue (rarely of red) color" (*MED*). The experts seem baffled by the medieval terminology of precious stones.

         smaragdynes. These are generally accepted to be emeralds. Either there was another green precious stone or the narrator in his enthusiasm is repeating himself. The whole catalogue is a bit helter-skelter, suggesting that A simply wanted to accumulate the names of many gems — or was as baffled as the modern experts.

2103   *Emastyce.* Bloodstones. "A name applied to certain precious stones spotted or streaked with red, supposed in former times to have the power of staunching bleeding," or "The modern heliotrope, a green variety of jasper or quartz, with small spots of red jasper looking like drops of blood" (*OED*). Again the narrator is either being exuberant or has some clearer characterization of gems in mind.

         charbokall. "A carbuncle, a precious stone said to glow in the dark" (*MED*). "In the Middle Ages and later, besides being a name for the ruby . . . applied to a mythological gem said to emit light in the dark" (*OED*).

2117–20 *Ne hart . . . for all Hysse.* An allusion to 1 Corinthians 2:9 (itself a paraphrase of Isaias 64:4): "That eye hath not seen, nor ear heard: neither hath it entered into the heart of man, what things God hath prepared for them that love him."

2122   The nine orders, or choirs, of angels were first enumerated by the man variously known as Pseudo-Dionysius the Areopagite or the Pseudo-Denys (late fifth century) as: angels, archangels, virtues, powers, principalities, dominions, thrones, cherubim, and seraphim. The idea is based on Psalms 96:7; 102:20; 148:2, 5 in the Vulgate; and especially on Daniel 7:9–10 and Matthew 18:10. The orthodoxy of the view is attested by St. Gregory the Great (c. 540–604) in his *Dialogues* and by Aquinas, *ST* 1.qu.108a6. Although angels are frequently cited in Scripture as messengers of God, the role of the nine orders is primarily to stand before the throne of God singing His praises.

2125   *Prevey wordys.* The phrase "Goddes privitee" was common to denote the knowledge possessed by God, angels, and the saved, which it was not proper for human beings to know.

2128   *opon thyn eyrus and here.* Compare Jesus' oft-repeated phrase in the Gospels, "He that hath ears to hear, let him hear" (Matthew 11:15, 13:9, 13:43; Mark 4:9, 4:23,

7:16; Luke 8:8, 14:35). A variation of the phrase is also repeated many times in the Apocalypse of St. John.

2176   *Renodan.* St. Ruadan (d. 584), abbot of Lothra. It is unclear what the special connection between Tundale and St. Ruadan could have been, especially in view of the chronological disparity. St. Ruadan was one of the "Twelve Apostles of Erin," who came to study with St. Finian in his School of Clonard, Meath, founded about 520.

2193   *Seynt Patryk.* St. Patrick (c. 389–461), the patron saint of Ireland, has pride of place in this series of prelates. He is believed to have been a Roman Britain taken as a captive to Ireland. He returned later to Ireland to convert the people to Christianity and to organize the Irish Church. Although a historical figure, he has myths, even magical qualities, associated with him; e.g., that he banished all snakes from Ireland and that he could release seven souls from Hell each Saturday.

2204   *Celestyen.* St. Cellach or Celsus, abbot of Armagh (1105), and later archbishop of Armagh until his death in 1129.

2207   *Malachye.* St. Malachy, Malachias O'Moore (b. 1094; archbishop of Armagh, 1132–1138). He was ordained by St. Cellach ("Celestyen") in 1119 and was confessor to Cormac MacCarthy ("Cormake"), king of Munster. Malachy, feeling that he had done what he could in the reformation of the Irish Church, resigned from the archbishopric of Armagh in 1138 and returned to Connor where he had been bishop earlier (1124–32). In troubled times he was welcomed by King Cormac, who was killed the same year Malachy resigned Armagh. On his second trip to Rome (1148), he fell sick while visiting his great friend St. Bernard of Clairvaux, founder of the Cistercian reform of the Benedictines, and he is said to have died in St. Bernard's arms. These connections tempt one to find a Cistercian influence on the poem, but no specific Cistercian imprint is apparent. St. Malachy prophesied the number of popes (112) to come before Doomsday. St. Bernard wrote his Life.

2209   *Pwope Celestyen.* Pope Celestine II was elected in 1143 and died in 1144 after a short reign of six months. His name here must be in error, since Malachy was consecrated archbishop of Armagh in 1132 during the reign of Innocent II (1130–1143). The Latin versions have Pope Innocent, but all English MSS that include this line (A, C, R) make the same error, perhaps influenced by the "Celestyen" in line 2204.

2213   *colagys*. Presumably colleges of canons whose primary purpose was to pray for the dead, though colleges composed of canons, who were priests, often attached themselves to nearby churches and assisted in the clerical work.

2217   See explanatory note to line 2076.

2222   *Crystyne*. Bishop of Clogher (1126–39) and older brother of St. Malachy. The Latin designation of his diocese, Lugdoniensis, accounts for *Lyon* in A and causes M to identify his see as Louth rather than Clogher.

2227   *Malachynus*. Latinate form of Malachy.

2230   *Neomon*. Nehemiah O'Morietach, bishop of Cloyne and Ross (1140–49). Sometimes he is erroneously identified as St. Neeman of Cluny, perhaps because of the Latin version of Cloyne — Cluanensis.

2232   *Clemy*. This is the bishopric assigned to *Neomon* by A; C has *Ylye*; P has *Ely*; R has *Clunny*. These seem to be various attempts to render the Latin "Cluanensis." See explanatory note to line 2230.

2235–38   Many scholars believe the empty seat to be reserved for St. Bernard of Clairvaux.

2381   *Hyheg*. Richard Heeg, who transcribed A and various other fifteenth-century MSS. According to M (p. 64), Heeg seems to have seen himself as more than simply a scriptor, or scribe, and therefore felt freer to modify his copy-text. His apparent use of a copy of Marcus, however, suggests a concern for authenticity.

Textual Notes to *The Vision of Tundale*

I have based my text on National Library of Scotland Advocates' MS 19.3.1 (**A**), the longest extant version. In the nineteenth century, A was purchased by the poet Robert Southey and given to Sir Walter Scott. The only edition of A, besides a diplomatic edition by W. B. D. D. Turnbull (1843), is Eileen Gardiner's doctoral dissertation (**G**). G lists variants from British Library MS Cotton Caligula A. ii (**C**), which has been edited with variants from all other MSS by Rodney Mearns (**M**), Bodleian Library MS Ashmole 1491 (**B**), Tokyo, Takamiya MS 32 (*olim* Penrose 10, *olim* Penrose 6, *olim* Delamere) (**P**), and British Library MS Royal 17. B. xliii (**R**), which has been edited by Albrecht Wagner with variants from A, B, C. I have made as few changes as possible to A consistent with making sense of the narrative. I have accepted and noted some alterations by G and a few of my own based on B, C, P, R. I have ignored G's changes that seem simply to tidy up the poem, because some rough passages in A contain a specificity that is an attractive characteristic of this MS.

I have silently expanded abbreviations and corrected obvious scribal errors such as "whet" for "when" (line 388), "bub" for "but" (837), and emended the scribal practice of occasionally hearing *g* and *k* interchangeably as in "styng" for "stynk" (333) and "lonke" for "longe" (1744). In the notes, as in the text, I have replaced obsolete Middle English graphemes with modern equivalents. Fuller manuscript and bibliographical detail precedes the text of the poem.

5	*ben awhyle*. A: *ben wyll awhyle*. I have omitted *wyll* as unusually clumsy and grammatically unnecessary.
10	*clanse*. A: *clanso*; C: *clense*; I have accepted G: *clanse* as doing least harm to A. Several times A has a mistaken *o* at the end of a word; subsequently I have corrected these without comment.
14	*yere*. A: *here*; G, following C, P: *yere*.
19	*is*. A frequently has *is* for *his* and vice-versa. I have retained this usage since it does not cause confusion.
24	*pride*. A: *pde* with *i* superscript.
37	*tyne*. A: *tyme*; G, following C, P: *tyne*.
59	*for his best*. G, following C: *as hym lest*, is plausible, but I have retained A.
70	*deray*. A: *aray*; G, following C: *deray*.
78	*at tho*. G, following C, P: *to*.
108	*corale*. A: *quale*; G, following C, P, R: *corale*. See explanatory note.
110	*flytte*. A: *had*; G, following C, P, R: *flytte*.

123   *payne.* A: *pyne*; G, following C, P, R: *payne. MED* lists *pyne* as a possible variant, but *payne* preserves the rhyme with line 124.

126   *nether.* A: *not ther*; G, following B: *nether.*

        layned. A: *laft*; G, following B, C, P, R: *layned.*

129–30 *But he sawe mony a hydwys payne / Or he come to the body agayne.* A lacks these two lines, which are important to the sense. G has soundly reconstructed them from B, C, P, R. It is likely that A simply skipped two lines of his exemplar.

133   The poem is divided into ten "passus," seven "gaudia," and the "reversio animae." They are marked in the margins of A. Because it makes more sense, I have begun Passus I here, as does G, rather than at line 135, where it is marked (*i passus*) in the margin of A. I, like G, have taken a similar liberty with Passus V, which is marked in A opposite line 433, Passus VI, which is marked in A opposite line 553, and Gaudium II, which is marked in A opposite line 1577.

155   *fete.* A: *face.* G, C, B, and P read *fete.*

167   *word.* A, G: *word*; B, C, R: *worlde. Word* is a common variant of *world* (*MED*).

176   *creidon.* A: *crendon*; B, R: *cried*; C: *cryde*; but G: *creidon* is a possible variant that changes A least.

191   *stryft.* A: *strft* is canceled before *stryft.*

204   *harneys.* A: *hornys*; G, following B, P: *harneys.*

215   *thought.* A: *thoyght*; G, following B, C, P, R: *thoughtes.* I prefer *thought*, preserving the singular and assuming a scribal error in one grapheme.

215–16 *That wykkyd thought that was in thi brest, / Woldyst thu never schowe it to no preste.* G, following B, C, P, R, places these lines after line 210. I have left them in their A position.

252   *uggly.* A: *ungdly*; G, following C, P, R: *uggly.* Perhaps A intended *ungodly.*

269   *thei.* A: *he*; C: *they.*

323   *the.* A: *that*; G, following B, C, R: *the.*

327   *brad.* A: *brdd*; C: *brode*; P, B: *brade.*

333   *stynk.* A: *styng*; C: *stynke.*

339   *dyd.* A: *dud.*

        than. Omitted in A. C: *thn.*

340   *pan.* A: *pon*; C: *panne.*

341   *ronnen.* A: *ronnon*; C: *ranne.*

        fyr and yron bothe. A: *that yron into the fyr bothe*; G, following B, P: *fyr and yron bothe.*

342   *As hit wer wax throw a clothe.* I have retained A, though G, following C, P is more felicitous: *As molton wax dothe throwe a clothe.*

347   *dight.* A: *ordent* has some support from C: *ordeyned*, but G, following B, P, R: *dight* makes slightly better sense and much better meter.

348	*or.* A: *and*; G, following B, C, P, R: *or.*
	yslayn. A: *bothe yslayn*; G, following B, C, P, R: *slayne.* To include A: *and* and *bothe yslayn* would make it necessary to have killed both parents. The reading in B, C, P, R makes it a matter of killing one parent. Surely, one is enough to deserve terrible torment.
353	*schall.* A: *schell*; C: *shall.*
357	*forth.* Omitted in A. C: *forth.*
363–64	*That was bothe darke and wan / And stank of pyche and brymston.* These lines are reversed in A but marked by the scribe *b, a* for correction.
376	*snowe.* C: *snawe*, which better suits the rhyme.
382	*This.* A: *Then This*, with *Then* marked for expunction.
389–90	*The angell ay before con pas, / And Tundale aftur that sore aferd was.* These lines are clumsy, but no obvious reconstruction from other manuscripts seems appreciably better without wholesale rewriting.
495	*this payne.* A: *he*; G, following C, R: *this payne* clarifies the line significantly.
529	*hys.* Omitted in A. G, following C, P, R: *hys.*
563	*Her ynee wer brode and brandon bryght.* A: *Therin wer brondus and brandon bright*; G, following C, P, R: *Her ynee wer brode and brandon bright* makes a substantial improvement in this line and makes line 564 more effective.
565	*waytud.* A: *waxoud*; G, following C, P, R: *waytud* is a more plausible action at this point in the narrative.
566	*pray.* A: *pay*; C: *pray.*
577	*sowles.* A: *sowlows*; G, following C, P, R: *sowles.*
614	*dystruccioun.* A: *dystruccoun*; G, following P, R: *dystruccioun.*
615	*turmentyd.* A: *turment*; G, following C, P, R: *turmentyd.*
626	*she.* A: *yee.* C: *she*; R: *ho.*
645	*Maygrey is chekys.* A: *Maygrey in is chekys.* I have omitted *in* since it is not ordinarily included in the proverb, though the person of the pronoun was variable.
647	*payne.* A: *pyne*; G, following C, P, R: *payne.* As in line 123, *pyne* is possible, but destroys the rhyme with the next line.
687	*And seyd.* A omits *seyd.*
699	*The angell seyd.* A: *and that*; G, following C, P, R: *the angell seyd.* Lines 699 and 700 are transposed in A. Accepting *The angell seyd* restores order to a confusing passage.
727–28	*The angelle . . . be noght aferd.* These lines are omitted in A. Some connection is needed. I have accepted G's use of B, P, R for line 727 and G's composite from B, C, P, R for line 728.
740	*hoke.* A: *hokeus*; G, following B, P: *hoke.* A destroys the rhyme and does not need *–us* to form a plural here.

743   *had he.* G, following B, C, P, R: *Tundal had*, but A frequently used the pronoun where other MSS use the proper name.

770   *bryght.* A: *bryt*; G, following B, C, P, R: *bryght*. This is probably a simple omission by A, but I have emended it because it would destroy the rhyme with line 769.

799   *That full.* A: *that fowle*; G, following B, C, P, R: *that full.* A was probably distracted by the appearance of *fowle* later in the line.

799, 801   *vermyn.* A: *venym*; G, following B, C, P, R: *vermyn. Venym* is a possible word, but *vermyn* better fits this narrative and the tradition of vision literature.

808   *cawdoron of drede.* A: *cawdoron of drede*; G, following B, C, P, R: *schadowe of dede.* The latter makes for an interesting allusion to Vulgate Psalm 22:4, but A makes sense as it is.

814   *tokenyng.* A: *thyng*, an eyeslip's repetition from the previous line. C: *tokenyne.*

816   *desseyves.* A: *dothe save*; G, following R: *desseyves.* Clearly, deception rather than salvation is required in the line, as suggested also by C, P: *begyles.*

860   *then.* A: *the.*

873   *lad hym.* A: *had hym*; C: *ledde hym*; P: *him ladde.*

903–04   *Then wax . . . and muche woo.* The manuscripts differ substantially. A makes as much sense as any other if we apply lines 905–06 to line 904 only and not to line 903.

910   *vermyn.* A: *venym*; G, following B, C, P, R: *vermyn.* See note to lines 799, 801.

916   *nygh fylled.* A: *fell neght to*; C: *nygh filled.*

933–34   *Her taylys . . . the oddes.* A: *Her naylus wer bothe gret and longe / All kene hokys wer ther hond.* G's reconstruction from B, C, P, R fits the descriptive and narrative situation better — and preserves the rhyme.

963–64   *For monkus . . . Holy Kyrke.* B, C, P, R all provide metrically smoother lines with better rhyme, but the specificity of A in line 963 and the inclusion of women in line 964 makes me prefer to leave A intact. Line 963 is missing in C.

969   *Thei.* A: *Iuwes*; G, following B, C, R: *thei.* The sentence needs a subject.

971   *the.* As a reminder of my procedure, A: *thei* is probably an error for *the* of the sort I do not ordinarily mention.

973   *thus.* A: *this*; C: *thus*, which the rhyme requires.

1002   *dongyll.* A: *dongyll* is unattested, but since A also uses it at lines 1029, 1031, I believe it is the word intended. See explanatory note.

1020   *longe.* A: *narow*; G, following C, P, R: *longe.* Some change is necessary to avoid the awkward repetition from line 1019.

1035   *The.* A: *thys*; G, following B, C, R: *the.* The noun is plural.

1062   *as hem liked best.* A: *at that best kast*; G, following R: *as hem liked best* not only preserves the rhyme but agrees in sense with B, C, P.

1079   *dre.* A: *dyre*, with *y* canceled.

1085	*Yet thei.* A: *This peyn*; G, following B, C, R: *Yet thei* avoids the repetition of *peyn* in A.
1094	*odur smythus.* A: *non boldly*; G, following C, R: *oder smythus.* A does not make sense without great contortions. C, R fit the context perfectly.
1097	*ynoghe.* A: *ynoght.*
1114	After line 1114, I have omitted two lines from A: *For why that same company / Foloyddyn the in foly.* These lines virtually duplicate lines 1115–16.
1148	*grevyd.* A: *gvyd*, with *e* written superscript.
1188	*they con falle.* A: *they dy con falle*, with *dy* canceled.
1192	*Have turned.* A: *Had ben*; emended by G, following C, P, R: *Have turned.*
1195	*clomsyd.* A: *closyd*; G, following C, P: *clomsyd.* This appears to be a simple omission of *m*, but I mention it because R also has *closyd.*
1198	*toryve.* A: *toryvy*; G, following C, P, R: *toryve.* A appears to have been distracted by "stryve" in line 1197 and spoiled the rhyme.
1234	*Too Satanas.* A: *too sanat satanas*, with *sanat* canceled.
1259	*on her krocus.* A: *on her he krocus*, with *he* canceled.
1262	*The.* A: *thei*; C: *the.*
1270	*than fast.* A: *than a fast*, with *a* canceled.
1288	*world.* A: *wold*, with *r* superscript.
1297	*Satanas.* A: *satans*, with *a* superscript.
1356	*hit had he.* A: *his tayle was*; G, following R: *hit had he.* The *tayle* in A in this line as well as in lines 1355 and 1357 suggests some confusion. G, R provide a significant improvement without changing meaning or rhythm.
1363	*gloand.* I have retained A: *gloand*; G, following R: *tatred*; P: *taterede*; C: *hyt were tatered.*
1376	*hondes.* The *d* is obscured.
1392	*ande.* A: *armus*; G: *ande* (meaning "breath"), based on R: *ende*, P: *?nde*, and C: *breth*, seems to make the best of a difficult situation. Certainly it is hard to see *armus* as suitable in A's own context.
1393	*the sowlys.* A: *the sowk sowlys*, with *sowk* canceled.
1407	*angyll.* A: *anglyll*; C: *angell.*
1420	*Adames.* A: *admes*, with *a* superscript.
1430	*That.* A: *And*; G, following C, P, R: *That.*
1447	*fayne.* A: *faynd*; C: *fayne.*
1457	*sumtyme.* A: *hor tyme*; G, following C, P, R: *sum tyme.* The A scribe may have had his eye on "hom" in line 1456.
1464	*Cheffe.* A: *Thyffe*; G, following P, R: *Cheffe.* Some word indicating leadership or authority is necessary.
1487	*have.* A: *hve*; C: *have.*

1534   After line 1534, A omits two beautiful lines that appear in C, R and are accepted by G: *Sone they feld a swete ayre / And* [C: *They*] *fond a feld was wonder fayre*.

1545   *That*. Omitted in A.

1570   *soo clere*. A: *soo here clere*, with *here* canceled.

1600   *and*. A: *and*; G, following C, R: *dyde* make the line clearer, but I have left A since it is intelligible and the pejorative adjective is with *Caym*.

1613   *a vow*. A: *aw vow*, with *w* canceled.

1628   *Therfor marcy behovus hom have*. A: *Therfor behovus hom to have marcy*. This line is a real oddity. I have replaced it with C.

1640   *ther*. A: *ther*; G, following C: *gud mon*. A can stand if one assumes that anyone who had reached that place was welcome. C, however, does make the situation clearer.

1643   *wonys*. A: *wowys*; C: *wones*.

1654   *Cormake*. A: *Cornale*; G, following C, R: *Cormake*. A makes the same error at line 1663, thereby suggesting that he genuinely mistook the name.

1690   *lege*. A: *lyke*; G, following R: *lege*.

1698   *oft*. A: *of*; R: *ofte*; C: *ofn*.

1699   *And sum wer*. A: *and wer*; G, following R: *and sum wer*. The *sum* is necessary to distinguish between the "pilgrims" and the "religious."

1706   *sufforyd*. A: *had sufforyd*. I have omitted *had*. A seems to have moved from indirect discourse to a quotation. Omitting *had* makes the whole a quotation.

1724   *hayre*. A: *yron*; G, following C, R: *hayre*.

1731   *brent*. A is missing a verb. I have supplied *brent* from R.

1738   *hayre*. A: *peyn*; G, following C, R: *hayre*. Perhaps A did not know what a "hairshirt" was?

1744   *longe*. A: *lonke*.

1750   *thore*. A: *throre*; C: *thore*.

1861   *schyre*. A: *cleer*; G, following C, R: *schyre*. I have accepted the change to avoid the repetition with line 1859.

1868   *world*. A: *wold*, with *r* superscript.

1899   *whylk*. A: *walle* does not make sense in this description. G, following R: *whylk*, or C: *whych* does.

1901–02 *And all . . . eyne myght see*. A: *And with all odur ryches hit was overwent / That noo eyne myght see ne hart myght thynke*. These lines are simply so ugly that I have substituted R, though I have retained A's second *myght* in line 1902.

1907   *On*. A: *And*; C: *On*.

        instrumentus. A: *instrumenstus*; C: *instrumentes*.

1923   *So much myrthe as thei made within*. This line is repeated in A.

1955–56 *But this . . . of that syght*. These lines are reversed in A.

1980   *swete*. A omits, but G, following C, R, accepts.

1995	*hyng.* A: *thing*; I have accepted G's emendation to *hyng*, which improves intelligibility greatly.
2034	*flowres.* A: *fruyt*; G, following C, R: *flowres*. The change must be accepted because tradition encourages and the context demands "flowers."
2053	*They.* A: *He*; G, following R: *They*.
2054	*He had hem.* A: *hym he had*; C: *he had hem*. The plural is needed.
2089	A makes sense but might be clearer without *wer feyr*.
2102	I have left the greatly imperfect rhyme. C and R have variants of lines 2099–2102 which provide a rhyme at line 2102, but require drastic changes in the names and order of the gems.
2132	*turne.* A: *tne*, with *ur* superscript.
2136	*angelles.* A: *angell*; C: *angelles*.
2142	*Renne.* A: *And renne* destroys the syntax.
2147	*angelles.* A: *angell*; G, following C, R: *angelles*.
2148	*dwelles.* A: *dwell*; G, following C, R: *dwelles*.
2157	*world.* A: *wold*, with *r* superscript.
2168	*syde.* A includes an ill-formed letter between *d* and *e*, which may simply be an error.
2181	*And seyd.* G, following C, R: *And seyd*. A omits *seyd*, and a verb is needed.
2189	*thes.* A: *this*; G, following C, R: *thes*.
2200	*namly.* A: *ma namly*, with *ma* canceled.
2220	*hym noght.* A: *hym noght*; G, following C, P, R: *but lytelle*. I have retained A, though the alternative makes more sense and better translates the Latin original.
2223	*Lyons.* A: *Lyon*; G, following C, R: *Lyons*.
2224	*possessyons.* A: *possessyon*; G, following C, R: *possessyons*. I have accepted the changes on the grounds that the plural is better in line 2224 and the name of the diocese in line 2223 is in some doubt. See explanatory note to line 2222.
2276	*holely.* A: *helely*; G, following C, R: *holely*.
2284	*body.* A: *bog body*, with *bog* canceled.
2304	*Thy marcé.* G, following C, R: *have on me marce*, but the nature of the outcry seems to allow the omission of the verb.
2360	*He repreved hem as Goddus lawe wold.* A: *How thei schuld be withdon as Goddes wyll wold*. I have rejected this line for its sheer ugliness and substituted C.
2381–83	*Explicit Tundale . . . coopy was.* These lines, the indication of the conclusion of the poem, are indented in A.

Glossary

abadde *hesitated*

abaysed, abayst *humiliated, abashed*

abite *habit*

aby *pay*

ac *but*

acordand *fitting*

acordaunce *accordance, parallel*

adrad *afraid*

adrede *to dread*

aferd *afraid, frightened*

aflight *afflicted, affected*

aght *ought*

ago *gone*

agrise *dread*

agrose *terrified*

alblast *siege engine*

ald *old*

aldermest *most of all*

alegge(d) *relieve(d)*

alkyn(s) *all kinds of, everything*

all and som *all and some, every one*

allane, all ane *alone*

alls *as*

allswa *also*

alltha(u)ff *although*

almosdede, almusdede(s) *almsdeeds*

als *as, also, as if, when*

alther hattest *hottest of all*

alther maste *most of all*

amayde *amazed*

amorwe *morning*

ande *breath*

ane *an, one, someone; alone*

aneli, anely *only, specifically*

angwis, angwysse *anguish*

ankyr *anchor*

annamelyd *decorated*

antem(e)s *anthems*

aperceived *realized, perceived*

apert *open*

apertely, apertliche *openly, plainly*

aplight *assured; assuredly, indeed*

aqueld *destroyed (spiritually)*

arayd *arranged, arrayed*

arase *arose*

ar(e) *before; already*

arliche *early*

arn *turned*

aros *arose*

aseth *reparation*

askus *ashes*

astone(y)d *astonished*

at, ate *at*

at(t) *that*

at(t)o(o)nus *at once*

atteryng *poisonous*

aubes *albs*

Austyn *St. Augustine*

Austyns *Augustinians*

auter *altar*

aventure *adventure, occurrence, experience, event*

aviis *advice, opinion; report*

avoutry, voutry *adultery*

avysede, avysud *considered*

aw *ought; befits, is fitting for* (impers.)

awen *own*
ay, ey *always, ever*
ayre *air*

bac *back*
bad *bade, ordered; prayed*
baelys *rods*
bagges *bags, pouches*
bald *assured, sure, certain, strong*
balder *bolder, more confident*
baldli, baldly *boldly, quickly, confidently*
bale(s) *distress, torment(s), suffering*
baly(w)s *bellows*
bandes *bonds*
bare *bore, carried*
bareyt *distress*
basseynus *basins*
bath(e) *both*
bathi *bathe*
baume *balm*
bayde *abided*
bayli(e), bayly *country*
baynly *obediently*
be, bi *by*
bede(s) *prayer(s)*
bede *to pray; bade*
bedene *completely*
Bedlem *Bethlehem*
behoves *must; it behooves, it is fitting for* (impers.)
beme *beams*
bendes *bands*
ben(e) *be; would be; been; are*
bere *commotion, uproar; tone; burden*
berell *beryl*
bere(s) *bear(s), wear; bore, wore*
berth *bears*

besantes *coins*
besom *swishing (sound)*
best *beast*
bete *beaten, hammered*
beth, beys *is*
beton *remedy, relieve; bite*
betyde *betide, occur*
bevereche *drink, beverage*
beymus *beams*
bi *by; according to; at the time of*
bicom(e) *become; became*
bidene *immediately, at once, forthwith*
bifell(e), byfyll *befell, occurred*
biheve *benefit*
bihove(s), byhovus *behoove(s), obliges, must*
biis *gray*
biknewe *revealed*
bileft *left*
bileve *belief; to remain*
bileved *left*
bise *ponder*
bitaught *commended, entrusted*
bithenche, bithinke *consider, imagine*
bituen, bituix *between*
bityd *occurred*
biwent *went*
blamed *blamed, convicted, found guilty*
bleryd *stuck out*
blew(e) *blue; blew*
blinne, blyn *cease, stop*
blo(o) *blue, livid*
blithe *glad, happy*
blytheliche *happily*
bocchere *butcher*
boiland *boiling*
bon *bound*
bond *bonds*

bone *help, gift, boon*
boron *born*
borowde *borrowed, redeemed*
bost *box (usually a pendant), pyx*
bostus *boasters*
bot *but, except, only*
boune, bowne *ready; bound, obligated*
bounté(s) *bounty, benefit; virtues*
bowsomly *obediently*
boxum *courteous*
brac *broke*
brad(der) *broad(er)*
bras *brass*
braste *overcome*
brawneschedyn *threatened*
brayd *shrieked*
bred(e) *bread; breadth;* **(all on) brede** *far and wide*
bredur *brother*
breke *broke; trilled*
brening *burning*
brend(on), brent *burnt, burned*
brenne *burn*
brerdes *rims*
brigge *bridge*
brithe *birth*
brochys *skewers*
brocking *calls of distress*
broddys *picks*
brond *brand*
bryd *woman*
bryg(g)e *bridge*
brymston, bronston, brunston, brimstone
brynand *burning*
bryn(s) *burn(s);* **brynt** *burnt*
bryst *burst*
burde *board, bench*

burd *would; would have to; must*
burdoun, burdown *bass; pilgrim's staff*
burges *burgess, citizen*
bus *must*
buxum *ready*
bwones *bones*
byd *bid, pray*
byde *abide, stay*
bystad *afflicted*
bytond *honed*

caghe *cage*
cald(e) *called, named; cold*
card *cared*
caroly *sing (carols)*
catell *possessions*
causteloines *chalcedony*
cawdoron *cauldron*
celestien *celestial, heavenly*
cessand *ceasing*
ceté *city*
chanoun(e)s *canons*
chantryse *chantries*
chapiter *chapter (meeting of friars)*
charbokull, charbukelston *carbuncle*
chargyd, chargytt *laden, burdened*
chaumber, chaumbre *chamber, room*
chaundelers *candle-holders*
chekus, chekys *cheeks*
chele *cold, chill*
chere, chyr *manner, disposition; countenance; cheer*
cheryschyd *took good care of*
chymné *furnace, chimney*
chyne *chin(s)*
chynus *chains*
clarkys *clerks*
clathes *clothes*

clen(n)es(se) *purity*

cleped *called (out), named;* **clepeing** *calling*

clepeth, clepi *call (out), name*

clere *bright, clear, shining*

clethyng *clothing*

cleyne *pure*

clombon *climbed*

clomsyd *enfeebled*

colagys *colleges*

cole *coal;* **colis, colys** *coals*

Colett(es) *Collect(s) (short prayer)*

colombin *columbine*

combret *clumsy*

comforth *comfort; comforted*

command *coming*

commounliche *commonly, generally*

compeynie *company, group*

con *did*

conjure *command, order*

con(ne)(n) *began to*

connyng *understanding, comprehension*

conscyons *conscience*

contakt *dissension*

conteyni *sustain*

contré *country*

contynanse *gesture*

coopy *copy, text*

cop *summit*

coper *copper*

coround *crowned*

corounes *crowns*

cors *corpse, body*

cosyn *cousin, kinsman*

cote *coat*

co(u)nsaile, conseil(y), consell, conseyl(e), cownsel(l) *counsel, advice*

co(u)ntynance *countenance, (facial) expression*

cours *part, course, iteration*

courtelage *garden*

couth(e), cowthe *knew, understood; could*

covand *promise*

cova(i)tise, covatyse, covetys(e) *covetousness, greed*

covent *convent*

covetand *coveting*

cowpus *bowls; cups*

cracched *scratched*

creaunce *faith*

crepand *creeping*

cresolyte *chrysolite*

Cristen *Christian*

croice, croyce *cross*

crounes *crowns (of the head)*

crouthe *croud (stringed instrument)*

cryand *crying*

cultorus *ploughshares*

cuntray, cuntré *country*

dart(es) *attack(s); barb(s)*

de(d)d(e) *death; dead*

dede *did; caused to (happen)*

dede(s) *deed(s), action(s), occurrence(s)*

ded(e)li, dedely *deadly*

defygurd *disfigured*

degrese *degrees*

del *times*

dele *bit, piece; dole, distress* (see also **dole**)

deme(d) *judge(d), deem(ed), direct(ed)*

departabill *set apart for an individual; separate, individual*

deppest *deepest*

deray *uproar*

dere(s) *harm(s), injure(s)*
derk *dark*
derur *more expensive*
desayvabill *deceitful*
descry *reveal, proclaim, announce*
dyscryve *describe, explain*
desmay *dismay; be dismayed*
desseyves *misleads*
dett *determined*
dett, deyt *debt, obligation*
develing *sprawling*
devine *figure out, divine*
devise(d) *describe(d); look(ed), examine(d)*
de(y)th(e) *death*
diamaunce *diamonds*
diche *ditch*
dight, dyght *set; built; ordered*
dispendes *to use, dispend*
dispysede *despised*
divynour *wise man*
do, don *do; cause to*
doctour *doctor, learned theologian*
dole *sorrow, pain, suffering*
dome *judgment*
Domesday, Domusday *Judgment Day*
dominical *Scriptural reading*
dong *beat*
dongyll *deep valley*
dorrus *doors*
dose *does*
dotaunce *doubt, uncertainty*
douhti *doughty*
dout, dowt(t)(e) *doubt, unease, confusion*
dowmpe *dumb*
drad *dreaded*
dredand *dreading*

drefull *sorrowful*
dregh *suffer*
dreynt *drenched*
Dright *Lord*
drof(f)(e) *drove, pursued*
droghe, drowgh, drowyn *pulled, drew*
drury *woeful*
dud(de) *did*
dueling *delay*
duelle *remain*
dwelland *dwelling*
dyamondus *diamonds*
dy(e)(y)(d) *die(d)*
dylfull *doleful*
dyppe *deep*
dysayvabyll *deceitful*
dyscryvynyn *describe*
dytte *fill up*

edderys, eddrys *adders*
ee(ne) *eye(s)*
eft *after; again*
eftsones *soon after*
eger *sharp, brusque, eager*
egge *edge*
eghtene *eighth*
eglentere *briar rose*
eighen *eyes*
eke *also*
eld *age*
elles *otherwise*
emastyce *bloodstones*
emer *guardian (angel)*
emeraudus *emeralds*
emperis, emperys *empress*
encheson *reason, intent*
encres(e) *increase*
ennamelyd *decorated*

285

enpayred *impaired, broken*
ensuample(s), ensaumpel(s)
  example(s), lesson(s)
entent *intention, purpose*
erbers *gardens*
erbes, erbys *plants*
er(e), erward *before*
er(t) *are*
ertheliche, erthely *earthly*
ertow *you are*
es *is, are*
eutes *newts*
evell, evyll *evil*
even, evon *straight, exactly, directly;*
  evening
evencristen *fellow Christian(s)*
evensang(e) *evensong (Vespers)*
everilk *each, every*
eydur *either*
eyn(e) *eye*
eyr(us) *ear(s)*

fabill, fabyll *fable, false story;*
  deception
fairhede *excellence, fairness*
fall *deadly*
falon *feel*
falshede *falsehood, deceit*
fand(e) *endeavor, undertaking; to*
  tempt; looked after; found
fandyng *temptation, troubling*
farly, ferly *wonder*
faulland *falling*
fawe *livid, angry*
fay *faith; source of doctrine*
fayn(e), feyn *glad, happy, pleased,*
  eager(ly); like to
febull, febyll *feeble*

feffed *endowed*
fekul *fickle*
fel *fall, fell*
feld *felt, sensed*
fele *many; avail*
fel(l), fyll *skin; destroy; feel; deadly*
fellawered *company, group, fellowhood*
felness *evil, treachery*
felyschepe *fellowship*
fend *defend*
fende(s), fend(us) *fiend(s)*
fer(e) *far; healthy; frighten; take as a*
  companion; companions; fire; **(in) fere**
  in a company, as a group
ferrede *company, crowd*
fetherfoy *chrysanthemum*
fe(y)t(t) *feet*
fine amour *perfect love; refined love,*
  courtly love
fithel *fiddle, violin*
flaumand *flaming*
flaumbe, flawm(m)e *flame*
flayd *frightened*
fleighe *flew*
fles(s)(ch)(e) *flesh*
fleyng *flaying*
flowe *fled, flew*
flowre delyce *fleur-de-lis*
flytte *moved, removed*
folowand *following*
foluydden *followed*
foly(e)(s), foli(es) *sin(s), folly/follies*
fond *found; tempt*
fonston *baptismal font*
forbrent *burnt severely*
force *strength, power*
fordo *prevent*
fore *assaulted*

forght(he) *forth*
forlast *lose, lost*
forlor(n)(e) *lost, loss*
forneise *furnace*
forsayd *aforementioned*
forst *frost*
for that *because*
forthi *therefore*
forthynkon *repent*
foryt *forth*
foulen, foulys, fowles *birds; bird's*
fowrte *fourth*
fra(m), fro *from*
frayne *ask*
fre *generous, gracious*
Frere Austines *Augustinians*
Frere Carmes *Carmelites*
Frere Menours *Franciscans*
Frere Prechours *Dominicans*
frere(s) *friar(s)*
fresand *freezing*
frete, fretud *bit; ate*
freyt *fretted; decorated*
fryst(yng) *delay(ing)*
frytte *fruit*
furgons *pokers*
fure, fuyr, fyr *fire*
fyoolys *bowls*

ga *go*
game(n) *game(s), delight, playing*
gan *go; did; became; began to; proceeded to*
gang *go; came; went*
gapus *gapes;* **gapud** *gaped open*
gase *go, goes; went*
gast(e) *ghost, spirit*
gatys *gates*

gavelers *usurers*
gederd, gederud, gedryd, geydoryd *gathered; re-formed*
gent *delicate*
ger *prepare; cause to*
gere *clothing*
gert *began to; caused to*
geyre *equipment*
ghate *gate*
gif *given*
ginne *engine, contrivance*
gle *joy, glee*
glow(e)and *glowing*
gnayst *gnash [teeth]*
gnowe *gnawed*
gobedys, gobettus *gobbets, chunks*
godspelle *gospel(s)*
go(i)nfa(i)noun *banner*
gon ga *began to go*
gonus *opens [his] mouth*
gowle(yng) *howl(ing);* **gowlyd** *howled*
gras *grace*
grayd *troubled*
grayde *prepared; performed; conveyed; given*
graythely *readily*
grede *crying, lamentation; cry out*
grediris *gridirons*
gredyron *gridiron*
grenned, grennyd *growled, grimaced, bared teeth*
gretand, gretyng *moaning, weeping, lamentation*
grete *great; wept*
gretton *greet*
grevd(d)e *grieved*
griseli(che), grysely *gruesome*
gronden *ground*

groonus *groans*
grucchud *grumbled*
gryn *grimace*
grysely, gryssly *horribly*
gud *good*
gun *began to; did*
gy *guide*
gyandys *giants*
gyf(en) *give(n)*
gylt *guilt*
gyn *means; engine*

haddestow *had you*
haght *have*
halden *held; considered; bound*
hale *whole; full; healthy*
halidom *relics*
halows *saints*
halvendel *half, a half part*
hame *home*
han *have*
harl *hurl*
harneys *armor*
has(e) *has, have*
hast *has, have; haste*
hate *hot*
hatter *hotter*
hautain *treble*
haylsed *greeted*
hayre *hairshirt*
hedder, hedur *hither, here*
hede *behead*
hedous *heads*
hegh, heighe *high*
heighe *hurry, hie*
hem(selve) *them(selves)*
hend *hands*
hende *courteous, gentle*

henge *hung*
hennes *hence*
hent *seize; taken, seized*
herd, hard *heard; praised*
here *here; hear*
hereyng *hearing*
herre *higher*
hert *heart*
herust *hear*
her(ys) *their; here*
hete, heyte n. *heat*
hete *commanded*
hetheing *abuse;* **to hetheing** *with abuse*
hethen, hethon *hence, away; here*
heved *head*
hewe *hew, color; bright (of complexion)*
heye *haste, quickness*
hider, hyder, hydour *hither, here*
hidous, hydous, hydwys *hideous, dreadful*
hight *high; height*
hight, hyght *was named, was called*
hing, hyng *hung*
hir *her; their*
ho *she*
hokes, hokys *hooks*
hole *hole; healed, whole*
holt *holds*
homerus *hammers*
hondryt *hundred*
honget *hung*
honging *hanging*
hootte *hot*
hor *their*
hosull, howsull *give the Eucharist;* **howsyld** *given the Eucharist*
howge, hogy, hugy *huge*
howsell *Holy Communion (Eucharist)*

288

Glossary

hows(es), howssus *house(s)*
hudde *hidden*
hund(e)reth, hundryd, hundryt
 hundred
hu(y)r *her*
hwond *hound*
hy(e) *quickly, hastily; haste; he; listen,*
 hear
hyde *hidden*
hyes *hie, gather*
hyld *held, believed*

iacyntus *zircons*
ich, yche *(the) very; each*
ich *I*
ichave *I have*
ichil *I will*
icy *comfort*
ilk, ylke *each, every; same, very*
ill *evil*
intil, intyll *into; unto*
iren *iron*
ise *ice*

Jacobins *Dominicans*
jogelars *deceivers; entertainers*
jowellys *jewels*
Jowes *Jews*
jugged *judged*

kalendes *calends (the first day of the*
 Roman month)
kan *know, understand; can*
kele *cool*
kelyng *cooling*
kend(e) *taught, explained; knowledge*
kene, keyn *sharp*
ken(ne) *know, understand, apprehend;*

teach
kennes *know(s)*
kest *cast*
kevered, keverdyn, keveryd *recovered*
knaw(yng) *know; knowledge*
kneland *kneeling*
kneld *kneeled*
kne(y)s, kneus *knees*
knottes *(decorative) knots*
krocus *crooks*
kyd(de) *known*
kyndam *kingdom*
kynde *nature; kind, kin*
kyndeli, kyndely *natural; naturally,*
 properly, according to nature
kyn(ne), kynnus *kind; kinds of*

ladde *led*
lane *grace*
laned *concealed, overlooked*
lappud *surrounded*
lare *teaching; learning*
lastand *lasting*
lat(es) *let(s), leave(s)*
lawed *uneducated* (see also **lewed**)
lectornes, lettornes *lecterns*
led(d)e *lead (metal)*
lede *nation, country, area*
lede(s) *lead(s)*
lef *leaf; willing, eager*
legge *lie, lay, place*
lem *gleaming*
lende *remain, reside*
leryd *learned*
les *lies; lost*
lesing *lying*
les(se) *less*
lest *last; least*

lest and maste *fully*

letany *litany*

lete *let; had; avoid, give up; leave out*

leten *forgiven; leave, give up*

lett *relieved; hindrance, obstruction, delay*

levand *living*

leve *dear, beloved; permission, leave, allowance*

levedust *lived*

levedy *lady*

levenyng *lightning*

lever *rather*

levon *live*

lewed, lewyd *uneducated*

leyd *placed*

leyn *lend*

le(y)ve *leave; believe*

libbe *live*

lic(c)houre *lecher*

lif *live*

ligge, lygge *lay*

lighting *lightning*

likeing, lykand, lykyng *liking, enjoyment*

liif *life*

lili *lily*

lite *little; light*

lodder *louder*

lod(d)ly, loghtly *terrifying, horrible, loathsome; angrily*

lond *land*

lo(o)gh(e) *laughed*

lopen *leapt*

lore *teaching*

lorn(e) *lost*

lotheliche, lothly *loathsome; hideously*

louken *lock*

low *flame*

luf(ed) *love; loved*

luke *look, see*

lychory *lechery*

lye *fire*

ly(es) *lie(s)*

lyf(and) *living; to live*

lyfed *lived*

lyf(f)(e) *life*

lygand *lying*

lyg(ges) *lie(s)*

lykkynyd *likened, compared*

lym(es) *limb(s)*

lythe *lies; joint*

lythur *evil*

lyveryt *delivered*

ma *to make; more*

mack *match*

maine, mayne *strength, power, might*

maister(s) *master(s)*

malycoly *melancholy*

manast *menaced*

manhede *manhood*

mankinne, mankyn(d)(e) *mankind*

mannes *men, people*

manslaghter *manslaughter*

marcé, marcy *mercy*

mare *delay; more, greater*

mare and lesse *more and less, all*

margarites *pearls*

marke *dark*

mase *make(s), made*

mased *amazed*

maste *most*

maygrey *despite*

mayn(e) *strength, power*

maynsweryng *perjury*

mayntene(d), mayntyn(iod)
  maintain(ed), support(ed), sustain(ed)
mayre *mayor*
mede *reward, solace; beverage;* **(to)**
  mede *for reward*
mele *meal*
mene *to mean, signify; melody (middle*
  part)
menegth *means*
meney *company, group*
meng *join, unite*
Menours *Franciscans*
mensk(ed) *honor(ed), worship(ped)*
menstracie *minstrelsy*
merknes *darkness*
merre *mar*
mervail(l)(e)(s), mervayle(s) *marvel(s),*
  miracle(s)
meschaunce *adversity, bad experience*
messe *mass*
mett *performed*
met(t)e *food; to dream; appropriate*
  (adj.)
mevand *moving*
meyne *mean, middle part; company*
michel, mekyll, mikell, muckyll,
  mykell, mykyll *great(ly), large, much*
midnerd *(middle-) earth, the world*
milde, myld(de) *mild, gracious*
miri(e) *merry*
misbileve *false belief(s)*
misgangyng *straying, going wrong*
misgilt *sin*
misours *sinners*
missays *misery*
mode *manner; mind, state of mind*
mold(e) *earth, world*
mon *must; attend to, mind*

mon(us) *man (men)*
mond *might*
montayn, monteyn(us), montteyn
  mountain(s)
mo(o) *more*
more and les *more and less, everything*
morwe, moron *morning*
mossel *morsel*
most, mott *must*
mot *motes*
myddelerd, mydylerde *(middle-) earth,*
  the world
mydes *middle*
myght, myghtes, myghttus *might,*
  strength, power
mylle *miles*
myn *less, lesser*
myne *mine*
mys *miss*
mysavysede *ill-advised*
mysgane *erred, gone astray*
mys(s)(e) *sin*
myster *need, needful*

nadder *adder, snake*
nakyn, nanekyn *no kind of*
nam *took*
nane *none, no*
naru *narrow*
nas *was not*
navylle *navel*
nawgeres *augers*
ne *not, no, nor*
neddren *adders, snakes*
neghand *nearing, approaching*
neghen *nine*
neighe *near; nearly*
nemon *name*

nempne *call out, name*
nerre *nearer*
nesche *flaccid, soft*
nether *deeper, farther down*
neven *explain, say, tell;* **(at) neven** *comparable, on a par*
nevend *mentioned, explained*
nis *is not*
nite *not know*
nithe *malice*
no *no; not; nor; did not*
nold(en) *would not*
noither, nouder, nouther *neither*
nom(e) *took, taken*
none *noon*
nones, for the nones *indeed*
non(e)skines *none at all*
nonnes *nuns*
nother *no other*
noure *nowhere*
noys *noise*
noy(se) *annoy(s), trouble(s), bother(s)*
nye *nearly*

o *of; one; on*
obeedyons *obedience*
obeydyand *obedient*
ocur *usury, high interest rate*
oddes *points*
odur, oodur *other*
of *off*
off *of*
oftok *overtook*
ogain *again; back*
ogain, ogaines, ogayne, ogayns *against; up to; towards*
oght *ever, at all; anything, aught*
okering *money-lending*

omell *among*
on *on, in; one*
onacles, onicles *onyx*
ond *spite; fierce*
onlyve *alive*
onone *at once*
onys *once*
or *or; before*
ordaine, ordeyn(yd) *command, arrange, ordain(ed)*
ordand *ordained, established*
ordans *ordains; guides*
ordenance *guidance*
order *religious orders*
ore *pardon*
orisoun(e), orysoune *prayer*
orybly *horribly*
ought *aught, at all*
ourn *arranged*
ous *us*
outher *either*
outrage *outrageous*
outtane *except*
overbrewe *knocked over*
overflé *pass over*
overschaken *passed by, overcome*
ovon *oven*
owhen *own*
owrys, oyres *hours*

payen(s) *pagan(s)*
par(a)cel(l)s *parcels, pieces*
parfyte, perfyte *perfect*
parti *portion, part; period (of time)*
party, ta party *one side*
partyse *parts*
paruink *periwinkle*

pas(s), passe *pass, leave, go away, go on; (at) pas to pass, to go*

Pasch *Easter; Passover*

passand *passing, temporary*

Pas(s)e *Easter; Passover*

payne *pain*

pays *peace*

pen(y)s *pence, coins*

perced *pierced*

pere *peer, equal*

persayved *perceived*

pes(e) *peace*

peté *pity*

pevertté, povertté *poverty*

peyn *pain*

piche, pyc(c)he, pykke *pitch*

pilers, pylers *pillars, columns*

pine, pyne *pain*

pittes *pits*

plas *place*

playne *fully*

playne pase *brisk pace*

pleyndon *lamented*

plough *land*

plyght *plight*

ponyst *punished*

pople *people*

pore *poor*

poudre *powder*

Poule *Paul*

poure *blameless, steadfast*

pourper *purple*

po(u)sté *power*

pouwere *power*

pover *poor*

poynt *point (of doctrine)*

prechours *preachers*

prede *pride*

prevely *secretly*

prevetese, privatese, priveté *secret, hidden knowledge, obscure matter; secrecy*

preve(y) *close, privy, confidential, secret*

prevyté *privacy*

prevytys *private parts*

priis *value, price*

primrol *primrose*

proved *tried, attempted*

prow *testing, proof, benefit*

pryd *pride*

purvayd(e), purveyed *provided; offered; conveyed; prepared*

putt *pit*

putton *pushed*

pyne(d) *pain; to pain, to be pained*

pynnes *pains*

quarel *missile*

queinte(r), quynte *clever; (more) skillful*

queyntaunce *acquaintance*

quic *caustic*

quic, quyk *alive, quick*

rad(de) *frightened*

raght *reached*

rampyng *leaping*

rasour *razor*

rathe(r)/(st) *(more, most) quickly; (more, most) promptly; soon(er/est)*

raw, on raw *in order (in a row)*

rays *raise*

reckys *care*

rede(s) *read(s); advise(s); to study*

re(e)de *red*

regnes *reigns*
reles(e) *release*
religioun *religious orders*
rennand *running*
renneth *runs*
repenti *repent*
repreved *reproved*
reprove *reproof*
resayved *received*
respyt *respite, relief*
reuthe, rewthe *pity, regret*
revescyd *vested*
rew(eful) *rue(ful)*
rewle *rule*
re(y)d(e) *advice, teaching*
reynyng *reigning*
ribaudie *foolishness*
ribes *rubies*
rigge, rygge *back*
rinneth *runs*
rode *cross; red*
rong *rang*
ros *rose, arose*
rout *bellow, shout*
rowte *rabble*
rugged *torn (up)*
ryfe *rigorous; well-known*
ryg *roof*
ryghtwes(s)nes, ryghtwisnes *justice*
ryghtwis *righteous*
rynand *running*
rysand *rising*
ryseing *rising, Resurrection*
ryve *tear;* **ryvon** *ripped*

sa *so, soever*
saferstones *sapphires*
salidoines *celadon*

sall *shall*
salud *saluted, greeted*
samen *together*
sampull *example*
saphere *sapphire*
sare *sad(ly), sore(ly), agonizing*
sartus *surely*
sary *sorry*
saul(e)(s), sawl(e)(s) *soul(s)*
saunfayle *without fail, without doubt*
Sauter *Psalms*
sautry *psaltery*
sa(u)wes *sayings, teachings, words*
saw *word*
sayand *saying*
schake *hurry*
schaltow *shall you*
schape *escape*
schappud *created*
scheld *shield*
schen *must*
schend(e) *destroy*
schent *overcome*
schet *shut*
schevus *sheaves*
schew(es), (ed) *show(s), (ed)*
scheynod *shone*
schire *entirely; brightly*
scho *she*
schon *shone*
schorpyonys *scorpions*
schriche *shrieking*
schrive, schryve *forgive; be forgiven (in the sacrament of Penance)*
schul *shall*
schuld *should*
schrevon *shriven*
schrist *shrieked*

Glossary

schryfen, schryven *shriven, forgiven*

schryft *(sacrament of) Penance, Confession*

schryll *clearly, brightly*

schynand *shining*

schyre *shining*

scole(s) *school(s)*

scrattyng *scratching*

scriche *screech, shriek*

scrippe *pilgrim's bag or pouch*

scryve *confess; renounce*

se *sea; to see*

seculeres *diocesan priests*

sede *said, taught*

seett *set, established*

sege *seat*

seighe, seyghe *saw*

seke *sick*

selly *remarkably, skillfully*

semand *appearing*

semlande *appearance*

semblaunce *comparison, resemblance*

semly *pleasing*

sen *since*

sensowrys *censers*

septurus *scepters*

se(e)r(e), seer *various, diverse*

serewyse *apart*

seriaunce *servants*

sertaine, sertayne *certain*

servydyst *deserve*

sese(s) *cease(s), stop(s), remit(s); sees*

sesoune *season, time*

sestow *do you see*

sete *sat*

sethen, sethyn, seython *since, later, afterwards*

sett *set, built*

seyn *seen*

seyner *sooner*

seyntwary *sanctuary*

seyrwyse *in various ways*

seyt *says*

seytt *seated; seat*

side *spacious*

sigge *say*

sikelatoun *silk woven with gold*

siker(liche), siker(ly), sycur(ly) *sure(ly), certain(ly), firmly*

sithen *afterwards, then*

sithe(s), sythus *time(s)*

skathe *harm*

sklaunder, sclandur *scandal, slander; sclanderyd slandered*

skorne *scorn, mock*

skyll *reason, rational capacity*

slane *slain*

slaveyn *pilgrim's cloak*

slete *sleet*

slewthe *sloth*

slowe *slow, sluggish*

slyke *such*

smal, smyll(e) *smell, odor, aroma; piece, bit*

smal(e) *small, fine, slender*

smert *painful, sharp; be pained*

smiche *smoke*

smylland *smelling*

smytheus, smythus *forges, blacksmith shops;* **smythy** *forge*

smythus *blacksmiths*

snaw *snow*

sobert *sobered, calmed*

sogettus, suggettus *subjects*

solemnyté *celebration*

sond *help*

soster *sister*

soth(e)(ly), soth(fastly), soghth, suthely
  truth; truly, correctly

sotyll *subtle*

souke *sucked*

sour *agonized*

sownes *leads (to)*

spac, spak *spoke*

space *a while, period of time*

sparthe *spear, battle ax*

spede *benefit, help, well-being; to*
  progress

spelle *teaching*

spended *spent, expended*

speyr *despair*

sponne *span*

spourged *purged, cleansed*

spowsage *marriage*

spyll(e) *kill, ravage, shake*

spylt *killed, destroyed*

spytyll forkus *pitchforks*

stabill, stabyll *stable, steadfast,*
  reliable, orthodox

stane *stone*

stark *strong*

sted *situated; treated*

sted(d)(e)(s), styd *place(s), location(s)*

stell *steal*

stel(l)(e), styll *steel*

stely *steal, sneak*

steron *stir*

ster(res) *star(s)*

steven(s) *voice(s), speech(es), sound(s)*

stighe *climbed, went up*

stille *firmly*

stin(c)kand *stinking*

stint *stopped*

stor *possessions*

store *powerful, potent, fierce*

stowt *staunch, sturdy*

stounde *time*

strem(es) *stream(s)*

strenkith, strynthe *strength*

stroy *destroy, overcome*

stryft *strife*

styf *sturdy, strong*

styr *stir, move*

suede *oppressed, afflicted*

suffrayne *(spiritually) beneficial; main,*
  principal

suffri *suffer*

suld *should*

sum *a; some*

sumdele *somewhat, a bit*

sumtyme *at one time, once upon a time*

swa *so*

swart, swert *black*

swepand *sweeping*

swere *neck; swear*

swete *adj., adv. sweat; sweet(ly),*
  comfortably

swetter *sweeter*

swevening *dreaming*

swiche *such*

swilk *such*

swithe, swythe *very, greatly; quickly;*
  firmly

swolo, swolewo *swallow;* **swollod**
  swallowed

swowyng *groaning*

sybbe *kinship*

syde *side, boundary*

syde-lyppud *wide-lipped*

sykande *sighing*

sykerer *more surely, more certainly*

sykud, sykyd *sighed*

sykurnes *security*
symple *frank, open, simple*
syngant *singing*
sythe(s) *time(s)*

ta *toe; take*
tak *take; took*
tak(e) (gud) tent *pay (close) attention*
takenyng *tokening, sign*
tald *told; counted; recounted*
tane *taken, caught; accepted, encompassed; the one*
tapaces *topaz*
teche(d) *teach (taught), show*
teght, teyt *teeth*
tempore *temper*
tene *suffering; ten*
tentes *pays attention, attends*
tenyd *accused*
terestri *terrestrial, earthly*
teythe *tithes*
tha *those*
thai *they*
thair *their*
thaire *these*
tham *them*
than *then*
thare, thore *there*
thaw(ye) *though*
the *the; thee, you, thyself; prosper*
thede *country, land*
thefus, theves *thieves*
thei *they; even if, although*
their *these*
thenche(n) *think*
thennes, thennus *thence*
ther *where; there*
thethen *thence*

thi *your, thy*
thider *thither, there*
thilche *these*
thin *thine, your*
thir *these*
thirl(ed) *pierce(d)*
tho *then; those*
thole *endure, bear, suffer*
thonder *thunder*
thonk(ed) *thank(ed)*
thratte *threatened*
thrawe *thrust*
thred, thridde *third*
throw *dangerous*
thrust *thirst*
thurgh *through*
thurt *need*
thurth(out) *through(out)*
thusgate *thus; thusly; as follows*
thyes *thighs*
tiding *tidings, news*
til(l), tyll *to, until*
tine, tyne *lose, harm, destroy; harmful, damnable*
titter *more quickly, quite quickly*
to *two; too; to*
tobrent *burnt fiercely*
todes *toads*
todrawyn, todrowe *torn apart*
toforn *before, in front of*
tokening *premonition*
tolys *tools*
ton *the one*
tong(us) *tongue; tong(s)*
tonicles *vestments, albs*
topes *topaz*
torent *tore, torn to bits*
toryfe *tear apart*

Glossary

toskus, toskys *tusks*
tothe *teeth*
tother *the other*
totore *tore up*
toucheth, towches *touches; is relevant*
tourn *turn*
touten *arses*
transyng *passing over, trance (unconscious state)*
travaild *troubled*
travayll *travail, hardship*
tremblyd *trembled*
trent *turned*
tre(u)(s) *tree(s); wood*
trispas(s)e *trespass, sin*
trone *throne*
trow(ed) *believe(d), trust(ed)*
trowestow *do you believe*
trowth(e) *truth, fidelity*
trowyng *opinion, belief*
trwe *true*
tuk *took*
tuk (gud) tent *paid (close) attention*
turmentri(e) *torment*
turmentowrus, turmentowrys *tormenters*
twoched *touched*
twybyll *pickax(es)*
twyne *part*
tyd, tyte *quickly*
tyde *time, liturgical season*
tyre *attire*
tysus *entices*
tyttest *most quickly*

uggod *shuddered*
umlappud, umsett *set around, surrounded*

uncouthe *uncivilized, savage*
undede *opened*
undernome *assumed, put on*
unkynd, unkyndely *unnatural, unkind*
unleylle *unfaithful*
unnethe *frighten; scarcely*
unnethes *lest*
unryghtwysse *unjust*
unskylfull *non-rational*
untyll *unto, to*
urn *flow*

valay *valley*
varely *verily*
vartu *power*
vayne *vain, useless, proud*
velany *villainy*
venjans *vengeance*
versickles *versicles (short, repeated prayers)*
vertu(s) *power(s), strength(s), virtue(s)*
vochensaffe, vochesave, vouchesave *promise, allow, grant*
volenté *desire*
voutry *see avoutry*
vys *vice*

wa *woe*
wait *know*
wald(e) *would*
walkand *walking*
walland *boiling*
walle *welled*
wan *dim*
wandes *fear*
wane *won, earned; one*
wanhope *despair*
wapen *weapon(s)*

298

war *was, were; aware; wary*

warand *(be) cursed*

warkus, warkys, werkes *works*

warld *world*

wast *wasted, useless*

wasted *washed, wasted*

wat(e), wot *know, understand*

wathes *perils, dangers*

wawys *waves*

waxand *waxing, growing*

wayly *wail*

wedla(y)ke *wedlock, marriage*

weld(es) *wield(s), control(s)*

welth *wealth, well-being, abundance*

wemen *women*

wend(e), wendust, wendyst *go, travel; lead; thought, knew*

wene *doubt; know, expect*

wennus *whence*

wenon *believe, think*

wepand *weeping*

weryed *troubled, wearied*

wether hokys *shepherds' crooks*

wetton *tell*

weved *quenched*

whare *where*

whase *whose, which*

wha som *whoever*

whatkyn *what kind of (sort of)*

whele *wheel*

whilk(e), whylk(e) *which*

whilom *once, at one time*

whys *wise*

wiche *what*

wick(e), wykud *wicked*

wif(e), wyf(e) *wife, woman*

wight(es) *creature(s), person(s)*

wimen *women*

winne *salvation; to win, prevail*

wirschepe, wirschip *worship*

wiseliche *wisely*

wist, wyst *knew*

wite, wytte *know, understand*

witerly, wyterly *truly*

withalle *withal, completely*

withdrawe *withdraw from, forsake; withdrawn, taken out*

witt, wytt, whytt *know*

wittes *wits, intelligence*

wlatsom *disgusting*

wod(e)(nes) *mad, crazy; fury, madness*

wode *waded*

wold *would*

woll *will*

wombe *belly*

won *one*

wond *moved; wander*

won(ne)(eth) *live(s); used to*

wonnyng *dwelling*

word(lyche) *world(ly)*

wost *would*

wott *know*

wox *grew, became*

wrayst *wrest, wrench*

wreche *vengeance*

wrenche *wiles*

wretyn, wryten *written*

wroght *wrought*

wryche *wretch*

wyle, wylye, wylys *while, times*

wyn *win, achieve, reach; winning, achievement;* **(at) wyn** *to win*

wys *know; explain, inform*

wyse *manner, way*

wytty *intelligent, learned*

Glossary

Y *I*

yalu *yellow*

yardys *rods*

yatys *gates*

ybe, ybyn *be, been*

ybent *bent, curved*

yblisced *blessed*

ybore, yborn *borne, carried*

ybounde *bound, imprisoned*

ybrought *brought*

ych(e)on *each one*

ycleped *called, named*

ycristned *christened, baptized*

ydelt *dealt, distributed*

ydight, ydyght *fitted out, constructed,*
shaped

ydo(n) *done, placed*

yede(n) *came, went, stood*

yeff(e) *if*

yefftus *gifts*

yeme *note, notice, care*

yemer *guardian*

yfere *gathered together*

yfeyll *feel*

yfilt *filled*

yha *yes*

yhe *ye, you*

yhede *went*

yheme *protect*

yherd *heard; praised*

yher(e) *year(s); hear*

yhing *young*

yhit *yet*

yhold *held*

Yhole *Yule (Christmas)*

yhong *young*

yhour *your*

yhow *you*

yhowth *youth*

yif *if*

yknawe *known*

ylete *let, undertaken, done*

yliche *like, equal to*

ylk(e)on *each one*

ymelt *melted, molten*

ynayled *nailed*

ynee *eyes*

ynome *taken*

yolow *yellow*

yo(o)d(e) *went*

ypilt *thrust*

yrke *troubled*

yschewed *showed*

yse *ice*

yse, gan yse *(began to) see; seen*

yseighe *saw, had seen*

ysett *attired*

yseyd *said, explained*

yseye *saw*

yvell *evil*

ywerd *protected*

ywis *indeed*

ywreked *compelled*

yye *eye*

Volumes in the Middle English Texts Series

The Floure and the Leafe, The Assembly of Ladies, and The Isle of Ladies, ed. Derek Pearsall (1990)

Three Middle English Charlemagne Romances, ed. Alan Lupack (1990)

Six Ecclesiastical Satires, ed. James M. Dean (1991)

Heroic Women from the Old Testament in Middle English Verse, ed. Russell A. Peck (1991)

The Canterbury Tales: Fifteenth-Century Continuations and Additions, ed. John M. Bowers (1992)

Gavin Douglas, *The Palis of Honoure*, ed. David Parkinson (1992)

Wynnere and Wastoure and The Parlement of the Thre Ages, ed. Warren Ginsberg (1992)

The Shewings of Julian of Norwich, ed. Georgia Ronan Crampton (1993)

King Arthur's Death: The Middle English Stanzaic Morte Arthur and Alliterative Morte Arthure, ed. Larry D. Benson and Edward E. Foster (1994)

Lancelot of the Laik and Sir Tristrem, ed. Alan Lupack (1994)

Sir Gawain: Eleven Romances and Tales, ed. Thomas Hahn (1995)

The Middle English Breton Lays, ed. Anne Laskaya and Eve Salisbury (1995)

Sir Perceval of Galles and Ywain and Gawain, ed. Mary Flowers Braswell (1995)

Four Middle English Romances: Sir Isumbras, Octavian, Sir Eglamour of Artois, Sir Tryamour, ed. Harriet Hudson (1996)

The Poems of Laurence Minot (1333–1352), ed. Richard H. Osberg (1996)

Medieval English Political Writings, ed. James M. Dean (1996)

The Book of Margery Kempe, ed. Lynn Staley (1996)

Amis and Amiloun, Robert of Cisyle, and Sir Amadace, ed. Edward E. Foster (1997)

The Cloud of Unknowing, ed. Patrick J. Gallacher (1997)

Robin Hood and Other Outlaw Tales, ed. Stephen Knight and Thomas Ohlgren (1997)

The Poems of Robert Henryson, ed. Robert L. Kindrick (1997)

Moral Love Songs and Laments, ed. Susanna Greer Fein (1998)

John Lydgate, *Troy Book: Selections*, ed. Robert R. Edwards (1998)

Thomas Usk, *The Testament of Love*, ed. R. Allen Shoaf (1998)

Prose Merlin, ed. John Conlee (1998)

Middle English Marian Lyrics, ed. Karen Saupe (1998)

John Metham, *Amoryus and Cleopes*, ed. Stephen F. Page (1999)

Four Romances of England: King Horn, Havelok the Dane, Bevis of Hampton, Athelston, ed. Ronald B. Herzman, Graham Drake, and Eve Salisbury (1999)

The Assembly of Gods: Le Assemble de Dyeus, or Banquet of Gods and Goddesses, with the Discourse of Reason and Sensuality, ed. Jane Chance (1999)

Thomas Hoccleve, *The Regiment of Princes*, ed. Charles R. Blyth (1999)

John Capgrave, *The Life of St. Katherine*, ed. Karen Winstead (1999)

John Gower, *Confessio Amantis*, Vol. 1, ed. Russell A. Peck; with Latin translations by Andrew Galloway (2000); Vol. 2 (2003)

Richard the Redeless and Mum and the Sothsegger, ed. James Dean (2000)

Ancrene Wisse, ed. Robert Hasenfratz (2000)

Walter Hilton, *The Scale of Perfection*, ed. Thomas Bestul (2000)

John Lydgate, *The Siege of Thebes*, ed. Robert Edwards (2001)

Pearl, ed. Sarah Stanbury (2001)

The Trials and Joys of Marriage, ed. Eve Salisbury (2002)

Middle English Legends of Women Saints, ed. Sherry L. Reames (2003)

The Wallace: Selections, ed. Anne McKim (2003)

Richard Maidstone, *Concordia (The Reconciliation of Richard II with London)*, ed. David R. Carlson, with a verse translation by A. G. Rigg (2003)

Other TEAMS Publications

Documents of Practice Series:

Love and Marriage in Late Medieval London, selected, translated, and introduced by Shannon McSheffrey (1995)

Sources for the History of Medicine in Late Medieval England, selected, introduced, and translated by Carole Rawcliffe (1995)

A Slice of Life: Selected Documents of Medieval English Peasant Experience, edited, translated, and with an introduction by Edwin Brezette DeWindt (1996)

Regular Life: Monastic, Canonical, and Mendicant Rules, selected with an introduction by Douglas J. McMillan and Kathryn Smith Fladenmuller (1997)

Women and Monasticism in Medieval Europe: Sisters and Patrons of the Cistercian Reform, selected, translated, and with an introduction by Constance H. Berman (2002)

Commentary Series:

Commentary on the Book of Jonah, Haimo of Auxerre, translated with an introduction by Deborah Everhart (1993)

Medieval Exegesis in Translation: Commentaries on the Book of Ruth, translated with an introduction by Lesley Smith (1996)

Nicholas of Lyra's Apocalypse Commentary, translated with an introduction and notes by Philip D. W. Krey (1997)

Rabbi Ezra Ben Solomon of Gerona: Commentary on the Song of Songs and Other Kabbalistic Commentaries, selected, translated, and annotated by Seth Brody (1999)

John Wyclif: On the Truth of Holy Scripture, translated with an introduction and notes by Ian Christopher Levy (2001)

Second Thessalonians: Two Early Medieval Apocalyptic Commentaries, translated with an introduction by Steven R. Cartwright and Kevin L. Hughes (2001)

Medieval German Texts in Bilingual Editions Series:

Sovereignty and Salvation in the Vernacular, 1050–1150, introduction, translation, and notes by James A. Schultz (2000)

Ava's New Testament Narratives: "When the Old Law Passed Away," introduction, translations, and notes by James A. Rushing, Jr. (2003)

History as Literature: German World Chronicles of the Thirteenth Century in Verse, introduction, translations, and notes by R. Graeme Dunphy (2003)

To order please contact: MEDIEVAL INSTITUTE PUBLICATIONS
Western Michigan University
Kalamazoo, MI 49008–5432
Phone (269) 387–8755
FAX (269) 387–8750

http://www.wmich.edu/medieval/mip/index.html

Medieval Institute Publications is a program
of The Medieval Institute, College of Arts
and Sciences, Western Michigan University

Typeset in 10.5 pt. Times New Roman
with Times New Roman display
Manufactured by Cushing-Malloy, Inc.—Ann Arbor, Michigan

Medieval Institute Publications
College of Arts and Sciences
Western Michigan University
1903 W. Michigan Avenue
Kalamazoo, Michigan 49008-5432
www.wmich.edu/medieval/mip/

 WESTERN MICHIGAN UNIVERSITY